D1478674

MAJOR
BIBLE TRUTHS

MAJOR
BIBLE TRUTHS

by
F. E. Marsh

KREGEL PUBLICATIONS
Grand Rapids, Michigan 49501

Major Bible Truths © Copyright 1979, 1969 by Kregel Publications, a division of Kregel, Inc. Formerly published as *The Structural Principles of the Bible.* By special arrangements with Pickering and Inglis, Ltd., Glasgow, Scotland. All rights reserved.

Library of Congress Catalog Card Number 68-58842

ISBN 0-8254-3246-4

First Kregel Publications edition 1969
Reprinted in 1979, 1984

Printed in the United States of America

CONTENTS

Contents / vii

viii / Contents

FOREWORD

F.E. Marsh loved the Bible and stated in this book, "There is a total structural unity in the Word of God." After one has carefully studied this work of Major Bible Truths, one can say the Bible is truly and more understandably "a lamp unto my feet and a light unto my pathway." As one searches for gold, he is rewarded with rich findings. The same applies to this book — as one seeks and digs into God's Word, one is richly rewarded. This study book on the important laws of Biblical interpretation covers many subjects including typology, the law of first mention, prophecy, prayer and the names of God among many others. All major doctrines are discussed.

Whether one uses this book as a guide for a Bible study method or as a handbook, because of the many fine outlines and collations of Bible truth, he will profit. A very readable book, the more one reads it, the more one wants to read. Here is a wealth of information about the Bible and its teachings. It is a most valuable tool for any pastor or Sunday School teacher. Surely it is a "must" for the study desk of every serious student, for it contains much material not commonly found in any text on hermeneutics.

A fascinating series of study unfolds before the reader's eyes. It was compiled in answer to a request for one book on the laws of Biblical interpretation and formerly entitled *Structural Principles of the Bible*. This author made the Scriptures his life's study. He has packed into this work the ripe fruit of his research. The teaching of the Bible is approached from many angles in such a manner as to make it a treasury of fine gold, to be shaped by the student into forms of spiritual wealth and beauty, that can be put into practical circulation. The subtitle, "How to Study the Bible", indicates the general nature of the book. The author seeks to guide his readers to see the principles which are woven tightly into the Scriptures so that they would have a clearer understanding of them. Such an illuminating book is a rare find!

Taking the Bible as a living organism, Marsh uses the

human body as a model for his twelve chapter headings and using metaphors entitles them, e.g. the body of a united organism, the soul of a breathing life, and a heart of a loving purpose.

Paul W. Bennehoff

PREFACE

MYLES COVERDALE, in his translation in speaking of the study of the Bible, writes :

" It shall greatly helpe ye to understand Scripture, if thou mark

>   not only what is spoken or wrythen,
>   but of whom
>   and to whom,
>   with what words,
>   at what time,
>   where,
>   to what intent,
>   with what circumstances,
>   considering what goeth before
>   and what followeth."

These wise and weighty injunctions are of paramount importance in studying God's Word. No better instructions could be given in a general way. Let us apply these rules. Instead of traversing the vast country of Scripture, let us go into the Garden of John's First Epistle, and pluck some of the rare flowers of expression.

"WHAT IS SPOKEN."

There are three great truths brought out in John's Epistle :

>   The manifestation of Life,
>   The manifoldness of Love,
>   The marvel of Light.

These are identified with the crisp, concise, and comprehensive mono-syllabic sentences :

>   " The Word of Life,"
>   " God is Love," and
>   " God is Light."

These are not given in the order in which they occur, but it is essential to recognise that order. Life precedes Light, and Light enables us to see Love.

Life is manifested, focused, and operates in the Son, Who is the Life. Life is revealed in and through the Son (1 : 1-4), and is climaxed in Him Who is the " True God and Eternal Life " (5 : 20). Light is the essential quality of God's being, for He " is Light," hence, the lustre of holiness and the beauty of righteousness eradiates from Him (1 : 5). Love is not a mere emanation from God, it is what He is, in the essentiality of His nature. " God is Love " (4 : 8, 16), not He *was*, nor He *will be*, but He *is*, and always was and always will be. Love does **not** move God, although **He in His** love moves.

Life must precede Light, as it was at the beginning. God created before He said, " Let there be light," then all was completed when the handiwork of love was revealed. This is true in Christian experience. When we are quickened from the death of sin, then we perceive the blood of God's Son cleansing, and we behold the manner of love in God's giving and grace.

" BUT OF WHOM."

John the Aged, and " The Disciple whom Jesus loved," in the solicitude of parental love was concerned about " The little children." Little children is a term of tender regard. John used two relative words for children, " Teknon," which means an offspring, hence, believers are not adopted merely, but those who are born into the family of God (3 : 1). John comes closer in his " Little children " by using the word " Teknion," which occurs seven times in the Epistle (2 : 1, 12, 28 ; 3 : 7, 18 ; 4 : 4 ; 5 : 21). Remembering it is an endearing word, how paternal are such sentences as the following :

" My little children . . . sin not " ; " My little children, your sins are forgiven for His name's sake " ; " Little children, abide in Him " ; " Little children, let no man deceive you " ; " My little children, let us . . . love . . . in deed and in truth " ; " Ye are of God, little children, and have overcome"; "Little children, keep yourselves from idols."

"WITH WHAT WORDS."

There is a variety of glorious truth which shines from the constellation of the sky of this firmament. Such words as "Truth," "Fellowship," "Know," "Born," "Of God," "This," "Manifest" illustrate. The great words are Life, Light, and Love. Of which we might say:

Life is the sum of all being,
Light is the sum of all knowledge,
Love is the sum of all moral excellence.

Beside these, there are seven things of God:

"The Word of God"—The Basis of all authority (2 : 14).
"The Love of God"—The Secret of all Godliness (2 : 5; 4 : 9; 5 : 2).
"The Will of God"—The Bliss of all Heaven's glory (2 : 17).
"The Children of God"—The Relationship of all privilege (3 : 1, 2, R.V. 10; 5 : 2).
"The Son of God"—The Centre of all revelation (3 : 8; 4 : 15; 5 : 5, 10, 12, 13, 20).
"Born of God"—The Involution of all life (3 : 9).
"The Spirit of God"—The Power of all ability (4 : 2).

The soul of these words glows with an intensity of meaning, and is vital with the energy of the Holy Spirit.

"AT WHAT TIME."

It is generally recognised that John's writings are the latest. Supposing the Gospel was written about 85 or 90, and the Epistles in 90, and the Revelation in 96, there is a sequence of thought and a world of suggestion in these dates. The Gospel takes us back to the Eternity of the past, the Epistles lead us into the life of the present, and the Revelation unfolds to us the glory of the future. The Gospel was written that we might believe "that Jesus is the Christ, the Son of God, and that believing we might have life in His name" (John 20 : 31). The Epistles were written that we

might have fellowship with the Father and the Son, that our
" joy may be full " (1 John 1 : 4), and that we may know we
have Eternal life (1 John 5 : 13). The Revelation was
written that we might know what is going to happen in the
" hereafter " (Rev. 1 : 19), and to show unto us, His servants,
the things which " must shortly come to pass " (Rev. 22 : 6).

" TO WHAT INTENT."

Every period has its blighting error and its blasting
heresy. In John's day there was the pernicious error of
Gnosticism, which taught that Christ did not actually come,
but He only seemed to, hence, John with cutting words
speaks of those who are " Deceivers," who " Confess not
that Jesus Christ is come in the flesh," and says of such, that
if any of them come, " Receive him not into your house,
neither bid him God speed " (2 John 7-11).

These Gnostics, like the modern Agnostics, say it is not
possible to know anything. We are not surprised to find
John stating the possibility of knowing things. Two words
are rendered " Know," the one indicating the Knowledge of
perception ; and the other, the Knowledge of personal
acquaintance. Looking back in the past, John frequently
tells his beloved ones, " ye have known " (2 : 13, 14), and
sometimes includes himself when he declares, " We have
known " (4 : 16). Emphasizing the present, he says, " Ye
know " (2 : 20, 21, 29 ; 3 : 5, 15), and " We know " (2 : 3, 3,
5, 18 ; 3 : 2, 14, 19, 24 ; 5 : 15, 15, 18, 20) ; when he
emphasizes the fact of knowing he says, " Hereby know ye "
(4 : 2, 6, 13) ; when he puts anything problematical he writes,
" If ye know " (2 : 29) ; and then when he intends them to
know something, he says, " That ye may know " (5 : 13, 20).
Thus the Spirit's intent is obvious, it is that we have the
enjoyment of knowing the things of God.

Without recounting the other points of Coverdale's
suggestions, as they are practically covered in what we have
said, we can see the importance of studying the principles
which he lays down.

MAJOR BIBLE TRUTHS

HOW TO STUDY THE WORD OF GOD

DEFINE your terms and then keep to the terms defined. Everything that God does is defined by His artistic skill, and He Himself defines Himself as " Love." " God is Love "! Who can define that revealing definition! " Structure " indicates that which is constructed, as a building, a machine, a bridge, hence, the relative parts which go to make up the whole. Principle speaks of the law which governs the making of anything, as when a builder constructs a building according to the prepared plan of the architect. To listen to some who speak of the Bible, we might suppose it was a hetergeneous conglomeration of atoms floating about in the clouds of tradition and hypothesis, and which are gathered into the crucible of human thought, and pounded by the pestal of human mentality in the mortar of reasoning probability, and which after ponderous labour is presented in a putty mass of problematic theories.

Law and order are seen everywhere, as Milton says :

> " Order is Heaven's first law—a glorious law
> Seen in those pure and beauteous isles of light
> That come and go, as circling months fulfil
> Their highest behest. Not less on earth discerned,
> 'Mid rocks snow-laid, or waste of herbless sand,
> Throughout all climes, beneath all-varying skies,
> Fixed for e'en the smallest flower that blooms
> Its place of growth."

With the many illustrations which abound in nature of order and design, it is difficult to fix on one in particular. Perhaps the beautiful and industrious bee is one of the most

1

illuminating. " The number three is seen in relation to the bee, from whatever point we view it. In three days the egg of the queen is hatched. It is fed for nine days (3×3). It reaches maturity in fifteen days (5×3). The worker grub reaches maturity in twenty-one days (7×3) ; and is at work three days after leaving its cell. The drone matures in twenty-four days (8×3). The bee is composed of three sections—head and two stomachs. The two eyes are made up of about three thousand small eyes, each (like the cells of the comb) having six sides (2×3). Underneath the body are six (2×3) wax scales with which the comb is made. It has six (2×3) legs. Each leg is composed of three sections. The foot is formed of three triangular sections. The antennæ consist of nine sections (3×3). The sting has nine (3×3) barbs on each side." Surely this is no chance ? Here is design, skill, order, and perfection.

Law and order are seen everywhere in God's world of good, and the same characterises His Word of Grace. Principles are primers to point to the pathway of power. To " hitch our car to a star " is no fancy flight of poet's imagination, for to hitch our car to the star of God's Truth is to find ourselves drawn upward and onward into the presence of God.

What is Law ? Law is the principle which governs anything. The principle of moral law is righteousness—doing right because it is the right thing to do. The principle of the law of gravitation is the gravity of every object to the earth, when not prevented by a higher power. The law of electricity is the electrification of the object it touches, to the movement and empowerment of some other object. The law of life is the reproduction of its species through the appointed channels. The law of the Gospel is the Spirit frees the sinner from the law of sin and death through faith in Christ, and makes him like to Him, to Whom he is united. The law of attraction is the power of any given thing to draw another object to itself, as the sun which keeps our planetry system in perpetual motion around itself ; and the law of Biblical interpretation and exegesis is to find out the mind of God through the Word of God under the teaching of the Holy Spirit. What are the principles which make the Bible an organic whole in its complete structure? Our purpose is to answer this question.

One of the most beautiful bird's-eye views of the Bible ever given is the following by the late Dr. Somerville, of Scotland, who compares it to a temple. He says, " We may compare these Holy Scriptures to a majestic temple, which took seventeen centuries to build. Its Architect and Maker is God, and everywhere about it you perceive the impress of the same hand that you can discern in the beautiful works of creation. This temple has sixty-six capacious, though unequally-sized, chambers. Every one of its 31,173 verses is a stone, a beam, more exceilent than was ever built by Solomon, or Zerubbabel. This beautiful Temple is the home of the whole family of God. Here they are nourished, tended, instructed, prepared for immortality. And not only is the Church of God found within this sacred enclosure, but God Himself is ever to be found there. Let us avail ourselves of the King's permission and step inside. We approach through a beautiful garden, the garden of Eden. The first building to which we come is the most ancient and venerable. It is made of five chambers; these are chambers of law and justice—the five books of Moses. These are the vestibule to the rest. Passing from them we come to a suite of twelve apartments, the library of the building, containing the historic records, the Churches' archives for a thousand years, from Joshua to Esther. Then we come to the saints' exercising ground, the gymnasium of the building—the book of Job. Then we all at once find ourselves in the orchestra of the building—the Psalms, where dwell all the sons and daughters of song, with cymbals and harps. Next we come to the chamber of commerce—the book of Proverbs; and close to that, a small, but important chamber, the penitentiary for defaulters—the book of Ecclesiastes. After that, there is a beautiful parlour, called sympathy with mourners— the Lamentations. And here and there about this part of the building are pretty conservatories of Oriental flowers— the book of Ruth, and the Song of Solomon. Then we have fifteen chambers of peculiar splendour. You enter, and you are surprised by the august magnificence that meets your eye—these are the halls of prophecy. Now we come to the more modern part of the building. We enter, and we find ourselves passing through four chambers of the most spotless marble ; and when we look on the walls we see four full-length portraits of the Lord of the building Himself, drawn by the Holy Spirit's inimitable hand—these are the four evangelists. On leaving them you hear extraordinary sounds, as of machinery in motion—wheels, cranks, and pinions—and everything exhibiting extraordinary activity. You look for the motive, but it is out of sight. It is above. This is the workroom of the building—the book of the Acts. Passing thence, we come to a very rich series of apartments, twenty-one in number, and we see no less than fourteen have inscribed over them one honourable name—the name of the Apostle to the Gentiles ; others have the names of John, James, Jude, and Peter. These are the halls of the Apostolic Epistles, in which the Lord has been pleased to lay up the very richest treasures of His house. And now we come to the extremity of the building, and we enter a mysterious gallery, with lights and shadows strangely blended, and sights of the most extraordinary description are presented to our eye. We are in the mysterious gallery of the Apocalypse. There we see the future of Christ's Church on earth, till Christ Himself, the Bridegroom, comes. Step out on the balcony and look abroad. There is a lovely meadow, with the pure river of the Water of Life, and beside it the Tree of Life, with its twelve manner of fruits, and its leaves for the healing of the nations. And high above us, crowning the everlasting hills, is a city all in gold, bathed in light and quivering in glory—the New Jerusalem—whose foundations are of precious stones, its walls of jaspar, and its gates of pearl, and that needs no sun nor moon, for the glory of the Lord doth lighten it, and the Lamb is the light thereof."

What a difference there is between the organization of a building in its structure, and the organism of the human body in its vitality. The former is dead matter, while the latter is living form. The books of men are products of the minds of living thought, but the words which make up their entirety are lifeless in their totality. The words of the Bible are living in their essence, and life-giving in their ministry, hence, "the words" are "the words which the Holy Spirit teacheth" (1 Cor. 2 : 13) ; "the words" which Christ spoke "are spirit and life" (John 6 : 63) ; "the words of Jehovah are pure or purified words" (Psa. 12 : 6) ; the Scriptures are the Breath of God (2 Tim. 3 : 16) ; the Word is living in its nature, and powerful in its effective working (Heb. 4 : 12) ; the Word is incorruptible in its substance (1 Pet. 1 : 23) ; and Christ-contained in its embodiment (John 5 : 39).

Taking the Bible as a Living Organism, we may use the human body as a model for our theme ; and as we do so we shall find—

The Body of a United Organism.

The Head of a Golden Wisdom.

The Spirit of an Intellectual Individualism.

The Soul of a Breathing Life.

The Heart of a Loving Purpose.

The Hands of a Working Design.

The Mouth of a Specific Utterance.

The Lungs of a Double Action.

The Ears of a Perpetual Attention.

The Feet of a Progressive Movement.

The Finger of a Distinct Direction.

The Eyes of a Prophetic Outlook.

We do well to think of the indestructibility of the spirit, and the vitality of the soul, but do not let us ignore the wonders of the body.

"Fearfully and wonderfully made."

All God's works are wonderful, but man is the most wonderful of all. Something of the care, thought, and ultimate purpose of God is suggested when the Psalmist declared, "My substance" (m., "body") "was not hid from Thee, when I was made in secret," that is, when the body was being formed in the womb. "Thine eyes did see my substance, yet being imperfect" (Psa. 139 : 13-16).

When we consider a few facts of the body we can see the skill of the Maker, and we marvel that—

> " A harp with so many strings
> Can keep in tune so long."

Think of the number of the bones which hold the body together, the elasticity of the bracing muscles, the rapidity of the movements of the different and fitting parts, the miracle of the corpuscles' of the vitalizing blood, the circulation of the blood as it touches every part of this hemisphere, the machinery of the digestive organs in their distributing work, the great air-shaft of the breathing bellows, the multiplicity of the working factory which we call the brain, the telegraphic system of the nerve-fibres of the many nerves, the thousands of receivers and distributors of the pores which are scattered all around, and many other things which go to make up the body.

" The whole body fitly joined together."

The human body in its compactness is used by the Holy Spirit to elucidate and illustrate the oneness of the spiritual organism of the Church (Eph. 4 : 16). Think of what the body means from the mere skeleton point of view : " For a man to stand upright, let alone walk or work, there must be a strong and firm though light bony skeleton. Thus he has some 250 bones wonderfully tied together by ligaments, whereby the 33 vertebræ of the spine, 64 bones of the upper limbs, 62 in the lower limbs, with 24 ribs, and 22 skull bones, are all made to subserve one organic whole."

As the body in its several members is dependent one upon the other, and all together go to make up the whole ; so each believer in Christ, and all together are needed to function to a single issue.

A Christian business man in a large co-operative firm in Pittsburgh, recently said in Buffalo : " The secret of business is ' De-centralize yourself, and absorb others ' " ; and " the customer is always right when he does not like the goods supplied." Give him what he wants, and he will want what you have.

Here is the secret too of real unity. When there is the unanimity of God's thought, and the heart unity of love, there will be the functioning of the union of Christ's mystical body.

" The hand " (1 Cor. 12 : 15)

The hand in its working is a miracle in its operation. " The bones, even if tied together, could do nothing without muscles, of which there are at least 500, with accompanying tendons. Does any imitator of Paderewski ever think how it is that he can practice for hours on stretch, or any admirer of Kriesler ask how that combined and effective motion of fingers, wrist, and forearm are possible ? Probably not. Yet it were all impossible but for the marvellous conjuncture of twenty bones in each hand, tied together firmly with eight more in the wrist, and three more above them."

Yet, what is the hand without the other parts of the body, and behind all and over and in all, the dominating will.

Other things may be said of the body, but it will suffice to indicate its wonderful organism. As the body is a unit and a pulsating organism, so the Word of God is a unit, and no part can be taken away without mutilating the whole.

1

THE BODY OF A UNITED ORGANISM

THE late Dr. A. A. Saphir has finely said, in referring to the Bible as an organism: "If the Bible were like a collection of stones, we might select some and put aside others, as less valuable and beautiful; and although in such selection we might make great mistakes, we should still be in possession of something more or less complete. But the Bible is like a plant, and all its parts are not mechanically or accidentally connected, but originally united, and hence a law of life rules here; and he who reveres life will neither add nor take away from the beautiful plant, which the Father hath planted in and through Christ by the Spirit."

There is one phrase which expresses the unity of the Scriptures, and that is the expression which occurs thirty-five times in Psa. 119, namely, "Thy Word." This is in the singular number, and accords with a common usage in the Book. There are three times thirteen books in the Old Testament, and three times nine books in the New Testament—sixty-six books in all, or three times twenty-two books. The time extends through sixteen hundred years in writing the Book, from Moses the Prophet to John the Apostle; and there are no less than thirty-six authors or human instruments through whom the Spirit wrote. Men of all grades and conditions were the human means of communication.

The Book was written in three different languages, and in many different places; and yet there is a unity which is perfect in its testimony.

There is a progressiveness in its revelation, but no contradiction, as may be seen in the names by which God gradually reveals Himself.

In Creation He is God-Elohim. God in creative skill, and artistic workmanship (Gen. 1).

8

In Proprietorship He is Lord God—" Adonahy-Jehovah," —and as such Abram recognises Him as The One Who can give the promised Seed (Gen. 15 : 2).

In Almighty Power He is El-Shaddai, the all-sufficient One, the One Who is enough, and as such He makes Himself known to Abram (Gen. 17 : 1).

In Covenant Relationship He reveals Himself to Israel as Jehovah (Ex. 6 : 3).

And in Christ He is revealed as The Father (John 14 : 9) ; and yet in whatever character He is made known He is but One Lord.

We shall note a sevenfold unity. The unity of the Book, unity of Prophecy, unity of the Books of the Bible, unity of Truth, unity of a Section, unity of a Book, and unity of Thought.

UNITY OF THE BOOK

The following inverse parallelism has been given as a bird's-eye view of the completeness of the Bible, which demonstrates beyond all question the design of a perfect plan :

1. The original creation in its beauty and perfection (Gen. 1 : 1). When the beginning was, we do not know, but as the watch tells of design and workmanship, so creation speaks of the Creator.

2. Creation ruined by sin (Gen. 1 : 2 ; see Isa. 45 : 18, R.V.). God did not create it " without form and void," but it became such as the verb indicates.

3. The earth blessed in the six days of creation and then cursed because of man's sin (Gen. 3 : 17).

4. Mankind dealt with as a whole from Adam to Abram.

5. The chosen nation called and blessed (Gen. 12 : 1).

6. Christ's first appearing (Heb. 9 : 26).

7. The Church taken out of the world (Acts 15 : 14).

When the Church is completed (Eph. 3 : 21), and Christ returns for the restitution of all things (Acts 3 : 21), then the reverse order will be followed :

7. The Church taken up to be with Christ (1 Thess. 4 : 13-18).

6. Christ's second appearing on earth (Heb. 9 : 28 ; Zech. 14 : 4).

5. The chosen nation blessed (Rom. 11 : 25 ; Acts 15 : 16).

4. Mankind dealt with as a whole (Acts 15 : 17).

3. The curse removed and the earth blessed and beautified (Amos 9 : 13-15 ; Isa. 35 : 1 ; Psa. 67 : 7).

2. Satan's final rebellion (Rev. 20 : 7-10).

1. The new heavens and the new earth (Rev. 21 : 1).

UNITY OF PROPHECY

Jesus is the Key of Prophecy. All Scripture centres in Him and is fulfilled in Him.

Among the many prophecies relating to Christ, let us take the following :

To **Adam** was made known Christ's miraculous birth, being called, not the " seed of man " but the " seed of the woman " (Gen. 3 : 15).

To **Abraham** was revealed the nation with which He would be identified (Gen. 12 : 3 ; Acts 3 : 25).

To **Jacob** it was made known that He would be of the tribe of Judah (Gen. 49 : 10).

To **David** it was communicated that He would be of his family (2 Sam. 7 : 12-14).

To **Daniel** was unfolded the time He would appear (Dan. 9 : 25).

To **Micah** was declared the town in which He would be born (Micah 5 : 2).

To **Malachi** it was stated that He would be preceded by a forerunner (Mal. 3 : 1).

To **Zechariah** it was shown that Christ would be betrayed for thirty pieces of silver (Zech. 11 : 12), and the way He would enter into Jerusalem (Zech. 9 : 9).

To the **Psalmist** was made known the manner of His death by crucifixion (Psa. 22 : 16) ; that not a bone of Him should be broken (Psa. 34 : 20) ; and that He would rise from the dead (Psa. 16 : 10).

And to **Isaiah** was revealed God's part in Christ's death (Isa. 53 : 10), and that He would be identified with transgressors and pray for them (Isa. 53 : 12).

UNITY OF THE BOOKS OF THE BIBLE

John's Gospel is associated with Genesis by the correspondent expression, " In the beginning."

Hebrews is joined with Leviticus by the parallel truths of worship based on the ground of atonement.

Romans is united to Exodus by the similar blessing of redemption by the Blood of Atonement through faith.

The pilgrim life of the believer, emphasized by Peter, is illustrated in Numbers.

The spiritual nature of the law laid down in Christ's teaching, as recorded by Matthew, finds its counterpart in Deuteronomy, and a further correspondence is seen in Christ's quotations from the Book in meeting Satan's temptations.

The book of Joshua is connected with Ephesians by the contrast between Israel's earthly inheritance and the believer's riches in heavenly things in Christ.

Daniel's sealed book is explained by the book of the Revelation.

And the apostasies recorded in the book of Judges are repeated in the Second Epistles of Peter and John, and in Jude.

UNITY OF TRUTH

The " eight feasts of Jehovah " are typical of the threefold cord of the Gospel, namely, Grace, Godliness, and Glory.

The Sabbath (Lev. 23 : 1-3) is typical of God's rest in Christ, as expressed in the Spirit of God abiding (resting) on Him, and the Father's acknowledgment of Him as the One in Whom He was well pleased (Matt. 3 : 16-17 ; John 1 : 33).

The Passover (Lev. 23 : 5) is typical of Christ's death for sin, and is expressive of the protection there is in Him Who was " sacrificed for us " (1 Cor. 5 : 7 ; Rom. 8 : 1-4, R.V.).

The Feast of Unleavened Bread (Lev. 23 : 6) represents the outcome of faith in Christ. He, by His indwelling presence, purges out the leaven of legality (Gal. 5 : 9), malice and wickedness (1 Cor. 5 : 7, 8).

The Firstfruits (Lev. 23 : 9-14) is typical of Christ's resurrection from the dead, as the firstfruits of those who sleep in Him (1 Cor. 15 : 20).

Pentecost (Lev. 23 : 15-21) is typical of the coming and dispensation of the Holy Spirit (Acts 2 : 1). He is gathering out from Jew and Gentile (two loaves) those who shall make up the mystical body of Christ (1 Cor. 12 : 12 ; Eph. 4 : 16).

The Feast of Trumpets (Lev. 23 : 23-25) is typical of the time when the trumpet of Christ's return shall be heard, as He gathers His own people to Himself in the Glory (1 Thess. 4 : 13-18 ; 1 Cor. 15 : 52).

The Day of Atonement (Lev. 23 : 26-32) is typical of Christ's manifestation to Israel as their Messiah when they shall "look upon Him Whom they have pierced " (Zech. 12 : 10 ; Rev. 1 : 7).

The Feast of Tabernacles (Lev. 23 : 33, 34) represents the Millennium, when the scene on the Mount of Transfiguration (Mark 9 : 2-7) shall be known over the whole earth, for the glory of the Lord will cover it (Hab. 2 : 14).

There is yet one other truth, the most important of all, and that is—all approach to God and all blessing from God is based upon vicarious sacrifice. From Genesis to Revelation this scarlet line is seen, and like the unseen bar in the Tabernacle (Ex. 36 : 33) holds all the Book, with its relative truths, together. Let us briefly embody New Testament statement with Old Testament type as found in the first three books in the Bible :

Abel's approach to God and acceptance was on the ground of sacrifice (Gen. 4 : 4, 5 ; Heb. 10 : 19, 20 ; 11 : 4).

Isaac's life was spared by the substitution of the ram (Gen. 22 : 13 ; 1 Pet. 2 : 24).

Judgment was averted by the slain paschal lamb (Ex. 12 : 6 ; 1 Cor. 5 : 7).

The clean animal redeeming the unclean (Ex. 13 : 13 ; Col. 1 : 13, 14).

The ransom money securing the Israelite (Ex. 30 : 13 ; 1 Pet. 1 : 18, 19).

The burnt offering accepted for the offerer (Lev. 1 : 3, 4 ; Eph. 5 : 2).

The sin offering answering for the sin of the sinner (Lev. 4 : 4-12 ; 2 Cor. 5 : 21).

The trespass offering was the basis of forgiveness (Lev. 5 : 6 ; Eph. 1 : 7, R.V.).

The peace offering was the ground of communion (Lev. 7 : 11-34 ; Col. 1 : 20).

The slain bird was the cause of the leper's cleansing (Lev. 14 : 5-7 ; 1 John 1 : 7).

The uplifted serpent was the bringer of life (Num. 21 : 8 ; John 3 : 14).

The offerings on the Day of Atonement were the makers of expiation (Lev. 16 : 3-16 ; Heb. 9 : 13, 14).

The ram of consecration was the inductor to the priesthood (Lev. 8 : 22-24 ; Heb. 9 : 12).

This is but a passing glance at what might be multiplied, but this goes to prove that—

> " The New is in the Old contained,
> The Old is by the New explained."

UNITY OF A SECTION

One of the striking sections of the Book is the 119th Psalm, and what it says of the Word of God in its many features. It gives an illustration of the law of full mention, that is, we shall find in a concrete section the full-orbness of a single truth.

In the Psalm we find a complete body of structural formation. As the hand is part of the body and yet connected with the whole, so this Psalm, while a part of the whole organism of the Bible, is compact and complete in itself, and might be summarized as a revelation of what the Bible is. This Psalm consists of 176 verses, divided into twenty-two sections. Each group has eight verses. There are twenty-two letters in the Hebrew alphabet, and each section commences with one of the letters of the alphabet, so there is one letter for each group. This may be seen in an ordinary Bible, as the letter is spelt over each section. " Aleph " is over the first, and " Beth " over the second

section. Another thing of moment is, each of the eight
verses commences with the letter of the section, as may be
seen in Rotherham's translation. This cannot be well given
in another language, but it may be illustrated. There is one
section which may be taken by way of illustration, namely,
the section from verse 65 to verse 72. Except in verses 67
and 71 each verse begins with the letter T, and it is a happy
coincidence that this section in the Hebrew is under and
identified with the letter " *Teth*." Let us see how the
section looks :

65. " Thou hast dealt with Thy servant,
      according unto Thy Word.
66. Teach me good judgment and knowledge :
      for I have believed Thy commandments.
67. Till (instead of " Before ") I was afflicted I went
      astray,
      but now I keep Thy Word.
68. Thou art good and doest good,
      teach me Thy statutes.
69. The proud have forged a lie against me,
      but I will keep Thy precepts with my whole
      heart.
70. Their heart is as fat as grease,
      but I delight in Thy law.
71. 'Tis good for me that I have been afflicted,
      that I might learn Thy statutes.
72. The law of Thy mouth is better unto me
      than thousands of gold and silver."

Another feature of the organism of the 119th Psalm is
the ten words, which cover the complete ground in telling us
what the Bible is and does. The ten words are—" Way,"
" Testimonies," " Precepts," " Commandments," " Word,"
" Law," " Judgment," " Statute," " Righteousness," and
" Word."

" WAY."

This word is derived from a root which means to tread,
hence, to walk, and is used to denote a track to a given
destination—" the *way* to the tree of life " (Gen. 3 : 24) ; a

course of conduct—" all flesh had corrupted his *way*" (Gen. 6 : 12) ; a journey—" three day's *journey*" (Ex. 3 : 18) ; and the mode of doing a thing—" *after the manner* of Egypt" (Isa. 10 : 24). What a descriptive word is this, as applied to the truth of God's Word. It is the track made for the journey of life along which we are to walk, and it also shows us how to behave as we tread the way. The word occurs thirteen times in the Psalm, and is rendered " way " and " ways " (verses 1, 3, 5, 14, 26, 27, 29, 30, 32, 33, 37, 59, 168), sometimes it denotes " the way of truth," and at other times to the Psalmist's conduct as he thinks of his " ways."

" TESTIMONIES."

This word comes from a word which signifies to go back again, to reiterate, hence, to testify, to witness. It occurs twenty-three times (verses 2, 14, 22, 24, 31, 36, 46, 59, 79, 88, 95, 99, 111, 119, 125, 129, 138, 144, 146, 152, 157, 167, 168). We find there are many who bear witness of God and to Christ. God's works testify of His power (Rom. 1 : 20). the seasons of His faithfulness (Acts 14 : 17), Moses of His righteousness (John 5 : 46), the Spirit of Christ's glory (John 15 : 26), John of His mission (John 1 : 32), the Scriptures of His personality (John 5 : 39), and the Apostles of His resurrection (Acts 4 : 33).

" PRECEPTS."

" Precepts " only occurs in the Psalms, twenty-four times in all, and out of them it is found twenty-one in Psalm 119 (verses 4, 15, 27, 40, 45, 56, 63, 69, 78, 87, 93, 94, 100, 104, 110, 128, 134, 141, 159, 168, 173 ; and Psalms 19 : 8 ; 103 : 18 ; 111 : 7, rendered " Statutes " and " Commandments "). The word is derived from a root which means to visit, to oversee, to charge, to care for, and denotes the mandate of God to command our obedience. If His precepts are fulfilled it means His promises are enjoyed.

" COMMANDMENTS."

" Commandments " is derived from a word which means to set up, to constitute, and is rendered " gave charge " (Num. 27 : 23), hence, in the command is recognised the

authority which gives it, therefore not to obey is an act
of rebellion. The word itself occurs twenty-two times
(verses 6, 10, 19, 21, 32, 35, 47, 48, 60, 66, 73, 86, 96, 98,
115, 127, 131, 143, 151, 166, 172, 176). God never gives
commands without the power to carry them out, therefore
all His commands are His enablings.

" WORD."

There are two words rendered "word." The first is
found in the following verses—11, 38, 41, 50, 58, 67, 76, 82,
103, 116, 123, 133, 140, 148, 154, 158, 162, 170, 172,—and
occurs nineteen times. It is derived from a root which
signifies to reveal or bring to light, as an utterance which
reveals the mind of a speaker. What a dark world this
would be but for the clear shining of The Sure Word of
Prophecy.

" LAW."

Law is expressed in the Decalogue. It is derived from a
word which means to project, as an arrow from a bow, or
water from a rock, hence, to point out or teach. It is
rendered " shot " in referring to an archer shooting an arrow
(1 Sam. 20 : 36), and " teach " by one who prays to be taught
(Psa. 27 : 11). From this root comes the word " law," and
signifies the direction of God in pointing out the rule of His
will. It occurs twenty-five times in the Psalm (verses 1, 18,
29, 34, 44, 51, 53, 55, 61, 70, 72, 77, 85, 92, 97, 109, 113,
126, 136, 142, 150, 153, 163, 165, 174). His law is binding
on our conscience and is to be recognised by our obedience.

" JUDGMENT."

The Hebrew word for judgment means to give a finding
which is just and right, and comes from a root which signifies
to set upright. Judgment, therefore, denotes God's verdict.
His judgments are said to be " righteous," " good," and
" right." The word occurs twenty-three times in the Psalm,
twenty-one times rendered " Judgments" and " Judgment,"
once " Ordinances," and once " as Thou used to do " (verses
7, 13, 20, 30, 39, 43, 52, 62, 75, 84, 91(" Ordinances "), 102,
106, 108, 120, 121, 132 (" as Thou used to do "), 137, 149,

156, 160, 164, 175). God's findings are final. They are not to be questioned, denied, nor distorted ; but to be accepted, loved, and followed.

" RIGHTEOUSNESS."

The word is translated " Righteousness " (verses 123, 142, second, 144, 172), " Righteous " (verses 7, 62, 106, 138, 160, 164), " Justice " (verse 121), " Right " (verse 75), and occurs twelve times. There are two akin words rendered " righteous " (verse 137), and " righteousness " (verses 40, 142). That which is right is the inherent meaning, just and true, hence, it is used of " just balances " (Lev. 19 : 36), that which is " even " (Job 31 : 6), and that which is in accordance with " justice " (Psa. 89 : 14). The straight ruler of God's Word is the instrument by which all our actions are to be lined.

" STATUTES."

" Statutes " comes from a root which is rendered " graven " (Isa. 49 : 16), and " pourtray " (Ezek. 4 : 1), and means to hack, to engrave ; therefore " statute " signifies that which is decreed in His revelation and engraven by His indelible pen. The word is rendered " decree " (Job 28 : 26), " portion " (Gen. 47 : 22), " bounds " (Job 14 : 5) ; and occurs twenty-two times (verses 5, 8, 12, 16, 23, 26, 33, 48, 54, 64, 68, 71, 80, 83, 112, 117, 118, 124, 135, 145, 155, 171). What Jehovah has engraven in His Word should be graven on our hearts, that it may be pourtrayed in clear type in our lives (see 2 Cor. 3 : 1-3).

" WORD."

This word (" Dābār ") is derived from a root which means to set in order, to arrange, hence it signifies to set forth in speech. It is rendered " word " and " words," and occurs twenty-three times (verses 9, 16, 17, 25, 28, 42, 43, 49, 57, 65, 74, 81, 89, 101, 105, 107, 114, 130, 139, 147, 160, 161, 169), and it is also translated " commandment " (2 Chron. 31 : 5), " promise " (2 Chron. 1 : 9), " report " (2 Chron. 9 : 5), " answer " (2 Chron. 10 : 6), " decree " (2 Chron. 30 : 5), " matter " (Ezra 10 : 4), and " message " (Prov. 26 : 6).

This Psalm amply illustrates the organism of a complete section. Let any nation, community, or individual follow, tread in the "way" of the Lord, hearken to His "testimonies," obey its "precepts," fulfil its "commands," listen to its "word," recognise its "law," bow to its "judgments," be regulated by its "righteousness," have its "statutes" graven upon the heart, and receive its message, and blessing will come to those who do so, and benediction will be bestowed on all around.

UNITY OF A BOOK

The same rule of perfect organism holds good in relation to a Book. Sometimes it is obvious and on the surface, like the order of the stars moving in their several orbits ; other times, the book is held together by an underlying thought of uniting cohesion, like the unseen bar which ran through the boards of the Tabernacle, and united them all on the foundation. The latter is illustrated in the Book of Genesis. The book is divided into ten sections, and is distinctly marked off by the word "Generations."* The significance of the word is important. The root from which it is derived signifies to beget, and invariably refers to results, not causes ; not to ancestry, but descendants ; not to origins, but to effects ; not to producers, but to what is produced. The importance of this is seen in the first occurrence of "Generations"— "The generations of the heaven and the earth" (Gen. 2 : 4). Some tell us that Genesis 2 is a second account of the creation, and that the "'Generations of the heaven and the earth' are the origin of the heaven and the earth," and therein they blunder, for on the contrary, they are the things for which the heavens and the earth were created, namely, they were made for man and the great drama of human history.

---

* There are two Hebrew words rendered "Generation" and "Generations." The two words occur twenty times. "Dor" occurs seven times (Gen. 6 : 9, second word ; 7 : 1 ; 9 : 12 ; 15 : 16 ; 17 : 7, 9, 12), and means a revolution of time, or an age, or generation ; it comes from a root which denotes a movement in a circle. The word is rendered "Posterity" in Num. 9 : 10. "*Toledoth*" or "*Toledah*" is found thirteen times in Genesis, and is rendered "according to birth" in Ex. 28 : 10.

The division of the book is as follows :

The Introduction, 1 to 4 : 26, giving an account of creation, and the reconstruction of things, and the Fall of man. " The Generations of the heaven and the earth."

The ten generations—

    5 : 1 to 6 : 8. " The Generations of Adam."

    6 : 9 to 9 : 29. " The Generations of Noah."

    10 : 1 to 11 : 9. " The Generations of the Sons of Noah."

    11 : 10 to 11 : 26. " The Generations of Shem."

    11 : 27 to 25 : 11. " The Generations of Terah."

    25 : 12. " The Generations of Ishmael."

    25 : 13 to 25 : 18. " The sons of Ishmael, according to their Generations."

    25 : 19 to 35 : 29. " The Generations of Isaac."

    36 : 1 to 37 : 1. " The Generations of Esau."

    37 : 2 to end of Genesis. " The Generations of Jacob."

There are three things which are of moment to recognise. First, the space covered by the references to the several individuals. This may be demonstrated by the number of chapters and verses found in relation to each. In the first section one chapter and eight verses are covered ; in the second, three chapters and fourteen verses ; in the third, one chapter and nine verses ; in the fourth, sixteen verses ; in the fifth, thirteen chapters and seventeen verses ; in the sixth, one verse ; in the seventh, six verses ; in the eighth, ten chapters and sixteen verses ; in the ninth, one chapter and one verse ; and in the tenth, thirteen chapters and thirty-five verses.

Two things are prominent in the above fact, the men of the flesh, such as Ishmael and Esau, and their descendants, are summarized in fifty verses ; while the men of faith and their seed, such as Terah, Isaac and Jacob cover no less than over forty chapters. From this we may gather, that those who are to play only a minor part in the drama of human history, while they are recognised, they and theirs are dismissed with a few statements of fact ; while those who are in the covenant of promise are prominent throughout.

Second, the undercurrent which runs through the strata of Genesis is, the men who are identified with the Promised Seed are to the front because of the Messiah with Whom they are associated. The others are in the formation of the human race, but the elect race is the foundation of the purpose of the Lord. Association with Christ makes all the difference whether we count or not.

Third, Genesis is divided into ten sections. The introduction embodies the sovereign act of God in creation, and here He stands alone, and illustrates the significance of the numeral one, which stands for the absoluteness of God. " The Lord our God is One Lord " (Zech. 14 : 9). Ten is the number of responsibility, or man's obligation to God, hence, the ten commandments, the ten virgins, and the ten words in Psalm 119 ; therefore the ten generations unfold God's recognition of man's ways and history. Another thing is of interest in the realm of numbers, there are three other references to prominent men in the Old Testament, namely, " The Generations of the Sons of Levi " (Ex. 6 : 16-19) ; " The Generations of Aaron and Moses " (Num. 3 : 1) ; and " The Generations of Pharez " (Ruth 4 : 18). This brings the generations up to thirteen, which is an imperfect number, we need one more to make a double perfection. Can we find one to complete ? Yes, the New Testament begins, " The Book of the Generation of Jesus Christ, the Son of David, the Son of Abraham " (Matt. 1 : 1). Why is Christ identified with David and Abraham ? These are the two men of which the Old Testament is full, and yet we do not read of " The Generations of David," or " Abraham " ! But they are not left out, for we find them in the Holiest of all with our Lord. Is this accidental ? We rather believe it is intentional, and reveals the master-hand of the Divine Builder, Who works on the plan of His will.

UNITY OF THOUGHT

The Prayer of the Lord Jesus in the Upper Room leads us into the Holiest of all, and we bow with lowly adoration as we listen to the holy words which fell from His holy lips, and we feel the holy pulsations of His holy heart of Love.

It is not without holy significance that the Holy Son addresses the Father as " Holy Father." Right through that holy Prayer we have the holy thought of the oneness which exists between the Holy Father and the Holy Son, and the consequent holy oneness which the Lord Jesus has brought about in making His own disciples one with the Holy Father and Himself.

Ponder this holy oneness in the light of the holy prayer, as recorded in John 17, and see how manifold and wonderful this comprehensive oneness is :

1. Oneness in Purpose

The momentous hour which ever struck came, when Christ said to His Father, " The hour is come " (ver. 1). The hour of His life was the goal of His passion. By His death, Christ would glorify the Father in His obedience unto death ; and the Father will glorify the Son in a peculiar way as a result.

2. Oneness in Gift

The Father gives the Son " authority over all flesh " (ver. 2) ; and of the Church as represented in the disciples, Christ says, " Thou gavest Me." He passes on the " given " word to them, and the given glory is passed on to them too, that is, the glory of being in His Father's presence, as He was in the eternal past.

3. Oneness in Knowledge   3, 7

Christ places us by His mediatorial grace within the circle of Him, Who is Eternal Life ; and this knowledge denotes a personal acquaintance with the Father and the Son.

4. Oneness in Work   4

The given work is fully accomplished. Hence the Son brought a glory to the Father " on the earth " beyond any previous glory.

5. Oneness in Deity and Position   5

" Before the world was," He was ; and since He was before the world was, He could not be a creature—created. Therefore, He was, and is, God the Creator. The conclusion to which we must come, is that He refers to the glory of oneness in the Godhead—as Deity.

6. Oneness in Manifestation   6

As the Son, Christ revealed the Father. His " Name " stands for His nature as the Father, with all that it implies, namely : the love of His heart, the grace of His care, the word of His promise, the joy of His peace, the peace of His joy, the strength of His power, and the home of His glory.

7. Oneness in Mission   8

How joyously and constantly Christ emphasizes that He was sent by the Father. All His goings were the Father's sendings, and all He did was the Father's doing.

8. Oneness in Possession   9, 10

Christ not only speaks of His own as " mine," but also as " Thine." Hence, He prays for them in a peculiar way. As Luther says, " What He must ask for the world is that it should be converted, not that it should be kept or sanctified."

9. Oneness in Glorification   10

What a meanful saying is " I am glorified in them." All that Christ did for His own and all that He made them, brought honour to Him, even as the watch and the painting speak of the skill of the workman and artist.

10. Oneness in Keeping   6, 11, 12, 15

For those whom Christ has kept, and who have kept His word, Christ prays for a twofold keeping. Negatively, that they may be kept from the evil of the world, or the Evil One ; and positively, that they " may be one."

11. Oneness in Scripture   12

Christ recognises the happenings which take place, even the treachery of Judas, as the fulfilling of the Scriptures. And how frequently He refers to " Thy words," " Thy word," and " Thy truth." The sacred writings were to Christ the voice of His Father's message to Himself and His disciples. When the Scriptures are the basis of our faith, there will be unity of action.

12. Oneness in Joy   13

" My joy fulfilled in themselves." Here is a gem of soul-brilliancy which flashes its light into the inner shrine of the spirit. He gives not in scanty measure, as the word " fulfilled " indicates.

13. Oneness in being Opposed   14

The cause of the hatred to Christ and His disciples is " Thy word." So Christ declares to His Father. The darkness hates the light. We are taken " out of the world " that we may shine in it.

14. Oneness in Separation   15, 16

Christ prays that His own may be kept from the evil of the world. The force of His request is better seen if we note the " εκ " which occurs twice, and if we render in each case " out of." " I pray not that Thou shouldest take them out of the world, but that Thou shouldest keep them out of the evil." They are not out of the world, even as I am not out of the world. The place of separation is always the place of power, the secret of soul prosperity and of progress in the spiritual life.

15. Oneness in the Truth   17

The preposition again adds force and fulness of meaning. Instead of reading " through," it would be better to read " *in* the Truth." The Truth is not merely a medium by means of which blessing comes, but it is a sphere in which we are to move, even as the bird lives in the air and the fish in the water.

16. Oneness in Commission   18

The pivotal words are the " as " and " so." As Christ was sent on His mission by the Father, even so He commissions us in His service. As Christ was essentially the Life, Light, Love, and Liberator, so we, His followers, are to be as recipients.

17. Oneness in Aim   19

" I "—" They." He set Himself apart in consecrated devotion to atone for the sins of His own ; and we are

" also " to set ourselves apart " in truth." " *In* truth " is
the correct reading, and not " through the truth." The
thought here is, not that we are to move in the sphere of the
truth, but in its reality ; to be set apart, so that there shall
be no falsity ; and for this we need, as Godet says, " the
communication which Jesus makes of His own sanctified
Person."

18. Oneness in Outlook   20

" I "—" Them "—" Their "—" Me." The pronouns are
pointers. The " I " of Christ's Loving Intercession ; the
" them " for whom He prays—all believers down the ages ;
the " their " of employed instruments, for it is by means of
the believer's testimony that others are blest ; and the " Me "
of the end in view, the others who will " believe on " Christ.
What a wonderful linking up and taking in we have in this
outlook of Christ's prayer !

19. Oneness in End   21

No less than five times do the words " in " and " one "
occur, giving us the sublime and mystic thought of inness in
oneness. Christ prays for His own " that they all may be
one, as Thou, Father, art in Me, and I in Thee, that they
also may be one in Us." Could anything be more concise ?
The result of this wonderful identification will be, the world
believing on Christ. When the end is reached, the result
will follow.

20. Oneness in Glory   22

The glory is what the Father is, in the essence of His
being, namely, Love. He that dwelleth in Love, dwelleth in
God, and God dwelleth in him.

21. Oneness in Love   23

There is still the wonderful inness of this oneness—" I in
them, and Thou in Me, that they *in*," may be " perfected
into." The added " *eis*," into, gives the thought of being
not only in the tabernacle of God's nature, but into the
Holiest Of All ; and there, and there alone, we learn the holy
secret, that the measure of Christ being loved by the Father
is the same for us.

22. Oneness in Place   24

" Father, I will that those whom Thou hast given Me be with Me where I am." Godet's comment is to the point : " Jesus no longer says, ' I pray, but I will !' This expression is found nowhere else on His lips. It is ordinarily explained by saying that the Son expresses Himself thus, because He feels Himself fully in accord on this point with the Father. This unique expression must be in harmony with the unique character of the situation. And the unique point in this latter is that it is a question of Jesus as dying. It is His testament which Jesus here places in the hands of His Father, and, as the expression of

HIS LAST WILL."

Christ here *wills ;* but He had previously promised (John 14 : 3).

23. Oneness in Fellowship   25

" I have known Thee . . . these have known." The world does not know the Father as such ; but the saints know Him because they know the Son. All acquaintance with the Father comes through fellowship with the Son.

24. Oneness in Intimacy   26

Christ makes known the Father. The Father is not knowable apart from the Son. He reveals God as Father. Mark the unique touches in His address to the Father. When it is Himself and the Father, He says " Father " and " O Father." When He prays for His own, it is " Holy Father." When He refers to the world, He says, " O righteous Father."

2

THE HEAD OF A GOLDEN WISDOM

THE wise man says, " The wise man's eyes are in his head " (Eccles. 2 : 14). The head stands for the seat of thought and understanding : therefore, the statement denotes the concentration of the man's mind upon the things that matter. Since that can be said of the ordinary man who is fulfilling the purpose of his intellectual being, how much greater the words can be applied to the God of Wisdom. We have to say of Him, as the bride said of her bridegroom, " His head is as the most fine gold " (Song of Solomon 5 : 11). That the God of wisdom can be any other than wise goes without saying, and it behoves us to remind ourselves that He is such. The wonderful God excites within us a sense of wonder, and it is well for us to be filled with awe and wonder as we think of Him, for that will call forth our praise and adoration.

The wisdom of God is seen in many directions, and we have to say of it that, like the grace of God, it is manifold. His wisdom is demonstrated in nature, as can easily be seen in any of God's beautiful flowers, if their make-up is studied and seen. His wisdom is illustrated in the creation of man and all his possibilities. His wisdom is seen in the history of the Church, for in spite of all her failures the ideal of God's purpose is exact and fitting. His wisdom is displayed in the Scriptures, for in them we find a revelation which is not made known in all the religious books of the religions of the world. His wisdom is made known in the Gospel, for that Gospel is a message of good news, telling how God has provided for the vilest, and that He in His grace can take even the scum of creation and make saints which shall glorify His Name. His wisdom is concentrated and demonstrated in Christ for He is essentially the Wisdom of God. Perhaps the Old Testament chapter in which He enunciates and enforces this, is in the wonderful description of Him that is found in Proverbs 8 ; and last, but not least, the wisdom of God is explicitly stated to be unfolded in the Cross of Christ's atoning death, for the Spirit's statement is that "Christ crucified is the power of God and the wisdom of God" (I Cor. I : 23).

We shall confine our study to this latter, namely, to see in the death of our Lord the mightiest display of God's wisdom that has ever been seen.

Wisdom may be summarized as intelligence seeing clearly, the fact of anything, and the right application of its use. Man in all his philosophy fails because he cannot see clearly, and he blunders again when he gets a conception of things because he lacks in wisdom, for wisdom is the right application of knowledge.

Paul was a master in philosophical reasoning, as well as a receiver of Divine revelation, and he was the former because he knew the Lord.

In his writings we often come across a full unfolding on a given theme as found in the section of his first letter to the saints at Corinth, when he makes known the difference between the wisdom of God in contrasting with it the wisdom of the world.

Man uses "enticing" words that he may make an impression upon others for his own glory and aggrandisement, and persuades his auditors to accept his dictum, but God seeks to convince us of the reality of things for our benefit (I Cor. 2 : 5). All God's wisdom and grace are centred in Christ, Who has ever been the embodiment and expression of it.

Man in his wisdom thinks he has the power to diagnose things, and has discernment of all things, but he has proven by his treatment of Christ that he is in the darkness of ignorance, and that all his wisdom comes to nought, and the crowning proof of it all, is in the crucifixion of the "Lord of Glory" (I Cor. 2 : 5-9).

The Christ on the Cross is to the cultured man in his wisdom, foolishness ; and to the religious man in his self-righteousness, a stumbling block ; but in God's grace and truth, as revealed in the glorified Christ, is the provision which He has made for man's salvation, for the Saviour on the Cross is God's answer for man's sin. And that same cross unfolds further, it is the power of God, for it lifts man from the defilement and degradation of iniquity (1 Cor. 1 : 20-24).

Man in his reasoning thinks that he can create an ideal and make himself answer to it, but he finds the folly of his schemes and the futility of his endeavour ; whereas, God in His wisdom can make Christ to be to the believer, righteousness, sanctification and redemption (1 Cor. 1 : 30, R.V.).

Man looks out into the future and creates a cult of his own speculation, as made known by the uncertainty of the darkness of spiritism, and forgets, or does not know, that " Eye hath not seen, nor ear heard, neither has entered into the heart of man, the things that God hath prepared for those that love Him ; " but the Holy Spirit opens up to us the future of all its glory and promise, hence the necessity to remember the future is made known in the revelation which the Spirit of God bestows, and is not found in the mind and wisdom of man (1 Cor. 2 : 9-16).

The wisdom of God is manifested in many ways, but it concentrates in Christ in Whom are " hid all the treasures of wisdom and knowledge " (Col. 2 : 3), and it irradiates in the glowing body on the cross of His atoning death.

> Without Christ all gain is loss ;
> All hope despair,
> That stands not in His Cross.

Godet has finely said : " The *wisdom* of God is the light which breaks on the believer's inward eye, when in the person of Christ he beholds the Divine plan which unites as in a single work of love, creation, incarnation, redemption, the gathering together of all things under one head, the final glorification of the universe. The believer thus finds himself, as Edwards says, in possession of ' a salvation which is at once the mightiest miracle in the guise of weakness (this for the Jew), and the highest wisdom in the guise of folly (this for the Greek).' "

Wisdom weighs the facts of the case, and meets the case in all its facts.

One of the greatest facts that faces humanity is the fact of sin. Canon Girdlestone, in his Synonyms of the Old Testament, in speaking about the language which God uses to describe sin, has given a brief summary as found in the following quotation :

" The pictorial power of the Hebrew language is seldom brought more prominently before the student than in its mode of designating the various aspects of evil. Every word is a piece of philosophy ; nay, it is a revelation. The observer of human affairs is painfully struck by the wearisomeness of life, and by the amount of toil and travail which the children of men have to undergo to obtain a bare existence ; he sees the hollowness, vanity, and unreality of much that seems bright and charming at first ; he notes that human nature, in its social and individual aspects, is distorted and out of course ; that the chain of love that ought to bind the great family in one has been snapped asunder ; that isolation and desolation have taken the place of unity and happiness ; that the relationship between man and his Maker has become obscured, and that even when man knows the will of God, there is something in his nature which prompts him to rebel against it ; lastly, he comes to the conviction that this state of things is not original, but that, like a dark cloud, it has intervened between the children of earth and the Sun of Righteousness, and has poured trouble upon humanity, opposing men's best instincts, and frustrating the original design of their creation."

God only knows the full facts about sin, and meets those facts as only He can. He meets them in the atoning sacrifice of Christ's death. This is seen in many ways, and not least in what the Spirit reveals in connection with the great red words of the Gospel, such as " Blood," " Love," " Grace," " Peace," " Cross," " Redemption," " Propitiation," " Forgiveness," " Justification," " Sanctification," " Passion," " Crucified," etc. The prominent star that shines out in connection with our Lord's death is, there is no word that is used in Holy Writ to describe sin but finds its full answer in that death for it.

We shall concentrate our study of this section by giving two lines of thought, namely, God's wisdom as seen in relation to Christ's death, first, that every truth of the Bible is associated with it ; and, second, in the offerings of the Old Testament, God's manifold wisdom is revealed in the way He minutely meets all the many questions that arise in relation to His glory and man's iniquity.

All the truths of the Bible centre in the atoning work of Christ. It is said of Bezaleel, who was the chief workman in the structure of the Tabernacle in the wilderness, that he was qualified for the work because there dwelt in him " The Spirit of Wisdom," and the wisdom of the Spirit of God is revealed as that Tabernacle is studied. We can only note one item, and that is that all the vessels of the Tabernacle could be enclosed in the area of the Altar of burnt offering, and surely this in its typical significance proclaims to us that all that Christ is in the heavenly sanctuary as our great High Priest, as He appears in the presence of God for us, is based on what He did for us in His atoning work on Calvary. The late H. W. Soltau has noted this fact in his book on " The Vessels of the Tabernacle." He says :

" The dimensions of the Altar of the Burnt Offering are such that all the other vessels of the Sanctuary could be included within it, and next, that there seems to be a manifest connection between its size and that of the Ark : for on referring to the measurements of the latter, we shall find that the height was one cubit and a half, just half the height of this altar : and the length was two cubits and a half, exactly half its length. May not these facts be intended to foreshadow, first, that every priestly ministration is involved in or connected with the death of the Lord Jesus, as every vessel of the Tabernacle was smaller than, and could be included in, the sacrificial altar ; and, secondly, that intercourse with God is a result from the fact of sacrifice, and is closely connected with it, as the size of the Ark is dependent on the size of the Altar ? One great object of God in giving His Son was to establish full and free intercourse with Himself ; so that the sinner, unhindered by his sins, might draw nigh, and might find and taste all the fresh springs of mercy and love flowing out from God abundantly through Christ."

As further illustrating all the truths of the Bible have their centre in the truth of Christ, we find that those truths are summarized under the following ten pivotal points, namely, the Bible, God, Man, Christ, Holy Spirit, Sin, Salvation, Church, Angels, and The Last Things. Everyone of these topics in their several bearings, finds its centre in the Man of Calvary.

THE BIBLE

The fact of Christ's death for our sins is said to be "according to the Scriptures" (1 Cor. 15 : 3, 4). This "according to" is full of suggestive meaning. The preposition "Kata" with the accusative suggests one object bending over another to meet its need, even as the nursing mother bends towards her babe to feed it. The Holy Spirit again and again, in referring to the death of our Lord, emphasizes that His death was the fulfilment of the Scriptures (Luke 24 : 27, 32, 45 ; John 13 : 8 ; 17 : 12 ; 19 : 24, 28, 36, 37 ; Acts 8 : 32, 35). Remove the atonement from the Bible, and we have a casket without the treasure ; a body without the spirit ; a tree without a root ; a house without the foundation ; a sky without the sun ; a cheque book without the balance at the bank ; and a gospel without the message.

GOD

There are seven great facts about the acts of God relative to Christ's death, each of which we find mentioned in the Epistle to the Romans.

The first fact is that God hath set Christ forth to be the Propitiation for our sins, and that by means of His Blood (Rom. 3 : 25, R.V.).

Second Fact. God's love is commended to us because Christ has died for us (Rom. 5 : 8).

Third Fact. God sent His Son in the likeness of sinful flesh (Rom. 8 : 3).

Fourth Fact. God condemns sin in the person of His Son on the Cross (Rom. 8 : 3, Margin).

Fifth Fact. God did not spare His Son when dealing with sin (Rom. 8 : 32).

Sixth Fact. God delivered Christ up for us when He gave Him over to death (Rom. 8 : 32).

Seventh Fact. The death and resurrection of Christ is God's answer to every charge that might be brought against us (Rom. 8 : 32, 34).

Therefore, at the Cross God is seen at His best in giving His Son for the worst, and in all that Christ did, God was acting, therefore in that death there is all the value of what He is in Himself. *God cannot die, but He Who died for us is God.*

MAN

At Calvary man is seen at his worst. We are told that " where sin abounded, grace did much more abound " (Rom. 5 : 20). This super-abounding of sin and grace is not a general statement, but a specific and formal one. Wicked hands nailed the Christ to the Cross (Acts 2). Mark, it does not say " sinful hands," but " wicked hands," which means rebellious hands, defiled hands, and shows man in the climax and concentration of his guilt. Man in the tripartite nature of his being is made up of spirit, soul and body. Man is identified with Christ, and Christ is identified with him in that He suffered in spirit and soul and body. His body was pierced for He was wounded for our transgressions (Isa. 53 : 5). His soul was poured out, for He is the Good Shepherd Who laid down His life (His soul) for the sheep (John 10 : 11). And He suffered in His spirit, for in anticipation of His death His spirit is said to be troubled on more than one occasion (John 12 : 27 ; 13 : 21).

CHRIST

Christ's goal was His death. His star of destiny was His death on Calvary. His death was no accident. On many occasions Christ in His teaching referred to His death on the Cross. If the Gospel of John alone is read with this thought in mind, it will be found that Christ directly and indirectly was indicating the nature and necessity of His death. There loomed before Him the momentous hour when He would pass through the awfulness of suffering for human guilt. Till the hour was come He could not die, but when it arrived He gave Himself up to answer for sin (John 17 : 1). There is one special occasion when Christ indicated the nature of His death. In the tenth chapter of the Gospel of John, five times over we find He stated that the Good Shepherd would lay down, or give, His life for the sheep (John 10 : 11, 15, 17, 18), and it is in the Gospel of John that we read of Christ's triumphant cry when He, in His sixth utterance on the Cross, exclaimed, " It is finished." Literally, He only uttered one word, " accomplished." How much was accomplished in that death ! If He had stopped one step short of the Cross His mission would have been a failure, for the Spirit of God has declared that the climax of Christ's ministry, as well as its nature, was " that He appeared to put away sin by the sacrifice of Himself " (Heb. 9 : 28).

THE HOLY SPIRIT

In many ways the association of the Holy Spirit with Christ in His death is seen. Generally speaking, we may say the Bible begins with a Brooding Dove in creation, and ends with a Bleeding Lamb in His glory and kingdom. Without multiplying Scriptures, we are most emphatically told that the Holy Spirit, as the Spirit of Christ, was associated with the prophets of old, as He made known to them the sufferings of Christ and the glory that should follow. The prophets did not always understand what the Spirit of God was revealing, hence they inquired and searched diligently what manner of time the Spirit of Christ which was in them did signify when it testified beforehand the sufferings of Christ and the glory that should follow (1 Pet. 1 : 10, 11). As the smitten rock in the wilderness brought forth the water that supplied the need of the children of Israel, so Christ, the Smitten Rock on Calvary, has obtained for us the Holy Spirit. Hence, we find in the Acts of the Apostles that the book opens with a passion of the Saviour's suffering, and is followed by the effectual power of the Holy Spirit.

SIN

If we may repeat the words of Canon Girdlestone when he refers to the words that were used to describe evil, " Every word is a piece of philosophy, nay, is a revelation." Sin, is a missing of the mark ; iniquity, is a distortion ; transgression, is going beyond the prescribed boundary ; rebellion, is the mailed fist of man's opposition ; trespass, is being unfaithful to a trust ; wickedness, is the turmoil of the tossing wave of man's unrest ; and unrighteousness, is the crookedness of man's actions. But the clarion note of the Gospel is, " Christ died for our sins." He died for us. He was " made sin " ; yea, as Benjamin Wills Newton says : " God damned sin in His Son !"

The above are only a few of the many statements and metaphors that are used to describe man's sin, but the wonderful revelation of Christ's death is this. There is no word that is used to describe human guilt, but finds its answer in the sacrifice of Christ for sinners.

SALVATION

The three-fold cord of salvation finds its fibre in the Cross. We are saved from condemnation through faith in Him Who gave Himself for us, hence, we are said to be saved from wrath through Christ (Rom. 5 : 9). Believers are being saved from the control of sin as the vitality of the risen life of Christ pulsates within them and overcomes the law of sin and death ; hence we read, " Much more being reconciled to God by the death of His Son, we shall be saved in His life " (Rom. 5 : 10), and believers will be saved from the body of sin and death when Christ comes back again. Hence we read, " God hath not appointed us to wrath, but to obtain the salvation by the means of our Lord Jesus Christ Who died for us, that whether we watch or sleep, we shall live together with Him " (I Thess. 5 : 9, 10, R.V.).

THE CHURCH

The Church always finds her basis in the Rock—the smitten Rock ; and it is her business to remember she has been purchased by Christ's Blood ; as Paul reminded the elders at Ephesus, when he charged them to tend the flock, which the Lord had " redeemed with His own blood." The late A. J. Gordon has well said : " The Church is Christian no more than as it is the continuous passion of Christ." This is proclaimed in the Lord's Supper and in the Believer's Baptism. Further, it is the Church's business to proclaim the Evangel of the Lord's Passion. Sir Robertson Nicol has said : " Not a few believers grow weakened and exhausted by sporadic efforts to assist in countless good causes. They forget in their breathless activity that Christ has not set His Church on earth primarily to do things, but to bear witness that He has done everything, and that the burden of humanity lies upon the Rock of Ages."

ANGELS

The objective fact of Christ's sufferings is always the object of the study of good angels. As the Cherubim is, made out of the same piece of gold which constituted the Mercy Seat, represented as gazing upon the Blood upon it (Ex. 25 : 18-22), so we read of the angels who desired to look into those things that related to Christ's sufferings and glory (I Pet. I : 12). Wicked angels, too, are found in association with Christ's death. The prince of the angels has been overthrown in his authority and power by means of the death of Christ (Heb. 2 : 14), and in the great battle which shall take place between Satan and his angels before Christ sets up His millennial kingdom, and those whom he sought to overcome, are able to overcome him by the Blood of the Lamb and by the word of their testimony, and they loved not their lives unto the death (Rev. 12 : 11).

THE LAST THINGS

The word of the last things, the Book of the Revelation, reveals Christ in a peculiar and unique character, namely, as a little Lamb. The word alone is found in the Book of the Revelation, for it is literally " a little Lambkin," and not a full-grown Lamb, as in four other places where He is mentioned as the Lamb of God. Twenty-eight times in the Book of the Revelation Christ is seen as the Little Lamb. As the

Lamb He is worshipped by all heaven's host. As a Lamb He makes His enemies to feel His power and indignation, for they are made to know the wrath of the Lamb ; and in the Golden Age, after the Millennium, Christ with His Bride is seen coming forth in His glory, and the glory is glorious in the heavenly city because the Light of it is the light of the glory of the Lamb.

CHRIST IN THE PASSOVER AND THE OFFERINGS

Is there not something unique, yea, we might say Divine, in the order in which the Books of the Bible occur ? At least we can see the order of experience in the spiritual life, in the sequence of their occurrence.

First, there is the *Genesis* of the new birth, the Spirit moving upon the chaos and darkness of our death and sin, and implanting the life of His own nature, and causing light to come and fruitfulness to be manifest.

Then there is the *Exodus* of redemption, the protection of the atoning blood from deserved judgment, the deliverance from the god of this world and the separation from world's doom and doings, and the Red Sea of Christ's death overcoming our enemies and cutting us off from the association of the evil of the Egypt of worldliness.

Then there is the *Leviticus* of worship on the ground of atonement. The blood of Christ's atonement is the ground of our blessing, and the God-given right of fellowship with Jehovah. He can speak to us from the blood-sprinkled mercy seat, because of the voice of Christ's completed work on Calvary.

Then there is the *Numbers* of the pilgrim life. The cloud of His presence and the fire of Jehovah's holiness are the shadow of His protecting love and the separating grace of His holy power. Armed by His armoury and shod by His grace, we walk amid the world of hostile influences unscathed and content.

Then there is the *Deuteronomy* of His instruction. Being dull of hearing and slow in learning the Lord has to call us into the School of His grace, that we may sit at His feet and hear His words. Uncircumcised ears have to be circumcised and dull senses have to be sharpened that we may learn to be wise and walk in His ways.

Then there is the *Joshua* of the fulness of the blessing of the promised land of abundance, which proclaims the fact that God hath blessed us with all spiritual blessings in Christ.

Then there is the *Judges* of conflict and also the equipment of the Spirit of Jehovah, who overcomes the enemies who oppose, and gives us the victory by His power.

Then there is the *Ruth* of Boaz's rest and redemption, which is found in the Kinsman Redeemer, to our heart's ease and enjoyment ; and

Then we are in the *Kings* of Christly rule, and find ourselves in the place of blessing and prowess by fellowship with David's greater Son.

The offerings are mainly dealt with, and the laws which regulate them, in the book of Leviticus. One significant omission impresses one, and that is, there is no mention of the Holy Spirit in the whole of the book. We can quite understand this speaking silence. It is the business of the Spirit to speak of Christ and to glorify Him. As He does this He hides Himself.

The keynote of the book of Leviticus is, worship on the ground of atonement. The outstanding truth of the offerings was the many-sidedness of Christ's atoning work, the meaning of which is, that all blessing from God and all approach to Him is on the ground of sacrifice. He who will not deal with the God of Calvary, will not find the God of grace with Whom he can deal.

The voice of Divine call in the book of Leviticus is, " Holiness to the Lord." The reason of the call to holiness of life is, because Jehovah is holy, hence, again and again the keynote is, " I am holy."

Absolute devotion and consecration are called for because of God's relationship to His people. Compromise with sin and association with sinners cannot be tolerated or allowed.

Separateness in dress, in food, in conduct, in dealing with others, in work, in worship, and in general deportment are all based on the fact that God's people are holy to Himself.

Another thing to recognize in the book of Leviticus and the offerings is, to note the " **forerunner, the after-comer, and the pivot-point.**" The forerunner is the Passover of God's delivering grace in the book of Exodus. Christ, our Passover, delivering us from the condemnation and control of sin, must be known before we can appreciate the many-sidedness of Christ's death in the offerings. Then the aftercomer of the offerings is, the ordinance of the red heifer in the book of Numbers (Num. 19). We ever need the cleansing of the blood of Christ as we are traversing this wilderness journey, for we are unconsciously contracting defilement, yea, even as we walk in the light and have fellow-ship with the Father and the Son, we need the cleansing of the blood to keep us fit for that holy place of fellowship, hence, the meaning of Hebrews 9 : 14, where we read, " How much more shall the blood of Christ, Who through the Eternal Spirit offered Himself without spot to God," etc. ; which, as Rotherham points out, means, not that Christ by the power of the Spirit offered Himself for us (although this is true), but that Christ in the eternalness of His own spirit projected Himself out for ever in an eternal efficacy of His own atoning death, hence, He lives in the power of an indis-soluble life (Heb. 7 : 16, R.V.M.), for He could not die again if He wanted to, and there is no need for Him to do so, for His death ever avails.

Then the pivotal point is the work of the great day of atonement. On that day, atonement was made not only for Aaron and his house and Israel, but also for the holy place, the tabernacle, and the altar (Lev. 16 : 15-18), in-dicating to us, in its typical application, that Christ's atone-ment avails for the house of the church, the nation of Israel, the holy place of the heavens (for they are not clean in His sight), the tabernacle of the old earth, and also the altar of heavenly worship and service. The tuning power which will cause all things to harmonize and act in perfect symphony, is the atonement of Christ.

One other thing it is well to notice is the order in which the offerings occur. First the burnt offering, then the meat offering, then the peace offering, then the sin offering, then the trespass, and then the drink offering.* The burnt offering of Christ's work to God in glorifying Him comes first because He must first be glorified. Then the meat offering of Christ's spotless Humanity. Then the peace offering of Christ's reconciling Ransom, upon the ground of which He keeps us in the place of fellowship with God. Then the sin offering of His being judged for our sin, in His death on the cross. Then the trespass offering of His bearing our sins in His own body on the tree ; and the drink offering of the wine of God's own joy in all that Christ did, and in all that it brings to us.

There are seven things in connection with each of the six offerings in Leviticus and Numbers, namely :

1. Jehovah and the offering.
2. The offering.
3. The offerer.
4. The priest and the offering.
5. The reason for the offering.
6. The blessing of the offering.
7. The practical teaching of the offering.

And Christ is seen in each point.

God's thought about Christ and His direction comes first, then Christ is the offering and the offerer, then Christ's official office is seen in relation to the offering, then the reason for the offering is to make an atonement, the blessings of the offering are various, and the practical outcome is what Christ can be in us, in the practicality of His love and grace.

THE PASSOVER

Before we can apprehend Christ in all the detail, all-sufficiency, and many-sidedness of His atoning death, we need to know Him as the One Who removes the condemnation of sin, as typified in the Passover.

---

* We recognise the drink offering is identified with the burnt offering, but we put it last, while we note its place and identity.

"Christ our Passover is sacrificed for us" (1 Cor. 5 : 7). When Jehovah was about to bring Israel out of Egypt, He said to Pharaoh, through Moses, " I will put a division," or a "redemption" (margin) "between My people and thy people " (Ex. 8 : 23). The Hebrew word rendered "Division" should be, as in the margin, rendered "Redemption." The word is translated "redemption" in Psa. 111 : 9, where we read, "The Lord sent redemption to His people." The word is also rendered "redemption" in Psa. 130 : 7—"With Him is plenteous redemption." The word means to sever by a ransom, hence, to release. Practically the same statement is repeated by Moses, when he proclaims what Jehovah is about to do, " That ye may know that the Lord doth put a difference* between the Egyptians and Israel" (Ex. 11 : 7). What that difference was, we are plainly told in Exodus 12, when the Lord passed over the children of Israel in grace, because of the shed blood of the Paschal Lamb, and passed through the midst of the Egyptians in judgment.

I. Direction

" Jehovah spake" (Ex. 12 : 1). "The Lord spake," settles all questions, solves all difficulties, scatters all doubts, sways all thought, sanctifies all service, satisfies all longings, searches all motives, and separates from all fears, to those who meet the Lord in the authority of His word by the faith of their hearts. One clear, concise direction to the children of Israel was, " Take every man a lamb and kill it on the fourteenth day of the month" (Ex. 12 : 6). There were many lambs killed on that day, but lambs are not

---

* The Hebrew word signifies " a difference in a marvellous and glorious manner," hence, " to separate and thus to distinguish." The word is so used in different relations. The word is rendered "separated " in Ex. 33 : 16, where Moses speaks of the Lord's presence with His people making a decided difference between them and other people. The same word is rendered " sever " and " set apart " in Ex. 8 : 22 ; 9 : 4 ; Psa. 4 : 3. The Hebrew word is also translated " shew marvellous " in relation to the Lord's exclusive " lovingkindness " (Psa. 17 : 7) ; and in Psa. 139 : 14, the Psalmist uses the same word, when he refers to his body as " wonderfully made." In each of these Scriptures there is the thought of distinction as well as difference.

spoken of : it is " the Lamb," clearly showing that the Lamb was typical of the Lamb of God, Who would in the fulness of time be slain for us.

Before the English took Quebec, under General Wolfe, the French thought themselves safe, in what seemed to them, an impregnable position. The city was poised, like some eagle in its nest, on an inaccessible height, as it proudly looked down upon the bosom of the flowing St. Lawrence. But the English had discovered a path, and in the silent midnight the army with muffled oars, floated on the ebb tide, scaled the heights, and the city taken. So Jehovah found a way to spare the first-born of Israel, not because the Israelites were any better than the Egyptians, but because He in His grace had loved them and had determined to save them (see the five references to Jehovah's love to Israel, and why He loved them, in Deut. 4 : 37 ; 7 : 7 ; 10 : 15 ; 23 : 5 ; 33 : 3).

The word of the Gospel is, as Elihu said long ago, " Deliver him from going down to the pit, for I have found a ransom," or as the Scripture might be rendered, " Release him by a ransoming price, for I have found an Atonement " (Job 33 : 24, margin). This is the message of the Divine Revelation of the Word, namely, " Christ died for our sins according to the Scriptures " (1 Cor. 15 : 3). Not according to men's opinions, nor men's thoughts, but " according to the Scriptures."

II. Provision

The slain Lamb was God's provision for Israel's safety : even as Christ's sacrifice on our account, is God's provision for the guilty race of man. The passover is significantly called " The Lord's Passover " (Ex. 12 : 27). So with Christ. God is no silent onlooker. His mind thought out the plan of salvation, His grace provided the sacrifice for salvation, His hand of power sustained Christ in His acting in salvation, His heart of love was manifested in the cross of salvation, His words of cheer encouraged Christ in His onward march to the goal of salvation, His walk of communion kept step with Christ in His obedience unto death to procure salvation, and in His Son there is the unfolding of all God's purpose

relative to salvation, for He is the Divine Word, " The
Logos," Who proclaims all the Father is and does.

The salvation of God's providing is gracious in its gift,
complete in its character, holy in its nature, sufficient in its
contents, perfect in its blessing, eternal in its bestowment,
powerful in its working, and answering to God in its outcome.

Many years ago a venturesome whale-ship, driven from
her course, found a deserted brig drifting among the ice-
floes of the polar sea.   Deserted by her crew, her rudder
guided by no human hand, she had sailed, like the ship of
the " Ancient Mariner," into that silent sea.   Her gallant
discoverers brought their prize through untold perils into
port.   But the tidings spread that the staunch ship, which
for well nigh two years had sailed among the frozen horrors
of the northern seas, without a living soul within her open
sides, was one of an English fleet that the British Government
had sent to rescue the heroic Franklin.   Then it was that the
United States did a beautiful, as well as a noble act.   The
U.S.A. Government fitted up the vessel in every minutest
detail.   From stem to stern her old aspect was restored.
On deck, in her cabin, not an article was lacking to render
her complete.   And then, with grateful courtesy, the costly
gift was sent across the ocean and given back, a freewill
offering to the Government of England.   The glory of the
deed belonged to America alone.   No British seaman had
helped to save her.   Not a farthing of English money had
aided in her restoration.   Even in her voyage across the
Atlantic, the crew that manned, the officers that commanded,
were of America's navy.   For England there remained
nothing to do.   She could only accept the salvation of her
vessel as a free and generous gift.   Bishop Cheney well says,
" Oh! type of God's work for man ; image of the simplicity
of men's accepting faith.   Brother, your soul has long been
like a ship abandoned to the seas.   God's mercy alone has
kept it so long afloat.   Drifting amidst icebergs, tossed on a
heaving sea, it is a miracle of Providence that it has not sunk
beneath the depths.   And now God would save it.   He
would rescue it from danger.   He would restore its long-lost
peace, its heavenly hope, its shattered purity, and give it

back to you redeemed and saved. But God will do it all. He will not give His glory to another. He will not let you add one solitary item to redeeming love, or pay one farthing for the blessings of salvation. There is absolutely nothing for you to do but to accept the gift. And this is faith. Oh take Him at His word!"

III. Application

It was not sufficient that the blood of the Lamb had been shed, it was to be placed by means of a bunch of hyssop on the side posts and lintel of the house. There had to be an application of the blood. The *sufficient* cause of God's salvation is found in the provision of His grace, but the *efficient* means of salvation is by virtue of our faith in Christ. The atonement of the Saviour only benefits those who accept the Saviour and His atonement.

There is a legend that on the night of the Exodus a young Jewish maiden—the first-born of the family—was so troubled on her sick-bed that she could not sleep. "Father," she anxiously inquired, "are you sure that the blood is there?" He replied that he had ordered it to be sprinkled on the lintel. The restless girl would not be satisfied until her father had taken her up and carried her to the door to see for herself ; and lo, the blood was not there. The order had been neglected, but before midnight the father made haste to put on his door the sacred token of protection. The legend may be false, but it teaches a very weighty and solemn admonition to every sinful soul who may be near eternity and is not yet sheltered under the atonement of Jesus Christ. It is not enough to know there is a Saviour provided, He must be the Saviour accepted.

IV. Salvation

Jehovah's word was, " I will pass over you " (Ex. 12 : 13). The Hebrew word " Pesak " comes from " Pasak," which means to *leap over*, or to move from one object to another. The noun, " *Pesak* " occurs 48 times in the Old Testament, and is always rendered " *Passover*." The verb, " *Pasak* " is translated " *Pass over* " in Ex. 12 : 13, 23, 27 ; and Isa. 31 : 5.

Lowth in commenting on Ex. 12 : 23, "The Lord will pass over the door," says, "The Lord will spring forward before the door "; or in his translation of Isa. 31 : 5, gives it, "As the mother bird hovering over its young, so shall Jehovah protect Jerusalem, protecting and delivering, leaping forward and rescuing her." The army of Sennacherib was invading Jerusalem, but the Lord assured His people, He would come over them and stand between them and the threatened danger. Thus the Lord not only passed over the children of Israel when He saw the blood, but He stood between them and any threatened danger ; yea, the Lord passed all over the children of Israel, even as the mother hen shelters her brood under her wings. Was it to this that our Lord refers in His lament over Jerusalem, when He exclaimed, "How often would I have gathered thee as a hen gathereth her chicken under her wings, and ye would not " (Matt. 23 : 37) ?

There is another thing that is worthy of our attention, and that is, the Angel of Judgment could not enter the houses where the blood was, for the blood (the symbol of death) prevented him. He could not enter from above, for the blood was on the lintel, he could not on the sides, for the blood was on the side posts, and he could not pass over the door step, for the blood was there too. "Blood on the door step !" exclaims someone. Yes, there was more blood there than anywhere else. The hyssop had to be dipped with the blood that was in the " bason " (Ex. 12 : 22). The word " *bason* " is unfortunate. The word rendered " *bason* " is the Egyptian word " *sap*," which means the step before the door, or the threshold of a house. The word is translated "*threshold*" in Jud. 19 : 27, and " *door* " in 2 Kings 12 : 9. The Septuagint version renders it, "The blood that is by the door." Strong says of the word, " In its original sense of containing a vestibule (as a limit)." Parkhurst says, " a threshold, which is swept or brushed by the door in shutting and opening." There was no direction given about the blood being put on the threshold for the simple reason the blood was already there, for that was the place where the lamb had been slain. Thus the blood of the lamb and the presence of Jehovah were Israel's salvation, so Christ not only in His atonement but Christ Himself is our Salvation. His Person and His work are the double securities of our salvation. We may well say, "God is my Salvation, I will trust and not be afraid."

V. Affirmation

God's "I will" of promise is enough for faith. His word was, "when I see the blood I will pass over you." The Word of God is faith's warrant and witness. God's witness to us of the worth of His Son is our assurance and authority. "He that believeth hath the witness in Him" (1 John 5 : 10, R.V.) ; that is, in Christ. The believer does not look within himself to find the witness, he listens to God as he looks at Christ, and finds it is in Him.

"One night I found," said a servant of Christ, "at a meeting, two lads of sixteen years of age sitting in a corner with their open Bibles. One had already been conversing with the other in an anxious state. 'Well, Johnny,' I said, 'what are you and George doing here?' 'I am trying to clear up his doubts,' said Johnny. 'What does he doubt?' 'His interest in Christ.' 'Well, what are you doing?' 'I am pointing him to the blood.' 'But is he not looking there already?' 'Perhaps he is, but I'm telling him to look till it grows on him.'" Ah, that is what we want : to look at the remedy till it so grows as to annihilate guilt ; to look at Christ and heaven till they so grow upon us as to outshine and eclipse the world. To look at the pattern He has set us till it grows in glory, and we grow through the power of the Spirit more and more "into the same image."

"When I see the blood," is what Jehovah says, "I will pass over you." Not when I see your good resolutions, your fine intentions, your earnest prayers, your much almsgiving, your zealous works, your extreme fasting, your penitent tears, your strong faith, and your consecrated purpose, but when I see the blood.

VI. Separation

Israel was not only protected in Egypt, but had to come out of it. They were separated from judgment by the blood.

They were separated to the Lord by His call, for they were to eat the Lord's passover with girded loins, shodded feet staffed hands, and in haste, hence, directly afterwards, it is said, "all the hosts of the Lord went out from the land of Egypt" (Ex. 12 : 11, 41). Some of them took Egypt out with them, although they came out of Egypt. They took out the bad taste of onions, garlic and leeks, and also some "dough" (Ex. 12 : 39 ; Num. 11 : 5). They had much better have left these things in Egypt, for they only went after more of them in the after days. It is a good thing to come clean out of the world, and let the Lord clean out the world from the heart. Separation to the Lord is the secret of the one, and occupied by the Lord's indwelling presence in the heart is the secret of the other.

VII. Communion

There is among the Hebrews a legend of two sisters who that night had, with the rest of their household, gone into their dwellings. One of them stood all ready to depart, and began quietly eating her portion of the roast body of the lamb (a type of the soul feeding on Christ), her mind at perfect peace and rest. The other was walking about the dwelling, full of terrible fear lest the Destroying Angel should penetrate therein. This one reproached her sister for being so careless and confident, and finally asked her how it was that she could be so full of assurance ; when the angel of death and judgment was abroad in the land. The reply was, "Why, sister, the blood has been sprinkled ; and we have God's word that when He sees the blood, He will pass over us. Now I have no right to doubt God's word. I believe He will keep His word. If I were in doubt about the blood having been shed ; or if I doubted either the integrity or ability of God in connection with His word, I should be uneasy. But, as I do not question the fact that the blood has been shed, and as I believe that God will be true to His word, I cannot but be at peace." They were both equally safe ; but one was at peace, while the other was not.

Peace is the result of communion. So long as any disturbing element worries the spirit, there can be no fellowship.

When there is nothing between the believer and the Lord, then the Lord has all things in common with him.

THE BURNT OFFERING

The Burnt Offering is typical of Christ in the Godward aspect of His atoning sacrifice, Who gave Himself an offering and a sacrifice to God for a sweet smelling savour (Eph. 5 : 2). Man had not only sinned, but come short of the glory of God (Rom. 3 : 23). Christ not only answered for sin, but He also glorified God, as He Himself said, " I have glorified Thee on the earth " (John 17 : 4).

I. Jehovah and the Offering

When man is first, he is always wrong, but when God is first man is right. Nothing was left to man's thought about the offering. In Lev. 1 Jehovah's name is mentioned again and again. The expressions are :

1. " The Lord called " (1 : 1). There is a general call to salvation, and a specific call to service.

2. " Before the Lord " (1 : 3, 5, 11). Consciousness of God's presence.

3. " Unto the Lord " (1 : 2, 9, 13, 14, 17), is significant of three things : The Lord's direction about the offering ; acting in the consciousness of Jehovah's presence, while offering the offering ; and the offering being given " to the Lord," it ascended to Him as " a sweet savour."

Christ was the One Who was directed in the work of atonement. It was His Father's word and work He fulfilled and accomplished (John 19 : 28, 30). What He did was in the consciousness of His Father's presence, hence, He was always about His business (Luke 2 : 49 ; John 4 : 34), doing the things pleasing to Him (John 8 : 29 ; Rom. 15 : 3), drinking the Father's cup (John 18 : 11), and ending His career as the One Who gave Himself to God for us (Heb. 9 : 14), in doing His will to benefit us (Heb. 10 : 7-10).

The three times the Father spoke to and of Christ, as recorded in the Gospels, are all associated with Christ's death and His pleasure therein. (1) After He came up from the waters of Jordan, typical of Calvary's baptism of judgment, the Father said, " This is My beloved Son in Whom I am well pleased " (Matt. 3 : 17). (2) At the transfiguration, when He spake of His decease, the Father said, " My beloved Son, in Whom I am well pleased " (Luke 9 : 31, 35). The other time was when Christ was troubled as to what He should say about His death. " What shall I say ? Father, save Me from this hour ? Father, glorify Thy name." Then there came a voice from heaven : " I have both glorified it and will glorify it again " (John 12 : 27, 28).

II. The Offering

A sevenfold description of the offering is given. The offering was to be (1) " without blemish " (Lev. 1 : 3, 10), typical of Christ in the sinlessness and the perfection of His humanity (1 Pet. 1 : 19). (2) It was to be wholly " consumed " (Lev. 1 : 9, 13, 15), typical of Christ Who gave Himself up to the will of God in death. He was " obedient unto death, even the death of the cross " (Phil. 2 : 8). (3) It was a " sweet savour offering " (Lev. 1 : 9, 13, 17), typical of Christ, Whose death brought glory and satisfaction to God (Phil. 2 : 11). (4) The offering was to be either a bullock, a lamb or a bird (Lev. 1 : 3, 10, 14), typical of Christ in the strength of His patient service (Luke 9 : 51), in His meekness and humility (Isa. 53 : 7), and in His weakness and innocence (2 Cor. 13 : 4). (5) It was to be offered on " the altar " (1 : 5, 11, 15), typical of Christ, Who offered His offering upon the altar of His Deity, " the Son of God, Who gave Himself for us " (Gal. 2 : 20). (6) Its blood was to be poured out—" drained " (Lev. 1 : 15, R.V.), and sprinkled (Lev. 1 : 5, 11), typical of Christ Who died to meet all requirements for us, and in Whom we find all we require (Heb. 10 : 1-10). (7) The burnt offering was cut and its parts specified—" the head, the fat, the inwards, the legs " (Lev. 1 : 8, 9, 12, 13), typical of Christ in His death in the " head " of His perfect knowledge about it (Matt. 16 : 21-23), in the " fat " of His healthful being (Acts 10 : 38), in the inness of His heart's affection (John 14 : 31), and in the " legs " of His determined way to the cross (Luke 13 : 33).

III. The Offerer

The offerer in some cases was different. If the offering was a beast the bringer of the offering was the offerer, but if the offering was a bird the priest acted for the offerer (Lev. 1 : 2, R.V. ; 1 : 15). The offerer is typical of Christ as man's representative, in whom man acts ; and the priest is typical of Christ as God's representative for whom He acts. There were seven things the offerer did : (1) Brought the offering to the door of the tabernacle for presentation (Lev. 1 : 3), typical of Christ Who presented Himself at His baptism and was accepted in the " well pleased " of Heaven (Mark 1 : 11). (2) It was presented by His own " voluntary will " as indicating there was no compulsion (Lev. 1 : 3), typical of Christ Who said of His life, " I lay it down of Myself " (John 10 : 18). (3) The offerer " put " his hand on the offering as indicative of his identification with it (Lev. 1 : 4), typical of Christ, Who cannot be separated from His work—the " Slain Lamb is the Sovereign Lord " (Rev. 5 : 6-9). (4) The offerer had to " kill " the offering (Lev. 1 : 5), typical of Christ Who surrendered Himself up to death (John 19 : 30). (5) The offerer had to " flay " the offering (Lev. 1 : 6), typical of Christ being stripped of all for us (2 Cor. 8 : 9). The word " flay " is the same as " stripped " in Job 19 : 9—" He hath stripped me of my glory," and in 1 Sam. 18 : 4, " Jonathan stripped himself." (6) The offerer " cut " the offering in pieces (Lev. 1 : 6), typical of Christ in the division of His service. See how this is illustrated in the seven sayings of the cross. His head of thought, His hands of service, His heart of love, His feet of passiveness. (The word " cut " is rendered " divided " in Jud. 19 : 29). (7) The offerer had to " wash " some parts of the offering—" his inwards and legs " (Lev. 1 : 9), typical of Christ, Who under the searching of the world and men and the devil, only revealed the perfection of His humanity. There was nothing of sin in Him, nor about Him (John 14 : 30 ; Heb. 7 : 26).

IV. The Priest and the Offering

The priest is typical of Christ in His official capacity acting for God as His representative, and also as the representative of believers acting to God for them.

There were some things the priest alone could do. (1) The priest alone had to do with the altar. He put the fire upon the altar, the wood upon the fire, the parts of the sacrifice upon the wood, and burned the sacrifice (Lev. 1 : 7-9), typical of Christ Who acted alone for us. He alone knew the worth of the altar of His Deity, the fire of Jehovah's majesty, the wood of human frailty, the details of God's requirement, and the glory of God. See how all this is brought out in Christ's priestly prayer of John 17. (2) The priest alone had the right to sprinkle the blood (Lev. 1 : 5, 11), typical of Christ, Who alone by means of His blood can cleanse our hearts from an evil conscience (Heb. 10 : 22). (3) The priest had to collect the ashes of the burnt offering and to carry them forth into a clean place (Lev. 6 : 11), typical of Christ, Who in the holy garments of His perfect priesthood, in the clean place of God's presence, has the ashes of His accepted sacrifice and thus the memorial of His atoning death, as He appears in the presence of God for us (Heb. 9 : 24). (4) The priest had to see there was a burnt offering offered every morning and evening (Ex. 29 : 38-42), typical of Christ Whose priestly service is of perpetual benefit (Heb. 7 : 25), because of the perpetual worth of His death (Heb. 10 : 14). (5) The skin of the burnt offering belonged to the priest (Lev. 7 : 8), typical of Christ Who fills the office of priest because He was stripped as the victim in death (Heb. 9 : 12). Christ can clothe us with His perfection, because He was stripped for us in propitiation.

V. The Reason of the Offering

" To make an atonement " is the terse and telling reason given, as to why the burnt offering was offered (Lev. 1 : 4) ; literally the word is " to give satisfaction." The word atonement is rendered " satisfaction " in Num. 35 : 31, 32. Atonement in connection with the burnt offering is typical of Christ giving satisfaction to God's glory. " We may satisfy a loving and holy requirement, or satisfy offending justice. Either would be satisfaction : the burnt offering is the former ; the sin offering, the latter."

VI. The Blessing of the Offering

The offering was accepted " before the Lord " (Lev. 1 : 3), that it might be " accepted for " the offerer (Lev. 1 : 4). There is not only the thought of something being accepted for the offerer in the word " accepted," but there is the thought of delight. The word is rendered " delighteth " in Isa. 42 : 1, in speaking of Christ in Whom God delighteth. The word is also translated " pleasure," " the Lord taketh pleasure in His people " (Psa. 149 : 4). Believers in Christ are comely in all the comeliness of His perfection (Ez. 16 : 14), complete in all the completion of His completeness (Col. 1 : 10), alive in all the livingness of His life (1 Pet. 2 : 4, 5), righteous in all the righteousness of His righteousness (2 Cor. 5 : 21), holy in all the sanctity of His holiness (Heb. 10 : 10, 14), rich in all the treasure of His riches (Eph. 1 : 3-7), precious in all the preciousness of His preciousness (1 Pet. 2 : 7, R.V.), and accepted in all the worth of His acceptance (Eph. 1 : 6).

VII. Practical Outcome of the Offering

As the offering was a " sweet savour unto the Lord," that is, that which was well pleasing to Him ; so we find there are certain things in the New Testament which are said to be acceptable or well-pleasing to Him.

1. A surrendered being to the Lord is well-pleasing or acceptable to Him (Rom. 12 : 1).

2. Consideration for others in the Lord is " well-pleasing to God " (Rom. 14 : 18, R.V.).

3. To minister to the need of God's servants is " well-pleasing to God " (Phil. 4 : 18, R.V.).

4. To recognize our responsibility in earthly relationships is " well-pleasing to the Lord " (Col. 3 : 20 ; Titus 2 : 9).

5. To have faith in God is to be " well-pleasing to Him " (Heb. 11 : 5, 6).

6. To do good to others is to be well-pleasing to God (Heb. 13 : 16).

7. To suffer wrongfully is to be acceptable to Him (1 Pet. 2 : 20).

We are saved and called to offer up these "spiritual sacrifices acceptable to God" (1 Pet. 2 : 5), we are exhorted to "offer service," after this kind "well-pleasing to God" (Heb. 12 : 28) ; and we should "make it our aim" to be "well-pleasing" to the Lord, for we have to stand before his judgment seat (2 Cor. 5 : 9, R.V.) ; and we may be assured that, as we allow the Lord to be "working in us that which is well-pleasing in His sight" (Heb. 13 : 21), we shall be "proving what is well-pleasing unto the Lord" (Eph. 5 : 10, R.V.).

MEAT OR MEAL OFFERING

(READ LEVITICUS 2)

The meat offering is typical of Christ in the perfection of His humanity, the holiness of His character, and the spotlessness of His beautiful life.

I. Jehovah and the Meal Offering

Eight times in Lev. 2 we have the expression, "unto the Lord" (1, 2, 8, 9, 11, 12, 14, 16).

Once we have the sentence, "the salt of the covenant of thy God" (verse 13) ; and twice the words, "the offerings of the Lord made by fire" (verses 3, 10).

In all Christ was and did, He ever was "unto the Lord."

He walked in His Father's ways (John 16 : 28).

He willed His Father's will (John 5 : 30).

He spake His Father's word (John 14 : 24).

He did His Father's work (John 17 : 4).

He rejoiced in His Father's love (John 10 : 17 ; 15 : 9).

He sought His Father's aid (John 11 : 41).

He aimed at His Father's glory (John 8 : 49).

"The salt of the covenant of thy God" is indicative of God on His part, keeping to His covenant promise to Christ (John 17 : 24), and on Christ's part indicative of His faithful service, seasoned with the salt of grace, in perfectly fulfilling our obligations to God and tasting death in so doing (Heb. 2 : 9).*

" The offering made by fire unto Jehovah," in its typical application, for this expression applies to other offerings as well as the meal offering (Lev. 1 : 9, 17 ; 3 : 3, 5, 9), proclaims Christ's endurance under the fire of trial, whether it be the fire of man's persecution (1 Pet. 2 : 23), the fire of the Spirit's testing under Satan's temptation (Luke 4 : 1, 2), or the fire of the Lord's judgment against sin (Rom. 8 : 3).

CHRIST, THE GOD-MAN

Nineteen hundred years ago,
   Upon Judean hills,
A character of wondrous blending
   Suddenly appears ;
The man of destiny ;
   Man destined to be,
In profile projected ;
   By prophets predicted ;
In symbol reflected ;
   Longed for—expected ;
By all ages desired ;
   By angels admired ;
Like man He walked ;
   Like God He talked ;
His words were oracles ;
   His acts were miracles ;
Of God, the best expression ;
   Of man, the finest specimen.
Full-orbed humanity,
   Crowned with Divinity ;
No taint of iniquity,
   No trace of infirmity.
" Ecce Homo !" Behold the Man,
" Ecce Deus !" Behold thy God.

---

* " To this day among the most diverse peoples, salt is the recognized symbol of incorruption and unchanging perpetuity. Among the Arabs of to-day, for example, when a compact or covenant is made between different parties, it is the custom that each eat of salt, which is passed around on the blade of a sword ; by which act they regard themselves as bound to be true, each to the other, even at the peril of life. In like manner, in India and other Eastern countries, the usual formula for perfidy and breach of faith is, literally, unfaithfulness to the salt ; and a man will say, ' Can you distrust me ? Have I not eaten of your salt ?' "

II. The Offering

The following general particulars may be noted :

1. " Fine flour " (Lev. 2 : 1), and " green ears of corn dried by the fire " (Lev. 2 : 14), are typical of Christ in the fineness of His holy character (Acts 3 : 14), and the full worth of His beautiful life, although scorched in the fire of trial (Acts 4 : 27, R.V.). Of Him the Holy Spirit says, that Holy Thing shall be called the Son of God (Luke 1 : 35).

2. Oil mingled with fine flour (Lev. 2 : 4), is typical of Christ being born of the Holy Spirit as to His perfect humanity (Matt. 1 : 20).

3. The oil poured upon the meal (Lev. 2 : 1) is typical of Christ being anointed with the Spirit (Acts 10 : 38).

4. Seasoned with salt (Lev. 2 : 13) is typical of the salt of grace (Col. 4 : 6), which seasoned all His words (Luke 4 : 22).

5. Frankincense is (Lev. 2 : 2) typical of the aroma of His life (John 8 : 29).

6. " No leaven " was allowed (Lev. 2 : 4, 5, 11 ; 6 : 17), which is typical of the fact that Christ was free from the leaven of wickedness (1 Cor. 5 : 8). Four things are said of Him. He " did no sin " (1 Pet. 2 : 22), He knew no sin (2 Cor. 5 : 21), " In Him is no sin " (1 John 3 : 5), and He was " undefiled " (Heb. 7 : 26).

7. No honey was to be associated with the offering (Lev. 2 : 11), and is typical of Christ, in Whom there was not the honey of sinful flattery and the unholy sweetness of the flesh (Prov. 5 : 3), nor the surfeiting of worldliness and its care (Prov. 25 : 16 ; Luke 21 : 34), but the life of unsullied consecration to God (John 17 : 19).

8. The offering was " most holy " (Lev. 2 : 3 ; 6 : 17), typical of Christ in the wholeness of His holy consecration to Jehovah. He was " Holy " as well as " undefiled " (Heb. 7 : 26).

9. Part of the offering was burnt by the priest on the altar when for an Israelite (Lev. 2 : 2 ; 6 : 15), but it was wholly consumed when for a priest (Lev. 6 : 23), and is typical of Christ, Who was only partially appreciated while

on earth as the Offerer (John 16 : 8-10), but Who is wholly appreciated in Heaven in His priestly service as the Man of men, acting for us (Rom. 8 : 34).

10. This offering was never disassociated from " the altar of burnt offering "—the place of sacrifice (Ex. 30 : 10 ; 40 : 29 ; Lev. 2 : 2, 8, 12 ; 6 : 15—" the altar " is always the altar of burnt offering),—and it was to be offered with the daily sacrifices (Ex. 29 : 40-42) and the burnt offering (Num. 15 : 3-12), typical of Christ in the combination of His life and death.   His perfect life qualified Him to act for us, but the act of His propitiatory death was the goal of His ministry (Rom. 5 : 18, R.V. ; Heb. 9 : 26).

III. The Offerer

The offerer did very little in connection with the meal offering.   Practically he only did two things.   He brought the offering to the priest, and then took a handful of it for the priest to offer as a memorial to the Lord.   The offerer is closely identified with the priest, it will be noticed.   Christ in the perfection of His manhood and His priesthood are intimately connected.   Very suggestively do we find these two things in the Epistle to the Hebrews when our Lord is spoken of by His human name " Jesus."   " We see Jesus," because of His death, crowned with honour and glory (2 : 9) ; we are privileged to enter the " holiest by the blood of Jesus " (10 : 19) ; we are exhorted to be " looking unto Jesus " as our Example (12 : 2) ; we are reminded that we have come " to Jesus the Mediator of the new covenant " (12 : 24), and that " Jesus . . . that He might sanctify " us, " suffered without the gate " (13 : 12) ; but our attention is also directed to Him as the " Apostle and High Priest, of our confession, even Jesus " (3 : 1, R.V.) ; for He is " the Fore-runner . . . even Jesus," having become a high priest (6 : 20, R.V.) ; and as " Jesus " has " become the surety of a better covenant " (7 : 22, R.V.).

While we may distinguish between what Christ was as the Offerer, and what He is as the Priest, we must not separate these offices, for they are essential the one to the other.

IV. The Priest and the Offering

The high priest had to offer a meat offering at his consecration to the priesthood (Lev. 6 : 19-23), this meat offering was wholly consumed on the altar : and is typical of Christ, Who, in the perfection of His holy humanity, and in the completeness of His atonement, has entered upon His priestly office. The Man of Bethlehem, Nazareth, Calvary, and Olivet is the " same Jesus." Mark the frequent expression in Hebrews, " This man " (3 : 3 ; 7 : 24 ; 8 : 3 ; 10 : 12), associated with His priesthood. The Man that was, is the Priest that is.

It was the business of the eldest son of the High Priest to take care of the meat-offering—" To the office of Eleazar pertaineth . . . . the daily meat offering " (Num. 4 : 16). Typical of the Spirit's work, Whose business it is to conserve the glory of Christ and to enhance His worth (John 16 : 13, 14).

In every meat offering the priest had his portion of what the offerer brought (Lev. 2 : 3 ; 6 : 16, 17), and not only Aaron, but his sons as well. Typical of the fact that believers are privileged to have fellowship with Christ, in feeding upon His holy character and thus in the spiritual feeding upon His flesh and blood to nourish the inner life.

One important thing must not be overlooked, it was to be " eaten in the holy place." It is only in the holy place of hallowed fellowship with Christ that we can feed upon Him.

V. The Reason for the Offering

One sentence sums up the reason for the offering. " The priest shall burn the memorial of it upon the altar, to be an offering made by fire of a sweet savour unto the Lord " (Lev. 2 : 2).

This offering is called " an offering of memorial " (Num. 5 : 15). It would recall the offerer's indebtedness to Jehovah for all His goodness. It was a " gift-offering " calling to remembrance. The very word " memorial," or words coming from the same root, is repeatedly used. " Give thanks at the remembrance (memorial) of His holiness " (Psa. 30 : 4 ; 97 : 12). " Thy remembrance (memorial) unto all generations " (Psa. 102 : 12). " Made His wonderful works to be

remembered " (lit., for a memorial, Psa. 111 : 4). "Thy
name endureth for ever, and thy memorial unto all generations " (Psa. 135 : 13). "The memory (memorial) of Thy
great goodness " (Psa. 145 : 7). " The Lord is His memorial "
(Hos. 12 : 5). The fragrance (the word "memorial" is rendered "scent" in Hos. 14 : 7) of Christ's life is appreciated
by God. His Beloved is a "sweet savour" to Him. The
BRANCH shall ever be "a memorial in the temple of the
Lord " (Zech. 6 : 14), and we do well to keep a book of
remembrance (memorial) as we think "upon His NAME "
(Mal. 3 : 16), for it is as ointment poured forth.

> The music of His matchless worth,
> It fills God's soul with joy and mirth.

VI. The Blessing of the Offering

As the offerer, Aaron and his sons and Jehovah were
identified with this offering ; so believers are identified with
God in His grace, and Christ in His priestly office, because of
Him Who lived and died for us. The blessing of His righteousness justifies us (Rom. 5 : 18, 19), the blessing of His
peace quietens us (John 14 : 27) ; the blessing of His love
inspires us (John 13 : 1) ; the blessing of His gift enriches us
(John 10 : 28) ; the blessing of His Word assures us (John
17 : 8) ; the blessing of His Spirit empowers us (John 16 : 7) ;
and the blessing of His example commands us (John 13 : 15).

One thing we need to keep ever in remembrance, and
that is, Christ's life is a blessing to us because the door of His
death has opened it to us. As Professor Charteris said,
" There was only one Christian life that began at Bethlehem,
and that was Christ's, every other Christian life begins at
Calvary and goes back to Bethlehem."

VII. Practical Teaching of the Offering

As Aaron and his sons (the consecrated ones, see Lev. 8)
were only allowed to eat the "remainder" of the offerer's
meat offering, with "unleavened bread . . . in the holy
place " (Lev. 6 : 16), so believers can only feed upon Christ
as they are separated from the leaven of wickedness and

dwell in the holy place of consecration to the Lord in the Spirit (Gal. 5 : 9, 22-25).

" Unto the Lord " (Lev. 2 : 2, 8, 9, 12, 14, 16) strikes another practical note. The gospel of " unto " is emphasized again and again in the New Testament.

Turning unto the Lord is the law of the believer's conversion (1 Thess. 1 : 9, R.V.).

Cleaving unto the Lord is the law of the believer's faith (Acts 11 : 23).

Living unto the Lord is the law of the believer's life (Rom. 14 : 8).

Making melody unto the Lord in the heart is the law of the believer's worship (Eph. 5 : 19).

Service done unto the Lord is the law of the believer's work (Col. 3 : 23, R.V.).

Ministering unto the Lord is the law of the believer's ministry (Acts 13 : 2).

Commending unto the Lord is the law of the believer's sympathy (Acts 14 : 23).

Giving unto the Lord is the law of the believer's consecration (2 Cor. 8 : 5).

Dr. S. H. Kellogg practically says : " A minister of the Word may with steady labour drive the ploughshare of the law and sow continually the undoubted seed of the Word in the Master's field ; and the apparent result of his work may be large, and even real, in the conversion of men to God, and a great increase of Christian zeal and activity. And yet it is quite possible that a man may do this, and still do it for himself, and not for the Lord ; and when success comes, begin to rejoice in his evident skill as a spiritual husbandman, and in the praise of man which this brings him ; and so, while thus rejoicing in the fruit of his labours, neglect to bring of this good corn and wine which he has raised for a daily meat offering in consecration to the Lord. Most sad is this, and humiliating, and yet sometimes it so comes to pass. And so, indeed, it may be in every department of religious activity."

THE PEACE OFFERING

The Peace Offering is typical of Christ Who, by means of His death, has made peace for us (Col. 1 : 20), reconciled us to God (Rom. 5 : 10), brought us into the place of possible enjoyment of the peace of God (Phil. 4 : 6, 7), and also of knowing the God of peace, and having fellowship with Him in the calm of His presence and the efficiency of His grace (1 Thess. 5 : 23 ; Heb. 13 : 20, 21). The peace offering is called " the food of the offering " (Lev. 3 : 11, 16). It was the food of God, and is typical of the satisfaction which the Father finds in Christ's death, for He and believers have fellowship with each other by means of it.

I. Jehovah and the Offering

As in the previous offerings, so in the Peace Offering, the expression, " unto the Lord," occurs (Lev. 3 : 3, 5, 6, 9, 11, 14 ; 7 : 11, 14, 20, 21, 25, 29 ; 19 : 5 ; 22 : 21, 22, 24). " Before the Lord " (Lev. 3 : 1, 7, 12 ; 7 : 30) is of frequent occurrence. To Jehovah and in the consciousness of His august presence all was to be done. This offering was also called " the hallowed Thing of the Lord " (Lev. 19 : 8), and in connection with it, emphasis is laid upon the fact that the " offerings " are the " offerings of the Lord " (Lev. 7 : 20), typical of Christ Who answered to God in the holiness of His nature, and Who is claimed by God to His own satisfaction.

" The LORD spake " (Lev. 7 : 22, 28) is again repeated. Typical of Christ Who acts under the authority of His Father. He had no works to perform, no words to utter, no will to act, and no work to accomplish, but what He had received from His Father (John 14 : 10 ; Luke 22 : 42 ; John 4 : 34).

" All the fat is the Lord's " (Lev. 3 : 16). The little word " all " is found in connection with each of the offerings. Of the burnt offering it is commanded, " Burn *all* on the altar " (Lev. 1 : 9) ; of the meat offering the priest had to burn " *all* the frankincense " on the altar (Lev. 2 : 2) ; of the sin offering it is said, " *all* his flesh " shall be burned outside the camp (Lev. 4 : 11, 12) ; in connection with the trespass offering, as to the blessing which came to the offerer, we read, " It shall be forgiven him for anything of *all* he hath done " (Lev. 6 : 7) ;

and of the peace offering " *all* the fat " was for the Lord. Typical of Christ in the entirety of His devotedness to God. In the burnt offering He was all for God ; in the meat offering He was all-pleasing to God , in the sin offering He was wholly consumed by God in answering for all our sin ; in the peace offering He was perfect in the devotion of His inner being ; and as the trespass offering He has procured for us a perfect remission from all the consequences of all our sins.

" I AM JEHOVAH " occurs four times at the end of the directions about certain peace offerings (Lev. 22 : 30, 31, 32, 33), indicating the absolute responsibility to do as He wishes and an intimation that being in the line of His will, He will enable the offerer to perform what He commands. It is not without significance that Christ is said to have been enabled to taste death for us, by the grace of God (Heb. 2 : 9).

II. The Offering

There are three special things to which we call attention : What the offering is called, the kinds of offerings presented, and the essential thing in the offering for Jehovah.

What the offering is called

1. Peace offering (Lev. 3 : 1), typical of Christ, Who sacrificed Himself in making peace with God on our account, hence, He is now our Peace (Eph. 2 : 14)

2. Holy offering, for it was to be " without blemish "— Christ our Holiness (1 Cor. 1 : 30).

3. " Sweet savour " offering (Lev. 3 : 5)—Christ our Acceptance (Eph. 1 : 6 ; 5 : 2).

4. Altar offering (Lev. 3 : 5)—Christ our Altar (Heb. 13 : 10).

5. Food offering (Lev. 3 : 11, 16)—Christ our Food (John 6 : 53-58).

6. Thanksgiving offering (Lev. 7 : 12)—Christ our Praise (Heb. 13 : 15),

7. Vow offering (Lev. 7 : 16, 17)—Christ our Responsibility (John 17 : 19).

The kinds of offerings presented

There are three kinds of offerings, namely, sacrifices of " thanksgiving," " vows," and " freewill offerings." The first was expressive of gratitude for blessings received (Psa. 116 : 16, 17). The second was in fulfilment of promise (Psa. 66 : 13, 15 ; 116 : 14, 18) ; and the freewill offering seems to have been generally offered in asking special favour of God (Jud. 20 : 26 ; 2 Sam. 24 : 25). All this is typical of Christ, Who freely gave Himself (John 10 : 15), Who answered for all our broken vows (Psa. 69 : 4), and Whose sacrifice was gladly rendered on our account (Psa. 40 : 6-8).

The fat and the inwards were specially the Lord's portion (Lev. 3 : 3, 4)—these are typical of Christ's inward excellence. Newton says, in speaking of " the *fat*," " The word for *fat* denotes the excess of excellence. ' Who filleth thee with the *finest* (fat) of the wheat' (Psa. 147 : 14). ' All the best (literally, fat) of the wine ' (Num. 18 : 12). . . . Where there is *vigour* in the powers of the inward being and where that inward vigour is found meet for the altar, there must indeed be perfectness. But where was such perfectness found ? Only in Him Who gave Himself for us, an offering and sacrifice to God, for a sweet smelling savour."

One other thing is worthy of note. The Hebrew word, " *Shelem* " (sacrifice), is confined to the peace offering, or as the peace offering should be called, " *peace sacrifice*." So in Psa. 40 : 6 (where all the four offerings of the first four chapters of Leviticus are enumerated, as set aside by being fulfilled in Christ Himself) the word " sacrifice " stands for peace sacrifice. The word " peace " is in the plural number, as if to betoken peace of every kind—perfect peace. Peace that shall answer every question of doubt or uncertainty.

III. The Offerer

Without enumerating the points of resemblance in the acts of the Offerer, between the peace and the other offerings, there is one which we may emphasize, namely, the offerer had his portion of the offering, upon which he could feed. Excepting " the fat, the blood, the inwards," which were the Lord's, the shoulder and the breast were for the priest and his family. The rest was for the offerer. " Christ as the Offerer stands as our Representative. Whether it be in the Sin-offering, the Burnt-offering, the Meat-offering, or the

Peace-offering, He is the man Christ Jesus " for us." He is
for us without the camp, for us put upon the altar, for us
bearing our sins, for us accepted and satisfied. And when
we say He did this for us, we mean that He did it *instead* of
us, nay, *as us*. Thus when He was judged, He was judged
as us. When He kept the law, He kept it as us. When He
was accepted, He was accepted as us ; and so when He was
satisfied, He was satisfied as us."

The offerer feasted with God, with the priest (Lev.
7 : 28-34), and with the priest's children (Num. 18 : 9-11),
for they all had their share in the same victim. So Christ
as our Representative has fellowship with His Father in
feeding upon His death (John 17 : 4) ; with Himself as the
High Priest, for He is satisfied with that death which gives
Him His present position and glory (Heb. 2 : 9) ; and we who
are associated with Him have communion with Him in the
satisfaction and supply of His death (1 Cor. 10 : 16).

IV. The Priest and the Offering

There are four things we may emphasize :

1. The priest sprinkled the blood upon the altar. The
blood on the altar always speaks of atonement (Lev. 17 : 11).
Christ's present priestly work is based upon His past atonement given by His death. His priestly service is always
coupled with His propitiatory sacrifice.

2. The Lord's portion of this offering is burned upon
" the altar upon the burnt sacrifice " (Lev. 3 : 5). Acceptance in Christ is the foundation of communion with God.
The burnt offering of Christ's worthiness in glorifying God
by means of which we are accepted, secures for us the place
of fellowship.

3. The shoulder of the peace offering was the portion of
the officiating priest—" It shall be the priest's that sprinkleth
the blood of the peace offerings " (Lev. 7 : 14, 32, 33). The
shoulder is always the symbol of power (see Isa. 9 : 6 ; Luke
15 : 5). Christ alone is the One Who lives, as our High
Priest, in the power of an endless life. (See the word
" *power*," *Dunamis*, in Heb. 1 : 3 ; 7 : 16 ; and the word
" *able*," *Dunamai*, in Heb. 2 : 18 ; 7 : 27.) The secret of His
power is His own inherent quality.

4. The breast of the peace offering was "for Aaron and his sons" (Lev. 7 : 31). The breast is the symbol of affection (Isa. 66 : 11 ; John 13 : 25). Believers and Christ can feed upon the affection which the cross displays, and find there the "meat indeed." The threefold love of God, namely, love *toward* us, love *in* us, and love *with* us (1 John 4 : 9, 12, 17, margin), is food enough for Him and us. Both the breast and shoulder are called offerings : the former a "wave offering" and the latter a "heave offering" (Lev. 7 : 30, 32). Everything has first to be presented "before the Lord" and given unto Him, then there can be received, that which is for us, from Him. Christ ascended to His Father in the heave offering of His resurrection and in the wave offering of His triumph, before He descended in the power of His Spirit and Word. "In and out" is God's order. "In" for fellowship, and "out" in blessing (John 10 : 9).

V. The Reason of the Offering

In Ezek. 45 : 15 we read of peace offerings with the burnt offering "*to make a reconciliation*," or more correctly, as the Revised Version, "*to make atonement*." The word is the primary root used in the Old Testament "to make an atonement," and in its typical application signifies Christ in the Godward aspect of His work giving satisfaction to God on account of sin, and therefore declares His work done for us. As found in connection with the peace offering, atonement may be used to illustrate a blessing which comes to us by means of it, namely, reconciliation. "*Kaphar*" is rendered "*reconciling*" and "*reconciliation*" in Lev. 16 : 20 ; Ezek. 45 : 15, 17 ; and Dan. 9 : 24. Christ died to reconcile us to God, *not* to reconcile God to us. God never went away from man, man went away from God. To sing—

> " My God is reconciled,
>   His pardoning voice I hear,"

is not correct, but to sing—

> " My soul is reconciled,
>   God's pardoning voice I hear,"

is to state the truth of being at one with God in the place of fellowship, by means of Christ's atonement.

VI. The Blessing of the Offering

The word for " *peace offering* " is " *Shelem,*" and is derived from the primary word, " *Shalem,*" which means to be safe, to be complete. The word " *Shalem* " is rendered, " *Be at peace,*" in Job 22 : 21 ; " *finished,*" in 2 Chron. 5 : 1 ; " *make prosperous,*" in Job 8 : 6 ; " *make restitution,*" in Ex. 22 : 5 ; and " *repaid,*" in Prov. 13 : 21. The use of the relative word may indicate some of the blessings which flow from Christ as our Peace offering. By His death He has finished the question of our sin (Heb. 9 : 26) ; by His death peace has been made (Col. 1 : 20), and we are at peace (Rom. 5 : 1) ; by His death the old life of sin is ended, and we are made prosperous in the new life of the new creation (2 Cor. 5 : 14, 17) ; by His death He has given to God, that which more than makes restitution for all our failure (Eph. 5 : 2) ; and by His death He has paid what we could never pay (1 Tim. 2 : 5, 6).

Dr. Kellogg says : " Man's idea always is, until taught by God, I will be religious and make God my friend, by doing something, giving something for God. God, on the contrary, teaches us in symbolism, as in all Scripture, the exact reverse ; that we become truly religious by taking, first of all, with thankfulness and joy, what He has provided for us."

VII. The Practical Teaching of the Offering

The Peace Offering is frequently called " a sacrifice of peace offering." In Num. 7, for instance, it is so described no less than 13 times, namely, in verses 17, 23, 29, 35, 41, 47, 53, 59, 65, 71, 77, 83, 88. The word " *Zebach,*" from " *Zabach,*" means to slaughter, and is rendered " *killed* " and " *slew* " in 1 Sam. 28 : 24 ; 2 Kings 23 : 20, hence it always means to put to death, therefore denotes the slaying of the animal for a peace offering. The Greek word for sacrifice, " *Thusia,*" from " *Thuo,*" has the same meaning. When applied to sacrifice it means to kill, and is rendered " *killed* " in Mark 14 : 12. When used in a Christian sense it suggests the thought of self-immolation. It is an axiom in the Christian life, that there can be no life truly Christian, without the renunciation of self.

There are three things we may ponder in thinking of the practical teaching suggested by the peace offering. These may be summed up under the words, Principles, Practice, Privilege.

1. Principles. The sacrifice of Christ must touch all sacrifices which we make. His sacrifice is the cause and pattern of our actions. While Amos 4 : 5 applies to Israel, we may take it to illustrate that we who believe in Christ have obligations to fill, by virtue of the covenant, that He has fulfilled for us, hence we are always directed to the Sacrifice of all sacrifices, as the reason and inspiration of any sacrifice we may make.

In Zech. 14 : 21 we read, " Every pot in Jerusalem, and in Judah, shall be holiness unto the Lord of hosts : and all they that sacrifice shall come and take them, and seethe therein." As the holy vessels will be used in the day of the Lord's millennial glory, in connection with the sacrifices, so the essential thing to make our sacrifices acceptable to the Lord is the vessel of a holy life.

Willingness on the part of the offerer was an essential thing in making the sacrifice of the peace offering—" Ye shall offer it at your own will " (Lev. 19 : 5). While the imperative mood is used in such Scriptures as Psa. 4 : 5 ; 50 : 14, where we are commanded to " offer the sacrifice," for love knows the obligation of command, yet it ever says, " I will freely sacrifice unto Thee " (Psa. 54 : 6).

2. Practice. In the Old and New Testaments there are sacrifices which the Lord expects His people to make.

(1) The sacrifice of a consecrated body (Rom. 12 : 1).

(2) The sacrifice of a broken spirit (Psa. 51 : 17).

(3) The sacrifices of thanksgiving and praise (Psa. 50 : 23, R.V. ; 107 : 22 ; 116 : 17 ; Heb. 13 : 15).

(4) The sacrifice of joy (Psa. 27 : 6).

(5) The sacrifice of a devoted life (Phil. 2 : 17).

(6) The sacrifice of righteousness (Psa. 4 : 5 ; 51 : 19).

(7) The sacrifice of loving help (Phil. 4 : 18 ; Heb. 13 : 6).

With such sacrifices God is well pleased, for their odour arises to Him as a smell of satisfaction as Noah's sacrifice did (Gen. 8 : 21).

3. Privilege. We are exhorted to offer up spiritual sacrifices. In 1 Pet. 2 : 5, the Greek word "*Anaphero*," rendered "*offer up*," means to take or offer up. It is a sacrificial term, and is used of the priest who "offered" sacrifices (Heb. 7 : 27), and is translated "*bear*" when applied to Christ Who "bear our sins in His own body on the tree" (Heb. 9 : 28 ; 1 Pet. 2 : 24). All believers are included in the holy priesthood, and being priests by Divine ordination and grace, it is their privilege to offer up the spiritual sacrifices already enumerated.

THE SIN OFFERING

The sin offering is typical of Christ, Who, in answering to God for our sin, was dealt with by Him in judgment. Christ was "made sin for us" (2 Cor. 5 : 21). He was "made a curse" in bearing the penalty of a broken law (Gal. 3 : 13 ; Deut. 21 : 23). He "bare our sins" as our Substitute (1 Pet. 2 : 24). He was "condemned" on our account (Rom. 8 : 3). He was "stricken" on our behalf (Isa. 53 : 8). Jehovah bruised Him and put Him to grief instead of us (Isa. 53 : 10) ; and He made to meet upon Him the seas of His wrath and justice against our iniquity (Isa. 53 : 6). Christ has answered for our sin and sins. Sin is the root, sins are the fruit. Sin is the source of iniquity, and lawlessness is the stream. Sin is the state, and sins are the acts. Sin is the nature, sins are the life. Sin is the inward condition, and sins are the manifestation of the evil. Being judged for the one and bearing the other, Benjamin Wills Newton says : "God sending His own Son in the likeness of sinful flesh, and concerning sin damned sin in the flesh, that is, our indwelling sin. Thus the wrath due both to our sin and our sins (I speak of believers) was borne by that Holy One. There it expended itself, there it burned until nought but ashes remained, there faith sees both the sin and sins of all believers ended for ever, as regards the judicial estimate of God. We may stand, as it were, by the side of that burning pile. We may see the flame raging in the full intensity of its devouring power, at length we behold it lessen, at last, flicker and decay, till it smoulders among the embers. We may watch the last expiring spark that glimmers there, and when that ends, when nothing but the cold ashes remain—we see an emblem of the relation which the fire of Holy Wrath bears to all the believing people of God. Its power is expended, it hath burned itself out, ashes only remain."

I. Jehovah and the Offering

Nothing was left to the caprice of man, everything was according to the Lord's direction—" The Lord spake, saying " (Lev. 4 : 1 ; 6 : 24). Typical of Christ acting as God directed Him in dying for sin, He said, " The cup which My Father hath given Me shall I not drink it ?" (John 18 : 11), and when that cup was pressed up to His lips, though His humanity shrank as He saw the bitter ingredients in it, nevertheless His cry was " not My will but Thine be done " (Luke 22 : 42 ; Heb. 10 : 1-10).

" Unto Jehovah " the offering was presented (Lev. 4 : 3, 31, 35), typical of Christ, Who offered Himself to God a sacrifice for sin. *He knew the holy requirement of the Lord, and He in His holy sacrifice fully met the Lord in His requirement.*

" Before Jehovah" (Lev. 4 : 4, 6, 7, 15, 17, 18, 24), namely, under His eye and in the consciousness of His presence everything was done. Typical of Christ, Who knew God's pleasure and demand, and Who in His life could say, " I do always the things that please Him " (John 8 : 29), and Who was never satisfied till He could say, of all the good pleasure of His purpose, " It is accomplished." " It is accomplished " is a better reading than " It is finished." The word " finished," in John 19 : 30, is rendered " accomplished " in John 19 : 28. A dead man's life is finished, but he may not have accomplished all he desired. Not so with Christ, He accomplished all He desired in His finished career.

" The Commandments of the Lord " are especially mentioned (Lev. 4 : 2, 13, 22), for although one might inadvertently break them, " yet is he guilty " (Lev. 5 : 17), and sin had to be answered for, whether known or unknown. Typical of Christ, Who in His atoning death, answered for our sins of omission as well as commission—our sins of ignorance as well as our sins of arrogance. " The blood of Jesus Christ His Son cleanseth us from all sin " (1 John 1 : 7), while we walk in the light, namely, while we may not be conscious of anything between ourselves and the Lord. He may see something, hence the need of the blood to keep us in the place of fellowship.

The fat of the sin offering was burned on the altar " for a sweet savour unto the Lord " (Lev. 4 : 31). Typical of Christ, Who, while being judged for sin, was in the inmost recesses of His being, bringing satisfaction and delight to God's heart. *The ill savour of our sin is overcome by the sweet savour of Him Who answered for it.* Christ did not say on the Cross, " My Father, why hast Thou forsaken Me ?" but, " My God, My God, why hast Thou forsaken Me ?" The Father in His delight never left Him. God in His righteousness against sin, did, for He was made the vile thing and Jehovah could not behold it with complacency (Hab. 1 : 13).

II. The Offering

Like every offering, the sin offering was to be "without blemish" (Lev. 4 : 3, 23, 28, 32). The perfection of His humanity was essential to the acceptableness of His offering Himself as the Sin Offering. As the Son of Man, it is said of Him, " Him hath God the Father sealed " (John 6 : 27). To this day, the Jew is only allowed to eat meat which has been examined by the Rabbi, and when he has done this, he seals it as fit for food. Christ was fit for the work He came to do.

Different animals were offered. " A young bullock " was offered for a priest (Lev. 4 : 3), and for the whole congregation (Lev. 4 : 14), a male kid for a ruler (Lev. 4 : 22, 23), a female kid or lamb for one " of the common people " (Lev. 4 : 32), and for specific sins " a female of the flock " (Lev. 5 : 1-6), and if the offerer was too poor to bring this, then two turtle-doves (Lev. 5 : 7, 8), or an " ephah of fine flour " (Lev. 5 : 11-13). Typical of Christ in the many-sidedness of His character answering for our sin. The strength of His Deity (Gal. 2 : 20), the manliness of His humanity (Heb.

12 : 3), the tenderness of His love, the gentleness of His manner, and the perfection of His life are all exhibited in Him Who died for us (1 John 3 : 16).

When the blood of the offering was brought into the Tabernacle the sin offering was wholly consumed, except the fat, outside the camp (Lev. 4 : 12, 21 ; 8 : 17). Typical of Christ, Who in the place of judgment suffered outside the camp for us (Heb. 13 : 11, 12). The death on earth is recognized in Heaven.

When the blood was not brought into the Tabernacle, the sin offering was eaten by the priest in the holy place (Lev. 6 : 26-30 ; 10 : 16-20 ; Heb. 13 : 11). The sin offering was either wholly burnt outside the camp, or wholly eaten by the priest in the holy place. It was wholly consumed either way. Typical of Christ and God finding perfect satisfaction in the offering for sin.

Where the sin offering was not wholly burned, it was eaten by the priest who offered it, and typifies Christ's satisfaction in His death, as He said, "With desire I have desired to eat this Passover with you before I suffer" (Luke 22 : 15). The eating of the sin offering signifies entering into that which makes atonement for sin, hence of necessity into the sin itself. In Christ it was necessarily found, when bearing our sin in His Body on the tree, and in this way part of the atonement itself (Lev. 10 : 17) ; but the fact that the priests could partake of it shows that it is not to be limited to this. " Daniel, confessing his sin and the sin of the people, was surely eating the sin offering ; and just such identification of ourselves with the sins of God's saints is a great need for all of us ; a realization which the knowledge of the Cross that we have as Christians will intensify, not in any wise lessen. Alas ! the slight knowledge of God's grace may indeed allow a light treatment of sin, perhaps also a bitter judgment of it : a real eating of the sin offering makes one as serious as tender ; who can harshly judge when Christ has borne the judgment ? Who can treat lightly what brought Him to the Cross ? "

In the cases of the priest and the whole congregation, the blood was brought into the holy place (Lev. 4 : 6, 7, 16, 17 ; see also the Great Day of Atonement, Lev. 16). But in the case of a ruler and one of the common people there is no mention of the blood being brought into the holy place (Lev. 4 : 25, 30, 34). Typical of the double fact, our sin is remembered and forgotten. Forgotten by the God Who forgave (Heb. 10 : 17), but remembered by Him Who answered for it to His glory (Heb. 2 : 9), and remembered by us in our gratitude to His praise (Rev. 1 : 5).

The offering was called " most holy " (Lev. 6 : 25, 29), or " holy of holies," the same expression as applied to the inner shrine of the Tabernacle (Ex. 26 : 33, 34). Typical of the fact that no sin could contaminate Christ, although He was " made sin."

All the blood of each offering was poured out at the altar of burnt offering (Lev. 4 : 7, 18, 25, 30, 34). It is Christ's absolute death, not His life, as associated with the altar of His Deity, that alone answers for our iniquity (2 Cor. 5 : 19).

III. The Offerer

There are three thoughts associated with the offerer of the sin offering, namely, Presentation, Identification, and Substitution.

1. *Presentation.* The offerer had to " bring," or to " offer," his offering unto the door of the Tabernacle (Lev. 4 : 4, 14, 23, 28, 32), evidently for examination to see that it was " without blemish." Typical of Christ in His personal worth, being fit to undertake the propitiatory work, His " obedience unto death " is the Spirit's summary of His worth and work (Phil. 2 : 8). Not His death apart from His life, nor His life apart from His death. The one was the complement of the other.

2. *Identification.* The offerer had to " lay " his hand upon the head of the offering (Lev. 4 : 4, 15, 24, 29, 33), as identifying himself with it. The word " lay " means to " lean upon," and is rendered " lieth hard " in Psa. 88 : 7, " stayed " in Isa. 26 : 3, and " sustained " in Gen. 27 : 37. Typical of Christ identifying Himself with His people, in that He stood with them in their guilt and speaks of their sins as " My sins " (Psa. 69 : 5).

3. *Substitution.* The offering had to be killed by the offerer (Lev. 4 : 4, 15, 24, 29, 33). The life's blood had to be shed. Typical of Christ, Who, as He said, " poured out " His blood for many, for the remission of their sins (Matt. 26 : 28 ; Luke 22 : 20). Christ's substitutionary work is the basis of salvation, the procurer of blessing, the spring of service, the igniter of love, the soul of faith, the glory of heaven, the overcomer of hell, the supplier of need, and the song of the saint.

IV. The Priest and the Offering

When a priest needed to offer a sin offering, he acted in his official capacity, when the priestly acts were required for himself (Lev. 4 : 5-12). When acting for himself and for the congregation, the blood was brought into the Tabernacle (Lev. 4 : 5, 16), sprinkled seven times before the vail (Lev. 4 : 6, 17), and put upon the horns of the altar of incense (Lev. 4 : 7-18). Typical of Christ, Who as the representative of His people, has entered upon His priestly work by virtue of His atoning sacrifice, and Who in the perfection of His atonement appears at the altar of intercession (Heb. 9 : 12-24).

In the case of a ruler or a private person (Lev. 4 : 22, 27), the blood was *not* brought into the Tabernacle, but was put upon the horns of the altar of burnt offering (Lev. 4 : 30-34), and in every case the blood was poured out at the bottom of the altar of burnt offering (Lev. 4 : 7, 18, 25, 30, 34 ; 5 : 9). Typical of Christ, Who ever recognizes the great fact of His atoning death on the cross, although His priestly service finds its basis and plea in the blood of remembrance.

In the case of the inadvertent sin specified in Lev. 5 : 1-5, the priest is the prominent person throughout (Lev. 5 : 6-13). We need the priestly service for us now, as well as the work of Calvary. They are intimately connected. The one is the outcome of the other ; and the one is possible because of the other. Typical of Christ Who, as our High Priest, has to base all His present service on the past fact of atonement.

The priest had to burn the sin offering, which was offered for himself and for the assembly outside the camp (Lev. 4 : 12-21), but in the other cases he and his sons were privi-

leged to eat the sin offering in the holy place (Lev. 6 : 26-30 ;
10 : 16-20). Typical of Christ Who, as our Offering, endured
the wrath of God for us, but Who finds, with His redeemed,
in the cross of His judgment, the food which satisfies His
own heart and theirs. "He shall see of the travail of His
soul and be satisfied," and we find His flesh is "meat indeed"
(Isa. 53 : 11 ; John 6 : 55).

V. The Reason for the Offering

Seven times over in Lev. 4 and 5, in connection with the
sin offering, we are told it was "to make an atonement . . .
concerning sin" (verses 20, 26, 31, 35 ; 5 : 6, 10, 13). The
meaning of the word "atonement" is to cover. Rotherham
in each case renders the sentence, "to make an atonement"
"Put a propitiatory covering over him because of his sin."
Atonement speaks of Christ giving to God on our behalf a
perfect sacrifice, and by that perfect sacrifice, we and our
offence are hidden from view. Godward, the atonement of
Christ is a work done for us, by means of which blessing
comes to us. "Underlying all these offerings there is the
conception that the persons offering are covered by that
which is regarded as sufficient and satisfactory to Jehovah."

VI. The Blessing of the Offering

The blessing which comes to the offerer is simply
expressed in the sentence, "It shall be forgiven" (Lev.
4 : 20, 26, 31, 35 ; 5 : 10, 13). But how intimately the
atonement and the blessing are associated may be gathered
from the meaning of the word to forgive, as one has said,
"The atoning lies behind the forgiving," yea, is the very
soul of the forgiveness. God's forgiveness is sure, for "There
is forgiveness with Thee" (Psa. 130 : 4) ; it is complete, for
"He forgiveth all our iniquities" (Psa. 103 : 3) ; and it is
waiting for all who will have it, for He is "ready to forgive"
(Psa. 86 : 5).

By implication one other thing is indicated, namely, as
"Whatsoever" touched "the flesh" became "holy" (Lev.
6 : 27), so believers, through contact with Christ, become like
Him. The holiness of the "most holy" offering communi-

cates its holiness to all it touches. Believers through the offering of the body of Jesus Christ once for all, have been sanctified, and by that one offering they " are perfected forever " (Heb. 10 : 10-14).

VII. Practical Teaching of the Offering

When we remember there was no provision under the law for the one who sinned " presumptuously " (margin, " with a high hand "), as in the case of the Sabbath breaker (Num. 15 : 30-40), and that the sin offering was for sins of ignorance, yet for all that the sinner was guilty (Lev. 5 : 17), we can see what an abhorrent thing sin is to Jehovah. The teaching of the New Testament as to the practical application of the death of Christ is, to take but one chapter (Rom. 6), we have quit sin's service as a master, its influence is destroyed as a power (verse 6), we are freed from its claim as a penalty (verse 7), we are unresponsive to its suggestions, so that we do not yield to its voice (verse 12), we rejoice in the " shall not " of the Lord's deliverance from its dominion (verse 14), we are separated from sin's pollution as we reckon we are dead to its sway (verse 11), and we no longer partake of its rations, (the word " wages " means rations, and is rendered " charges " in 1 Cor. 9 : 7, in speaking of a soldier's rations or allowance), and we have our fruit unto holiness (verse 23). The cross that frees from condemnation, cuts off all sin's associations with the world (Gal. 1 : 4), the flesh (Gal. 5 : 24), the devil (1 John 3 : 8), and self (Gal. 2 : 20).

THE TRESPASS OFFERING

The typical teaching of the Trespass Offering is, Christ not only suffered for sin but for sins. He not only was judged for what we *are*—sinners with a sinful nature,—but He died for what we *did*, hence we are told in the New Testament He " was delivered for our offences " (Rom. 4 : 25) or " trespasses." The word " offences " is rendered " sins " and " trespasses " in Eph. 1 : 7 and Col. 2 : 13, where we are told our sins and trespasses are forgiven on the ground of Christ's substitutionary sacrifice.

I. Jehovah and the Offering

The one thing which stands out prominently in relation to Jehovah and this offering is, the offering was to be estimated according to the requirement of the Lord—" If a soul commit a trespass and sin through ignorance in the holy things of the Lord : then he shall bring for his trespass unto the Lord a ram without blemish out of the flocks, with thy estimation by shekels of silver, after the shekel of the sanctuary, for a trespass offering " (Lev. 5 : 15).

Many might think anything would do for the Lord, as they did in the days of Malachi (Mal. 1 : 7, 8), but Jehovah allows no human to estimate the things Divine. God's " estimation " of His Son is unequalled in its appreciation. Again and again the Spirit speaks of Him as the " Precious One." The Greek word " timee " means honourable, and is rendered " price " in Matt. 27 : 9 ; " sum of money " in Acts 7 : 16 ; " honour " in 2 Pet. 1 : 17 ; and " precious " in 1 Pet. 2 : 7. " Timios " is derived from " timee," and means that which is valuable, costly, honoured, and esteemed, and is rendered " reputation " in Acts 5 : 34 ; " dear " in Acts 20 : 24 ; and " precious " in 1 Pet. 1 : 19. " Entimos " means that which is invaluable, and is rendered " precious " in 1 Pet. 2 : 4, 6. Christ is the One Who is costly beyond all valuation, and dear to God in His Divine estimation. This Precious One has redeemed us with His costly, precious blood : a price which God truly estimates and appreciates, and which meets all the requirements of His holiness and justice.

II. The Offering

The Trespass Offering pointed in two directions, namely, Godward and manward. Godward, in man's trespass of the holy things (Lev. 5 : 14-19) ; and manward, in trespass against another (Lev. 6 : 1-7).

1. Named Offering. This offering is distinctly called " a Trespass Offering." The Hebrew word for trespass means guilt, and by implication signifies a fault, and is derived from a primary root which means to be guilty. The primary word is rendered " *guilty* " in Lev. 4 : 13, 22, 27 ; 5 : 2, 3, 4,

5, 17. Some have called the offering a " guilt offering," as in Lev. 5 : 15, R.V., Christ is our Guilt Offering. The words, " Thou shalt make His soul an offering for sin," should be, " Thou shalt make His soul a trespass offering," for the words, " an offering for sin," are the same as rendered " trespass offering." The margin of Isa. 53 : 10, R.V., renders the same word, " a guilt offering."

2. Specified Offering. Excepting in the case of the cleansing of the leper (Lev. 14 : 12-14, 21), and the restoration of the Nazarite who had broken his vow (Num. 6 : 12), the offering was always to be " a ram " (Lev. 5 : 15 ; 6 : 6 ; 19 : 20-22). There are no grades of offering in connection with the trespass offering as in connection with the other offerings. One animal and one alone had to be brought, and that one, not any one, was to be a ram which was to be valued according to the thought of God. There is One and only One Who can answer for our trespasses, and He is the perfect One of God's choice, Who in the perfection of His nature has offered Himself for our guilt in His death : hence we read, " When He had offered one sacrifice for sins, forever sat down at the right hand of God " (Heb. 10 : 12, R.V.M.). Christ will never need to rise up again to deal with the question of sin : hence the marginal reading is correct, when it puts the comma after " sins " instead of after " ever."

3. Over-plus Offering. In addition to the offering, restitution had to be made, both in the trespass of holy things and in the wrong to another (Lev. 5 : 16 ; 6 : 5). The principal was not only to be restored, but " a fifth," a double tithe, was to be " added thereto." Its typical application is, Christ has not only answered for our sins in their offence against God, but that there is a super-abundance of merit in His atoning death. There is a " much more " in His sacrifice than is indicated in the " fifth part added thereto " (Heb. 9 : 13, 14), and also a superabounding of God's grace beyond human guilt (Rom 5 : 20). An old Puritan once said, " Sin has made a great sore, but God in His grace provides a larger plaster."

4. Associated Offering. The trespass offering had to be killed in the place where the burnt offering was killed, and

also the fat and certain other parts were to be offered on the altar of burnt offering. Those parts of the trespass offering were to be burned on the altar, and while they are distinctly associated with the sin or trespass, their burning on the altar and their association with the burnt offering, indicates that they went up to God as a sweet smelling savour, for the word to burn means to burn as incense (Lev. 7 : 1-5). Christ in offering Himself for our sins has not only answered for our guilt, but has glorified God in all His sacrificial work. His obedience unto death delighted the heart of God, although that obedience meant for Him the death of the Cross (Phil. 2 : 8).

5. Holy Offering. Like the sin offering the trespass offering is called " the Holy of Holies " (Lev. 7 : 1). The holiness of the Holy One must necessarily be communicated to all that He did : hence He could answer for sin as He has. This substitutionary fact is emphasized repeatedly by the Holy Spirit. The Just suffers for the unjust (1 Pet. 3 : 18) ; the Christ dies for the ungodly (Rom. 5 : 6) ; the Saviour takes the place of the sinner (Rom. 5 : 8) ; the Strong stands in the place of the weak (Rom. 8 : 3) ; the Peacemaker reconciles the enemies by His blood (Col. 1 : 20, 21) ; the debtor is ransomed by the Mediator (1 Tim. 2 : 5, 6) ; and the offender has his offence cancelled because of Him Who stood in His place (Rom. 4 : 25).

III. The Offerer

There are two expressions which sum up the duty of the offerer in connection with the trespass offering, and these are, he shall bring his guilt offering unto the Lord, and he shall make amends because of the harm which he has done (Lev. 5 : 15, 16 ; 6 : 5, 6). The Hebrew word translated " the harm which he hath done," is the same as is rendered " sinned " and " committed " (Lev. 4 : 3, 14, 23, 28, 35 ; 5 : 5, 6, 7, 10, 11, 13, 14, 16), and in some cases it might be read, the sin of his trespass, or the trespass of his trespass. His ignorance of his trespass did not make him any the less guilty, for we read, " though he wist it not, yet is he guilty." He had to bring, in making amends for his trespass, an estimated ram as a trespass offering, in addition to the restitution he had to make. All this is typical of Christ Who in the adorableness of His personality, has given to God in His vicarious atonement a perfect offering for our failure in holy things, and who has so identified Himself with us in our sin that He makes our sin His own. In Psa. 69, that Psalm of descriptive outline of Christ's intense and inner suffering, we hear Him say, " Then restored I that which I took not away." He made restitution for us. He paid the price in full on our behalf, and sacrificed Himself in His substitutionary death. Five times in the Revised Version of the New Testament we have the words, " He gave Himself up." As the Lover of the Church in dying for her (Eph. 5 : 25), as the Substitute for the individual believer (Gal. 2 : 20), as the Bearer of sins (Gal. 1 : 4), as the Separator from iniquity and the Purchaser of the redeemed (Titus 2 : 14), and as the Ransomer Who paid the invaluable price of His own blood (1 Tim. 2 : 6). The latter Scripture is very significant. Alford renders it, " He gave Himself a payment in recompense."

IV. The Priest and the Offering

There are three things we specially emphasize in the action of the priest in relation to this offering.

The offerer brought the offering to the priest—" He shall bring a ram without blemish . . . unto the priest " (Lev. 5 : 18 ; 6 : 6). Christ as the Offerer knew the requirements of the sanctuary of Jehovah and complied accordingly. The ram of His consecrated humanity, the unblemished perfection of His character, and the holiness of Jehovah's presence were all estimated and given by Him. What is said of the peace offering was required of every offering, namely, " It shall be perfect to be accepted " (Lev. 22 : 21). Christ was the Perfect One, Who knew perfectly the perfection of God's claim, hence He could say, " I have glorified Thee on the earth." He alone knew what God was, and He was all God asked for or could demand, hence He is now in His priestly glory, as the One Who was crucified, made of God unto us " Wisdom, Righteousness, Sanctification, and Redemption."

Wisdom is the right application of Knowledge : Righteousness is conformity to God's law.   Sanctification is conformity
to God's nature, and Redemption is conformity to God's
glory.   Therefore, Christ is God's communicated knowledge
of Himself.   Christ is the Perfect Answer to His law for us.
Christ is the Perfect Conformer to His nature in us, and the
Perfect Saviour to make us like to God Himself.

Certain parts of the offering were to be burned by the
priest on the altar.   The parts are given in detail in Lev.
7 : 3-5, and it is distinctly stated the priests shall burn them
(Lev. 7 : 5).   The word to burn means to burn as incense,
and the specified parts being especially those which were
identified with " the inwards " of the animal are typical of
the inward perfection of the Lord Jesus.   To take but one of
the specified parts, namely, the kidneys.   The Hebrew word
for kidneys is used frequently in a moral sense, and is translated " reins " : hence, " God trieth the heart and reins "
(Psa. 7 : 9 ;   Jer. 17 : 10).   We hear Christ saying in the
prophetic word in relation to His willingness to answer for
sin and to glorify God, " I delight to do Thy will, O My God,
yea, Thy law is written within My heart, or in the midst of
My bowels " (Psa. 40 : 8, margin).   Christ in the priestly act
of His present service continues to bring out the perfection
of His inmost Being, as He lives in the presence of God for
us.   This is strikingly illustrated in the beautiful combination of Christ's past work on the Cross and His present service on the throne, as detailed in Heb. 9 and 10.

The Priest's Portion.   We have noticed the portions for
Jehovah which were burned on the altar : the rest of the
offering belonged to the priest—" the priest that maketh
atonement therewith shall have it " (Lev. 7 : 7 ;   14 : 13),
and with him his sons were privileged to eat of the sacrifice
(Lev. 7 : 6 ; Num. 18 : 9, 10).   When a man trespassed in
the holy things he had to add a fifth to the value of the ram
which he brought for a trespass offering, which became the
priest's property (Lev. 5 : 15, 16), and when a man trespassed
against his neighbour he had to restore to him the principal,
and also add a fifth part in addition to what he had taken
away, besides bringing the ram to atone for his sin, for his

trespass was against the Lord as well as his neighbour (Lev. 6 : 5-7). Should the person not be living, the trespasser was not excused from making restitution. The next of kin were to be recompensed on his behalf ; and should there be no kinsman to whom restitution could be made for the guilt, the restitution for guilt which is made unto the Lord shall be the priest's ; besides the ram of the atonement whereby atonement may be made for him (Num. 5 : 6-8, R.V. ; 2 Kings 12 : 16). This is typical of the satisfaction which Christ finds now as He presents to God on our behalf the value of the perfect sacrifice He gave to God in our stead. As when the tax-gatherer came to Peter for the tribute money, Christ met the requirement of the law by telling Peter he would find the money in the fish's mouth which, as He said, " shall be for Me and thee," so Christ has given all that was required to meet every claim of God against us, and now we with Him delight to dwell upon this fact, even as Aaron and his sons were privileged to feed upon the trespass offering.

V. The Reason of the Offering

The reason of the offering was because of trespass, and trespass in two directions : trespass toward God in holy things, and trespass against others in personal things.

Trespass against Jehovah in the holy things is a solemn subject. The following are cases in point :

1. The adopting of one's own methods in God's service, as in the case of Moses, who struck the rock when God told him to speak to it ; hence Jehovah said to him, " Because ye trespassed against Me . . . ye shall not go into the land " (Deut. 32 : 51).

2. Taking to one's own self anything that has been devoted to the Lord, as exemplified in the case of Achan taking the devoted things of Jericho, for he is said to have committed a trespass in the devoted thing (Josh. 7 : 1 ; 22 : 20, R.V.).

3. Compromising with God's specific directions as is sadly illustrated in King Saul and Amalek, for in not obeying the Lord he committed a trespass against Him (1 Chron. 10 : 13, R.V.).

4. Failure to inquire of the Lord in prayer, as seen in Saul when he inquired of a familiar spirit instead of Jehovah, for in so doing he committed a trespass against Him (1 Chron. 10 : 13, 14).

5. Relying on one's own strength instead of resting on God's Word, as in the case of Israel under Rehoboam, who trespassed against the Lord (2 Chron. 12 : 2, R.V.).

6. Presumption in the worship of God in acting on self-authority, as in the case of Uzziah, when he presumed to act in the priest's office, as Azariah reminded him, when he said to him, " Thou hast trespassed " (2 Chron. 26 : 18).

7. Failure to render to Jehovah what is His right, as when Judah did not worship Him and give to Him what His law required, as Hezekiah confessed, " Our fathers have trespassed " (2 Chron. 29 : 6, 7).

8. And distinct disobedience to the commands of the Lord, as when the people of Israel, under Ezra, married strange women of the nations, which action is designated as " This trespass " (Ezra 9 : 2 ; 10 : 2, 10, R.V.).

In each of the above Scriptures the word " trespass " occurs, and is the same as is found in Lev. 5 : 15.

Trespass against others is given in specific detail. There are five illustrations given to us in Lev. 6 : 2, 3, R.V. :

1. Unfaithfulness to a trust, as when one entrusts something to the keeping of another, and the entrusted one unlawfully uses for himself the deposit committed to him, as the Word says, " deal falsely with his neighbour in a matter of deposit " (Ex. 20 : 16).

2. The second case is that of two persons in a business transaction. The text says in " fellowship," the R.V., " of bargain." In every true business transaction there should be fellowship, but when one takes advantage of another's ignorance and sells an article beyond its worth, or represents it to be what it is not, then he deals falsely. Too many are like the man in Prov. 20 : 14, and not like Abraham, who would give Ephron the price of the land (Gen. 23).

3. The third instance is called " robbery." A case in point would be when one, under the plea of legal form, takes

from another more than is due to him, as did Ahab with Naboth's vineyard (1 Kings 21 : 1-16).

4. The fourth instance is when a man "oppressed his neighbour." An employer exacting more than his due from his employee illustrates it : or taking from a neighbour more than the law allowed, when in personal need (Deut. 23 : 24, 25) ; or as Zaccheus did when, like the tax-gatherers, he unlawfully took taxes from them (Luke 19 : 2-8).

5. The last example is when one finds something which belongs to another and then declares he has not found it. In each of these cases the important thing to notice is that there was not only a trespass against the neighbour, but a trespass against the Lord ; and there were three things which were requisite before forgiveness could be obtained. A full restitution, a double tithe, and a trespass offering (Lev. 5 : 15, 16 ; 6 : 4-6), were requisite in order that the priest might "make an atonement" for the offence committed. Christ's atoning work is the only thing which can adjust things before God, whether wrong be done to another or offence against Himself. Three times the sentence occurs, "make an atonement," in referring to any form of trespass, for it was only by the offering of the "Trespass Offering" that the offence could be forgiven, and that too after restitution had been made (Lev. 5 : 16, 18).

VI. The Blessing of the Offering

As in the sin offering, so in the trespass offering, the significant blessing is forgiveness. "It shall be forgiven him" is the Spirit's clear and emphatic testimony on the ground of the atonement made for the trespass committed against the Lord. The New Testament is unmistakeable in its teaching on the forgiveness of sins.*

---

* The word "Aphiemi," rendered "forgiven" in Matt. 9 : 2, signifies "to let go." It is used to describe the disciples who "left" their nets (Matt. 4 : 20) ; "sent away," in speaking of Christ sending away the multitudes (Matt. 13 : 36) ; of Lazarus being "let go" from the bonds which held him (John 11 : 44) ; and of Christ when He "yielded up" His Spirit into the hands of His Father (Matt. 27 : 50).

The Gospel is the proclaimer of forgiveness (Luke 24 : 47 ; Acts 13 : 38).

God is the Author of forgiveness (Acts 5 : 31 ; Mark 2 : 7).

Man is the receiver of forgiveness (Matt. 9 : 2).

The Blood of Christ is the ground of forgiveness (Col. 1 : 14 ; Eph. 1 : 7 ; Heb. 9 : 22).

Faith in Christ is the instrument to obtain forgiveness (Acts 10 : 43 ; 26 : 18).

The Word is the assurance of forgiveness (1 John 2 : 12 ; Jas. 5 : 15 ; Luke 7 : 47).

Liberty is the meaning of forgiveness (Luke 1 : 77 ; 3 : 3 ; 4 : 18). The words remission, deliverance and liberty, in Luke, are the same as is rendered forgiveness in Eph. 1 : 7.

The condition of forgiveness is a forgiving spirit (Matt. 6 : 12-15 ; Eph. 4 : 32).

VII. The Practical Teaching of the Offering

The practical teaching is threefold. First, there has to be confession of the wrong done. Second, there has to be full restitution made as the double tithe added. And third, the ceasing to trespass again as is typically suggested in the cleansing of the leper, by the blood of the trespass offering, being placed on the different members of the man's body, saying in so many words that he was henceforth wholly separated in the entirety of his being, in consecration to the Lord (Lev. 14 : 14).

" Fools make a mock at sin," or " the trespass offering " (the word " sin " is the same as " trespass offering "), " but among the righteous there is favour" (Prov. 14 : 9). The righteous hold with " favour" the truth of Christ as their trespass offering, for they feel the need of His grace and atonement, but the fools, like Ishmael mocking Isaac, mock at the vicarious work of Christ. What a lot of fools there are in the Church and out of it !

THE DRINK OFFERING

(READ NUM. 28 AND 29.)

The drink offering consisted of strong wine (Num. 28 : 7), and is typical of the joy which the death of Christ gives to

God, and brings to Christ and the believer, for wine is repre-sented in the Scriptures as the symbol of joy. It is said to cheer the heart of God and man, and to make the latter glad (Jud. 9 : 13 ; Psa. 104 : 15).

I. Jehovah and the Offering

Like all the other offerings this one was presented " unto the Lord." The expression, " unto the Lord," occurs eighteen times in Num. 28 and 29, and is frequently used in connection with the drink offering, which is significantly said to be " poured unto the Lord " (Num. 28 : 7).

The purpose Christ had in view in pouring out His soul in death for us was infinitely greater than to save us from hell and bring us to heaven. It was to bring us to God. The Holy Spirit emphasizes this again and again in the New Testament when He speaks of Christ's death and sacrifice, hence believers are said to be " reconciled to God " (Rom. 5 : 10 ; 2 Cor. 5 : 19), " alive unto God " (Rom. 6 : 11), " redeemed to God " (Rev. 5 : 9), and " priests unto God " (Rev. 1 : 6), for His offering to God (Eph. 5 : 2 ; Heb. 9 : 14) was to bring us to God (1 Pet. 3 : 18). To know we have been brought to the centre of all blessing is to be in touch with all God is, has, does, promises, and will yet do.

II. The Offering

There are three special things we may ponder in relation to the drink offering.

1. It was an associated offering. It was not an offering like some of the other offerings which could be offered alone, but was always identified with the burnt offering (Ex. 29 : 40, 41 ; Num. 15 : 5-24).

In the interesting details regarding the burnt offerings which were to be offered daily (Num. 28 : 1-8), on the Sabbath (Num. 28 : 9, 10), at the beginning of the month (Num. 28 : 11-15), at the passover (Num. 28 : 16, 24), at the feast of the firstfruits (Num. 28 : 26-31), in the seventh month and the seven days associated with it (Num. 29 : 1, 32), and on the eighth day of the seventh month (Num. 29 : 35-39), we read continually of *his* drink offering and *their* drink offering.

Especially is it emphasized in speaking of the daily burnt offering in the repeated " a continual burnt offering and his drink offering " (Num. 28 : 10, 15, 24, 31 ; 29 : 11, 16, 19, 22, 28, 31, 34, 38). The association of these offerings in their typical import tells us that the joy of the Lord, and our joy in Him, spring from the atonement of His death. It was after the shepherd had found the sheep that he said, " Rejoice with Me," and from other Scriptures we know how far He had to travel, even to the death of the cross, before He could find us and lift us up to the place of oneness with Himself.

" But none of the ransomed ever knew
How deep were the waters crossed ;
Nor how dark was the night that the Lord passed through,
Ere He found His sheep that was lost."

The believer has no joy but that which is born of the sorrow of Christ. " We rejoice in God through our Lord Jesus Christ, through Whom we have received the reconciliation " (Rom. 5 : 11), and the awakener of heaven's melody is found in Him Who has redeemed us to God by His blood (Rev. 1 : 5). The silence of His awful cross is the songster that makes us sing in the sunshine of His glory.

2. The drink offering is essentially a Canaan Offering. The directions regarding this offering seem to localize it in the land of Canaan, for God's direction is, " Speak unto the children of Israel and say unto them, when ye come in the land of your habitations . . . and will make . . . a burnt offering . . . then shall he that offereth . . . bring . . . the fourth of a hin of wine as a drink offering " (Num. 15 : 1-5). There was no joy or gladness when Christ was passing through the wilderness of Gethsemane and suffering on the rugged hill of Calvary. His soul was exceeding sorrowful even unto death, and His " I thirst," and " My God, My God, why hast Thou forsaken Me," tell out how He suffered and the hell of agony He endured. The joy was in the afterward of His Easter and His Ascension, as He seems to indicate it would be, as He passed the sacramental cup and said to His disciples, " I will not drink of the fruit of the vine until the kingdom of God shall come " (Luke 22 : 18). While we recognize the fulfilment of this word of Christ points to the

joy which He will have in His millennial glory, still there was a *filment* of it on the Day of Pentecost, as the gladdening Spirit came upon the disciples, as even the world recognized when they tauntingly said, " These men are filled with new wine."

3. Proportionate Offering

The drink offering was a proportionate offering. When a lamb was offered for a burnt offering the fourth part of a hin was the quantity specified for a drink offering (Ex. 29 : 40 ; Lev. 23 : 13). When a ram was offered, a third part of a hin of wine was the quantity, and when a bullock was given as a burnt offering, half of a hin of wine constituted the drink offering (Num. 28 : 14). As the different animals typify Christ in the various aspects of His death, so the various quantities of the wine speak of the degrees of His joy. There was a joy He might have had apart from His cross, as we read in *Heb. 12 : 2, but the joy which was born of His cross was greater than any other joy could possibly be. Is there not something of this suggested in the salutation of Christ to the women on the morning of the resurrection, when He said to them, " All hail " (Matt 28 : 9), or as the word might be rendered, " Rejoice," for it is so given in Matt. 5 : 12. He had passed through the throes of death and would now enthuse them with the joy of His triumph.

We may say Christ has a sevenfold joy :

The joy of anticipation for His delights were with the sons of men in the past eternity (Prov. 8 : 31).

The joy of incarnation, for the angelic song at His birth was, " Behold I bring you tidings of great joy " (Luke 2 : 10).

The joy of fellowship which Christ had with His Father (Luke 10 : 21).

The joy of confidence, for He could say, even in the pains of death, " My heart doth rejoice," for He knew His Father

---

* " Who instead of the joy which was set before Him, endured the cross." The Greek preposition " Anti " justifies this reading, for the sentence should read, " instead of the joy," in place of, " for the joy which was set before Him." What that joy was we are not told, but He refused to have that joy and chose the cross instead.

would raise Him up from among the dead (Acts 2 : 24, 26, 28).

The joy of victory, for His word to John on the Isle of Patmos was, " I am He that liveth, and was dead : and, behold, I am alive forevermore, Amen ; and have the keys of hell and of death " (Rev. 1 : 18).

The joy of salvation, which He proclaims, is the joy of the three persons (Luke 15 : 6, 9, 24).

The joy of satisfaction, for " He shall see of the travail of His soul, and shall be satisfied " (Isa. 53 : 11).

III. The Offerer

The offerer brought his drink offering as an expression of his glad appreciation of the Lord's goodness to him (Num. 15 : 3-5 ; 1 Sam. 1 : 24, 28 ; 2 : 1). There was no compulsion brought to bear upon Christ to make Him give His life a ransom for many. There are seven words which shine out in the sky of Christ's voluntariness in relation to His death. These are " delight," " set," " give," " lay," " led," " shed," " offered."

The " I delight " of His willing obedience—" I delight to do Thy will " (Psa. 40 : 8).

The " set " of His determined purpose—" I set My face like a flint " (Isa. 50 : 7).

The " I will give " of His holy sacrifice—" the bread which I will give is My flesh " (John 6 : 51).

The " I lay " of glad surrender—" I lay down My life for the sheep " (John 10 : 15).

The " led " of His patient submission—" Led as a lamb to the slaughter " (Acts 8 : 32).

The " shed " of His poured life—" My blood . . . which is shed for many " (Matt. 26 : 28).

The " offered " of His sufficient atonement—" Offered one sacrifice for sins " (Heb. 10 : 12-14).

All these speak of the perfection of His substitutionary work. All that will come to Him in the day of His coming glory, as well as the triumphs of His past achievements, is because " He hath poured out His soul unto death " (Isa. 53 : 12).

IV. The Priest and the Offering

The priest is not very prominent with this offering. He was responsible to see that all the requirements of the Sanctuary were met, and among them was one which we might specially consider, namely, the quantity of the wine, for the drink offering was always to correspond to the quantity of the oil. Thus when a lamb was offered, the fourth part of an hin of wine was required, and the same quantity of oil; when a ram was offered a third part of an hin of wine was specified and the same of oil; and when a bullock was presented half an hin of oil was commanded and the same of wine (Num. 28 : 7, 14). The oil is mentioned first and then the wine. The oil is an emblem of the Holy Spirit, and the wine, of joy. One aspect of the ministry of Christ is to remind us of our dependence upon the Holy Spirit, and that there can never be the enjoyment of the joy of the Lord, but as we are governed by the Spirit of the Lord. We are reminded of this in the following passage : "Now the God of hope fill you with all joy and peace in believing, that you may abound in hope, through the power of the Holy Ghost" (Rom. 15 : 13).

A Spirit filled life is always a gladdened life, which glows with the Lord's joy. "Gladness of heart" is the outcome of Pentecost (Acts 2 : 46); "rejoicing they were counted worthy to suffer shame for His name," is consequent upon a Spirit indited testimony (Acts 5 : 41); "the face of an angel" is the outcome of the Spirit possessing Stephen (Acts 6 : 15); "He went on his way rejoicing," is the result of the Spirit's working through Philip to the Eunuch (Acts 8 : 39); Barnabas was "glad" when he saw what God had been doing through others, and the secret cause was because he "was full of the Holy Ghost" (Acts 11 : 24); the disciples were "filled with joy," because they were filled with the Holy Spirit, when persecuted at Antioch (Acts 13 : 52); and the consequence of being filled with the Spirit is, "Speaking to yourselves in psalms and hymns and spiritual songs, singing and making melody in your heart to the Lord" (Eph. 5 : 19).

V. The Reason of the Offering

Reading between the lines and remembering that wine is said to cheer the heart of God and man, the drink offering suggests the delight that God and Christ find in the work of Calvary. We miss much if we do not see the pleasure as well as the pain which the Godhead has in the mutual sacrifice of the cross. " It pleased Jehovah to bruise Him." He knew the necessities of the case, and met the case in all its necessities. The Hebrew word " pleased " in Isa. 53 : 10 means " to be inclined to," and " to bend towards an object with ardent desire and delight." The word is frequently translated " delight " (Num. 14 : 8). The use of the word as associated with the Father and the Son in relation to atonement will illustrate the joy of fellowship they had in Calvary. I give a few Scriptures and italicize where the same word and its cognate occurs :

" Sacrifice and offering Thou didst not *desire* " (Psa. 40 : 6). " I *delight* to do Thy will" (Psa. 40 : 8). " It *pleased* the Lord to bruise Him " (Isa. 53 : 10). " The *pleasure* of the Lord shall prosper in His hands " (Isa 53 : 10). Christ delighted to do the Father's will, and the Father delighted in Him as He did it. We are such creatures of sense and circumstances, that we are more concerned with consequences than terminals, but Christ's aim was to glorify His Father by doing His will. He died to have us that we might have Him. The mother does not think of the anguish which the child's birth caused her. Her joy is in the child born. Christ delighted to carry out the will of the Father. The Father delighted in the Son when He was crushing Him in death for us, and now the Father can honour the Son and delight in Him, in a way He never did before. The eyes of carnal reason see only a bloody scene of cruel enactment on the cross, but the eyes of appreciative love behold a consecrated fulfilment of Divine intent.

VI. The Blessing of the Offering

There are certain words and phrases which are specially identified with Christ's death, which have their reflex blessing in the experience of the believer. One such word in the Old

Testament is the word " poured," and one in the New Testament is the word " shed," for both of them are not only identified with Christ in the typical drink offering, but also with the blessing which flows from His death. The Hebrew word " poured " in Isa. 53 : 12, means to make bare, to empty out. It is rendered " emptied," 2 Chron. 24 : 11, and " make bare " in the margin of Psa. 137 : 7. Christ in His death emptied out Himself and was bare in His utter destruction, that He might enrich us with the treasury of His grace and the splendid robes of His glory. In Isa. 32 we have given to us the sad consequences of the curse and desolation of sin, and then there is a transformation scene which is the result of the Spirit being poured from on high (see Isa. 32 : 15-18).

The New Testament word " shed " (Mark 14 : 24) is equally associated with the Spirit and Christ. The Greek word means to pour out, or to empty out. It is used of the Holy Spirit four times, and is rendered " poured out " and " shed forth " (Acts 2 : 17, 18, 33 ; 10 : 45) in speaking of His presence and power, and it is also translated " shed " in speaking of His renewing grace (Titus 3 : 6), and " shed abroad " in speaking of the love of God shed abroad in the hearts of believers (Rom. 5 : 5). How wonderful God's giving is. The Father emptied Himself out when He gave His Son, the Son emptied Himself out when He gave His life for us, and now the Spirit waits to empty Himself out in enriching us. Nothing is too great for the Father to give to us since the Son gave Himself for us.

VII. Practical Teaching of the Offering

Paul, in writing to the Church at Philippi, says : " Yea, and if I be *offered upon the sacrifice and service of your faith, I joy, and rejoice with you all " (Phil. 2 : 17), and at the end of His earthly career he said to Timothy, " For I am now ready to be *offered, and the time of my departure is

---

* The word " offered " in both these passages is a sacrificial term, and means to pour out as a libation, and in a figurative sense signifies one who gives himself over to death, and in the Gospel sense, one who is wholly devoted to Christ's cause.

at hand " (2 Tim. 4 : 6). In the first instance, he views the Philippians in their character as consecrated believers, as a holocaust or burnt offering to God, and upon the sacrifice of their devotion he was willing to pour out his own life's blood as a drink offering in his endeavour to make known the Gospel which he had preached to them ; and he expresses the same thought to Timothy as he looks death in the face from his prison in Rome.

The secret which will make us willing to sacrifice everything and to be sacrificed is the sacrifice of Calvary. It is well to say :

" If thou couldst in vision see,
The man God meant ;
Thou wouldst not be, the man
Thou art, content."

But there is something better, for the above lines but throw man back upon himself, and that means discouragement if not despair. God ever directs our thoughts to the Christ, that in His example we may find our inspiration and in His indwelling we may have the secret force which makes us follow the perfect ideal. We might well covet the spirit that young McCall, of the Livingstone Congo Mission, had when, in the midst of his work in Africa, he was suddenly struck down and called upon to give up his life. His last words were : " Lord, I gave myself to Thee, body, mind and soul. I consecrated my whole life and being to Thy services ; and now, if it please Thee to take myself, instead of the work which I could do for Thee, what is that to me. Thy will be done."

THE RED HEIFER

(READ NUM. 19 AND HEB. 9 : 13, 14.)

The typical teaching of the Red Heifer is, the application of the atoning work of Christ to the conscience and life, removing contracted defilement from both, by the power of the Holy Spirit.

The book where the ordinance of the Red Heifer occurs, namely, the book of Numbers (the book of the Pilgrim Life), is suggestive. While treading the wilderness of life, believers may contract defilement, and while we do not need to be saved from the wrath to come, for that took place when we believed in Christ, we do need to recognise that the same atoning blood is needed ; for if we need the cleansing blood to keep us clean while we are walking in the light, how much more we need that atoning death when we get defiled. Yea, the true servant of Christ feels he needs the cleansing blood to cleanse his service, yea, even his sanctification needs the cleansing of the sanctifying blood, yea, we need the perfect Holiness of our Great High Priest to bear the iniquity of our holy things, as well as to bear our sins (Ex. 28 : 36-38).

An old writer has written to the point, " The impious lives of the wicked are as contagious as the most fearful plague that infects the air. When the doves of Christ lie among such pots, their yellow feathers are sullied. You may observe that in the oven the fine bread frequently hangs upon the coarse ; but the coarse very seldom adheres to the fine. If you mix an equal portion of sour vinegar and sweet wine together, you will find that the vinegar will sooner sour the wine, than the wine sweeten the vinegar. That is a sound body that keeps healthy in a pest-house. It is a greater wonder to see a saint maintain his purity among sinners, than it is to behold a sinner becoming pure among saints. Christians are not always like fish, which retain their freshness in a salt sea ; or like the rose, which preserves its sweetness among noisome weeds ; or like the fire, which burns hottest when the season is coldest. A good man was once heard to lament, ' that as often as he went into the company of the wicked, he returned less a man from them than he was before he joined with them.' The Lord's people, by keeping evil company, are like the persons who are much exposed to the sun, insensibly tanned."

I. Jehovah and the Offering

As in all the offerings, the directions come from Jehovah Himself ; and those directions are distinctive and direct. " And Jehovah spake unto Moses," is the ringing and introductive mandate (verse 1), and said, " Speak unto the children of Israel." It was to a redeemed people, whom the Lord had chosen and called to Himself. The Lord has a message for His people, which is essentially for them.

Then how simple and yet how arresting is His message
to them. There is no uncertainty in its tone, and no equi-
vocation in its appeal. Like a clarion note of command,
which peals out to the soldier and bids him to march, the
Lord again and again in the chapter says, " Ye shall " ; and
" shall " (verses 3, 3, 4, 5, 5, 6, 7, 7, 7, 7, 8, 8, 9, 9, 10, 10,
11, 12, 12, 12, 13, 13, 14, 16, 17, 17, 18, 19, 19, 19, 20, 20,
20, 21, 21, 21, 22, 22) occurs no less than thirty-eight times
in the chapter. The Lord will not allow His people to be
living in a state of defilement, hence He holds them responsible to be clean ; and not to be pure is to frustrate His
purpose, " Christ also loved the Church, and gave Himself
for it ; That He might sanctify and cleanse it with the
washing of water by the word, That He might present it to
Himself a glorious Church, not having spot, or wrinkle, or
any such thing ; but that it should be holy and without
blemish " (Eph. 5 : 25-27). He acts on the same principle
when He restores His people Israel, for He says, " Then will
I sprinkle clean water upon you, and ye shall be clean :
from all your filthiness, and from all your idols, will I cleanse
you " (Ezek. 36 : 25).

Sir Robert Anderson explains and points this searching
truth : " If a citizen be guilty of a crime, his conviction and
sentence will dispose of the judicial question raised by his
offence ; and yet if he formerly enjoyed the right of entrée
at the palace, nothing short of a royal pardon will restore to
him that privilege. This parable may serve to illustrate one
aspect of the truth here in question. Although the believer
has vicariously suffered the judicial consequences of his sin,
that sin would none the less bar his ever again approaching
God, were it not that by confession and the atoning work of
Christ he obtains forgiveness. But even though a citizen
may have an acknowledged right to appear at Court, he may
not enter the royal presence mud-splashed or travel-soiled ;
and wilderness defilement, even though contracted inno-
cently, precluded the Israelite from entering the sacred
enclosure. And for this also there was full provision. But
no special sin offering was needed. The unclean person was
purged, first by being sprinkled with ' the water of purifica-

tion '—water that owed its efficacy to the great sin offering,—
and then by bathing his entire body. The ritual is given in
detail in Num. 19. The victim was burnt to ashes. The
ashes were preserved, and water that had flowed over them
availed to cleanse. A sin required blood-shedding, defilement was purged by this water (Heb. 9 : 13). And, as we
have seen, the blood-shedding was the act of the man who
had sinned; so here, no priest was needed; any clean
person could perform the rite (Num. 19 : 13), thus indicating
that the sprinkling and the washing are not the work of
Christ for us, but indicate our own responsibility to seek the
restoration of communion with God by faith and repentance."

II. The Offering

There are at least twelve features of the Red Heifer
sacrifice.

1. *Red in Colour.* " Bring thee a red heifer " (verse 2).
Red is suggestive of fulness of life, as Keil says : " The
blood-red colour points to the colour of the most intensive
life, which has its seat in the blood, and shows itself in the
red colour of the face." Besides the Hebrew word " *Ad-
dohm*" comes from " *Adam*," which means " *Red earth*."
The Bride says of the Bridegroom in the Song of Solomon,
" My Beloved is white and *ruddy*." Law tersely remarks :
" What is Adam but red earth ? Hence the ruddy type
manifests our Lord, as Adam's Offspring. Yes, He is truly
man, that He may take man's place, and bear man's guilt,
and pay man's curse, and suffer in man's stead."

2. *Perfect in Structure.* The animal was to be " without
spot," or as Young renders, " A Perfect One." The word is
rendered " Perfect "—" His way is perfect " (Psa. 18 : 30) ;
" Complete "—" Seven Sabbaths shall be complete " (Lev.
23 : 15) ; " Whole "—" A whole day " (Josh. 10 : 13) ;
" Full "—" A full year " (Lev. 25 : 30) ; " Sound "—" Let
my heart be sound in Thy statutes " (Psa. 119 : 80) ; " Undefiled "—" Blessed are the undefiled " (Psa. 119 : 1) ,
" Upright "—" The Lord knoweth the days of the upright "
(Psa. 37 : 18) ; and " Without blemish "—" Offer a male
without blemish " (Lev. 1 : 3).

Two things were true about Christ, He was perfectly human, and a Perfect Human. There was not anything wanting in Him.

3. *Spotless in Nature.* The red heifer was to have " no blemish." The word " no blemish " signifies freedom from disease and infirmity, without a stain or blot. The word is rendered " without spot "—" Lift up thy face without spot " (Job 11 : 15), and " blot "—" The wicked man getteth himself a blot " (Prov. 9 : 7).

There was no blot on Christ's character, nor blemish in His nature. Hell testified to His holiness (Mark 1 : 24), Paul to His sinlessness (2 Cor. 5 : 21), John to His freedom from sin (1 John 3 : 5), Peter to His spotlessness (1 Pet. 1 : 19), the Father to His well-pleasingness (Matt. 3 : 17), the Holy Spirit to His perfection (Heb. 7 : 26), and He could challenge men and hell to find anything defiling within Him (John 8 : 46), and said, " The prince of this world cometh, and hath nothing in Me " (John 14 : 30).

4. *Yokeless in Service.* The yoke was for the controlling of the animal and indicates the necessity of its being under a power outside of itself. The subsidiary thought is a compelling force to make the animal work, and is used in Scripture as a grievous burden, and being free from a burden speaks of absolute liberty (1 Kings 12 : 4-14 ; Isa. 9 : 4 ; Ezek. 34 : 27). As applied to man the yoke indicates that which he imposes upon himself by his own folly (Lam. 1 : 14). No yoke ever rested upon Christ which compelled Him to do things. He said, " I delight to do Thy will, O My God." " My meat is to do the will of Him that sent Me, and to finish His work," and even when the bitter cup of Gethsemane was about to be pressed up to His sacred lips, He said, " The cup which My Father giveth Me, shall I not drink it ? " There was no compulsion upon Him other than the constraining love that He had for His Father.

5. *Presented in Offering.* The red heifer had to be brought by the offerer and given to Eleazar (verses 2, 3). The word is, " give her to Eleazar," and the word " give " means to give absolutely over to a given purpose, and is rendered " commit " in Isa. 22 : 21, when speaking of the government

being committed from one person to another. Christ absolutely gave Himself over when He gave Himself up to the suffering of the Cross, that His precious Blood might cleanse our conscience from guilt and our life from defilement. He is the Offerer and the Offering, as He Himself said more than once, " I lay down My life of Myself."

6. *Separated to Death.* The red heifer had to be taken outside the camp and there slain in the presence of Eleazar (verse 3). Without the camp indicates the place of death (Num. 5 : 3), the place of uncleanness (Lev. 14 : 40, 41), the place of the curse (Lev. 24 : 14, 23), and the place of judgment (Num. 15 : 35, 36). Christ suffered without the camp (Heb. 13 : 12), and went for us into the place of the uncleanness of our sin, the death we deserved, the curse we had merited, and the judgment we ought to have borne. When the animal was in the outside place, the specific command was, " One shall slay her before his face." We cannot emphasize too strongly that it is in the death of Christ, for that is the typical import of the slaying of the animal, that provision is made for the removal of any defilement that believers may contract during their pilgrimage life.

7. *Slain in Substitution.* The red heifer had to be slain before the face of Eleazar (verse 3). It is specifically stated that " one shall slay her," and this is more than merely killing. The word which means to slay is used to describe an animal that is sacrificed as an offering, hence to slaughter, to kill. It is rendered " kill " in relation to the passover lamb (Ex. 12 : 6), of Abraham when he took the knife to " slay " his son (Gen. 22 : 10), and as a participle it is translated " beaten " and " shoot out " in describing " beaten " work and the shooting of an arrow (2 Chron. 9 : 15 ; Jer. 9 : 8). As associated with the offerings it also represents one dying for another. We recognise the fact that Christ's death alone is that which answers for our sin, whether it be for the salvation of the sinner, or the cleansing of the saint. Bunyan in his book, " The Holy War," represents Emmanuel saying, " Wherefore, when Mansoul had sinned I became a surety to my Father, body for body and soul for soul, that I would make amends for Mansoul's transgressions ; and my

Father did accept thereof. So when the time appointed was come, I gave body for body, soul for soul, life for life, blood for blood, and so redeemed my beloved Mansoul."

8. *Burnt in Judgment.* The Divine direction is, "One shall burn the heifer in his sight, her skin, and her flesh, and her blood, with her dung shall he burn" (verse 5). There are two words for burn, one meaning to burn as incense, and thus to cause to ascend to the Lord as a sweet smelling savour (see use of word in Lev. 1 : 9, 13, 15, 17). The other word, the one used in relation to the heifer, signifies to consume utterly, often as an act of judgment, as in the case of the "accursed thing" of Jericho (Jos. 7 : 15, 25), and the sin offering (Lev. 4 : 12, 21), and to burn rubbish (Neh. 4 : 2). The Hebrew word here rendered "burn" is not that which is generally used of the sweet savour offerings, but one that signifies to utterly consume, and fitly expresses the fire of Divine judgment. This twofold action of slaying and consuming tells of a twofold suffering on the part of the Holy One of God. There was not only that which He bore at the hands of man, and much else which must have been anguish to His holy and sensitive soul, but there was that judgment of God upon sin, the wrath and the curse due to those in whose stead He suffered.

9. *Specified in Application.* "And Eleazar the priest shall take of her blood with his finger, and sprinkle her blood directly before the tabernacle of the congregation seven times" (verse 4). "Directly" in relation to the place of Jehovah's dwelling was the blood to be sprinkled. Typical of the directness and straightness of the Lord's act in meeting His requirements, and yet the blood was sprinkled towards the tabernacle, which is called "the tabernacle of the congregation," as meeting the need of the people. Seven times was the blood sprinkled, as typical of the perfection (seven being the perfect number) of Christ's death. The blood was "sprinkled." The blood of sprinkling, to which we have come (Heb. 12 : 24), represents the application of the blood of our Lord, in meeting God's requirements as the blood sprinkled on the mercy seat (Lev. 16 : 14) ; and the cleansing

of the defiled one, as is typified in the blood being sprinkled on the leper to be cleansed (Lev. 14 : 7).

10. *Applied in Atonement.* " And for an unclean person they shall take of the ashes of the burnt heifer of purification for sin " ; or as The Revised Version, " The burning of the sin offering." The offering was " for sin," mark " for sin." Man would have written " for defilement " ! And only " the sin offering " (R.V.) could answer " for sin." Thus the defilement is viewed as " sin." The principle holds good right through, the sin must be atoned for before the defilement can be removed. This is what the Seraph said to Isaiah when he confessed to his uncleanness, " Thy sin is purged (atoned for), and thine iniquity is taken away " as a result. Too often the words are misquoted and the Seraph is made to say, " Thine iniquity is purged and thy sin is taken away." What he said was, " Thy sin is atoned for and thine iniquity is taken away " (Isa. 6 : 7).

11. *Associated with Living Water.* " Running water," or as the Hebrew, " Living waters shall be given thereto in a vessel " (verse 17). The word " running " means " living," and is rendered " living creatures " in Ezek. 1 and " life " in Gen. 1 : 20, and comes from a root which means to live, hence fresh. Five times the water is called, " The water of separation " (verses 9, 13, 20, 21, 21). The " ashes " of the burnt animal were associated with the water (see ashes in verses 9, 10, 17). The Living Water is typical of the Living Truth of God's Word, and reminds us that He loved the Church and gave Himself for it, that He might sanctify and cleanse it by the washing of water by the Word (Eph. 5 : 25, 26) ; and the water and ashes being called " The water of separation," reminds us that the blood and word of Christ assure us that the confessed defilement is removed from the conscience and cleansed from the life.

12. *Identified with Different Things.* " The priest shall take cedar wood and hyssop, and scarlet, and cast it into the midst of the burning heifer " (verse 6). The cedar wood and hyssop suggest natural things in the entire range of nature, as we read of Solomon's wisdom of natural things, " From the cedar tree that is in Lebanon to the hyssop that springeth

out of the wall" (1 Kings 4 : 33). "Scarlet" is connected
with the earthly glory of man, hence we read of the daughters
of Israel, whom Saul "clothed with scarlet," and the great
whore of the world who will be "arrayed in purple and
scarlet" (2 Sam. 1 : 24; Rev. 17 : 3, 4). Do not these
things in their typical import suggest the cause of the saints'
defilement? For the world's contamination, and the natural
products of earthly things are the causes of defilement.

III. The Offerer

The offerer is described "as one shall slay her before his
face"; "one shall burn the heifer in his sight"; "and a
man that is clean shall gather up the ashes of the heifer"
(verses 3, 5, 9, 10). The offerer in this case seems to be, not
a type of Christ, but rather one (perhaps one of the Levites)
who is called to occupy a place of responsibility in God's
assembly. Paul seems to embody this thought in the
following sentences out of his Epistles:

"Take heed . . . to all the flock, over the which the Holy
Ghost hath made you overseers" (Acts 20 : 28); "There are
differences of administration but the same Lord" (1 Cor.
12 : 5); "I have espoused you to one husband, that I may
present you as a chaste virgin to Christ" (2 Cor. 11 : 2);
"Ye which are spiritual restore such an one" (Gal. 6 : 1);
"Yea, and if I be offered upon the sacrifice of your faith"
(Phil. 2 : 17); "That we may present every man perfect in
Christ Jesus" (Col. 1 : 28); "We were gentle among you,
even as a nurse (nursing mother) cherisheth her children"
(1 Thess. 2 : 7); "If any man obey not our word . . . have
no company with him" (2 Thess. 3 : 14); "O man of God,
flee these things" (1 Tim. 6 : 11).

These sentences embody the thought of personal fitness
for the Lord's service; a fulfilment of a sacred trust of
responsibility; and a service to others in seeing that others
are right, and if not, then a ministry which ends in their
restoration to the Lord.

To revert to those who acted apart from the priest, we
can see what service they rendered:

1. Acting in the presence of the priest. " One shall slay her before his face " (verse 3). Eleazar is a type of the Holy Spirit, and the one who acts in His presence is called upon to do so under His direction, and in fellowship with Him, as Paul indicates when he charges the saints in Corinth, when dealing with one in discipline, to see that they act in the Name of the Lord (1 Cor. 5 : 7).

2. Acting in relation to the offering. " One shall burn the heifer in his sight . . . without the camp " (verses 3, 5). It was in the place of judgment, action was to be taken— "without the camp." We are exhorted to go outside the camp to Christ bearing His reproach (Heb. 13 : 13), and we are exhorted to " judge ourselves " (1 Cor. 11 : 31), in the several associations with the observance of the Lord's death, and if we do not we come under His discipline.

3. A clean person had to gather up the ashes of the heifer, and place them in a clean place (verses 9, 18, 19). Only those who are sanctified and clean are fit for the Lord's service. This was urged by Paul in writing to Timothy about the Lord's service, when he said, " If a man purge himself . . . he shall be a vessel unto honour, sanctified and meet for the Lord's use and prepared unto every good work " (2 Tim. 2 : 21).

4. Those who were dealing with others needed a constant cleansing themselves (verses 8, 10, 21). We cannot come in contact with defilement without being defiled. The late Professor Drummond once remarked upon the fact, that after he had listened to some confession of sin, he felt polluted himself. How true it is even when we walk in the light, we need the cleansing of the blood of Christ to keep us in the place of fellowship (1 John 1 : 7).

IV. The Priest and the Offering

The priest in relation to the ordinance of the red heifer was not the high priest, but Eleazar his son, and is a type of the Holy Spirit, in His administration in applying the benefits of Christ's death in removing defilement from the conscience and life of the believer. The priest as " the priest " is mentioned five times (verses 3, 4, 6, 7, 7,).

The red heifer was under the control of the priest—" Ye shall give her unto Eleazar the priest, that he may bring her forth without the camp" (verse 3). The Divine record of the things and vessels and offerings in relation to the Tabernacle are summarised by the words, "The Holy Ghost signifying" (Heb. 9 : 8-14), for it was " through the Eternal Spirit " Christ accomplished all His atoning and substitutionary work.

V. Reason of the Offering

" A purification for sin " (verse 9). What a host of meaning is found in those two words " for sin." Sin ! Sin is viewed, not only as guilt, but as sin. Sin is a polluting thing. It pollutes the mind (Rom. 8 : 7), defiles the heart (Matt. 15 : 19), corrupts the imagination (Gen 6 : 5), debases the will (John 5 : 40), warps the ways (Rom. 3 : 12-15), injures the soul (Micah 6 : 7), stains the lips (Isa. 6 : 5), and blinds the eyes (Mark 8 : 18).

If we trace the word " unclean " in verses 11-16, we shall see for whom the offering was provided. Any one who touched a dead body was unclean for seven days. If he purged himself from sin within the three days (margin, ver. 12); then on the seventh day he would be clean, but if he did not then he was still unclean. Which seems to imply, that three days were given for the removal of the cause of defilement and the application of the offering for it ; but if action was not taken within the time limit, then the unclean one was still unclean ; and if action was still delayed, then the unclean one was cut off from Israel, and the reason was, because he was not sprinkled with the " water of separation " (verse 13). Uncleanness is not tolerated in the Lord's people for one moment by the Lord, and further, the end in view was not only the cleansing away of the guilt from the conscience, but the removal of it from the life. The Holy Spirit finely expresses it in the following words : " For if the blood of bulls and goats, and the ashes of an heifer sprinkling the unclean, sanctifieth to the purifying of the flesh : how much more shall the blood of Christ, Who through the Eternal Spirit offered Himself without spot to God, purge your conscience from dead works to serve the living God?" (Heb. 9:13, 14). Mark the "from" and the "to." The conscience purged "from dead works," and "to serve the living God." "Serve" means worship. There can be no worship unless we are clean.

VI. Blessing of the Offering

"He shall be clean" (verse 12). If we were to go by what we feel we would likely say, as many have, "I can never forgive myself," but surely we are not having fellowship with the Lord if we so speak. As we think of ourselves, and we have a growing sense of our unworthiness, we shall be inclined to say with holy John Fletcher: "I am nothing, I can do nothing, I compare myself with Lazarus, with this difference, his sores were all outside, but mine are all inside." But there is a danger in self contemplation and thinking of our unworthy selves, lest we should not believe what the Lord says. He says, "If we confess our sins, He is faithful and just to forgive us our sins, and to cleanse us from all unrighteousness." Sins confessed are sins forgiven, and sins forsaken is the secret of enjoyment of the Lord's promises. "Having therefore these promises, dearly beloved, let us cleanse ourselves from all filthiness of the flesh and spirit, perfecting holiness in the fear of the Lord" (2 Cor. 7:1).

VII. Practical Application of the Offering

Without reiterating the thought of cleanness, there are two thoughts which we focus in the practicality.

1. The open vessel should be covered to keep it clean. It seems strange, and yet it is connected with a defiled tent. We read: "And every vessel, which hath no covering bound upon it, is unclean" (verse 15). Everything was contaminated by the presence of the contaminating one. On the other hand it is suggested, that if the vessel was covered it was not defiled. Is not this thought suggested by the frequent reference in the Psalms of being covered? How this is brought out in Psa. 91, the Psalm which speaks of dwelling in the secret place of the Most High, and to those who make the Lord their Refuge and Fortress, the "He shall's" of His promise and protection apply.

" He shall deliver thee " ; " He shall cover thee " ; " There shall no evil befall thee " ; " He shall give His angels charge over thee."

2. If we are unclean we shall make others unclean. " Whosoever toucheth the dead body of any man that is dead, and purifieth not himself, defileth the tabernacle of the Lord ; and that soul shall be cut off from Israel : because the water of separation was not sprinkled upon him, he shall be unclean ; his uncleanness is yet upon him " (verse 13). The person who was unclean, and did not get cleansing, " defiled the sanctuary of Jehovah " (verse 20). An Achan in the camp not only causes us to be defeated by our enemies, but pollutes the Lord's temple. Individual condition is either a bane or a blessing. One weak link in a chain means a broken chain. One sinner destroyeth much good. The Apostle felt this when he addressed the saints at Corinth and reminded them that " a little leaven leaveneth the whole lump " (1 Cor. 5 : 7). What a difference there would be in God's assemblies if each member recognised his or her obligation to be right for each other's sake as well as for their sake, and above all for the Lord's sake.

3

THE SPIRIT OF AN INTELLECTUAL
INDIVIDUALISM

THE questions of the Bible are full of far-reaching
suggestion, and are answered in the revelation which
God has given therein. The following terse and telling
" what " is connected with Individualism and Intellectualism,
" What man knoweth the things of a man, save the spirit
of man which is in him ?" (1 Cor. 2 : 11). Self-consciousness
and self-determination are both suggested in summing up
what man is. As man knows he exists by his consciousness
of being, and knows what he knows ; so God only knows
what He is, and knows what He knows, therefore we are
dependent upon what He says to us in His Word about
Himself.

Theology in its restricted sense means the doctrine of
God. Theology comes from *Theos*, God ; and *logos*, speech;
therefore the word means the doctrine of God. In the
deeper spiritual sense, we understand theology to be the
knowledge of God in Jesus Christ, by means of the Spirit,
through the Word (John 17 : 3).

Intuitively man feels there is a God. Every heathen
religion is a declaration of man's quest for Him. It is a law
in nature, that for every intuitive faculty there is a fitting
correspondent. As the fluttering nestling finds its answer
in the supporting air ; so man, moved by the instinct of his
need of God, seeks to find the God he needs. Paul recognized this when he looked upon the erected altar to the
unknown God at Athens (Acts 17 : 23-28), for that erected
altar was a mute appeal to God for His salvation, and that
altar also was a masterly argument against the unreality of
the 30,000 false gods of the Athenians.

It requires more faith *not* to believe in God than to
believe in Him. Carlyle, in writing to Frederick of Prussia,

said: Atheism he never could abide; to him it was flatly inconceivable that intellect, moral emotion could have been put into him an Eternity which had none of its own. Man is an intelligent being: can intelligence spring from non-intelligence? Man is a sympathetic being: can feeling be evolved from material which is utterly destitute of feeling? Man is a free agent: can freedom of action proceed from that which is incapable of choice? Man has a sense of right: can that sense proceed from an insensible force? "From our own consciousness of will we infer a supreme originating will; of intelligence, a supreme constructing mind; of morality, a supreme righteous Lawgiver; of affection, a supreme Father."

What does God say about Himself? God only can reveal Himself. The Unknown and the Unknowable can only make Himself fully known.

There are three great names and their relatives in the Old Testament, and one in the New Testament, by which God has been pleased to reveal His character. The three in the Old Testament are "Elohim," "Adonai," and "Jehovah"; and the one in the New Testament is "Father." These names form a beautiful and expressive cube of God's nature. George Macdonald says: "The name of our Lord God should lie a precious jewel in the cabinet of our hearts, to be taken out only at great times, and with loving awe." Jehovah Himself sets a great store upon His name. He prohibits us from taking His name in vain (Ex. 20:7), and attaches significance and meaning to the several names by which He calls Himself (Ex. 6:3).

The English reader can generally distinguish the three names of Elohim, Jehovah and Adonai, in the ordinary version,—I say generally, not always,—for they have been translated interchangeably at times; but generally God stands for Elohim and its relatives, Jehovah is given in small capitals, LORD, and Adonai is given Lord in the ordinary way. Sometimes Jehovah is rendered GOD, as in Ezek. 37, and can easily be recognised because it is given in small capitals.

Elohim and its relatives—Eloah, El, Elah, El-Shaddai.

1. Elohim, God in the unity of His divine personality and power.

2. Eloah, God in the exclusiveness of His Deity, as the Supreme object of worship.

3. El, God in the expressiveness of His character and action.

4. Elah, Chaldee form of Eloah.

5. El-Shaddai, God in the sufficiency of His grace and government.

GOD (HEBREW, ELOHIM)

Elohim occurs about 2,500 times. In 2,310 instances it is applied to God, and elsewhere is used in a secondary sense and is applied to idols (Ex. 34 : 17), to men (Psa. 82 : 6 ; John 10 : 34, 35), and to angels (Psa. 97 : 7), and is rendered " gods " (Gen. 3 : 5), " judges " (Ex. 22 : 8), and " angels " (Psa. 8 : 5). Elohim means the Putter Forth of Power, hence in its first occurrence we have its meaning, " In the beginning God " (Gen. 1 : 1). Canon Girdlestone on this title says, " It is the title of the Creator and Ruler of the world, as such, and it indicates the power and majesty of that Being to Whom every creature owes his existence, his daily life, and his habitation." (See Gen. 5 : 1 ; Deut. 4 : 38 ; Isa. 45 : 18). In Gen. 1 to 2 : 3, Elohim occurs 35 times in describing God as the Putter Forth of Power in creation. The title occurs in ten ways, as descriptive of His power.

" God created " (verses 1, 21, 27). His power to bring into being. The word " created " (" Bara ") means to bring into existence, without the aid of pre-existing materials.

" God made " (verses 7, 16, 25, 31 ; 2 : 2, 3). His power to fashion and beautify. The word " asah," rendered " made," means to fashion out of what already exists. It is used to describe the building of a ship (Gen. 3 : 14), the dressing of a calf (Gen. 18 : 8), the preparing of a meal (Gen. 19 : 3), and the erection of a house (1 Chron. 15 : 1).

" The Spirit of God moved " (verse 2). His power to bring into life.

" God said " (verses 3, 6, 9, 11, 14, 20, 24, 26, 28, 29). His power to speak and cause to be.

"God saw" (verses 4, 10, 12, 18, 21, 25, 31). His power to discern and appreciate.

"God called" (verses 5, 8, 10). His power to describe and name.

"God divided" (verse 4). His power to separate and distinguish.

"God set" (verse 17). His power to place and keep.

"God ended" (2 : 2). His power to accomplish and complete.

"God blessed" (1 : 28 ; 2 : 3). His power to enrich and sanctify.

The books in which the name Elohim most frequently occurs, are Deuteronomy and Psalms. In Psa. 68 it occurs 26 times and practically covers all the truths of salvation. This Psalm is also remarkable because the name of JAH, LORD (Jehovah), **Lord** God (Jehovah Adonai), Lord (Adonai), God (El), Almighty (Shaddai), and **Lord** God (Jehovah Elohim) are also given.

The passage which most strikingly illustrates the meaning of Elohim is Gen. 1 : 26, "And God (plural) said, Let us (plural) make man in our image" (singular). Elohim is the plural of Eloah, and therefore the above gives us the Trinity acting in unity, for the creation of man is the act of the Father (Ex. 20 : 11), Son (Col. 1 : 16) and Spirit (Job 26 : 13) ; and yet man is made in the image, not the images, of God, for there is only one God, therefore the unity of the Godhead is made known. Trinity in unity, and unity in Divine personality are beautifully blended, even as there are light, heat and colour in the rays of the sun, and yet there is only one sun.

Psa. 62, illustrates in a suggestive way the thought embodied in this title.

Salvation—" My soul waiteth upon *God*, from Him cometh my salvation."

Expectation—" My soul wait thou only upon *God*, for my expectation is from Him."

Exultation—" In *God* is my salvation and my glory."

Foundation—" The Rock of my strength . . . is in *God*."

Protection—" *God* is a Refuge for us."

Revelation—" *God* hath spoken " ; and

Enduement—" Power belongeth unto *God.*"

What a stimulus to faith and an inspiration to love, is found in this title of God, for looking at it in the light of the New Testament, we find the Father in the power of His love, the Son in the provision of His grace, and the Spirit in the potentiality of His strength.

The spiritual truth for us is, we have the power of God in the God of power, hence we have the arms of " the eternal God " beneath us to sustain (Deut. 33 : 27), " God " as the refuge around us, for protection (Psa. 46 : 1), God as the sun above us to warm (Psa. 84 : 11), and God behind us, that we may say with the Psalmist, " I may walk before God " (Psa. 56 : 13).

GOD (HEBREW, ELOAH)

" Eloah " is formed from a root, not in use, namely, Ahlah, which means to worship. It is the singular form of Elohim, and denotes, when used of God—the one living and true God,—Who alone is worthy of adoration. It is put, therefore, in direct contrast with false gods, or the many gods of the heathen.

Eloah occurs 57 times, and except in six instances (2 Chron. 32 : 15 ; Prov. 30 : 5 ; Dan. 11 : 37, 38, 39 ; Hab. 1 : 11), is applied to the true God. No less than 41 times is Eloah found in the book of Job. Its first occurrence is in Deut. 32 : 15, 17, " He forsook God (Eloah) Who made him . . . they sacrificed unto devils and not unto Eloah," and this gives the clue to its meaning, for Eloah is set over against the demons. The same contrast is seen in Neh. 9 : 17, 18. Eloah is a " God ready to pardon . . . they made them a molten calf, and said, This is thy god (Elohim) that brought thee out of Egypt." The true and the false, the living and the dead, and the One and the many gods are here contrasted. The most striking passage is that used by Job, when he anticipates the coming of his Kinsman Redeemer, and in the expectation of his faith says, " though after my skin worms destroy this body, yet in my flesh shall I see God " (Eloah). He does not say, I shall see Elohim, but Eloah, for as Christ

was God manifest in the flesh, so He will be the only manifestation of the Godhead in the glory, hence it is fitting
Eloah (singular) should be used. The concrete verses which
summarize "Eloah" are the questions in Psa. 18 : 31 and
Isa. 44 : 8. "Who is Eloah save the Lord?" "Is there an
Eloah beside Me?" Thus as in Elohim we have Trinity in
unity, so in Eloah we have absolute Deity, for both the Old
and New Testaments emphasize, "The Lord our God is one
Lord," or as Newberry renders it, "Jehovah, the Ever-
existing One, our Elohim, our Triune God, is one Jehovah"
(Deut. 6 : 4 ; Mark 12 : 32 ; 1 Tim. 2 : 5). There is none
beside Him in His Deity, and there should be none beside
Him in our lives.

GOD (ELAH, CHALDEE)

Elah is the corresponding title to Eloah, in the Chaldee
language. It occurs 90 times—43 times in the book of Ezra,
46 times in Daniel, and once in Jer. 10 : 10. Thus the
Living and True God is identified with His people in captivity. The first occurrence of Elah is in Ezra 4 : 24, where
attention is called to the fact that the work of rebuilding
the "house of Elah" was made to cease, and called forth
the ministry of Haggai and Zechariah, for we read, "Then
the prophets, Haggai the prophet, and Zechariah the son of
Iddo, prophesied unto the Jews that were in Judah and
Jerusalem in the name of Elah of Israel, even unto them."
What was the effect? "Then arose up Zerubbabel, and
began to build the house of Elahah" (ah, emphatic) . . .
" and with them were the prophets of Elahah helping them."
The authorities tried to make them cease working, but the
" eye of Elahah was upon the elders of the Jews," and they
were conscious of His presence and help.

The most interesting verse in which the name of Elah
occurs is Dan. 6 : 23, where we read of Daniel—"He believed
in his Elah." The book of Daniel strikingly illustrates faith
in God as Elah, in connection with Daniel and the three
Hebrews. We have—

The worship of faith—"Daniel blessed *Elah*" (2 : 19).

The unconcern of faith—" Our *Elah* is able . . . but if not " (3 : 17, 18).

The companion of faith—" Four . . . fourth like the Son of *Elah* " (3 : 25).

The prayer of faith—" Daniel . . . prayed . . . before *Elah* " (6 : 10).

The finding of faith—" Found Daniel praying . . . before *Elah* " (6 : 11).

The reward of faith—" My *Elah* hath shut the lion's mouths " (6 : 22).

The honour of faith—" The *Elah* of Daniel " (6 : 26-28).

The history and use of this title of God is most instructive. Earthly mandates, fiery furnaces, scheming courtiers, persecuting men, and lions' dens cannot deter God's servants, to whom He is the Living One, for John Brown's cause ever goes marching on, when it is the cause of the Lord.

GOD (EL, HEBREW)

The title El occurs about 250 times, and always in the singular. It signifies strength, and denotes God as the Strong One and First and Only cause of things, and being in the singular emphasizes the essence of the Godhead. The attributes of God are generally associated with this title, hence, as to His *duration* He is the " *Everlasting God* " (Gen. 21 : 33) ; as to His *power*, He is the " *Almighty God* " (Gen. 17 : 1) ; as to His *exclusiveness*, He is the " *jealous God* " (Ex. 20 : 5) ; as to His *holiness*, He is a " *Consuming Fire* " (Deut. 4 : 24) ; as to His *pity*, He is a " *merciful God* " (Deut. 4 : 31) ; as to His *fidelity*, He is a " *faithful God* " (Deut. 7 : 9) ; as to His *vitality*, He is the " *Living God* " (Josh. 3 : 10) ; as to His *greatness*, He is the " *Terrible God* " (Neh. 1 : 5) ; and as to His *compassion*, He is the " *Gracious God* " (Jonah 4 : 2).

This title occurs mostly in the Psalms, occurring over 70 times, and among the number is found the expression of faith, namely, " My God " (Psa. 18 : 2 ; 22 : 1, 10 ; 63 : 1 ; 68 : 24 ; 89 : 26 ; 102 : 24 ; 118 : 28 ; 140 : 6). The first time El is used is in connection with Melchisedek, who is said to be " priest of the most high El " (Gen. 14 : 18). It is often found in connection with other words, such as " El-elohe-Israel" (God the God of Israel, Gen. 33 : 20) ; " El-beth-el" (God of Bethel, Gen. 35 : 7) ; "El-Shaddai" (The Almighty God, Gen. 48 : 3) ; and "Immanuel" (God with us, Isa. 7 : 14). The most expressive use of El is found in Psa. 22 : 1, where Christ appeals to El in His agony on the cross—" My God, My God," etc. The Son of God in His suffering, had not God the Son to His helping, but because of that death, He is to us " The mighty God " (El, Isa. 9 : 6), therefore we can say, " Behold God (El) is my salvation " (Isa. 12 : 2), and we can bear our testimony, " Happy is he that hath the God (El) of Jacob for his help, and whose hope is in Jehovah his Elohim " (Psa. 146 : 5).

ALMIGHTY GOD (HEBREW, EL-SHADDAI)

El-Shaddai, which means Almighty God, occurs 8 times in the Old Testament. Shaddai (Almighty) occurs 40 times, thus Shaddai, with and without El, occurs 48 times. Shaddai is found 31 times in the book of Job, and is rendered "Almighty" in each case. The other instances where Shaddai is mentioned are Num. 24 : 4, 16 ; Ruth 1 : 20, 21 ; Psa. 68 : 14 ; 91 : 1 ; Isa. 13 : 6 ; Ezek. 1 : 24 ; Joel 1 : 15. The eight passages where El-Shaddai occurs are Gen. 17 : 1 ; 28 : 3 ; 35 : 11 ; 43 : 14 ; 48 : 3 ; 49 : 25 ; Ex. 6 : 3 ; Ezek. 10 : 5. The equivalent expression occurs 10 times in the New Testament. Once He is called " Lord Almighty " (2 Cor. 6 : 18), once " The Almighty " (Rev. 1 : 8) ; five times " Lord God Almighty " (Rev. 4 : 8 ; 11 : 17 ; 15 : 3 ; 16 : 7 ; 21 : 22), once " God Almighty " (Rev. 16 : 14), once " Lord God Omnipotent "—same word as rendered " Almighty " (Rev. 19 : 6), and once " Almighty God " (Rev. 19 : 15). The New Testament word rendered " Almighty " is a compound one, one part meaning " *all*," and is so rendered when Christ says, " *All* power is given unto me " (Matt. 28 : 18) ; and the other part signifies " *power*," and is so rendered in Eph. 1 : 19 ; 6 : 10 ; in the sentences, " His mighty *power* " and the " the *power* of His might." It signifies the All-Powerful One, the Absolute Sovereign.

The Hebrew word " Shaddai " comes from the root " Shad," which means a breast, and is so rendered in Gen.

49 : 25 (the first time it occurs)—" the blessings of the
breasts." The word Almighty is in the plural, but the title
" El " is in the singular, so we have again trinity in unity,
and yet only one Divine personality. El-Shaddai, in the
depth of its meaning, signifies the many-breasted God, Who
is able to supply every need, the One Who is enough. The
first time " the Almighty God " is mentioned is in Gen. 17 : 1.
Abram had been walking before Sarah for thirteen years in
scheming to get the promised seed according to her idea, when
God comes to His servant, and says, " I am the Almighty
God, walk before Me, and be thou perfect." He says in so
many words, " I am all-sufficient to perform My promise
without your projects." Impossibilities according to man
are possibilities according to God. The last time " God
Almighty " is mentioned in the Bible is in relation to judgment, when Christ is described as the One Who " treadeth
the winepress of the fierceness of Almighty God " (Rev.
19 : 15). God is All-Bountiful to supply the need of His
people, His promise is sure, His grace is sufficient, His love is
satisfying, His truth is sanctifying, His joy is uplifting, His
word is certain, and He Himself is enough ; but it is equally
true He is All-Powerful to crush the devil, to destroy the
anti-christ, to overthrow evil, to stamp down oppression, and
to consign the wicked to their own place.

The most suggestive passage where Shaddai occurs, apart
from El, is Psa. 91 : 1. " He that abideth under the shadow
of the Almighty," and the New Testament promise to those
who obey in being separated to Him, speaks not only of
protection from all evil, but the positive power of a consecrated life, for what greater promise can we have than " I
will dwell, I will walk, I will be their God, I will receive, I
will be a Father . . . saith the Lord Almighty " (2 Cor.
6 : 14-18). Here is victory, power, progress, usefulness,
happiness, holiness, and heaven.

LORD (HEBREW, ADON, ADONAI)

Adon and Adonai are found in the following combinations :

Adon—The Lord (Josh. 3 : 11). The Absolute Owner of
all.

Adon-Jehovah—The Lord God (Ex. 23 : 17). The Proprietor Who is also in covenant relationship.

Adon-Jehovah-Elohim—Thy Lord, the Lord and thy God (Isa. 51 : 22). Thy Master, the Unchanging One, the Powerful One.

Adon-Jehovah-Sabaoth—The Lord, the LORD of Hosts (Isa. 19 : 4). The Master, the Unchanging Leader of armies.

Adonai—O my Lord (Ex. 4 : 10, 13). My Masters.

Adonai-Elohim—O Lord my God (Psa. 86 : 12). My Masters, my Creators.

Adonai-Jehovah—O Lord God (Deut. 3 : 24 ; 9 : 26). My Masters, the Ever Existing One.

Adonai is from Adon, and means Master or Owner. Adonai is the possessive plural of Adon, and therefore signifies, " My Masters." Adon is applied to God and man, and is rendered " *Sir* " in Gen. 43 : 20 ; " *Lord* " in Gen. 18 : 12 ; ' *Master* " in Gen. 24 : 12 ; and " *Owner* " in 1 Kings 16 : 24. It is only applied to the Lord 28 times, and mostly in the Psalms. The first occurrence of Adon is in Ex. 23 : 17, where Israel is reminded of their responsibility " to appear before the Lord,'' and because He was their Master, they were responsible to fulfil their obligations to Him. Five times the expression, " The Lord of all the earth," occurs (Josh. 3 : 11 ; Psa. 97 : 5 ; Micah 4 : 13 ; Zech. 4 : 14 ; 6 : 5), denoting what is His property. " The Lord . . . will suddenly come to His temple " (Mal. 3 : 1), why ? Because He comes to claim His own. Perhaps the most striking verse is in Psa. 110 : 1, " Jehovah said unto Adon, Sit Thou on My right hand, until I make Thine enemies Thy footstool." Christ uses this verse to emphasize His Lordship (see Matt. 22 : 42-45).

Adonai. This title is used of the Lord exclusively. The first time Adonai occurs is in Gen. 15 : 2, " And Abram said, Lord." Abram takes the place of humble inquiry when he asks how the Lord will fulfil His promise to make him the head of a great nation.

The following thoughts are suggested by the use of this title :

1. *Authority.* Two hundred times in the book of Ezekiel we have the expression, " Saith the Lord God," literally it is Adonai-Jehovah. Study its use in Ezek. 16, where the sentence occurs eleven times (verses 3, 8, 14, 19, 23, 30, 36, 43, 48, 59, 63), and it will be found that all the authority of the Great Jehovah as Lord and Master is behind Ezekiel in giving the Divine Message.

2. *Power.* " The Lord God (Jehovah-Adonai) is my strength, and He will make my feet like hind's feet, and He will make me to walk upon mine high places " (Hab. 3 : 19) Here Jehovah is before Adonai because it is a question of personal relationship to Jehovah in giving strength as Lord. " The Spirit of the Lord God (Adonai-Jehovah) is upon me " (Isa. 61 : 1). Here Lord is before Jehovah, because it is Christ acting for God in power to others. " The Lord (Adonai) hath made the host of the Syrians to hear a noise " (2 Kings 7 : 6). The flap of an eagle's wing acting for God had more power in it than the whole army of the Syrians. " The hand of the Lord God (Adonai-Jehovah) fell upon me, then I beheld " (Ezek. 8 : 1). In these four Scriptures we have power to walk, power for service, power for victory, and power to see.

3. *Deity.* In Psa. 35 : 23, we have another combination of Adonai, namely, " My God (Elohim) and my Lord " (Adonai), and in Psa. 38 : 15, " O Lord (Adonai), my God " (Elohim). These are the very words which fell from the lips of Thomas as he recognised the Deity of Christ, " My Lord and my God."

4. *Reverence.* The Lord as Adonai is appealed to in Daniel's confession of national sin, eleven times. Once as " Adonai-Elohim " (Dan. 9 : 3) ; once in the expression, " the Lord's sake " (verse 17) ; twice in the sentence, " Lord our God " (verses 9, 15) ; and seven times in the exclamation, " O Lord " (verses 4, 7, 8, 16, 19). " Elah " is not used by Daniel in his prayer : that title will do when speaking about God to the heathen (Dan. 6 : 22), or for the heathen in speaking of God (Dan. 3 : 28) ; but nearer and more expressive terms are on the lips of holy reverence and trustful love, hence Daniel speaks of God as " Jehovah-Elohim " (Dan.

9 : 4, 13), as "Adonai-Elohim" (Dan. 9 : 15), as "El" (Dan. 9 : 4), "Elohim" (Dan. 9 : 17, 18, 19), and "Jehovah" (Dan. 9 : 13). Right through the prayer of confession the man of God is on his knees, and in the inness of his being recognises the Lordship of Jehovah (Dan. 9 : 19). Listen to his closing words, "O Adonai, hear ; O Adonai, forgive ; O Adonai, hearken and do."

5. *Ownership.* "The Lord (Adonai) God (Jehovah) hath opened mine ear" (Isa. 50 : 5). The prophetical reference is to Christ's willing service (see Psa. 40 : 6-8 ; Heb. 10 : 7), and the typical reference is to Ex. 21 : 5, 6, where the slave loves his master to such an extent, that he will not avail himself of the right of freedom which the jubilee gives, and says, "I love my master . . . I will not go out free." The word "*master*" is "*Adon*," which is the singular form of "Adonai." When the slave gave up his freedom, we read, "Then his master (Adon) shall bring him . . . unto the door post, and his master (Adon) shall bore his ear through with an awl, and he shall serve him for ever." His Adon had an absolute right of ownership to the slave, even as Christ has an absolute right to us who are His bond-servants.

6. *Relationship.* The expression of faith is, "O my soul, thou hast said unto Jehovah, Thou art my Adonai" (Psa. 16 : 2). The relationship of a servant to the Lord and the Lord to the servant is recognised.

7. *Responsibility.* After the cleansing of the prophet by Jehovah, he heard "the voice of Adonai saying, Whom shall I send and who will go for Us ?" After he had responded to the call and heard the message he was to deliver, he said, "Adonai, how long ?" (Isa. 6 : 8-11). The prophet was found in the attitude of responsible service, as every true servant of the Lord is. The Lord has a right to our absolute obedience (Mal. 1 : 6), and we have a grace-given right to His loving protection, since we are His own and we can say, "Adonai-Jehovah will help me" (Isa. 50 : 7, 9).

LORD (JEHOVAH.)

There are many combinations of Jehovah with other titles and names, some of which are as follows :

Jehovah—LORD (Ex. 6 : 3). His Being and Immutability.

Jehovah-Adon—The LORD our Lord (Neh. 10 : 29). The unchanging One, Who is the Owner of the redeemed.

Jehovah-Adonai—LORD God (Psa. 109 : 26). Relationship to His servants as Master.

Jehovah-El—O LORD God (Psa. 31 : 5). The unchanging One, Who is supreme in His strength.

Jehovah-Elohim—LORD God (Gen. 2 : 4). Relationship to man as Creator.

Jah—The LORD (Psa. 68 : 4). The Independent One.

Jah-Jehovah—The LORD Jehovah (Isa. 26 : 4). The unchanging One, Who will never fail.

Jehovah-Elohim-Sabaoth-Adonai—The Lord, the God of Hosts, the Lord (Amos 5 : 16). The Unchanging One, the Leader of heaven's host, the Owner of all.

Jehovah, Jehovah-El—The LORD, the LORD God (Ex. 34 : 6). The Unchanging One, the Unchanging One in all His might.

Jehovah-Sabaoth-Elohim—The Lord of Hosts, the God (Jer. 27 : 4), the Unchanging One, the Leader of heaven's Army, the Putter Forth of power.

I AM THAT I AM (Ex. 3 : 14). His independence

The name of Jehovah is generally printed (LORD) in small capitals, and is thus distinguished from the other Hebrew words that are translated Lord. This wonderful name occurs about 7,000 times in the Old Testament. A few times it is given Jehovah, as in Gen. 22 : 14; Ex. 6 : 3; 17 : 16; Jud. 6 : 24; Psa. 83 : 18 ; Isa. 12 : 2 ; 26 : 4 ; and several hundred times it is rendered "God." Many definitions have been given as to the meaning of this name, but Jehovah is beyond a mere definition. Newberry defines it, "He that always was, that always is, and ever is to come." Rev. 1 : 4 reveals God as expressing Himself thus, " From Him which is " (the ever Existing One) " and which was " (the One Who always was) " and which is to come " (Who always will be). When Moses asked for God's name, He replied, " I Am that I Am," or as it might be rendered, " I Am what I Am," expressive not merely of Self-Existence, but of unchangingness of character. He always was what He is, He is what He was ;

He will ever be what He was and is. He is unchanging in
character, purpose, promise, and love. As the Spirit says
of Him, " With Whom is no variableness, neither shadow of
turning " (Jas. 1 : 17). He is the same in the yesterday of
the past, in the to-day of the present, and in the forever of
the future. Bonar expresses the thought admirably in the
well-known lines—

> " I change He changes not,
> The Christ can never die,
> His love not mine the resting place,
> His truth not mine the tie."

When spoken of Him *personally*, Jehovah refers to the
independence of His being and the immutability of His
character ; when used of Him in *relation* to man as His
creature, Jehovah refers to His relationship as Creator ; and
when found in connection with His *redeemed people*, Jehovah
refers to His faithful and covenant love.

The name of Jehovah is used with special significance.
When coupled with Elohim, Jehovah refers to His relationship to man as Creator. " Lord God " (Jehovah-Elohim)
occurs 19 times in Gen 2 and 3. Among those references will
be found the following thoughts, the earth made for man
(2 : 4), man made for the earth (2 : 7), a home made for man
(2 : 8), man put into the home (2 : 16), woman made for man
(2 : 21, 22), man hiding from God and called by Him (3 : 8, 9),
God's provision for man (3 : 21), God's statement about man
(3 : 22), and God's mercy in keeping man from the tree of
life (3 : 23). The whole story of man's creation, man's fall,
and God's provision for him in grace is thus summed up.
When Jehovah is used without any other name, His covenant
and redemptive relationships are emphasised. When He is
about to bring Israel out of Egypt He reveals Himself as
Jehovah. He speaks to Moses and says, " I am Jehovah " ;
then He reminds him, He was not known to Abraham, Isaac
and Jacob as Jehovah, but as El-Shaddai, but He was going
to fulfil the covenant made with them because He was
Jehovah, hence He commissions Moses to tell the children of
Israel, " I am Jehovah " ; then He gives five " I wills " of
promise, and says, " Ye shall know I am Jehovah your

Elohim " ; then He gives two more " I wills " in declaring He will keep to the promise made to their fathers about the land of promise, and sums all up by saying, " I am Jehovah " (Ex. 6 : 2-8). Again, when the LORD leads His people ou of Egypt, it is as Jehovah He goes before them (Ex. 13 : 21), but when He stands between them and the Egyptians He is said to be Elohim (Ex. 14 : 19), for He is prepared to exercise His power. Again, in the book of Judges, where we have recorded the repeated failure of Israel, the Spirit in qualifying the men who delivered the nation is not spoken of as the Spirit of God, but always as " the Spirit of the LORD " (Jehovah), for the reason of His grace is because of His covenant relationship (Jud. 3 : 10 ; 6 : 34 ; 11 : 29 ; 13 : 25 ; 14 : 6, 19 ; 15 : 14).

Jehovah denotes Jehovah exclusively, therefore God and Lord are not interchangeable titles. " In the name of Jehovah the personality of the Great I Am is distinctly expressed. It is everywhere a proper name, denoting the person of God. The Hebrew may say, ' *the* Elohim,' the true God, in opposition to all false gods ; but he would never say ' *the* Jehovah,' for Jehovah is the name of the true God only. He says again and again ' *my* God,' but never ' *my* Jehovah,' for when he says ' my God,' he means Jehovah. He speaks of the ' *God of Israel*,' but never of ' *the Jehovah of Israel*,' for there is no other Jehovah. He speaks of ' *the Living God*,' but never of ' *the Living Jehovah*,' for He cannot conceive of Jehovah other than living." There is no adjective to describe Him, for He is beyond description. The sentence, " Jehovah, He is God," is of frequent occurrence (see Deut. 4 : 35, 39), but not, " God, He is Jehovah." The whole contest on Mount Carmel between Elijah and the 400 priests of Baal was, whether Jehovah or Baal was God. Elijah said, " If Jehovah be God follow Him, if Baal, follow him. . . . The Elohim which answereth by fire, He is God the Elohim " (Newberry, 1 Kings 18 : 24). Jehovah proved He was God by the descending fire, as the people said, " Jehovah, He is God ; Jehovah, He is God," but nothing could prove He was Jehovah. White is white, and nothing can prove it is black, white proves itself.

To know Jehovah as Jehovah in an experimental sense, is to know that He can, and will, perform what He commands. One asks the question, " What does the name of Jehovah mean ?" It is a very ancient form of the verb *to be.* Jehovah signifies, *He will cause it to happen, He will cause it to be, He will cause it to pass.* The expression, " I am Jehovah," and " I am the LORD your God," occurs over 40 times in the book of Leviticus. The passages group themselves around the words, prohibition, promise and performance. *Prohibition—* " Therefore shall ye keep My commandments and do them, I am Jehovah " (Lev. 22 : 31), is the summary of what Israel were not to do and what they were to do, as emphasized in chapters 18-22. *Promise—*" I am the LORD that bringeth you up out of the land of Egypt, to be your God, ye shall therefore be holy, for I am holy " (Lev. 11 : 45 ; 1 Pet. 1 : 16). Redemption by God, relationship to Him, and responsibility to Him, also bring regard from Him, for He says, " I am . . . to be your God " (2 Cor. 6 : 17, 18). *Performance—*" I am Jehovah which sanctify you " (Lev. 20 : 8). The Lord's precepts are illuminated with His promises, and His promises are the assurances of His performance. " I am Jehovah " is the signature upon the cheque of promise, and is to be honoured by the Cashier of performance at the Capital Bank of Heaven's precept.

The name of Jehovah reminds us of His immutability. He says, " I am Jehovah " ; then He explains what it means, " I change not " ; then He gives the application, " Therefore the sons of Jacob are not consumed " (Mal. 3 : 6). Being what He is, He cannot do other than He does. How often in the Psalms do we find the Spirit playing upon the words, " Jehovah is," as coupled with the believer's faith. He is the Rock upon which we rest. " Jehovah is my Rock " (Psa. 18 : 2) ; He is the Defence in which we can hide, " Jehovah is my Defence " (Psa. 94 : 22) ; He is the Garrison by which we are preserved, " Jehovah is my Keeper " (Psa. 121 : 5) ; He is the Shield behind which we are protected, " Jehovah is my . . . Shield " (Psa. 28 : 7) ; He is the Deliverance by which we are saved, " Jehovah is my Light and Salvation " (Psa. 27 : 1) ; He is the Shade by which we are refreshed, " Jehovah is thy Shade " (Psa. 121 : 5) ; and He is the Pastor to Shepherd, " Jehovah is my Shepherd " (Psa. 23 : 1). Since Jehovah is what He is, we may well come to the conclusion of faith as expressed in Psa. 37.

" Trust in Jehovah " (verse 3), for He supplies all needs.

" Delight in Jehovah " (verse 4), for He fulfils all desires.

" Commit unto Jehovah " (verse 5), for He accomplishes all things.

" Rest in Jehovah " (verse 7), for He looks after all His saints.

" Wait upon Jehovah " (verse 9), for he bestows all blessing.

" Look to Jehovah " (verse 34), for He rewards all waiters.

" Trust in Jehovah " (verse 40), for faith sees all grace.

The relative titles found in connection with the name of Jehovah proclaim the manifold service of His grace. There are

FOURTEEN TITLES OF JEHOVAH

" Jehovah is His name " (Ex. 15 : 3). " They that know Thy name will put their trust in Thee : for Thou, Jehovah, hast not forsaken them that seek Thee " (Psa. 9 : 10). The name of the LORD stands for His nature, His character. The meaning of Jehovah is the Unchanging One, namely, the One Who always was, is and is to come (Rev. 1 : 4). Jehovah Himself explains it by I AM THAT I AM, or I AM WHAT I AM (Ex. 3 : 14).

There are fourteen titles of Jehovah. I take Newberry's rendering of the Hebrew words for the English reader.

Jehovah-Hoseenu

Jehovah-Hoseenu is the LORD our Maker—" O come, let us worship and kneel before Jehovah our Maker " (Psa. 95 : 6). Dr. Parkhurst in his Hebrew Lexicon, points out that the word " asah," is used of God in a variety of ways in speaking of Him as the Maker. To produce as a tree " *yielding* fruit " (Gen. 1 : 11) ; to prepare a meal, as when Manoah " *made* ready a kid " (Jud. 13 : 15) ; to observe an ordinance, as when Israel were told to " *keep* " the Passover (Ex. 12 : 47) ; to " *pare* " the nails, as when one dresses them (Deut. 21 : 12) ;

to consecrate, as when Israel were commanded "*to do*" all the Lord's commandments (Deut. 28 : 1) ; and to fashion, as when the things of the tabernacle were "*made*" according to the Divine pattern (Ex. 36 : 10-38). When therefore reference is made to Jehovah our Maker it does not refer to Him as the Creator, causing things to come into being ; but His fashioning out of what already existed. As He is the Fashioner of the material universe, so He is the Artificer of His Spiritual Tabernacle.

Jehovah-Jireh

Jehovah-Jireh is the " LORD will see or provide " (Gen. 22 : 14). The word for Jireh is rendered " *saw* " in speaking of Abraham as he journeyed with Isaac to the place of sacrifice and " *saw* " it " afar off," and " *provided* " when Abraham assures Isaac "God will *provide* Himself a lamb," and " *looked* " as the patriarch " *looked* " and saw the ram caught in the thicket (Gen. 22 : 4, 8, 13). The LORD is the universal Provider for His people. He looks out and sees there is ample provision, hence before we were, He had provided life for our death, salvation for our sin, atonement for our guilt, health for our sickness, joy for our sorrow, strength for our weakness, and heaven instead of our hell, and all this in the Lamb of Calvary (Rom. 8 : 32).

Jehovah-Ropheca

Jehovah-Ropheca means the Lord that healeth, or as Rotherham renders, the Lord the Physician (Ex. 15 : 26). The word means to mend as a garment is mended, to repair as a building is reconstructed, and to cure as a diseased person is restored to health. The word is rendered " *make whole* " in Job. 5 : 18, " *physician* " in Jer. 8 : 22, " *cure* " in Jer. 33 : 6, " *heal* " in Psa. 60 : 2, and " *repaired* " in 1 Kings 18 : 30. Sometimes it is used to express God's grace in restoring the spiritual life, hence, " He healeth all our diseases " (Psa. 103 : 3), He healeth the broken in heart (Psa. 147 : 3), and the backslider from his backslidings (Jer. 3 : 22) ; and sometimes it is used to express healing of bodily infirmity as in the case of Abimelech (Gen. 20 : 17), and Hezekiah (2 Kings 20 : 5) ; and the reason of the healing is found in

Him, by Whose " stripes we are healed." Christ's wounding on Calvary is the cause of our wholeness by grace, in spirit, soul and body.

Jehovah-Nissi

Jehovah-Nissi means "the Lord our Banner" (Ex. 17 : 15). "*Nissi*" signifies a token, and is rendered "*sail*" in Isa. 33 : 23 ; Ez. 27 : 7 ; "*Standard*" in Isa. 49 : 22 ; 62 : 10 ; "*Ensign*" in Isa. 5 : 26 ; 11 : 10, 12 ; "*Banner*" in Psa. 60 : 4 ; "*Sign*" in Num. 26 : 10 ; and "*Pole*" in Num. 21 : 8, 9. It is not without suggestion that the word "*Pole*" is "*Nissi*" in connection with the brazen serpent lifted up upon it to give life to Israel, for our Saviour was lifted up upon what He was in Himself, and by means of that cross we get victory over self, the flesh and the world, for we are crucified to all of these by means of it (Gal. 2 : 20 ; 5 : 24 ; 6 : 14), hence the Lord Himself is the Victory over the Amalek of our foes, and He as our Banner leads us always in triumph. The Lord in His death for us is our Banner in victory, our Standard in life, our Ensign in testimony, our Sail for progress, and the Sign to all that He is our Triumphant Lord.

Jehovah-Mekaddeshcem

Jehovah-Mekaddeshcem means "the Lord that doth sanctify." The expression, " I am the Lord which sanctify you," occurs in several connections. It is found seven times in the Book of Leviticus.

Sanctified to Keep. " Ye shall keep My statutes and do them ; *I am the Lord which sanctify you*" (Lev. 20 : 8). Obedience to the Lord is possible because of the operation of the Lord. The measure of our sanctification is guaged by our obedience.

Sanctified to Purity. The priest was prohibited from taking to wife an impure woman, and a twofold reason was given, because " he is holy unto God," and because of what Jehovah is, for He says, " For *I the Lord, which sanctify you*, am holy" (Lev. 21 : 7, 8).

Sanctified to God. The command about the pure woman for wife is repeated. It might be all right for any one else to marry a widow, or a divorced person, but not for a priest, for he was not to " profane his seed among his people, *for I the Lord do sanctify them*" (Lev. 21 : 15). A soul sanctified to the Lord, is one who is wholly for the Lord, hence he cannot do what would be allowable in others.

Sanctified to Wholeness. No one with any bodily blemish was allowed to fill the office of priest, although he was allowed, being Aaron's seed, to eat of the " bread of his God " ; and the reasons given are twofold, first, " because he hath a blemish," and, second, " that he profane not My sanctuaries : for *I the Lord do sanctify them* " (Lev. 21 : 16-24). A saved soul feeds on Christ as the Bread of Life, but it is the wholly sanctified one who has the right to approach the Lord and touch His holy things.

Sanctified to Distinguish. The priest was not allowed to eat anything " which died of itself " ; nor that was torn by beasts ; these would have the blood in them and were prohibited. That which disease had touched, or violence seized, was not to be eaten. The sanctified soul cannot feed upon the diseased and dead things of the world, nor the violent things of sin and angry saints. He feeds upon the prescribed Christ of the Word and the things of the Spirit of Peace (Lev. 22 : 8, 9).

Sanctified to Guide. Should a man " unwittingly eat of the holy bread which was for the priest and his family, then the priest had to tell him of his fault, and tell him what to do, for such were not to profane the holy things of the Children of Israel, which they shall offer unto the Lord ; or suffer them to bear the iniquity of trespass, when they eat their holy things, for *I the Lord do sanctify them* " (Lev. 22 : 15, 16).

Sanctified to Remember. " *I am the Lord which hallow you* " (same word as rendered sanctify in the other Scriptures), " *that brought you out of the land of Egypt, to be your God* " (Lev. 22 : 32). Israel was redeemed by Jehovah, hence He had a right to all He asked from them.

Jehovah-Eloheenu

Jehovah-Eloheenu means the " Lord our God " (Psa. 99 : 5, 8, 9). As " Our Father " reminds all God's children of their common relationship with Him and each other, so " The Lord our God," speaks of the commonwealth of God's people in Him. Nineteen times the expression, " The Lord our God," occurs in the book of Deuteronomy, and in the following associations : (1) *What He is*—" The Lord our God is one Lord " (Deut. 6 : 4). The Ever-Existing One is all powerful in the Trinity of His being, and sufficient in Himself for all He needs, but He is ours. (2) *Where He is*—" The Lord our God is in all things that we call upon Him for " (Deut. 4 : 7). Obedience in prayer always finds the Lord there for it ever brings Him near. (3) *What He said*—" The Lord our God spake " (Deut. 1 : 6, 19 ; 2 : 37 ; 5 : 25, 27 ; 6 : 20, 24). Prohibitions for protection, precepts for direction, and promises for inspirations, cover the Lord's injunctions. (4) *What He did*—" The Lord our God delivered " (Deut. 2 : 33, 36 ; 3 : 3 ; 23 : 14). His deliverances and blessings mean victory and rest. The rest of faith consummated in the triumph of faith. (5) *What He gave*—" The Lord our God doth give " (Deut. 1 : 20, 25). God's givings are the secret of our living. He gives with a generous hand and a loving heart. There is no cold comfort in His bestowments, they are all warm and rich. (6) *What He has*—" The secret things belong unto the Lord our God " (Deut. 29 : 29). He tells us what is good for us, and He tells us more as we are good to Him. The heart-throbs of our love, move Him to reveal the heart thoughts of His purpose. (7) *What He shows*—" The Lord our God hath showed us His glory " (Deut. 5 : 24). He is not a show to gratify our curiosity, but He is a majesty to command our wonder. The glory of His nature is love, the glory of His character is holiness, the glory of His acts is grace, the glory of His truth is promise, the glory of His Word is knowledge, the glory of His power is usefulness, and the glory of Himself is Christ.

Jehovah-Eloheka

Jehovah-Eloheka signifies " The Lord thy God." It is of frequent occurrence in the book of Deuteronomy, and is found 20 times in chapter 16. Taking its use from the book of Exodus, we find it denotes Jehovah's relationship to His people and their responsibility to Him. There are four definite thoughts, namely, redemption, relationship, responsibility, and reward. "*Redemption by the Lord*"—"I am Jehovah thy Elohim which brought thee out of the land of Egypt" (Ex. 20 : 2). Ransom by the blood of atonement procures redemption by the hand of power. *Relationship to the Lord*—"Lord *thy* God." Relationship is secured by redemption. The Son of God was our Ransom, that we might become the sons of God by His grace. *Responsibility to the Lord* (Ex. 20 : 3, 7, 10). Privilege beings responsibility: there is no blessing of the Gospel, but has an attendant obligation. *Reward by the Lord* (Ex. 20 : 12). Obedience always brings blessing, as well as bringing its own reward.

Jehovah-Elohay

Jehovah-Elohay means, "The Lord my God" (Zech. 14 : 5). The personal pronoun expresses personal faith in the God of Power. The language of faith is, "O Lord my God, in Thee do I trust" (Psa. 7 : 1) ; the outlook of faith is, "The Lord my God will enlighten my darkness" (Psa. 18 : 28) ; the testimony of faith is, "O Lord my God, I cried unto Thee and Thou hast healed me" (Psa. 30 : 2) ; the worship of faith is, "O Lord my God, I will give thanks unto Thee" (Psa. 30 : 12) ; the consecration of faith is, "I wholly followed the Lord my God" (Josh. 14 : 8) ; the stay of faith is, "The hand of the Lord my God was upon me" (Ezra 7 : 28) ; and the hope of faith is, "The Lord my God shall come" (Zech. 14 : 5).

Jehovah-Shalom

Jehovah-Shalom means, "The Lord send peace" (Jud. 6 : 24). The comprehensiveness of the word "*Shalom*" in its use in Isaiah tells out what Jehovah is as our Peace. He is the *Procurer of Peace*, for "the chastisement of our peace was upon Him" (Isa. 53 : 5) ; He is the *Personification of Peace*, for He is "The Prince of Peace" (Isa. 9 : 6) ; He is the *Publisher of Peace* (Isa. 52 : 7) ; He is the *Perfection of Peace*, for He keeps in "perfect peace" those who trust Him (Isa. 26 : 3) ; He is the *Power of Peace*, for "He will ordain peace" and work all our "works in us" (Isa. 26 : 12) ; He is the *Promise of Peace*, for He says, "The work of righteousness shall be peace, and the effect of righteousness, quietness and assurance forever" (Isa. 32 : 17) ; and He is the *Perpetuator of Peace*, for He declares "His covenant of peace" shall not be removed, and of the increase of His government and peace there shall be no end (Isa. 9 : 7 ; 54 : 10). The inscription on the altar of our worship means more to us than Gideon's altar did to him, for our Jehovah-Shalom does more for us.

The consequence of knowing the Lord as Jehovah-Shalom may be illustrated by the renderings of the word " *Shalom.*" It is translated " *Welfare* " in Gen. 43 : 27 ; " *Good health* " in Gen. 43 : 28 ; " *All is well* " and " *Safe* " in 2 Sam. 18 : 28, 29 ; " *Prosperity* " in Psa. 35 : 27 ; " *Favour* " in Song of Solomon 8 : 10 ; and " *Rest* " in Psa. 38 : 3. The following blessings are found and enjoyed through personal acquaintance with Jehovah : " *Welfare*," for He sees we fare well ; " *Good health*," for His grace tones the body as well as tempers the soul ; " *All is well*," for the lights and the shadows are blended in the all things of His workings ; " *Prosperity*," for the prosperity of the soul is the soul of all prosperity ; " *Favour*," for the smile of His face makes our face to smile ; " *Rest*," for the calm of the Eternal Rest fills the being with the rest of the Eternal Calm ; and all is " *Safe*," for we cannot be safer than when we have the circle of His protecting presence.

Jehovah-Tsebahoth

Jehovah-Tsebahoth means, "The Lord of Hosts." Tsebahoth is rendered " *armies* " in Num. 1 : 3, " *the service* " in Num. 4 : 23, and " *appointed time* " in Job 14 : 14. It is essentially the Lord's military name and frequently He loves to assure His people of the fact that " The Lord of Hosts is His name " (Isa. 47 : 4 ; 48 : 2 ; 51 : 15 ; 54 : 5). A frequent formula of expression is, " Thus saith the Lord of Hosts," especially in Jeremiah. In the book of Zechariah, " The Lord of Hosts " occurs 53 times, and being found in this book, which declared God's action in judgment and blessing upon Israel, is of peculiar interest. Take but three passages : Zech. 4 : 6—" Not by might " (margin, " army "),

" nor by power, but by My Spirit, saith the Lord of Hosts."
The wealth of earth and the armies of the nations cannot
hinder the working of the Spirit of the Lord of Hosts. Every
" mountain " of difficulty and opposition will become a
" plain," over which He will walk in triumph. Zech. 13 : 7—
" Awake, O Sword, against My Shepherd and against the Man
that is My Fellow, saith the Lord of Hosts." The cross was
the place where all the armies of darkness congregated to
overthrow the purpose of Jehovah, but they were only the
instruments to fulfil His will. The cross has an inner meaning beyond the hate of man and the rage of hell, it satisfies
the heart of Jehovah, hence from the place of wounding
comes the wealth of blessing ; and in that seeming cross of
defeat was accomplished the most crucial triumph ever
obtained. Zech. 14 : 21—" Holiness unto the Lord of Hosts,"
is the sentence which describes the climax of millennial
blessing. When the Lord is in possession, every possession
has the name of Jehovah stamped upon it.

Jehovah-Rohi

Jehovah-Rohi means " The Lord my Shepherd " (Psa.
23 : 1). The many sidedness of His Shepherd-office is illustrated in the use of the word rendered " *Shepherd.*" It is
translated " *Feeder* " in the margin of Gen. 4 : 2, and
" *Keeper* " in the text ; " *Companion* " in Prov. 28 : 7 ;
" *Friend* " in Jud. 14 : 20 ; " *Pastor* " in Jer. 17 : 16 ;
" *Herdman* " in Gen. 13 : 7 ; and " *Shepherd* " in Psa. 23 : 1.
As our Shepherd, the Lord is the Feeder to provide, the
Keeper to protect, the Companion for fellowship, the Friend
for help, the Pastor for comfort, the Herdman to gather,
and the Shepherd to lead.

Jehovah-Heleyon

Jehovah-Heleyon means " The Lord Most High."
Heleyon means highest, and is rendered " *uppermost* " in
Gen. 40 : 17 ; " *high* " in Neh. 3 : 25 ; " *higher* " and
" *highest* " in Ezek. 9 : 2 ; 41 : 7. As denominating the Lord
in the ordinary version, He is—

Highest (Psa. 18 : 13 ; 87 : 5).

Most High (Num. 24 : 16 ; Deut. 32 : 8 ; 2 Sam. 22 : 14).

Most High God (El) (Gen. 14 : 18, 19, 20 ; Psa. 78 : 56).
God (Elohim) Most High (Psa. 57 : 2).
Jehovah Most High (Psa. 7 : 17 ; 47 : 2).

Under the title of " The Most High," Jehovah is distinctly said to be " The possessor of heaven and earth " (Gen. 14 : 18, 19) ; and the distributor of the earth among the nations (Deut. 32 : 8) ; and fittingly as having to do with the Gentiles, He is designated " The Most High " in the book of Daniel no less than 12 times (Dan. 3 : 26 ; 4 : 2, 17, 24, 25, 32 ; 5 : 18, 21 ; 7 : 18, 22, 25, 27). It is not without significance that this title has to do with the Most High as the Ascended One Who is in the highest place, guiding and over-ruling all things and making everything work to one given end, to set His Son as the King-Priest, after the order of Melchisedec, upon His throne, to rule in the millennial glory of His power and majesty (see Psa. 110 : 4-7 ; Zech. 6 : 13 ; Heb. 5 : 6 ; 6 : 20 ; 7 : 17, 21).

Jehovah-Tsidkeenu

Jehovah-Tsidkeenu means " The Lord our Righteousness " (Jer. 23 : 6 ; 33 : 16). " *Righteousness* " is rendered " *right* " in Psa. 17 : 1 ; " *Just* " in Deut. 25 : 15 ; and " *justice* " in Prov. 1 : 3, and signifies that which is right, just and true. It is descriptive of what Jehovah is. The Lord cannot communicate to us His attributes, but He can in His grace make us right with Himself, because of the Christ Who was made sin for us (2 Cor. 5 : 21), and put to our faith's account, as He did to Abraham, what Christ is as His righteousness, and reckon us righteous.

The passages in Jeremiah are peculiar in their forecast of Christ as the Regal Branch reigning over Israel, and when in His millennial rule " He shall execute judgment and justice in the earth," the " Name whereby He shall be called " is " The Lord our Righteousness." And not only shall He be thus called, but of God's people, as represented in Jerusalem, it is said, " This is the name by which *she* shall be called, The Lord our Righteousness." What the Lord is in Himself to His glory, they become in Him by His grace.

Jehovah-Shammah

Jehovah-Shammah means "The Lord is there" (Ezek. 48 : 35). It is the title by which Jehovah designates Himself as the dweller in the millennial city of Jerusalem. In the past the tabernacle and the temple were His dwelling places, but in the future He will move into the wider sphere of the City. In the millennium there will be the temple and the city ; but in the New Jerusalem there is no temple, but the Lord Himself.

"The Lord is there." The Old Testament's question to fallen man is, "Adam, where art thou?" The first question in the New Testament is, "Where is He?" The reply to the question in the New Testament, as given by the Holy Spirit, in the past, present and future is,—

Where *was* He ?

In the manger of humiliation, at His incarnation.
In the wilderness of temptation, at His testing.
In the hall of judgment, at His rejection.
On the cross of atonement, at His death.
In the will of His Father, in His service.
Outside the tomb of death, at His resurrection.
On the mount of triumph, at His ascension.

Where is *He ?*

On the throne of acceptance, with His Father.
In the surrendered child of God, by His Spirit.

Where *will* He be ?

On His throne of glory, at His coming.

What shall we say of this wonderful name of Jehovah ? Let us remember that His name is "*Holy* and *Reverend*" (Psa. 111 : 9), therefore holiness and reverence become us who bear His name ; His name is *Pleasant* (Psa. 135 : 3), therefore let us gladly praise Him, for He is "full of delight" (Rotherham) ; His name is "*glorious*" (Psa. 72 : 19), therefore let us exult in Him forever ; His name is "*Excellent*" (Psa. 148 : 13), therefore let us speak well of Him ; His name is "*Exalted*" (Isa. 12 : 4), therefore let us proclaim Him as the supreme One ; and His name is "*Everlasting*" (Isa. 63 : 16), therefore let us count upon Him for continued blessing, for as Rotherham renders the passage, " Our Redeemer from the Age-time past is Thy name."

What do we find in this name ? Let me give you seven blessings and give Rotherham's reading of the Scriptures :

Safety. " A tower of strength is the name of Jehovah, thereinto runneth the righteous and is safe " (Prov. 18 : 10).

Joy. " They may leap for joy in Thee who are lovers of Thy name " (Psa. 5 : 11).

Supply. " Jehovah . . . a refuge for times of destitution : thus let them who know Thy name put confidence in Thee " (Psa. 9 : 10).

Power. " I will make them mighty in Jehovah, and in His name shall they march to and fro, declareth Jehovah " (Zech. 10 : 12).

Inspiration. " I have remembered in the night Thy name, O Jehovah, and have kept Thy law " (Psa. 119 : 55).

Victory. " Jehovah is a warlike One. Jehovah is His name. The chariots of Pharaoh and His train hath He cast into the sea " (Ex. 15 : 3, 4).

Presence. " In every place where I may mention My name will I come in unto thee and will bless thee " (Ex. 20 : 24).

FATHER

In Elohim we have revealed the glory of God's power, in Adonai the glory of the Lord's possessions, in His name of Jehovah we have made known the glory of His Divine Person, and in Father we have brought to us the glory of His loving Paternity. In the first there is made known the skill and strength of His hands as Creator ; in the second there is made known the claim and call of His authority as Lord and Master ; in the third we see the grace and constancy of His immutable purpose as the unchanging One ; and in the fourth we have the hand and heart of our Father's love and aid. " The Father of Glory " (Eph. 1 : 17) is one of the designations of Himself, but the glory of the Father is only known as we are in intimate fellowship with the Father of Glory.

" I cannot see," Huxley once wrote to Charles Kingsley, " one shadow or tittle of evidence that the great Unknown underlying the phenomena of the universe stands to us in the relation of a Father—loves us and cares for us, as Christianity asserts." If we only look where Huxley looked, we shall see that " Nature is red in tooth and claw with ravening," but when we see Jesus we behold " the Only Begotten of the Father, full of grace and truth."

The Gospel of John is specially the Gospel which reveals the Father. In Matthew, " the Father " is mentioned 44 times, in Mark 5 times, in Luke 17 times, and in John 122 times. Tracing through John's Gospel, a definite thought may be emphasized in each chapter where the Father is mentioned.

1. *The Father's Unfolding* (1 : 1-14). The Divine Word reveals the loving Father in His grace and truth. Christ is all He was in the living expression of what the Father is. The Gospel opens with the Son in the Father's bosom, and before it closes it reveals a saved sinner in the bosom of the Son (1 : 18 ; 13 : 25).

2. *The Father's House* (2 : 16). When the Son comes to the Father's house He finds it polluted and possessed by religious sinners. Cleansing is the first act, for there can be no compact in grace till the usurper is cast out from his government.

3. *The Father's Trust* (3 : 35). The Beloved Son has given to Him the wealth of the Father's treasure. Adam was trusted and failed. Christ was trusted and was faithful. This Gospel reveals Christ as constantly giving. Look up His " I gives." He has so much to give the sons, because, as the Son, He has received all the treasures of the Father.

4. *The Father's Worship* (4 : 23). The spirit nature of the Father seeks the spiritual worship of His children. The locality of place and the hollowness of form are not recognized by Him, while the heart of faith and the reality of love's gratitude are food and satisfaction to His being.

5. *The Father's Will* (5 : 17-42). There breathes through Christ's references to His Father, working, loving, honouring, committing, sending, witnessing, and fitting, one thought, namely, His delight to do all the Father wishes. He wills

and walks in His Father's will, hence the Father is with Him in all His ways.

6. *The Father's Provision* (6 : 27-57). As the Bread of God, Christ is God-sealed, God-given, and God-satisfying. He that wants Christ wants the Father and everything, while he that has Christ wants nothing, for in the Father's provision he has everything.

7. *The Father's Commission* (8 : 16-54). Sent by the Father, His vocation was to please Him, He spake of Him, for He enjoyed His company, and the Father honoured Him in consequence.

8. *The Father's Fellowship* (10 : 15-38). Mutual knowledge, mutual love, mutual service, mutual preservation, mutual action and mutual possession are some of the heart throbs which the finger of faith feels as it is placed on the pulse of this chapter.

9. *The Father's Response* (11 : 41). The upward gaze of Christ's appeal brings the unloosing act of God's power, which causes the corrupting Lazarus to glide forth from the grip of death's grasp in the vitality of Christ's life. No power can withstand the Son's prayer and the Father's potency.

10. *The Father's glory* (12 : 26-50). The goal of the Father's command had its consummation in the gore of the fiery cross of Calvary. The hour of all hours was the hour of Calvary's darkness, for then did Christ meet God's claim and glorify His name, and fulfil every iota of the Father's will.

11. *The Father's Confidence* (13 : 1-3). The consciousness of the Father's confidence was the fuel that kept the flame of Christ's continuance burning brightly. The hate of men, the desertion of friends, the blackness of the cross, and the ire of God's judgment could not hide the smile of the Father's face.

12. *The Father's Image* (14 : 2-31). The Visible Son was the Invisible Father. There is no question about God, the past, the present, the future, the claim of love, the coming of the Spirit, and the unknown, but finds its answer in Christ.

13. *The Father's Ministry* (15 : 1-26). The ministry of the Fatherly Husbandman is the cause of the fruitfulness of the vine and the branches. The sap of the Spirit's life, the

glow of the Divine love and the flow of the Son's joy are all
due to the grace of the Father's attention.

14. *The Father's Love* (16 : 3-32). The income which
Christ has brought to us, the outcome of Christ's work for us,
all we have become in His grace, and all the enemies we
overcome in His power, are because the Father has come to
us in His love, and lives in us in His power.

15. *The Father's Keeping* (17 : 1-24). The priestly prayer
of Christ is a portraiture of His pleading as He now pleads
for the Father's preservation of His own. The finished work
of the cross is the basis of His prayer, and the final entrance
into His glory is its terminus.

16. *The Father's Cup* (18 : 11). The cup of our woe was
pressed by the hand of love to the lips of grace, that grace and
love might press to our lips the cup of blessing and salvation.

17. *The Father's Presence* (20 : 17-21). To the sublime
heights of the Father's presence He ascends, after going into
the depths of intense suffering, and now He sends us forth to
make known the riches of His grace.

In addition to the general survey of the Fatherhood of
God in Christ as revealed by the Spirit in John, we find the
Father's specific acts severally mentioned.

His definite seeking (4 : 23).

His earnest working (5 : 17).

His ardent loving (5 : 20 ; 10 : 17 ; 16 : 27).

His powerful raising (5 : 21).

His specific sending (5 : 36 ; 8 : 16-18).

His Divine sealing (6 : 27).

His holy giving (6 : 32, 37 ; 10 : 29 ; 13 : 3).

His attractive drawing (6 : 44).

His recognized honouring (8 : 54 ; 12 : 26).

His appreciative knowledge (10 : 15).

His distinct command (10 : 18 ; 14 : 31).

His consecrating act (10 : 36, R.V.).

His unmistakable message (12 : 50).

His manifested indwelling (14 : 10).

His sufficient bestowment (14 : 26 ; 15 : 26).

His fruitful tending (15 : 1).

His safe keeping (17 : 11).

And further to these specific acts, which speak of the Father's active ministry on behalf of the Son and the sons, we have certain things which are said to belong to the Father.

The " Only Begotten of the Father," or what Christ became for us (1 : 14).

The bosom of the Father, or the affection in which the Son lives (1 : 18).

The home of the Father, or the place in which He dwells (2 : 16 ; 14 : 2).

The life of the Father, or the vitality of His being (5 : 26).

The will of the Father, or the desire of His heart (5 : 30 ; 6 : 39).

The name of the Father, or the expression of His nature, or His authority (5 : 43 ; 10 : 25 ; Matt. 28 : 19).

The hand of the Father, or the keeping of His power (John 10 : 29 ; Luke 23 : 46).

The works of the Father, or the activities of His ministry (10 : 37).

The commandment of the Father, or the requirement of His love (15 : 10).

The cup of the Father, or the requirement of His holiness (16 : 11).

The knowledge of the Father, or the tenderness of His care (Luke 12 : 30).

The face of the Father, or the consciousness of His presence (Matt. 18 : 20).

The pleasure of the Father, or the intention of His love (Luke 3 : 22).

The glory of the Father, or the display of His worth (Matt. 18 : 27).

The grace and peace of the Father, or the gift of His mercy (1 Cor. 1 : 3).

The blessings of the Father, or the provision of His grace (Eph. 1 : 3).

The promise of the Father, or the enduement with His power (Luke 24 : 49 ; Acts 1 : 4).

The love of the Father, or the affection of His heart (1 John 2 : 15 ; 3 : 1).

The witness of the Father, or the appreciation of His Son (John 5 : 36, 37).

The foreknowledge of the Father, or the purpose of His grace (1 Pet. 1 : 2).

The kingdom of the Father, or the future of His plan (Matt. 24 : 34 ; 1 Cor. 15 : 24).

There are several relative expressions which shine out in the New Testament, and which bring out the many-sidedness of the Fatherhood of God.

"*Father.*" Christ's revelation of God as Father (John 1 : 14-18).

"*A Father.*" God's relationship to the Son and sons (Heb. 1 : 5 ; 2 Cor. 6 : 18).

"*The Father.*" Personal glory of the Father (1 John 1 : 2 ; 3 : 1 ; 4 : 14).

"*My Father.*" Christ's personal relationship to the Father (John 15 : 1, 8).

"*Your Father.*" Responsibility of the children to the parent (Matt. 5 : 16, 45, 48).

"*Our Father.*" Responsibility because of common relationship (Luke 11 : 2).

"*God the Father.*" His exclusive relationship (2 Tim. 1 : 2 ; 2 Pet. 1 : 17).

"*God our Father.*" The saints' commonwealth and confidence (Eph. 1 : 2).

"*God and Father of our Lord Jesus Christ.*" The relationship of Christ and His own (Eph. 1 : 3).

"*Holy Father.*" Christ's priestly service for His saints (John 17 : 11).

"*Righteous Father.*" Christ and the world (John 17 : 25).

I. " Father."

When " Father " is used alone it speaks of intimate relationship, hence, when Christ speaks to His Father He says, "*Father*" (Luke 22 : 42 ; 23 : 34, 46 ; John 11 : 41 ; 12 : 27, 28 ; 17 : 1, 21, 24) ; or "*O Father*" (Matt. 11 : 25 ; John 17 : 5) ; or "*Abba, Father*" (Rom. 8 : 15 ; Gal. 4 : 6).

In the above Scriptures, Christ as the Son is seen in seven relations to the Father, as—

1. The Willing Son (Mark 14 : 36 ; Luke 22 : 42 ; John 12 : 27, 28).
2. The Confident Suppliant (Matt. 11 : 25).
3. The Satisfied Intercessor (John 11 : 41).
4. The Earnest Worker (John 17 : 1).
5. The Holy Priest (John 17 : 5, 21, 24).
6. The Pleading Substitute (Luke 23 : 34).
7. The Surrendered Spirit (Luke 23 : 46).

II. " My Father."

Christ uses the words, " My Father," in one or two relationships, either in the fellowship of their mutual love or service, or else as they are mutually acting for believers.

Mutual Work. Christ speaks of " *My Father's* business " (Luke 2 : 49), and the works He did as done " in *My Father's* name " (John 10 : 25), and says, " *My Father* worketh hitherto and I work " (John 5 : 17). The sphere of His service, the authority for His action, the plan which He followed, the business in which He was engaged, and the fellowship of His work, were all begun, continued and ended from, in, through, with, and to the Father.

Mutual Purpose. The requirement of the Father was met by the ransom of the Son, hence, in referring to the direction of the Father in relation to His substitutionary death, Christ says, " This commandment have I received of *My Father* " (John 10 : 18). Christ's death was no accident, it was Love's sending and suffering, and thus the accomplishment of Divine decree.

Mutual Keeping. The double grip of grace tells us that Love's fingers are interlaced in the warmth of their embrace for the keeping of the sheep in the place of the Lord's preservation, for the Lord assures us we are not only in His hand, but " My Father," Who gave them, He is greater than all : and no man is able to pluck them out of My Father's hand " (John 10 : 29). Preserved in the hand of Power, we are kept safe from sin's pollution.

Mutual Indwelling. There is a mystic union between the sons and the Son with the Father. Wonderful are the words, " Ye shall know that I am in *My Father*, and ye in Me and I in you," and to those who know Him by their obedience, Christ further says, " If a man love Me, he will keep My words : and *My Father* will love him, and We will come unto him, and make Our abode with him " (John 14 : 20-23). The word " *abode* " is the same as rendered " *mansion* " in John 14 : 2. God's home is in the obedient child, and the obedient child is at home in God.

Mutual Obedience. The Son and the sons have one path to tread, namely, the way of obedience. The appreciation of love's complacency comes through response to Love's commands. " If ye keep My commandments ye shall abide in My love, even as I have kept *My Father's* commandments and abide in His love " (John 15 : 10).

Mutual Bestowment. " Behold I send the promise of *My Father* upon you " (Luke 24 : 49). The purpose of the Father culminated in the Passion of the Son, and the Passion of the Smitten Son brought the Power of the Spirit's grace, even as the struck rock of Horeb resulted in the gushing water.

Mutual Thought. " In *My Father's* house are many mansions, if it were not so, I would have told you " (John 14 : 2). The place Christ is preparing is in the house of the Father's many abodes. The home-coming of the children from the school of life will find many surprises of the Father's thinking and the Son's working.

III. The Father

When the Father is referred to as " The Father," the exclusiveness of His being is emphasized as, " He that hath seen Me, hath seen *the Father* " (John 14 : 9) ; to the sovereignty of His grace : " No man can come to Me, except *the Father* draw him " (John 6 : 44) ; to the claim of His Deity : " Worship *the Father* " (John 4 : 21) ; to the revelation of His love : " The only begotten of *the Father*, full of grace and truth " (John 1 : 14) ; to the holiness of His love : " *the Father* loveth " (John 3 : 35 ; 16 : 27) ; to the power of His Spirit : " Whom *the Father* will send in My name " (John 14 : 26) ; and to the character of Christ's service : " *the Father* which sent Me " (John 12 : 49 ; 14 : 24).

The Father as " the Father " is referred to again and again in the Gospel of John. Take but one section, namely,

John 5 : 19-21, as illustrating the Father in relation to the exclusiveness of His being as the source of things.

1. *Source of Action* (verse 19). Being in the subordinate position as the Son, He cannot act apart from the Father as His servant, therefore all His actions were the acts of the Father. The lowly dependence of His Spirit declares the holiness of His character and His fitness for His Father's service, for as all independence of God is in the virus of sin, so dependence upon Him is the virtue and vitality of service.

2. *Source of Love* (verse 20). The love of the Father to the Son shows itself in three ways—in His confidence in Him (John 3 : 35), in His communion with Him, and in the communication through Him. His tender regard is manifest in the feelings of His heart's love, and in the fulness of hand's liberality, for all that comes from the Father to the Son comes through the Son to us.

3 *Source of Power* (verse 21). The " as " and " so " of the verse show community of action. " The work belongs to the Father," as Luthardt says, " in so far as it proceeds from Him ; to the Son, in so far as it is accomplished by Him in the world."

The student will find ample reward for his pains if he will ponder the Paternity of God along this line. For instance, take John's epistle for a further study.

IV. " Your Father "

These words embody with them, the thought of responsibility. Fourteen times the couplet occurs in Matthew's Gospel :

Shining to glorify (5 : 16).

Proving the relationship by kindness to persecutors (5 : 45, 48).

Helping the needy, unseen (6 : 1).

Praying to purpose (6 : 8).

Forgiving to be forgiven (6 : 14, 15).

Trusting to be fed (6 : 26, 32).

Praying and receiving (7 : 11).

Allowing the Spirit to speak (10 : 20).

Trustful because cared for (10 : 29).

Looking after the little ones (18 : 14).

The One to be recognized (23 : 9).

The privilege of being God's children brings a corresponding responsibility, but when we respond to His ability we can fulfil every responsibility.

What does this Christly relationship to the Father mean to those who are the children of God ?

1. *Nature of the Father.* There are two principal words translated " sons," or " children," in the New Testament, namely, " *Huios* " and " *Teknon.*" The former is always used in an adoptive sense, and refers to the dignity of sonship, and the latter expresses kinship, a descendant, and denotes nature. " *Huios* " is used in Rom. 8 : 14, 19 ; Gal. 3 : 26 ; 4 : 6 ; Heb. 12 : 5, 6, 7, 8 ; and " *Teknon* " in 1 John 2 : 12 ; Rom. 8 : 16, 17, 21 ; 1 John 3 : 1, 2, 10. As the child owes its being to its parents, so being begotten from above by the Spirit we possess the nature of God, and that nature is love.

2. *Named by the Father.* " Called the sons " (children) " of God " (1 John 3 : 1), that is, we are named children. The word (*Kaleo*), rendered "*called,*" is frequently used in the giving of names : " *called* His name Jesus " (Matt. 1 : 25), " *called* the Son of The Highest " (Luke 1 : 32), " *call* his name John " (Luke 1 : 60), " Mary, *called* Magdalene " (Luke 8 : 2), " A man *named* Zacchæus " (Luke 19 : 2), " a place which is *called* Calvary " (Luke 23 : 33), " that old serpent *called* the devil " (Rev. 12 : 9). The title by which believers are designated is that of children. Life makes us children and character and conduct prove we are such.

3. *Provision from the Father.* There are three New Testament Scriptures beginning with the sentence, " Blessed be the God and Father of our Lord Jesus Christ " (2 Cor. 1 : 3, R.V. ; Eph. 1 : 3 ; 1 Pet. 1 : 3), which accentuate the largeness of the Father's provision. All comfort in all tribulation is found in the first, so every circumstance in the outer life is met ; all blessing for all need is assured in the second, so every requirement of the inner life is bestowed ; and all the future for all time and eternity is provided for in the third, so the life infused is the earnest of the life to come, in all its incorruptibility and purity.

4. *Fellowship with the Father.* " Our fellowship is with the Father " (1 John 1 : 3). The word for " fellowship "

(*Koinonia*) is rendered "*communication*" in Phile. 6, "*communion*" in 2 Cor. 13 : 14, "*distribution*" in 2 Cor. 9 : 13, and "*contribution*" in Rom. 15 : 26, and comes from the word *Koinonos*, which means one who shares something with another, hence we read of those who were "*partners*" with Simon (Luke 5 : 10). Fellowship with the Father means *mutual communication*, for we bless Him with our grateful praise, and He blesses us with His gracious provision ; *mutual distribution*, for He gives to us the blessing of His love, that we may love others with the love of His blessing ; *mutual contribution*, for He makes us partakers of His holiness, that we may by our holiness prove we are partakers of His nature. We are partakers in all His business, and He is a partner in all ours, so there is fellowship, fellow-help, fellow-feeling, fellow-work, fellow-purpose, fellow-company, and fellow-care.

5. *Assurance in the Father.* " Because ye are sons, God hath sent forth the Spirit of His Son in your hearts, crying, Abba, Father " (Gal. 4 : 6 ; Rom. 8 : 15). The Spirit by the Word assures the surrendered sinner that He is God's own child. The act of our faith, acting according to God's Word, meets the assurance of God's voice in that Word, that the believers are God's children. The witness within is the entrance of the Word of God without, even as the sun-lighted and sun-warmed room is proof positive of the shining sun outside.

6. *Obedience to the Father.* " If ye call on Him as Father " (1 Pet. 1 : 17, R.V.), then certain obligations rest upon us, and especially *the* obligation of obedience, for we cannot have the privileges of the Gospel without their attendant responsibilities. Obedience is the medium of blessing (1 Pet. 1 : 2, 22), the meaning of faith (Rom. 15 : 18 ; 16 : 19), the soul of love (John 14 : 15), the evidence of holiness (Rom. 6 : 16), the heart of consecration (Rom. 6 : 17, margin), the answer of trust (Heb. 11 : 8), and the secret of confidence (1 John 3 : 19). The word " *assure* " is given " *may obey* " in Jas. 3 : 3, and " *confidence* " in Phile. 21.

The word in Heb. 11 : 8, rendered " *obeyed*," is rendered " *hearken* " in Acts 12 : 13. Literally it is " to answer."

" Rhoda came to the door, to ask who was there " (R.V., " came to answer " ; margin, " to ask who was there ").

7. *Loved and Preserved by the Father.* " Beloved in God the Father and kept for Jesus Christ " (Jude 1, R.V.). One of the fundamental principles brought out in the New Testament is the unity of operation of the three persons of the Godhead, and yet their distinctive ministries. The Father bears witness to the Son and the Son to the Father, the Spirit reveals the Son and the Son speaks of the Spirit. The Spirit leads to the Son that we may know the Father, and the Father keeps us for the Son that we may share His glory. The redeemed are not only kept *in* Christ as the place of their safety, but they are preserved *for* Him as a trophy of His grace.

There is a threefold way by which Christ is glorified in His saints : (1) In what He has done for them, for the Father, hence He says, " I am glorified in them " (John 17 : 10) ; (2) In what the Spirit does in them, as they know Christ in the effectiveness of His grace, hence the Apostle prayed, " That the name of our Lord Jesus Christ may be glorified in you " (2 Thess. 1 : 11, 12) ; (3) and what the Father is yet going to do when He recompenses His own at the coming of Christ with His saints in judgment, when " in that day " He shall " be glorified in His saints " (2 Thes. 1 : 6-10). To the time of His return when we shall be mutually satisfied, and to the day of His manifested glory when we shall be admired by the world, we are kept by the Father.

We may come to a sixfold conclusion from this study :

1. That the Father is made known in Christ alone, therefore if we would know the Father we must know the Son, for " no man," He explicitly says, " cometh unto the Father but by Me " (John 14 : 6).

2. That while all men are the " offspring of God " (Acts 17 : 29) by creation, they are only His creatures and not His children, for all humanity has sinned and all are under condemnation (Rom. 3 : 23), hence the necessity of a new birth to become members of the family of the Father (John 3 : 3, 5 ; 1 : 12, 13).

3. That it was essential the Son of God should taste death in a substitutionary sense for those who should become the sons of God, for the mystic key to open the door of sonship, as well as salvation, is the atoning death of Calvary. Christ's word was, " The Son of man *must* be lifted up " (John 3 : 14). The Son of man on the cross is the procuring cause to make the sons of men one with Him in the commonwealth of His Fatherhood.

4. That believers in Christ are the children of God in a double sense : spiritually by the new birth, for by the Spirit we are born into God's family (John 1 : 12, 13 ; 3 : 3, 5), and receive His nature (2 Pet. 1 : 4) ; and adoptively we are the children of God as to place, for He has given us all the privileges of sonship (Rom. 8 : 15-17).

5. That the evidence we are the children of God, is not by profession, but by following two things : (1) *Negatively,* separation from sin, for we read, " He that committeth sin is of the devil . . . whosoever is born of God doth not commit sin . . . in this the children of God are manifest, and the children of the devil " (1 John 3 : 8-10). (2) *Positively,* love to the Lord in loving others. " Every one that loveth is begotten of God " (1 John 4 : 7, R.V. ; 5 : 1).

6. That it is the privilege of every child of God to experience all that is meant by God being the Father. A Father thinks of His children, cares for them, watches over them, succours and keeps them. Our Father provides for our need (Matt. 6 : 8, 26, 30), answers our requests (Matt. 7 : 11 ; John 14 : 13), watches over our welfare (Matt. 10 : 29-31 ; John 13 : 1), takes pleasure in giving (Luke 12 : 32), protects in danger (John 10 : 29), secures a home (John 14 : 2), loves His own (John 16 : 27), and trains in discipline (Heb. 12 : 7-9).

When the second son of the writer was lying on his death bed in Sunderland, as we surrounded his bed, we thought he had fallen asleep, when he suddenly opened his eyes, and, seeing me, quietly said, " Father !" O that in all our life we might ever look up to the Lord, and say to Him in the love of obedience and the trust of faith, " Father " !

4

THE SOUL OF A BREATHING LIFE

"HE breathed upon them," and said, "Receive ye the Holy Spirit," and by that act Christ came into contact with His disciples in a new relationship and power. In the life-giving power of a breathing life, He endowed His own for life and service.

Christ, as the Breather of the Holy Spirit, reveals the intimate relationship there is between them, and shows the Life-giver, and the Life given. Therefore "Breath" as an emblem of the Holy Spirit speaks of Him in the livingness of His Divine inspiration.

The thought is happily expressed in the following lines :

> " Breathe on me, Breath of God,
>   Fill me with life anew,
> That I may love what Thou dost love,
>   And do what Thou wouldst do."

There are three main embodying thoughts found in connection with Breath in the Scriptures :

Inspiration, or The Inbreathing of Life.
Invigoration, or The Power to Perform.
Exhalation, or The Breathing out of Blessing.

I. Inspiration

Inspiration signifies in-breathing, or the power which gives life to anything, hence Channing says, " One great thought breathed into a man may regenerate him."

Man owes his natural life to the Spirit. Elihu declared long ago, " The Spirit of God hath made me, and the Breath of the Almighty hath given me life " (Job 33 : 4). Man's spirit-nature was created before his body was formed, and after his body was formed, God breathed into his nostrils the breath of life, and man became a living soul. Man was a created spirit before he was a living soul, for the image of God in man is, as Dr. Dale says, " The nature of God," that is, man, like God, is a spirit-being. The soul or breath unites the spirit and body. Angels are spirits, but have no soul or animal life; but man has, and is, a spirit, soul and body. Therefore a man is a breathing personality, as a live human being under present conditions. When he dies, like the son of the widow of Zarephath, there is " no breath left in him " (1 Kings 17 : 17). Things that are dead are again and again described as having " no breath " (Psa. 104 : 29 ; 135 : 17).

Spiritual life is essentially the impartation of the Spirit, as Christ declares, " That which is begotten of the Spirit is spirit." Perhaps no finer illustration of the Spirit's living work can be found than that which we find in Ezek. 37, where the restoration of Israel's national and spiritual life is depicted, under the metaphor of a valley of dry bones, and how they live by His operation.

First, God promises in relation to the dry bones, " I will cause breath to enter in you, and ye shall live." Then there was a shaking among the dry bones, and they are adjusted to each other, and covered with sinews and flesh, but there " was no breath in them." Then the prophet was commanded to prophesy to the " Breath " (margin) and to say, " Thus saith the Lord God, come from the four winds, O Breath, and breathe upon these slain, that they may live. So I prophesied as He commanded me, and the Breath came into them, and they lived " (Ezek. 37 : 4-10).

The spiritual resurrection of Israel is a type of the Spirit's quickening of dead sinners. Like Israel, sin has slain us, death has mortified us, and we are dry and helpless. There may be, as the vision suggests, the shaking of the dry bones of conscience and interest in Divine things : there may be the place-ment of bone to bone, in a clear conception in the mind of how we may be saved ; there may be the covering of the dry bones by the flesh of religious profession and the sinews of self-determination, but these are not life. The sinner has sense-consciousness in his body, life-consciousness in his soul, and self-consciousness in his spirit, but the one thing which makes the saint to differ from the sinner is *God-consciousness*. As long as the sinner is without God, he

is without at least seven things. Without the blood of
Christ, which alone can remit the past and release the sinner
from the hold of sin (Heb. 9 : 22) ; without Christ, Who alone
can save, sanctify and satisfy (Eph. 2 : 12) ; without peace
which alone can calm the mind and silence the conscience
(Isa. 57 : 21) ; without hope, which alone can clear the
vision and make the future bright with coming glory (Eph.
2 : 12) ; without life, which alone can qualify to see and
enter the kingdom of God (John 3 : 3, 5) ; without strength,
for the sinner has no ability to rise to higher things (Rom.
5 : 6) ; and without the Spirit, for those who are not the
Lord's are summed up in the destitution of their need, as
" having not the Spirit " (Jude 19).

On the other hand, how much is expressed by the pregnant statement, " alive unto God." The Greek word rendered " alive " in Rom. 6 : 11 is " *Zao*," and is a primary
verb, and means to live. An interesting study is suggested
by the use of the word as applied to the spiritual life. It is a
God-imparted and a Christ-secured life, for Christ came by
way of the Cross that we might " live through Him " (1 John
4 : 9).

It is a Christ-identified and a Christ-associated life, for
He says, " Because I live ye shall live also " (John 14 : 19).

It is a God-derived and Christ-sustained life, as Christ
declares : " As the living Father hath sent Me, and I live by
(because of) the Father, so he that eateth Me, even he shall
live by (because of) Me " (John 6 : 57).

It is a self-displacing and a Christ-centred life, for all
those who know Him cease to " live unto themselves, but
unto Him " (2 Cor. 5 : 15).

It is a Spirit-inscribed and a Spirit-indited life, for
believers are the epistle of the living God, and He inscribes
His character on their inner being (2 Cor. 3 : 3).

It is a Christ-indwelt and a Christ-revealing life, for each
indwelt believer recognizes what the Apostle said, " I live,
yet not I, but Christ liveth in Me " (Gal. 2 : 20).

It is a brethren-considerate and a Lord-controlled life,
hence brethren who " live unto the Lord " do not despise nor
judge each other (Rom. 14 : 7-9).

It is a saint-helping and a missionary-loving life, for it ever hears the voice of the missionary plea, "Now we live if ye stand fast in the Lord" (1 Thess. 3 : 8).

And it is a God-controlled and a God-goaled life, for being "alive from the dead" we recognize we are "alive unto God" (Rom. 6 : 11, 13).

II. Invigoration

Scott speaks of—

> "Two dogs of black St. Hubert's breed,
> Unmatched for courage, breath, and speed."

Here he used "breath" to indicate ability and freedom of action. The potential fact of Christianity is, God never asks from us anything without giving us the power to perform it.

What is indicated when Christ breathed on His disciples and said, "Receive ye the Holy Spirit?" There is no article in the original, therefore it should read, "Receive ye Holy Spirit." Godet says, "The absence of the article before Holy Spirit, shows that the question is not yet the sending of the Paraclete promised," but the "receive" indicates "He puts their will in unison with His own, that they may be prepared for the common work."

The promise of Pentecost was to "be endued with power from on high" (Luke 24 : 49), and that power was the accompaniment of the Spirit. "Ye shall receive power, the Holy Spirit coming upon you" (Acts 1 : 8).

"There is," says one, "a magnetism in a personal appeal, which no words conveyed through another can possess." Every personality wields a power for weal or woe : therefore, personality means power. Christ especially emphasizes this when He says : "Ye shall receive power, after that the Holy Ghost is come upon you" (Acts 1 : 8). He brings the power, and is the power. He does not give us the power that we may use it, but He is the power that He may use us. There is a sevenfold power that believers need : namely, power to be, power to do, power to suffer, power to keep, power to pray, power to give, and power to speak.

Power to be "strengthened with all might, according to His glorious power, unto all patience and longsuffering with

joyfulness" (Col. 1 : 11); or, as Rotherham renders it,
"with all power being empowered, according to the grasp
of His glory, unto all endurance and longsuffering with you."
As the potter by the power of his skill is able to form the
beautiful vase, so the Holy Spirit, as He grasps us in the
hands of His grace, can form our character in such a manner
that the traits of patient love and enduring grace shall be
evident in all our life, for these graces are the development
of His work within, and not the accretion of work without.

Power to do. The greatest work ever performed was that
which God performed when He put forth "the strength of
His might" in raising Christ from the dead (Eph. 1 : 19,
R.V.), which we are exhorted to "know" through the
Spirit's enlightening grace (Eph. 1 : 18-20). "Give me a
grip of your conquering hand," was the request of an officer
to his commanding general, when commissioned to carry out a
difficult task. He felt that if he had a grasp of the hand
which had obtained so many victories, it would be an
inspiration to him. We not only want to grip the hand of the
Spirit, but we need to be gripped by Him: then we can do,
because He does. The grasp of His might will give us such
a grip, that we shall grip to some purpose.

Power to suffer. Many of God's people are so con-
tinuously occupied with their own comfort, and so frequently
complain against suffering, that they miss the special
empowerment which comes to those who are equipped to
endure by the sufficient grace of the Lord. Paul's summary
of the lesson which he learnt in the school of suffering,
through prayer and faith, was: "I rather boast in my
weaknesses, that the power of Christ may spread a tent over
me" (Rotherham, 2 Cor. 12 : 9). That enveloping power
would never have been known, but for the blast of trial.
Out of the "eater" of suffering comes the sweetness of
grace. Bethel's hard pillar is the bottom rung in Heaven's
cast-up way of promise. Joseph found that Egypt's throne
was reached by the prison.

Power to keep. "I need to get all the religion I can, to
keep what I have got," said a believer in relating his experience. Surely he was occupied with the endeavours of his

own attainments. The true and effectual keeping is to be "kept by the power of God." His keeping is instant, like the eyelid preserving the eye (Psa. 17 : 8) ; His keeping is incessant, like the stream which keeps clean the stone lying in its bed (Psa. 19 : 13) ; His keeping is invulnerable, like the warrior who is encased in bullet-proof armour (1 Pet. 1 : 5).

Power to pray. The reason why the Lord is able to do above anything we ask or think, is because of " the power that worketh in us " (Eph. 3 : 20). That power, the Spirit Himself, must be effective in His working within, if we would know the exceeding abundance of God's supply from above. We prevail so ineffectively with Heaven, because we allow so little of the Spirit's effectiveness within. " The Spirit Himself maketh intercession," and for this we need to be in the Spirit, that is, in ungrieved communion with Him. Praying in the Holy Spirit is the pre-requisite for the Holy Spirit to pray in us, even as the atmosphere is essential for the transmitter of wireless telegraphy to send the message.

Power to give. Paul, in calling attention to the liberality of the churches in Macedonia, says : " According to their power, I bear witness, yea, and beyond their power, they gave of their own accord " (R. V., 2 Cor. 8 : 3). The moving power which caused them to give so frankly and fully was " the grace of God bestowed " (2 Cor. 8 : 1). When the life of God is low in the experience of the child of God, then the giving will be small ; but when the warm heart of love is throbbing, then the willing hand of giving is liberal. It is not then, how little can be given, but how much is He worthy ! The principle that the spiritual believer observes is found in the words of Christ's prayer to His Father, when He said, " All Thine are Mine, and Mine are Thine." When we know that what He has is ours, we recognize that what we have is His.

Power to speak. " They were all filled with the Holy Spirit . . . and with great power gave the apostles witness of the resurrection of the Lord Jesus " (Acts 4 : 31, 33). Speaking without the Spirit is like talking in a foreign tongue to those who do not know the language ; while speaking in the Spirit every word is intelligible to those who hear.

Looking to ourselves, we shall say with Jeremiah: "I cannot speak, for I am a child"; but filled with the Spirit, we shall know the Lord's assuring word as He says: "Behold, I have put My words in thy mouth" (Jer. 1 : 6, 9).

How many men owe everything in life to one young heart that trusted them when all was doubtful, one faithful love that kept them company as long as ever it could! "I never was anything till I knew you," wrote Tom Hood to his wife. How true are those words, "I never was anything till I knew you," applied to the Holy Spirit, every believer testifies! And we shall never be anything, nor continue to be anything, except we "know Him"—know Him in the power of His life, in the strength of His might, in the glow of His love, in the lowliness of His humility, in the sanctity of His holiness, in the wisdom of His guidance, in the inspiration of His Word, and in the glory of His Personality.

III. Exhalation

Exhalation describes the act of out-breathing. One expresses the thought in speaking of Nature being clothed with the beauty which comes from the dawn:

> "Clothing the palpable and familiar
> With golden exhalations of the dawn."

Speaking of the death of a man in his helplessness, we read, "His breath goeth forth, he returneth to his earth" (Psa. 146 : 4). In general operation exhalation expresses the fragrance of the flowers, the ministry of the trees in purifying the air, and the action of heat drawing forth the vapours of the earth. Taking these thoughts only: we may say, they metaphorically express the work of the Spirit. He draws forth the natural powers from the swamp of our sinfulness. He causes to come forth the graces of His holiness, and He brings forth the fragrance of His flowers of character.

The Spirit draws forth the natural powers from the swamp of our sinfulness, and changes them into the garden of His productiveness. "The heavens remit in bountiful showers what they had exhaled in vapour," so says one in writing of the action of the sun in drawing the vapours from the earth. We can imagine if the sun could reach the malarious swamp with its miasma the poison of the gas would be dissipated, and the swamp annihilated. The same change can be accomplished in the realm of moral and spiritual spheres of the heart and life.

A working man, who had spent his life in dissipation, but was turned to God, and made a new creature in Christ, was twitted by an atheist, who denied the miraculous by saying, " You don't believe that Christ turned water into wine !"

" Oh, yes I do," replied the saved man, " and what's more, if you will come to my home, I will show you something more wonderful !"

" What's that ?" was the ready question.

" Why, in my home, He's turned beer into furniture !"

Sin will cause men to change the glory of the incorruptible God into man-made images of their own creation, and cause them to walk in all unholy and unnatural living (Rom. 1 : 23-32) ; but the Holy Spirit can change the mind of thought, so that we are transformed into the likeness of Christ, even as He was transfigured in His body. (See the words " Transfigured " in Matt. 17 : 2, " Transformed " in Rom. 12 : 2, and " Changed " in 2 Cor. 3 : 18, which are one and the same in the original.)

The Spirit can cause to come forth from Himself in us the graces of His holiness.

One has said, " The under side of every leaf is furnished with thousands of tiny mouths, through which the leaf breathes back upon the world the air it has purified and sweetened for human uses. And so the foliage of a mighty forest is like a cluster of fountains from which health and quickening alchemies are ever pouring, which supply the needs of all those kingdoms of life gathered under its shadow. And in the same way the Holy Spirit of God breathes upon us from every point of our environment. Through countless mouths His soul-quickening influences flow silently unto us, neutralising the doubt, sloth, and sin exhaled from the lower nature, so that we can breathe back our souls to God in faith and desire continuous as the river from God's throne."

What a difference between Paul as Saul " breathing out threatenings and slaughter" against the disciples of the Lord, and the benedictions of his Christly service on behalf of others.

We often see a notice of a shop to let : " These premises will be converted to meet the wishes of the incoming tenant " : thus if a grocer takes the shop which had been occupied by a butcher, the whole place has to be converted. Try and think what Saul was as Saul, and what Paul became as Paul.

Saul *versus* Paul

1. Did much evil (Acts 9 : 13). Did much good (2 Tim. 4 : 7).

2. Causing others to suffer (Acts 9 : 14). Suffering with Christ (2 Cor. 11 : 23-28).

3. Breathing out threatenings (Acts 9 : 1). " Behold he prayeth " (Acts 9 : 11).

4. Kicking against the pricks (Acts 9 : 5). Serving the Lord (Acts 27 : 23).

5. Journeying towards Damascus with ill-intent (Acts 9 : 3). Pressing towards the mark for the prize (Phil. 3 : 14).

6. Self-righteous in his religion (Phil. 3 : 4-6). Gaining Christ (Phil. 3 : 7-9).

7. A malignant persecutor (Gal. 1 : 13). A mighty witness (Gal. 1 : 15-24).

An old soldier in Cornwall once described conversion as " Halt. Attention. Right about face. Quick march." Halting in the course of sin : paying attention to the call of the Gospel : turning to the Lord : and then going onward in the Divine life ; and that going forward is only possible as we are energised and equipped by the Holy Spirit.

The Spirit brings forth the fragrance of the flowers of His character.

An author, in describing the work of another, says : " A breath of beauty and noble feeling lives in and exhales from the whole of his great work like the fragrance from a garden of flowers." And another has sung of flowers :

" Sweet letters of the angel tongue,
   I've loved thee long and well,
And never have failed in your fragrance sweet
   To find some secret spell,—
A charm that has bound me with witching power,
   For mine is the old belief,
That, 'midst your sweets and 'midst your bloom
   There's a soul in every leaf."

Where there is the soul of the Spirit's reality, there will be the fragrance of soul-lifting influence. So many Christian lives are not attractive. They are more like bare trees in the winter time. They lack the beauty of foliage and flowers. There is life, but no fragrance. It is said of Sir Isaac Newton, that he had " the flower of a blameless life." When blamelessness is wedded to fragrance there will be the offspring of appreciation. A little girl was once sitting opposite a Quaker lady in a tramcar, and noticing the sweet face of the latter, she suddenly exclaimed, " Do let me kiss you !" " Yes, my dear, certainly," she replied. A friendship sprang up between the kissed and the kisser. In the afterwards the girl said, " Were you not surprised that day in the tram when I asked you to let me kiss you ?" " Oh no, dear, they often asked me that." One commenting upon the incident remarks, " The purity and sweetness of her life shone from her face, and made her so winsome and bonny that people could not help wishing to kiss such a face. Her life had flowered."

God breathes in His life, that He may breathe out His blessing to others. Through His in-breathing life and His indwelling presence, He out-breathes what He asks us to do.

All the Spirit can breathe into us, and out-breathe from us, is by means of that Word which is said to be " God-breathed," for " All Scripture is given by inspiration of God " (2 Tim. 3 : 16). The word rendered " inspired of God " is literally " God-breathed." The Scriptures are the Breath of God, therefore, if we would inbreathe God we can only do so by breathing in the Word. We do well, therefore, to in-breathe the Word of God, for it is not only God-breathed, but *God breathing*, and as we do so we shall become like it.

THE PERSONALITY OF THE HOLY SPIRIT

" The Holy Ghost descended in a bodily shape " (Luke 3 : 22). " The Lord is the Spirit " (2 Cor. 3 : 17, R.V.). " The Lord . . . the Spirit " (2 Cor. 3 : 18, R.V.). " The Spirit of Christ which. was in them did point unto " (1 Pet. 1 : 11, R.V.).

When John saw the Holy Spirit descending upon Christ, he beheld Him as a Dove. That it was no vapoury, shadowy apparition is emphasized by Luke, for he says, " The Holy Ghost descended in a *bodily* shape " (Luke 3 : 22). The Greek word " *Somatikos* " occurs in two other places in the New Testament, and in each the word is applied to a body. In referring to the exercise of the body, the Apostle says, " Bodily exercise profiteth little " (1 Tim. 4 : 8) ; and in calling attention to the corporate fact of Christ being the treasury of Deity we read, " In Him dwelleth all the fulness of the Godhead *bodily* " (Col. 2 : 9). In the fact that each of the evangelists records that the Holy Spirit was seen in *organic form*, we have the assurance of His divine personality. Godet has finely summarized in his comment upon it : " By the organic form which invests the luminous ray, the Holy Spirit is here presented in His absolute totality. At Pentecost the Holy Spirit appeared under the form of divided tongues of fire, emblems of special gifts ; but in the baptism of Jesus it is not a portion only, it is the fulness of the Spirit which is given."

We cannot be too emphatic, or emphasize too often, the personality of the Holy Spirit, for as the body without the Spirit is dead, so the Father and the Son are not without Him, for " God is a Spirit." All that the Father is, as such : all the Son is, as the Son : is because the Spirit is. A foreign writer has said :

" The Spirit is so far from being, as with us, something belonging to God, that it is said, God is Spirit, the Lord is the Spirit, so that it really is just the Spirit, through Whom God is the Person that He is. The Divine Spirit is not only, as with us, something belonging to and in the Father and the Son, but that very thing through which Father and Son is God : *the Spirit is the personal being of God in Father and*

Son. Therefore He is called the Holy and Holy making, the Power and the Quickener: in Him the very own personal being of the Father and the Son is begotten into man. It is just in the Spirit that the personal life of God is centred: so little can He Himself be anything impersonal."

A Christian worker in Scotland was once being catechised as to how many persons there were in the Godhead. She was known for her love of the truth and love for souls. The minister was a broad man in thinking. He put the question to her, "How many persons are there in the Godhead?"

To the astonishment of the minister and those assembled, she replied, "There are two persons in the Godhead, the Father and the Son."

Again, the minister put the question, this time with a caution, and she gave the same reply. Whereupon he turned to his elders and those present and said, "You see what comes of high flown zeal and hypocrisy. This woman seeks to teach others, and is herself more ignorant than a child. What ignorance! Woman, don't you know that the correct answer is, 'There are three persons in the Godhead, the Father, the Son, and the Holy Ghost'?"

"Sir," replied the woman, "I ken verra well that the catechism says so, but whether am I to believe the catechism or yersel'? We hear you mention the Father, and sometimes, but *nae* aften, ye mak' mention o' the Son in yer preachin', but wha ever heard you speak aboot the Holy Ghost? 'Deed, sir, ye never sae muckle as tauld us whether there be ony Holy Ghost, lat alane oor need o' His grace."

No honest reader of the Old or the New Testament can deny for one moment the personality of the Holy Spirit, for all that constitutes personality is applied to Him. The question arises, "What constitutes Personality?" Individuality, intelligence, independence, character.

I. Individuality

A literary critic says of authors: "The author has no right to project himself into his characters, and give different proper names to one personality." Many might question the statement of the critic, but what he means to say is, an individual should be himself and not impersonate another, and no one character should assume two parts. Individuality means personality and no more. Christ is not impersonating anyone when He speaks of "another Comforter." He means a distinct individuality apart from Himself. The personal pronouns which the Lord uses about the Spirit bring this out with unmistakable clearness. Take the personal pronouns of John 14 and 16, and there we find :

The Personal Helper abiding—" *He* may abide with you."

The Personal Friend known—" Ye know *Him*."

The Personal Companion indwelling—" *He* dwelleth . . . in you."

The Personal Teacher instructing—" *He* shall teach you all things."

The Personal Witness testifying—" *He* shall testify of *M*e."

The Personal Ambassador coming—" I will send *Him* unto you."

The Personal Comforter arriving—" When *He* is come."

The Personal Reprover convicting—" *He* will reprove " (convict).

The Personal Title proclaiming—" When *He*, the Spirit of truth."

The Personal Guide directing—" *He* will guide you."

The Personal Voice declaring—" *He* shall not speak of Himself."

The Personal Ear attending—" *He* shall hear."

The Personal Tongue rehearsing—" That *He* shall speak."

The Personal Revealer unfolding—" *He* will show you."

The Personal Glorifier enhancing—" *He* shall glorify Me."

The Personal Receiver initiating—" *He* shall receive of mine."

These personal pronouns tell us plainly of the personality of the Spirit, especially when we remember their connection and association. He was to take the place of Christ— " Another Comforter "—Who would be to His disciples all He had been. As Christ had been a personal Helper to His disciples, so the Holy Spirit is to God's people. His divine personality means personal and individual blessing.

There is a story of a man whom his wife urged to begin family prayers. It was hard the first time. A Bible chapter had been read, and the two were on their knees, but there was silence—the prayer did not begin. The wife at length cried out, " O God, give John a lift." He got the lift and prayed. There is no more manifest fact in the Acts of the Apostles than that the great lifting power was the Holy Spirit. He lifted the early disciples from the low level of creature sufficiency on to the high level of Christly action : and in all He did His personality is brought out in the personal way He dealt with individuals. The divided tongues of fire " sat upon each of them," and each spoke as " *the* Spirit gave them utterance " (Acts 2 : 3, 4) ; Peter has the invincible face of boldness in his unswerving testimony, for He had received the power of Him, Who is called " *My* Spirit " (Acts 2 : 14-36) ; Stephen has the illumined face of heaven's light because of the shining grace of the Spirit within (Acts 6 : 5, 15) ; Philip, the evangelist, guides the Eunuch to the Saviour because he is under the direction of the directing Spirit (Acts 8 : 29-39) ; the church at Antioch knows whom to send forth into the mission field for their ears were anointed with the unction of the Holy One (Acts 13 : 2) ; Paul and his fellow-labourer know where to go and where not to go for they are sensitive to the Spirit's guiding hand, and they respond at once to Him (Acts 16 : 6-10) ; and the Apostle is so imbued with that same power that He is able to detect at a glance the frauds and unreality of such men as Elymas the Sorcerer (Acts 13 : 9, 10). He Who lifted them in the time of their need is able and willing to lift us in the need of our time.

> " He Who waters meadow lilies
>   With the dew from out the sky ;
> He Who feeds the flitting sparrows
>   When in need of food they cry,
> Never fails to help His children
>   In all things both great and small ;
> For His ear is ever open
>   To our faintest far off cry."

II. Intelligence

Matthew Arnold asserts, " We say that no one has discovered the nature of God to be personal, or is entitled to assert that God has conscious intelligence." Such an assertion brings God down to blind force, hard law, and unthinkable action. The wonder is that any man who has " conscious intelligence " should be able to think, that unconscious force can possibly produce the man who makes such an unintelligent statement. One has said :

" I heard the other day two butterflies, on the edge of a flower, discussing. One said, ' We cannot know there is any honey in the flower : no butterfly ever found it there, no butterfly ever will.'

" The other said, ' Well, nevertheless, I think there must be some.' And while they debated it, Gnostic and Agnostic, a humming bird flew in and ran its long bill into the flower, sipped the sweet, and was gone. To debate whether there is beauty and truth in the Word of God, whether there is beauty and truth in the world, whether there is beauty and truth in the Christ that came from God,—this is not religion. ' Oh taste and see that the Lord is good,'—that is religion."

As God in His being cannot be known by mere speculation, neither can the deeper things of the gospel be known but through the teaching of the Spirit. There must be the spiritual intelligence born of the Spirit, to know the Spirit in the intelligence of His personality. Many professed ministers of the Gospel, who get on the plain of carnal reason, speak of the Holy Spirit as " an emanation from the Father and the Son, like the breath which proceeds from the body." Those who make such a statement demonstrate that they know nothing of the Spirit in His personality. We may know what He does without knowing Him. Edison cannot be known by an electric lamp ; Marconi is not known by a telegraph pole ; nor is Lord Kelvin known by reading one of his lectures in the newspaper. Although, on the other hand, the phonograph, the wireless telegraphy, and the findings of the scientist prove their personal existence. The same is true as we think of the Holy Spirit. His works prove

Himself, and as we come in contact with Him, we know Him, not by His works, in Himself.

As we read through the Acts we find the Holy Spirit is spoken of in an indefinite manner, such as when we read of Peter being " filled "* with the Holy Spirit (Acts 4 : 8) ; and He is also spoken of in a very definite way whenever the definite article is used. Personal intelligence may not be suggested by such an expression as " filled with Spirit " ; but personal intelligence is certainly present when we read " *the* Holy Spirit spake " (I give Rotherham's translation), " *the* Spirit was giving," " shouldst deal falsely with *the* Holy Spirit," " witnesses of those things, also the Holy Spirit," " *the* Spirit caught away Philip," " *the* Spirit bade me go," " sent forth by *the* Holy Spirit," " *the* Spirit of Jesus suffered them not," " *the* Holy Spirit hath set you as Overseers " (Acts 1 : 16 ; 2 : 4 ; 5 : 3, 32 ; 8 : 39 ; 11 : 12 ; 13 : 4 ; 15 : 28 ; 16 : 6, 7 ; 20 : 28). Such words can only describe the action of an intelligent person. Blind force, and a mere emanation cannot speak as He did through David, nor give the gifts bestowed at Pentecost, nor be lied against as Ananias did, nor be a confirmative witness, nor catch away a person as Philip was, nor direct an Apostle as Peter was, nor send forth missionaries as Paul and Barnabas were, nor approve of an action as He did of the charge given to the Gentiles by the assembly in Jerusalem, nor hinder a person's action as the apostles were when they were prevented from going to Asia and Bithynia, nor appoint Elders as He did in the church in Ephesus. All these actions are personal and intelligent and proclaim the minute interest and care which the Spirit took, and takes, in the affairs of the church and the individual believer.

A young lady was asked on one occasion if she knew a certain book written by a popular author, and she replied, " No," and showed but little interest. But on a subsequent occasion she was asked the same question, and replied with

---

* Rotherham's translation gives the definite article when it occurs in the Greek, and leaves it out, as above, when it does not occur. Newbury indicates the same by putting the " the " in italics in his Englishman's Bible.

much zest and interest. One who had heard the question on both occasions expressed surprise at the different way in which she had replied. " Well, you see," she answered, " since the first time the question was put to me, I have read the book and married the author." They who are acquainted with the Holy Spirit know Him in the intelligence of His strengthening grace, comforting love, enabling power, sanctifying truth, inspiring influence, gladdening joy, and victorious achievements.

III. Independence

Another trait of personality is independence. Being independent of all, the Holy Spirit is dependent on none. Shakespeare makes one of his characters say :

> " I'll never
> Be such a gosling to obey instinct ; but stand
> As if a man were author of himself,
> And knew no other kin." (Coriolanus. Act V., Scene 3.)

Coriolanus would not be swayed by anyone or anything, but would be an independent man to act in an independent manner. Certainly the Holy Spirit ever did, and ever will, act as " author of Himself." Christ's statement is very emphatic. We read, " The Spirit where it pleaseth doth breathe " (Rotherham, John 3 : 8) ; and in the chapter which describes the Holy Spirit in His unity and sovereignty as the Administrator in the body of Christ, we read, He divides His gifts " to every man severally as *He* will " ; but while there is a diversity of gift and administration, He is referred to seven times over as " *the same Spirit*," etc. (1 Cor. 12 : 4-11). Godet well says, " The deliberate will here ascribed to the Holy Spirit seems to me to imply His personality, as the act of giving supposes His Divinity."

His will is never self-will, nor is His independence selfishness, as too often is the case with us. He is absolutely disinterested in His actions, and unbiassed in His determinations. His claims and calls are never for His own aggrandisement, but they are always for our blessing and benefit ; hence, the way to secure the independence of the Spirit is to be under the sway of the independent Spirit. Those who knew the late Mr. Moody intimately could not help being impressed with his independence of man, while he always recognized that which was of God in his fellow believers. What was the cause of this ? On a certain occasion he heard these words : " The world has yet to see what God will do—with, and for, and through, and in, and by the man who is fully and solely consecrated to Him." When Mr. Moody heard that he said : " The speaker did not say a great man, or a learned man, or a rich man, or a wise man, or an eloquent man, or a smart man : but simply a man. I am a man, and it lies with the man himself whether he will or will not make that entire and full consecration. I will try my uttermost to be that man." And he became that man, and the world has proved what God can do with, and for, and through, and in, and by men and women who are fully and entirely consecrated to Him.

IV. Character

Robertson, of Brighton, says in one of his sermons, " Personality is made up of three attributes : consciousness, character, and will."

Character is the sum total of what a person is, by virtue of what he has done. Every one is the son of his own works, or as the boy said, when he was asked what character was : " I should think it was a dictionary of our actions while on earth." As we think of character as the sum total of what a person is, by virtue of what he has done, we have opened up before us a large country of truth, as we ponder the personality of the Spirit. One of the titles by which He is made known is the Spirit of Christ, and He is this in many ways.

He is the Spirit of Christ because He rested upon Him (Luke 4 : 18).

He is the Spirit of Christ because He testified of Him (1 Pet. 1 : 11).

He is the Spirit of Christ because He unites to Him (1 Cor 12 : 12, 13)

He is the Spirit of Christ because He is given by Him (John 1 : 33).

He is the Spirit of Christ because He acts for Him (John 14 : 16).

He is the Spirit of Christ because He will gather us to be with Him (Rom. 8 : 11).

He is the Spirit of Christ because He makes us like Him (2 Cor. 3 : 18).

Especially in the latter sense He communicates Himself to us, and in so doing communicates Christ, and makes all He did and was not only facts to be believed, but living factors to form our life (Eph. 3 : 16, 17). One has well said : " We have the Holy Spirit to interpret the story, so that Christ is more than the Lord of the ancient tale, but the Lord Who holds word with us now."

Bunyan tells us how the Holy Spirit revealed to him the way " from the birth and cradle of the Son of God to His ascension and second coming from heaven to judge the world. Truly, I then found upon this account, the Great God was very good unto me : for to my remembrance, there was not anything that when I cried to God to make known and reveal unto me but He was pleased to do it for me : I mean not one part of the Gospel of the Lord Jesus but I was orderly led into it. Methought I saw, with great evidence, from the revelation of the four evangelists, the wonderful work of God, in giving Jesus Christ to save us, from His conception and birth, even to His second coming to Judgment. Methought I was as if I had seen Him born, as if I had seen Him grow up, as if I had seen Him walk through this world from the cradle to the Cross : to which, also, when He came, I saw how gently He gave Himself to be hanged and nailed on it for my sins and wicked doings. Also, as I was musing on this, His progress, that dropped on my spirit, He was ordained for the slaughter."

Thus to muse upon the Christ, in the Spirit, is to find that we are moulded after Him, even as the metal is formed like the mould into which it runs.

PREPOSITIONS OF THE SPIRIT

A missionary related in my hearing how he got to know the language of a certain people in Africa among whom he was sent to labour. First, he got the nouns by pointing to certain objects and asking what they were. Second, he got the verbs by asking what the objects did. And third, he got the prepositions by asking the relationship of one object to another. In pondering the prepositions which are used in relation to the Holy Spirit in the New Testament, we shall see what His relationship to us is, and what He expects our relationship should be to Him. The Spirit is found in connection with the following prepositions :

" Apo " means from, as when a tourist goes from one place to another.

" Dia " means through, as when a lawyer is a medium through whom the prisoner's case is advocated.

" Eis " means into, as when a bird flies to its nest and nestles down into it.

" Ek " means out of, as the life of the child is derived from and comes out of the parent.

" En " means in, as a person who dwells in a house, or the fish lives in the sea.

" Epi " means upon, as when the electric current comes upon the arm of the car and moves it on its way.

" Kata " means down, as when the snow comes down from the clouds to the earth.

" Meta " means with, as when one friend walks with another and they converse together.

" Para " means beside, like the two horses hitched to a carriage beside each other.

" Peri " means around, as when a teacher goes around a lesson that the whole of it may be apprehended.

" Pros " means towards, as when one person comes towards another.

" Huper " means over, as when a mother bird bends over her young and acts on their behalf.

" Hupo " means under, as when the strong arms of the parent are under the child.

The late Bishop Wescott says : " The whole force of the Revelation is contained in two letters—the Greek preposition for ' in '—' en.' " This preposition is found more than 2,700 times in the New Testament. What the Bishop said of the one preposition may be said of the others, for the wine of the Kingdom is found in every one of them. Of one thing I am perfectly convinced, that the clouds of ignorance, mis-statement, and misunderstanding, will be swept away if we allow the wind of the Spirit to blow through our minds through the medium of the Word, for His light shines in His truth, which we shall see if we are illuminated by Him.

It would be impossible for me to go into all the different senses in which the prepositions are used. The plan I shall adopt will be to state in a general and broad sense the meaning of a preposition, then call attention to the case with which it is associated, and then note the spiritual sense in which it is used of the Spirit and the believer. A well-known authority lays down the general rule regarding the cases: " The cases are determined, not by the preposition, but by the idea to be explained." It may be as well to say, that the genitive implies *motion from*, whence? The dative implies *rest in* or connection *with*, where? The accusative implies *motion towards*, whither?

" Pros."

The Coming of the Spirit towards the Believer. " *Pros* " occurs twice in connection with the Spirit with the accusative, and signifies the coming of one person to another, as Nicodemus, who came " to Jesus " (John 3 : 2). Christ said of the Spirit, "The Comforter will not come unto (pros) you. . . . I will send Him unto (pros) you " (John 16 : 7). Christ promised the Comforter or Advocate to carry on His work while He was away. As Eliezer was sent by Abraham to get a bride for Isaac, after Isaac was bound upon the altar for sacrifice, so the Holy Spirit was commissioned to come and get the Church for Christ after He had given Himself up in His atoning death, for it is the Spirit's work to unite believers to Christ, the Head of the Church, by His immersing grace.

" Peri."

The Spirit in the Compass of His Ministry as the Testifier. " *Peri* " occurs three times in connection with the Spirit with the genitive, and signifies what is said or written concerning a person, as Christ said of the Scriptures " concerning Himself " (Luke 24 : 27, 44).

" This spake He of (peri) the Spirit " (John 7 : 39).
" He shall testify of (peri) Me " (John 15 : 26).
" Teacheth you of (peri) all things " (1 John 2 : 27).

The preposition would be better rendered " concerning," as Newberry gives it, rather than " of." Christ spake concerning the Spirit in the operation of His ministry, and the Spirit speaks concerning Christ, and all things. The largeness of His ministry is suggested by the " all things," and the concentration of it in the Christ.

" Ek."

The Spirit as the Life Giver. " *Ek*," governing the genitive, signifies " out of," as Christ said of His disciples, they were given Him " out of the world " (John 17 : 6).

" With child of (ek) the Holy Ghost " (Matt. 1 : 18, 20).
" God giveth not the Spirit by (ek) measure " (John 3 : 34).
" Of (ek) the Spirit " (Gal. 6 : 8).
" By (ek) the Spirit " (1 John 3 : 24).
" He hath given us of (ek) His Spirit " (1 John 4 : 13).
" Spirit of Life from (ek) God " (Rev. 11 : 11).

The spiritual life which the believer receives is not an evolution from the natural man, but an involution from the Spirit through faith in Christ, which produces a revolution in the heart and life, and in its evolution shows itself by growth in grace.

" Apo."

The Spirit Coming in His Authority from God to us. " *Apo*," in connection with the Spirit, occurs with the genitive only, and signifies the going from a place, as when Christ " departed from (apo) Galilee " (Matt. 19 : 1).

The Spirit's authority in speaking—" He shall not speak of (apo) Himself " (John 16 : 13).

The Spirit's authority in blessing—" I will pour out of (apo) My Spirit " (Acts 2 : 17, 18).

The Spirit's authority in transforming—" As by (apo) the Spirit (2 Cor. 3 : 18).

The Spirit's authority in testimony—" Holy Ghost sent down from (apo) heaven " (1 Pet. 1 : 12).

The Spirit's authority in administration—" From the seven spirits " (Rev. 1 : 4).

As the Ambassador goes from his own country to another and acts as the medium between both : so the Spirit comes from the court of heaven to the court of His earthly temple on earth.

" Eis."

The Spirit as the Inductor. Immersed into (*eis*) His name—" In the name . . . Holy Ghost " (Matt. 28 : 19).

Insight through His power—" Paul filled with the Holy Ghost, set his eyes on (eis) him " (Acts 13 : 9).

Identified into the body—" One Spirit . . . baptized into (eis) one body " (1 Cor. 12 : 13).

Included in the family—" Spirit of His Son into (eis) your hearts " (Gal. 4 : 6).

Influenced by His leading—" Soweth to (eis) the Spirit " (Gal. 6 : 8).

Introducing the Christ in His indwelling—" His Spirit in (eis) the inner man " (Eph. 3 : 16).

Indwelling of His presence—" Given unto (eis) us His Holy Spirit " (1 Thess. 4 : 8).

" Meta."

The Spirit as the Identifier. " *Meta* " signifies to be identified with another or something, to be associated with a person, as in the apostolic benediction, when Paul says, " The Lord Jesus be with thy spirit. Grace be with you " (2 Tim. 4 : 22). As found in association with the Spirit, " meta " is used twice with the genitive.

" That He may abide with (meta) you for ever " (John 14 : 16).

" Communion of the Holy Ghost be with (meta) you " (2 Cor. 13 : 14).

The Spirit identifies Himself with us as the Companion for fellowship, that we in all things may have fellowship with the Companion.

" Para."

The Spirit in His Care. " *Para* " signifies to be beside another, to be in close proximity, to proceed from the side or vicinity of one, or from one's sphere of power, or from one's wealth or store. It means to come from beside one : with the dative it means to be at the side of a person : and with the accusative it denotes motion towards another. The genitive is illustrated by Christ's saying, " I came from the Father " : the dative by Peter lodging " with one Simon the tanner " (Acts 10 : 6) : and the accusative by Saul of Tarsus, who was " brought up . . . at the feet of Gamaliel " (Acts 22 : 3). " Para," as associated with the Spirit, occurs three times. Once with the dative and twice with the genitive (John 16 : 28).

" He dwelleth with (para) you " (John 14 : 17).

" Send . . . from (para) the Father " (John 15 : 26).

" Proceedeth from (para) the Father " (John 15 : 26).

The Spirit has come from the Father in response to the request of Christ to care for His disciples, and to take the place of Christ, and carry on His work ; hence, the Spirit is the other Comforter, and comes from the Father as such. The Spirit is in accord with the Father and the Son, therefore if we would keep in accord with them we need to be in the concord of the Spirit.

" Kata."

The Spirit the Standard of our Actions. " *Kata* " denotes motion from the higher to the lower. With the genitive it signifies down from, against, and in opposition to, as when the swine " ran violently down (kata) a steep place " (Luke 8 : 33) ; and as Christ says in His message to the Church at Ephesus, " I have this against (kata) thee " (Rev. 2 : 4). With the accusative it means down towards, down upon, throughout, according to. It is often used to represent anything done according to a standard, as when Moses made the tabernacle " according to (kata) the fashion " of the plan he had seen (Acts 7 : 44).

" Kata " is used twice with the genitive in relation to the Spirit, and six times with the accusative. The first are : Matt. 12 : 32, and Gal. 5 : 17. The sin " against (kata) the Holy Ghost " is a terrible sin, because it is man in his assumption setting himself above the Spirit instead of the

Spirit being recognized in His sovereignty. The Spirit in the life of the surrendered believer acts " against (kata) the flesh," even as the flesh acts " against (kata) the Spirit."

The passages with the accusative are :

Rom. 1 : 4—" According to (kata) the Spirit of holiness."

Rom. 8 : 4, 5—" After (kata) the Spirit."

1 Cor. 12 : 8—" By (kata) the same Spirit."

Believers are to act in the Spirit, in the commands of His Word, in accord with His nature, and according to the leading of His directions.

" Epi."

The Spirit in the Activity of His Power. " *Epi* " generally means on, resting upon. With the genitive, proceeding from, resting upon as a basis, thus of Christ as the One Who " sat on (epi) the throne " (Rev. 6 : 16) : with the dative, resting in or upon, as when Christ " sat on (epi) the well " (John 4 : 6) : and with the accusative, as coming upon with implied motion and intention, as when God makes His " sun to rise on (epi) the good and evil " (Matt. 5 : 45). The Holy Spirit is only mentioned, and significantly so, with the accusative.

" Lighting upon (epi) Him " (Matt. 3 : 16).

" Descending upon (epi) Him " (Mark 1 : 10).

" I will put My Spirit upon (epi) Him " (Matt. 12 : 18).

" Holy Ghost shall come upon (epi) thee " (Luke 1 : 35).

" The Holy Ghost was upon (epi) him " (Luke 2 : 25).

" Spirit of the Lord is upon (epi) Me " (Luke 4 : 18).

" I send the promise of My Father upon (epi) you " (Luke 24 : 49).

" It abode upon (epi) Him " (John 1 : 32).

" Upon (epi) whom thou shalt see " (John 1 : 33).

" Remaining on (epi) Him " (John 1 : 33).

" Holy Ghost is come upon (epi) you " (Acts 1 : 8).

" Sat upon (epi) each of them " (Acts 2 : 3).

" I will pour out of My Spirit upon (epi) " (Acts 2 : 17).

" On (epi) My servants," etc. (Acts 2 : 18).

" Great grace was upon (epi) them all " (Acts 4 : 33).

" Holy Ghost fell on (epi) all them " (Acts 10 : 44).

" Holy Ghost fell on (epi) them " (Acts 11 : 15).
" As on (epi) us " (Acts 11 : 15).
" Holy Ghost came on (epi) them " (Acts 19 : 6).
" He shed on (epi) us " (Titus 3 : 6).
" Resteth upon (epi) you " (1 Pet. 4 : 14).

The Scriptures undoubtedly refer to a definite crisis in the lives of those upon whom the Spirit came with signs following : and the case in which the preposition occurs proclaims a process based on that crisis.

" Dia."

The Effective Working of the Spirit. " *Dia.*" Its primary significance is through, throughout. It occurs with the genitive and accusative. With the genitive it indicates the instrument by means of which an action is accomplished, hence, it is said of Christ continually that blessing comes " through our Lord Jesus Christ " (Rom. 5 : 1, 9, 11). With the accusative, " dia " indicates the reason of an action, hence, the reason why many believed in Christ after He had raised Lazarus from the dead was " by reason of " him (John 12 : 11). The preposition occurs only once with the accusative in relation to the Spirit and the believer, and that is in Rom. 8 : 11—" Quicken your mortal bodies by (dia) His Spirit." The reason of God's action is because of the Spirit's indwelling.

With the genitive, " dia " occurs as follows :

Christ commanding by means of the Spirit—" Through (dia) the Holy Ghost had given commandment " (Acts 1 : 2).

Agabus prophesying by means of the Spirit—" Signified by (dia) the Spirit " (Acts 11 : 28).

Disciples warning Paul by means of the Spirit—" Who said to Paul through (dia) the Spirit " (Acts 21 : 4).

The Spirit speaking by means of Esaias—" Well spake the Holy Ghost by (dia) Esaias " (Acts 28 : 25).

The love of God shed abroad in the heart by means of the Spirit—" Love of God shed abroad in our hearts by " (dia) (Rom. 5 : 5).

The united prayer of the saints by means of the Spirit— " For (dia) the love of the Spirit " (Rom. 15 : 30).

God making known spiritual things by means of the
Spirit—" By (dia) the Spirit " (1 Cor. 2 : 10).

The gifts conferred by means of the Spirit—" To one is
given by (dia) the Spirit " (1 Cor. 12 : 8).

Strength imparted by means of the Spirit—" Strengthened
with might by (dia) His Spirit " (Eph. 3 : 16).

Keeping sacred by means of the Spirit—" Keep by (dia)
the Holy Ghost " (2 Tim. 1 : 14).

Christ offering Himself by means of the Spirit—" Who
through (dia) the eternal Spirit " (Heb. 9 : 14).

Purified in obedience by means of the Spirit—" Purified
your souls in obeying the truth through (dia) the Spirit "
(1 Pet. 1 : 22).

Whether the Spirit does an act through another, or
another accomplishes something through Him, He is seen as
the active and energetic worker, even as the water moves the
mill wheel and the willow growing by the side of the stream
grows by its fertilizing flow.

" Huper."

The Spirit as the Gracious Intercessor. This preposition
only occurs in relation to the Spirit with the genitive, and
signifies, over and separate from, as though bending over to
protect, hence, it is often used to denote Christ's substitutionary work on our behalf. " Christ for (huper) us " (Rom.
5 : 8). Of the Spirit's work in us as the Pleader it is said,
" The Spirit maketh intercession for (huper) us " (Rom.
8 : 26). The Spirit cannot always utter through human lips
the sighing of His requests, but His sighs are interpreted by
the other Intercessor at God's right hand.

" Hupo."

The Spirit in His Leading. This preposition occurs with
the genitive as relating to the Spirit and the believer, and
denotes a position under something higher, the place " from
under which anything comes forth," or " the agent from
under whose hand a thing is accomplished," often used in the
sense of " by," hence we read of Paul being " left in bonds
by (hupo) Felix " (Acts 25 : 14). Five times the preposition
occurs in connection with the Spirit and us.

Led by the Spirit to be tempted—" Led of (hupo) the Spirit " (Matt. 4 : 1).

Led to see by the Spirit—" Revealed by (hupo) the Spirit " (Luke 2 : 26).

Led forth in Christian service—" Sent forth by (hupo) the Holy Ghost " (Acts 13 : 4).

Led not to go to a certain place—" Forbidden by (hupo) the Holy Ghost " (Acts 16 : 6).

Led to do as the Spirit impelled—" Spake as they were moved by (hupo) " (2 Pet. 1 : 21).

Under the Spirit's wisdom we act, under His power we are upheld, and under His instructions we go forward, conscious He is under us to carry the responsibility.

" En."

The Holy Spirit as the Indweller and the Infiller. Preposition governing the dative, with the primary idea of rest in any place or thing. As compared with " eis " and " ek," " en " stands between the two, " eis " implying motion into, " en " the being or remaining in, and " ek " motion out of. Christ uses " en " again and again in John 15 in calling attention to the mutual abiding of vine and branches. " Abide in Me and I in you." As applied to the Spirit, we find " en " occurs eight times with reference to His indwelling in the believer, and twenty-six times in calling attention to Him as the element which infills the spiritual being and surrounds it too.

The Spirit as the Indweller. Christ's promise—" He shall be in (en) you " (John 14 : 17).

Mark of new birth—" If so be the Spirit of God dwell in (en) you " (Rom. 8 : 9).

Quickener of body—" If the Spirit . . . dwell in (en) you " (Rom. 8 : 11, margin).

Consecrator of body—" Spirit of God dwelleth in (en) you " (1 Cor. 3 : 16).

Holiness of character—" Holy Ghost which is in (en) you " (1 Cor. 6 : 19).

Guardian of trust—" Keep by the Holy Ghost which dwelleth in (en) us " (2 Tim. 1 : 14).

The Spirit as the Infiller. The highest form of expression and the most expressive and inclusive of all found in the Word is " in the Spirit." To the experience implied in being " in the Spirit " we are continually exhorted. " In the Spirit " comprehends all the experiences embodied in being " baptized with," " full of," " filled with," " possessed by," " poured out," " resting upon," " welling up," " power," " flowing out," etc. Let the following pointers, pointed by the Scripture, speak for themselves :

1. Bestowment of the Spirit—" Baptize you with (en) " (Matt. 3 : 11 ; Mark 1 : 8 ; Luke 3 : 16 ; John 1 : 33 ; Acts 1 : 5).

2. Power of the Spirit—" Cast out demons by (en) " (Matt. 12 : 28).

3. Insight of the Spirit—" David in (en) Spirit call Him Lord " (Matt. 22 : 43).

4. Revelation of the Spirit—" He came by (en) the Spirit " (Luke 2 : 27).

5. Guidance of the Spirit—" Led by (en) the Spirit " (Luke 4 : 1).

6. Gladness of the Spirit—" Rejoiced in (en) Spirit," R.V.., " In the Holy Spirit " (Luke 10 : 21).

7. Environment of the Spirit—" Baptized with (en) the Holy Ghost " (Acts 1 : 5 ; 11 : 16).

8. Witness of the Spirit—" Conscience also bearing me witness in (en) the Holy Ghost " (Rom. 9 : 1).

9. Joy of the Spirit—" Joy in (en) the Holy Ghost " (Rom. 14 : 17).

10. Sanctification of the Spirit—" Being sanctified by (en) the Holy Ghost " (Rom. 15 : 16).

11. Prompting of the Spirit—" No man can say, Jesus is the Lord, but by (en) the Holy Ghost " (1 Cor. 12 : 3).

12. Inspiration of the Spirit—" Speaking by (en) the Spirit " (1 Cor. 12 : 3).

13. Faith of the Spirit—" Faith by (en) the same Spirit " (1 Cor. 12 : 9).

14. Healing of the Spirit—" Gifts of healing by (en) " (1 Cor. 12 : 9).

15. Union of the Spirit—" By (en) one Spirit " (1 Cor. 12 : 13).

16. Enablement of the Spirit—" By (en) the Holy Ghost "
(2 Cor. 6 : 6).

17. Access of the Spirit—" Access by (en) one Spirit "
(Eph. 2 : 18).

18. Cohesiveness of the Spirit—" Habitation of God
through (en) the Spirit " (Eph. 2 : 22).

19. Unfolding of the Spirit—" Made known . . . by (en)
the Spirit " (Eph. 3 : 5).

20. Encompassing of the Spirit—" Filled with (en) the
Spirit " (Eph. 5 : 18).

21. Praying of the Spirit—" Praying . . . in (en) the
Spirit " (Eph. 6 : 18 ; Jude 20).

22. Love of the Spirit—" Love in (en) the Spirit " (Col.
1 : 8).

23. Ministry of the Spirit—" In (en) the Holy Ghost "
(1 Thess. 1 : 5).

24. Vindication of the Spirit—" Justified in (en) the
Spirit " (1 Tim. 3 : 16).

25. Anointing of the Spirit—" Preached . . . with (en) the
Holy Ghost " (1 Pet. 1 : 12).

26. Outlook of the Spirit—" In (en) the Spirit " (Rev.
1 : 10 ; 4 : 2 ; 17 : 3 ; 21 : 10).

No one can honestly ponder these passages of Holy Writ
without being conscious of three things :

The difference between the ideal and the actual.

The crisis necessary to make actual the ideal.

The process based on the crisis which makes the ideal
actual and permanent.

THE SPECIFIC REVELATION ABOUT THE SPIRIT
IN THE ACTS

Christ not only revealed the Father, but He made known
the Person and Work of the Holy Spirit ; and His work and
Personality is made known in what is known as The Book of
the Acts, but which is the record of the Personal Acts of His
operations.

There are four ways in which the Holy Spirit is spoken
of in The Acts, namely, as " The Spirit," " Holy Spirit,"
" the Holy Spirit," and " the Spirit, the Holy."

" The Spirit."

When He is said to be " the Spirit," His Personality is revealed. Nine times He is spoken of as " The Spirit."

As the *One Who gave* " *utterance* " to the disciples on the Day of Pentecost : " The Spirit gave them utterance " (2 : 4).

As the *Guide in dealing with others* for their soul's salvation : " The Spirit said unto Philip, ' Go,' " etc. (8 : 29).

As the *Director in the Lord's Work :* " The Spirit said unto Peter, Behold, three men seek thee " (10 : 19). " The Spirit bade me go with them " (11 : 12).

As the *Foreteller of coming events :* " Agabus . . . signified by the Spirit there should be a great dearth throughout all the world " (11 : 28).

As the *Preventer in Christian service :* " They assayed to go into Bithynia, but the Spirit suffered them not " (16 : 7).

As the *Qualifier to teach :* " Apollos . . . being fervent in the Spirit, he spake and taught diligently the things of the Lord " (18 : 25).

As the *Indicator of suffering :* " I go bound in the Spirit unto Jerusalem " (20 : 22).

As the *Communicator to warn :* " Who said to Paul, through the Spirit, that he should not go up to Jerusalem " (21 : 4).

" Holy Spirit."

Where there is no article in the original, the power of the Spirit is to the front, therefore " Holy Spirit " and " Power " are equivalent.

Power to communicate : " After that He through Holy Spirit had given commandments " (1 : 2).

Power to baptise : " Ye shall be baptised with " (in, " εν ") " Holy Spirit " (1 : 5).

Power to fill : " They were all filled with Holy Spirit " (2 : 4).

Power to speak : " Peter filled with Holy Spirit, said " (4 : 8).

Power for confidence : " When they had prayed . . . they were all filled with Holy Spirit, and they spake the Word of God with boldness " (4 : 31).

Power for office: " Seven men of honest report, full of Holy Spirit and wisdom, whom we may appoint over this business " (6 : 3).

Power to serve: " They chose Stephen, a man full of faith and Holy Spirit " (6 : 5).

Power to see: " He, being full of Holy Spirit, looked up steadfastly into heaven, and saw the glory of God, and Jesus standing on the right hand of God " (7 : 55).

Power to qualify: " Prayed for them, that they might receive Holy Spirit . . . they received Holy Spirit . . . he may receive Holy Spirit " (8 : 15, 17, 19).

Power to endue: " Be filled with Holy Spirit " (9 : 17).

Power to do good: " God anointed Jesus of Nazareth with Holy Spirit . . . Who went about doing good " (10 : 38).

Power to unify: " Ye shall be baptised with Holy Spirit " . . . " The like gift as He did unto us " (11 : 16).

Power to discern: " He was a good man and full of Holy Spirit " (11 : 24).

Power to detect: " Paul, filled with Holy Spirit, set his eyes on him and said," etc. (13 : 9).

Power to rejoice: " The disciples were filled with joy and Holy Spirit " (13 : 52).

Power to possess: " Have ye received Holy Spirit ?" (19 : 2).

The Holy Spirit

" The Holy Spirit," as so expressed, occurs seven times, and reveals His character as the Holy One.

Holy in Testimony: " Ye shall receive power after that the Holy Spirit is come upon you " (1 : 8), " and ye shall be witnesses unto Me." The Holy One comes upon the holy ones to bear witness to the Holy One.

Holy in Promise: " Received of the Father the promise of the Holy Spirit " (2 : 33). The three persons of the Holy Godhead are seen acting.

Holy in Gift: " The gift of the Holy Spirit " (2 : 38).

Holy in Ministry: " The churches . . . were edified, and walking in the fear of the Lord, and in the comfort of the Holy Spirit, were multiplied " (9 : 31).

Holy in Endowment : " On the Gentiles also was poured out the gift of the Holy Spirit " (10 : 45).

Holy in Discretion : " Seemed good to the Holy Ghost " (15 : 28).

Holy in Authority: " Forbidden of the Holy Spirit to preach the Word in Asia " (16 : 6).

" The Spirit, The Holy."

This double expresses His Personality and His Character, and occurs fifteen times. We may view Him in this double sense, and see in every instance where the Spirit, the Holy, is mentioned He is so declared.

His Holy Word : " The Spirit, the Holy, by the mouth of David spake " (1 : 16).

His Holy Nature : " Why hath Satan filled thine heart to lie to the Spirit, the Holy " (5 : 3).

His Holy Witness: " We are His witnesses of these things " (Christ's unholy death), " so also is the Spirit, the Holy " (5 : 32).

His Holy Ministry : " Ye do always resist the Spirit, the Holy " (7 : 51).

His Holy Presence : " The Spirit, the Holy was given " (8 : 18).

His Holy Confirmation : " The Spirit, the Holy, fell on all them which heard the Word " (10 : 44).

His Holy Possession : " Received the Spirit, the Holy " (10 : 47).

His Holy Coming : " The Spirit, the Holy, fell on them " (11 : 15).

His Holy Direction : " The Spirit, the Holy, said, Separate Me Paul and Barnabas " (13 : 2).

His Holy Commission : " Being sent forth by the Spirit, the Holy " (13 : 4).

His Holy Bestowment: " Giving them the Spirit, the Holy . . . purifying their hearts by faith " (15 : 8).

His Holy Equipment : " The Spirit, the Holy, came on them " (19 : 6).

His Holy Warning : " The Spirit, the Holy, witnesseth " (20 : 23).

His Holy Appointment: " The Spirit, the Holy, hath made you overseers " (20 : 28).

His Holy Word: " The Spirit, the Holy, saith " (21 : 11).

His Holy Prophecy: " Well spake the Spirit, the Holy, by Esaias, the prophet " (28 : 25).

To rightly recognise the Holy Spirit is to be regulated in all things by Him.

If the above is carefully pondered it will be seen that the definite way in which the Spirit is spoken of, is unfolded in the setting of each reference. For instance, the sin of Ananias was an affront to the Spirit, and also a reflection on His character, hence the glaring act in sinning against " The Spirit," " The Holy."

THE NAMES AND TITLES OF THE HOLY SPIRIT

The names and titles which are ascribed to the Spirit stand for His personality, nature, and activities.

He is *" The Spirit "* in the sum of His personal totality (Mark 1 : 10). As breath is the vital principle of the body, so the Spirit is the inmost life of God, for " God is Spirit."

He is *" The Spirit of God "* in the association of His Deity (Matt. 3 : 16 ; 12 : 28). All that God is, the Spirit is, in His character and attributes.

He is *" The Spirit of the Lord "* in the claim of His authority (Isa. 11 : 2 ; Luke 4 : 18). He claims His own in divine right because they are His own to claim.

He is *" The Spirit of the Living God "* in the vitality of His ministry (2 Cor. 3 : 3). The legibility of His work is seen by the love-light which shines out of a holy heart in the life.

He is *" The Spirit of Christ "* in the sphere of His testimony. He brings Christ to us in His revelation (1 Pet. 1 : 11), and brings us to Christ by His association (Rom. 8 : 9).

He is *" The Spirit of His Son "* in the relationship of His paternity (Gal. 4 : 6). The Spirit assures believers they are sons in the Son, and in Him they are children of the Father.

He is *" The Spirit of Jesus Christ "* in the supply of His bounty (Phil. 1 : 19). All that Jesus Christ *is, has,* and *can do* are ours since we are His by the Spirit.

He is " *The Spirit of our God* " in the grace of His adaptability (1 Cor. 6 : 11). The extremity of our sinful case is met in the suitability of God's grace.

He is " *The Spirit of your Father* " in the love of His sympathy (Matt. 10 : 20). The pressure of our circumstances may be trying, but the Father will meet us in our need with His sufficient grace.

He is " *The Holy Spirit* " in the character of His sanctity (Rom. 15 : 16). He could not be any other than Holy, and therefore wherever He is, holiness is the evidence of His presence.

He is " *His Holy Spirit* " in the sacredness of His Divinity (1 Thess. 4 : 8). Uncleanness and unrighteousness are not tolerated by the Giver of the Spirit, nor by the Spirit given. Where they are, He either leaves the indulger, or consumes them in the fire of His holiness.

He is " *The Holy Spirit of Promise* " in the earnest of His glory (Eph. 1 : 13, 14). All He promises is like Himself, holy. The Mohammedan paradise of sensual indulgence is impossible in the realm of His glory.

He is " *The Holy Spirit of God* " in the affection of His sensibility (Eph. 4 : 30). Recognizing Who the Spirit is, and what He is, we cannot grieve His holy love.

He is " *The Spirit of Holiness* " in the power of His ability (Rom. 1 : 4). The form of expression is peculiar in relation to this title. It denotes the essential attribute of God as the sunlight speaks of the sun.

He is " *The Spirit of Truth* " in the Word and His veracity (John 14 : 17 ; 16 : 13 ; 1 John 5 : 7, R.V.). He is the Author of truth, He is its Essence, and He is also its Communicator.

He is " *The Spirit of Life* " in the operation of His vitality (Rom. 8 : 2). He is the Source of life in Christ. He is the Strength of life in Himself. He is the Sustainer of life by His Word. And He is the Goal of life in God.

He is " *The Spirit of Wisdom* " in the revelation of His mystery (Eph. 1 : 17). He is the Initiator into the full knowledge of God Himself. To know Him is eternal life, eternal love, eternal peace, and eternal satisfaction.

He is " *The Spirit of Grace* " in the pleading of His ministry (Heb. 10 : 29). He acts in grace, to communicate grace, to place in the sphere of grace, and to make us to correspond to grace.

He is " *The Spirit of Love* " in the glow of His intensity (2 Tim. 1 : 7). He unfolds the God of love and sheds abroad the love of God in the heart. All the fruit of the Spirit is love in a nine-fold character.

He is " *The Spirit of a Sound Mind* " in the sense of His intelligence (2 Tim. 1 : 7). His appeals are not contrary to reason, although at times they are beyond it. He has the best of reasons for all His actions.

He is " *The Spirit of Power* " in the might of His strength (2 Tim. 1 : 7). Disease, demons, and death cannot resist His might. Christ's ministry and resurrection are witnesses thereto.

He is " *The Spirit of Adoption* " in the benefit of His assurance (Rom. 8 : 15). He assures us we are God's children when we believe in Christ by His Word ; and He assures us we are pleasing to God as we are obedient.

He is " *The Eternal Spirit* " in the existence of His immutability (Heb. 9 : 14). He is eternal in the character of His being, in the faithfulness of His love, and in the Word of His promise.

He is " *The Spirit of Burning* " in the glow of His zeal (Isa. 4 : 4). He searches by the fire of His Word, He inspires by the glow of His love, He moves by the prayer of His intercession, and quickens by the zeal of His power.

He is " *The Spirit of Prophecy* " in the utterance of His testimony (Rev. 19 : 10). He rests us in Christ's past work on the Cross. He leads us to the Christ of the Word in the present, and He assures us of the future glory to come.

He is " *The Seven Spirits of God* " in the perfection of His personality (Rev. 4 : 5 ; 5 : 6). The seven titles mentioned in Isa. 11 : 2 illustrate this perfection.

He is " *The One Spirit* " in the bond of His unity (1 Cor. 12 : 13). He invites believers to Christ and to each other. Division and dissension are not consistent with His presence, but love and fellowship are.

He is " *The Spirit of Understanding* " in the illumination of His teaching (Isa. 11 : 2). Only the Spirit-taught mind can understand the Spirit-given Book.

He is " *The Spirit of Counsel and Might* " in the strength of His guidance (Isa. 11 : 2). He not only gives the needed counsel for direction, but He carries us through to the place of designation.

He is " *The Spirit of Knowledge and the Fear of the Lord* " (Isa. 11 : 2). He holds up the lamp of knowledge to enlighten us, and then hedges us with holy awe lest we should fail to fear Him Who loves.

He is " *The Good Spirit* " in the care of His actions (Neh. 9 : 20). He leads by His truth, He feeds by His promises, He prunes by His discipline, He inspires by His love, and instructs by His acts.

He is " *Thy Free Spirit* " in the upholding of His grace (Psa. 51 : 12). He liberates from sin, self, the world, the flesh, Satan, care, and fear, and keeps in the liberty of His truth and love.

He is " *The Spirit of Grace and Supplication* " as the cause of intercession (Zech. 12 : 10). To pray in the Spirit proves a consecrated heart, and for the Spirit to pray in us proclaims a prevailing intercessor.

He is " *The Spirit of the Living Creatures* " in the wheels of His providence (Ezek. 1 : 20, 21). The mysteries of life are the makers of life. Angel faces are seen by the eye of faith in the dark clouds.

He is " *The Promise of the Father* " in the power of Christ's bestowment (Acts 1 : 4). He was promised to Christ as a reward of His toil, and Christ promised Him to His own to obtain in all things their triumph.

He is " *The Comforter* " in the help of His advocacy (John 14 : 16). Believers have two Advocates. One in heaven looking after our interests (1 John 2 : 1), and one on earth looking after God's interests.

He is " *The Spirit of Glory* " in the outlook of expectancy (1 Pet. 4 : 14). There is a twofold waiting. Christ is waiting to be with us, and we are waiting to be with Him.

Each of these points suggests a Bible study in itself. For example, see the seven times " The Spirit of the Lord " is mentioned in Judges ; and the four references to " The Comforter " in John's Gospel.

The use of the definite article as found in connection with the Spirit declares His personality. There are two ways by which the Holy Spirit is spoken of, namely, with and without the definite article. Many places where the Holy Spirit is spoken of as such, the definite article is omitted. As a rule where " *Hagion Pneuma* " (Holy Spirit) occurs the reference is to what the Spirit does and gives. Take one passage. " They were all filled with Holy Spirit and began to speak as the Spirit gave them utterance " (Acts 2 : 4). There is no article before Holy Spirit because His gift is referred to, but there is in the second use of *Pneuma*, because the Giver is mentioned. Rotherham, in his translation of the Acts, recognises the original throughout. The following is a list where the Spirit is referred to in the Acts with the definite article, proclaiming His personality. I give Rotherham's translation.

The Spirit coming—" The Holy Spirit cometh upon you " (1 : 8).

The Spirit inditing—" The Holy Spirit spake beforehand " (1 : 16).

The Spirit inspiring—" Speaking . . . as the Spirit was giving " (2 : 4).

The Spirit fulfilling—" The promise of the Holy Spirit " (2 : 33).

The Spirit promised—" Ye shall receive the free gift of the Holy Spirit " (2 : 38).

The Spirit insulted—" Thou shouldest deal falsely with the Holy Spirit " (5 : 3).

The Spirit affronted—" Put to the proof the Spirit of the Lord " (5 : 9).

The Spirit witnessing—" Witnesses . . . also the Holy Spirit " (5 : 32).

The Spirit enabling—" The Spirit with which he was speaking " (6 : 10).

The Spirit resisted—"Against the Holy Spirit do strive" (7 : 51).

The Spirit bestowed—"The Spirit was being given" (8 : 18 ; 15 : 8).

The Spirit speaking—"The Spirit said" unto Philip (8 : 29 ; see also 10 : 19 ; 11 : 12 ; 13 : 2 ; 28 : 25).

The Spirit removing—"The Spirit of the Lord caught away Philip" (8 : 39).

The Spirit received—"The Holy Spirit they have received" (10 : 47).

The Spirit prophesying—"Through means of the Spirit" (11 : 28).

The Spirit sending—"Sent forth by the Holy Spirit" (13 : 4).

The Spirit directing—"Seemed good unto the Holy Spirit" (15 : 28).

The Spirit forbidding—"Forbidden by the Holy Spirit" (16 : 6, 7).

The Spirit intimating—"The Holy Spirit . . . doth bear me full witness" (20 : 23 ; 21 : 11).

The Spirit appointing—"The Holy Spirit hath set you overseers" (20 : 28).

The Personality of The Spirit is implied by His association with the Father and the Son. What is ascribed to the Father and the Son in the personal acts, is also said of The Spirit.

The Work of Creation. "By His Spirit He hath garnished the heavens" (Job 26 : 13). The word "garnished" means to adorn, and is rendered "goodly" in Psa. 16 : 6, hence, something beautiful and pleasant. The world is now a cosmos (adorned with beauty) instead of a chaos (waste and empty) because of His action (Gen. 1 : 2).

The Person of His Deity. "The Lord the Spirit" (2 Cor. 3 : 18, R.V.). *Kurios* is applied to God in Matt. 22 : 37, and to Christ in the oft repeated sentence, "In the Lord" (see Phil. 1 : 14 ; 2 : 19, 24, 29 ; 3 : 1 ; 4 : 1, 2, 4, 10), and means the One Who is the Proprietor ; hence, has the right to rule and command. The same title is given to the Spirit ; hence, the sin of Ananias was against the Spirit as Lord (Acts 5 : 9).

The Operation of His Providence. " Thou sendest forth Thy Spirit, and they are created : and Thou renewest the face of the earth " (Psa. 104 : 30). The word " renewest " means to repair, to make anew, to restore. It is translated " repair " in 2 Chron. 24 : 4, 12. The Spirit repairs all waste in nature and gives to the earth a new appearance.

The Omniscience of His Knowledge. " The things of God knoweth no man, but the Spirit of God " (1 Cor. 2 : 11). Man cannot see nor understand the things of God, but the Spirit is cognisant of all. He is the Custodian of all God's secrets and the Revealer of all He is.

Omnipresence of His Being. " Whither shall I flee from Thy Spirit " (Psa. 139 : 7). In the heaven of immensity, in the hell of mystery, and in the earth of secrecy, He is alike present.

The Omnipotence of His Power. " The power of the Holy Spirit " (Rom. 15 : 13). The literal reading of this sentence is, " power of Holy Spirit," as though He was the embodiment of all power. All the power of God is located in the Spirit.

The Eternalness of His Character. " Eternal Spirit " (Heb. 9 : 14) He never was any other than He is. He cannot be any other than He is. And He can never be any other than He was.

The Enabler of Christ's Atonement. " Who through the eternal Spirit offered Himself without spot to God " (Heb. 9 : 14). The Greek preposition " *dia*," rendered " *through*," signifies " *by means of*," and therefore indicates that the active agent behind Christ's act was the Spirit.

The Raiser of Christ's Body from the Dead. " The Spirit that raised up Jesus from (out of) the dead " (Rom. 8 : 11). The working of God's power displayed in the quickening of Christ's dead body (Eph. 1 : 19, 20) is the concentrated act of the Spirit (1 Pet. 3 : 18).

The Secret of Christ's Ministry. " God anointed Jesus of Nazareth with the Holy Ghost and power, Who went about " (Acts 10 : 38 ; Luke 4 : 1, 18). The thoroughness of Christ's energised ministry is suggested by the Greek word, " *went about* " (*Dierchomai—Dia*, through ; and *chomai*, to traverse), which means, to go through.   It is rendered "*go through*" (Matt. 19 : 24) and "*passed through*" (Luke 19 : 1).   Being thoroughly equipped, He thoroughly accomplished.

The Approver of Christ's Worth.   The Spirit in Dove-form rested upon Christ at His baptism (Matt. 3 : 16) as the Father's voice commended His Son.   The Bible opens with a Brooding Dove, and ends with a Bleeding Lamb.   The Dove approves the Lamb.   When He rested upon Christ it was as the Dove, and when He came upon the disciples He came as fire.

The Inaugurator of Pentecost.   The promise of the Father was the bestowment of the Spirit by Christ (Acts 1 : 4; 2 : 33), Who takes charge of things for God during Christ's absence.

The Bestower of Blessing.   The Source of blessing is God in His love, the Channel of blessing is Christ in His grace, and the Secret of blessing is the Spirit in His fellowship (2 Cor. 13 : 14).

The Spirit's personality is further stated in the operation of God's grace (Rom. 5 : 5; 1 Cor. 6 : 11; Eph. 1 : 13), in the ordinance of believers' baptism (Matt. 28 : 19, 20), in the prayers of the believer (Rom. 8 : 26, 27), in the relationship of God's children (Gal. 4 : 6), in the worship of the saint (Phil. 3 : 3; Eph. 2 : 18), and in the witness of the Trinity (1 John 5 : 7).

In most of the above Scriptures it will be found that the three Persons of the Godhead are mentioned; and in others where an action is specifically stated about the Spirit, His personality is implied, for what is said of Him is also said of the Father and the Son.

DIAGRAM

ILLUSTRATING THE USE OF THE GREEK PREPOSITIONS

IN CONNECTION WITH

THE HOLY SPIRIT

The Holy Spirit coming down from Heaven (Acts 2 : 1-4).   The Ascent of the Spirit with the Church (II. Thess. 2 : 1, 6).

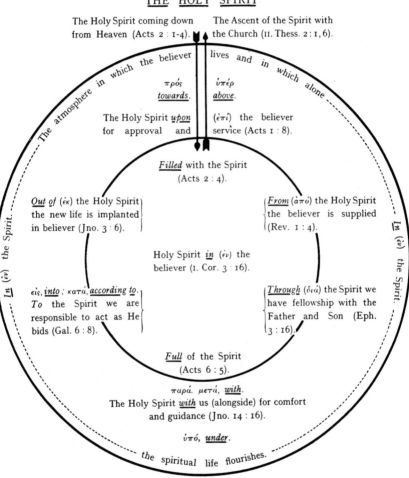

The atmosphere in which the believer lives and in which alone

In (ἐν) the Spirit.

πρός *towards.*   ὑπέρ *above.*

The Holy Spirit *upon* for approval and   (ἐπί) the believer service (Acts 1 : 8).

Filled with the Spirit (Acts 2 : 4).

Out of (ἐκ) the Holy Spirit the new life is implanted in believer (Jno. 3 : 6).   *From* (ἀπό) the Holy Spirit the believer is supplied (Rev. 1 : 4).

Holy Spirit *in* (ἐν) the believer (I. Cor. 3 : 16).

εἰς, *into* ; κατά, *according to.* *To* the Spirit we are responsible to act as He bids (Gal. 6 : 8).   *Through* (διά) the Spirit we have fellowship with the Father and Son (Eph. 3 : 16).

Full of the Spirit (Acts 6 : 5).

παρά. μετά, *with.* The Holy Spirit *with* us (alongside) for comfort and guidance (Jno. 14 : 16).

ὑπό, *under.*

the spiritual life flourishes.

In (ἐν) the Spirit.

5

THE HEART OF A LOVING PURPOSE

THE heart in a metaphorical sense stands for the inness of things, hence the " issues of life " are said to come out of it (Prov. 4 : 23) ; and God's dealings with Israel in the wilderness were to " prove " what was in their heart (Deut. 8 : 2) ; and " out of the heart," Christ said, proceeds everything that is wrong (Matt. 15 : 19). The heart denotes the inward determination expressed in action : the workers who brought their gifts and work for the tabernacle, were those whose hearts were willing and stirred up (Ex. 35 : 5, 26, 29, 34, 35). The heart expresses the inward affection of the soul. The call to Israel was to love the Lord with all their heart (Deut. 6 : 5). The heart speaks of the inward thought of the mind. The Lord commanded Israel to lay up His words in the heart (Deut. 11 : 18). The heart stands for the inward conclusion of a judicial finding, hence, Solomon prayed he might have a heart of understanding to judge aright (1 Kings 3 : 9). The heart represents the inward inclination of the desires : " He shall give thee the desires of thine heart " is the promise of the Lord as we delight in Him (Psa. 37 : 4). The heart sometimes denotes the inward anguish of the soul. The apostle said to the saints at Corinth, he was in " anguish of heart " about them (2 Cor. 2 : 4). The heart reveals the inward attitude of the will, hence, if any man shall believe on the Lord Jesus and confess Him as Lord he shall be saved (Rom. 10 : 9, R.V.) ; and the heart expresses the inward dealing of love's affection, hence the apostle said to the saints at Philippi, " I have you in my heart " (Phil. 1 : 7). In a general sense, the heart represents the will of God's loving purpose. We shall confine this study to three thoughts—The loving purpose of God in giving Christ for the world's salvation ; His loving plan in relation to Israel ; and His purpose in regard to the Church as revealed in the Epistle to the Ephesians.

183

The revelation of all revelations is, " God is Love." The religions of the world have no such revelation, therefore their light is darkness in the light of Christianity. " God is Beauty," says the Greek. " God is Strength," states the Roman. " God is a Despot," asserts the Barbarian. " God is Law," avows the Jew. " God is Everything," proclaims the Pantheist. " God is Force," says the Scientist. But " God is Love," reveals the Spirit.

As we listen to men, how confused we become. John Morley declared, " Christianity is the struggle after an ideal." Christ revealed the Father as running to meet the prodigal while he was yet a great way off. The prodigal's conception of the Father's love was to be made a " hired servant." The Father treated him as a son.

We ask, " Is the Gospel a revelation or a discovery ?" When the apostle was at Athens, he found the Athenians had erected an altar to " The unknown God " ; but he was able to declare, " He whom ye ignorantly worship I declare unto you." Nothing can be plainer than the message the apostles preached. It was a message which declared something new— something done outside of man,—so we say with Oliver Cromwell, " Shall we seek for the roots of our comforts within us ? What God hath done, what He is to us in Christ, is the root of our comfort : in this is stability : in us is weakness. I think I am the poorest wretch that lives, but I love God, or rather I am beloved of God." That God loved and gave is the revelation which Christ makes known.

One has said, " Religion has changed, like everything else. The creed in our day was simple and severe. To us right or wrong meant heaven or hell, neither more nor less. Now what is Christianity ? Who can show us ?" That is all the world can say, and many pulpits re-echo ! It gives us a question mark ! Unless we look to Divine revelation, as found in Christ and the Word, we are floundering in the bog of speculation. Man has no adequate reply to man's need, and Nature is no better, for Nature, " red in tooth and claw," only intensifies the question. Christ alone answers the question, " What is Christianity ?" It is focused in Himself. How sublime, soul-stirring, and sufficient is His embodying revelation : " For God so loved the world, that He gave His only begotten Son, that whosoever believeth in Him should not perish, but have everlasting life." These wonderful words of life and beauty, as one has said, naturally divide themselves into four parts :

<blockquote>
The Lake, The Love of God.
The River, The Son of God.
The Pitcher, The Faith in Him.
The Draught, Everlasting Life.
</blockquote>

I. The Lake

Looking out over the beautiful Lake Erie, at Erieside, in Ohio, U.S.A., one lovely Summer's day in July, and musing on its gentle, heaving bosom, as the sun was kissing it in its life-giving warmth, I recalled the words of Bernard, who, gazing with absorbed intent on Lake Geneva, in Switzerland, asked the question, " Has anyone seen the Lake ?" " We have no answer," says one. " No man has seen the Lake at any time, and yet we know all God's awful attributes—

<blockquote>
" Are ministers of love,
And feed its Sacred Flame."
</blockquote>

So says not the Spirit of God, for He reveals the Divine Logos, the Word, in John's unfolding Gospel, for although the word " Gospel " does not occur in John's Gospel, that Gospel is full of Gospel, for it reveals to us Christ in its genesis in " the Bosom of the Father," and in its revelation unfolds to us a saved sinner in the bosom of the Son.

How utterly wanting are all the definitions of God ! The Apostles' Creed leads us to " God the Father, Maker of heaven and earth," and the Shorter Catechism speaks of Him in His being as " being holiness, justice, goodness, and truth," and " Infinite, eternal and unchangeable." But not a word about Love. Sir Robertson Nicoll has rebukingly written in speaking of this grave omission in the Creeds of Christendom, " 'God is Love.' These words do not occur, as far as I remember, in any of the confessions of the Reformed Church."

<blockquote>
God is Love, not Love He was, nor He will be,
But He is, and always was, and always will be.
Here is fact, pulsating, warm,
Trust Him and see.
</blockquote>

" God is Love : God is Love !" so exclaimed, in his dying moments, the late Professor Emslie. " I will go and tell the world. They do not know it." Oh, if men would only recognize the fact, how they would realize its benediction ! This is the panacea to heal the feuds of men. This is the power to inspire the devotion of saints. This is the soul to move the sinner from the haunts and habit of sin. This is the salt to preserve society from the putrefaction of lust. This is the soil to nourish the character with the fruit of the Spirit. This is the substance of Christianity as found in Christ ; and this is the essence of God's being and eternal life : for, as Westcott has finely said, " Eternal life is that which has to do with the Being of God," and God, in the essence of His being, " is Love."

This Lake is deeper than man's sin. The prodigal had a glimmering of this when he said, " How many hired servants of my father's have bread enough and to spare ?" At least if he did not get the " enough," he got what was found in the " to spare." What a poor conception he had of the Father's bounty ! When God gives He does not give us a crust. He gives us the Bread of Life—the Christ.

What wonderful contrasts Christ reveals of the Lake of God's love in the parable of the prodigal son !

The prodigal in his self-will demanded the " portion of goods that falleth " to him. The Father in Love's giving " divided " unto him " His living," literally " His life."

The prodigal in his self-action " gathered all together." The Father in His Love was waiting on the look-out for the wanderer's return.

The prodigal in his self-destination went into the " far country." The Father in His Love's sight saw the ungrateful one while he was yet " a great way off."

The prodigal in his self-waste " wasted his substance in riotous living." The Father in His Love's heart had " compassion " on him.

The prodigal in his self-folly " spent all " he possessed. The Father's Love's desire moved Him to run to welcome the wanderer. " He ran." The only time we read of God being in a hurry.

The prodigal in his self-destitution began " to be in want." The Father in His Love's embrace fell on his neck and took him to His heart.

The prodigal in his self-association " joined himself to a citizen of that country." The Father in His Love's kiss lavished upon the swine-feeder the many kisses of His affection.

The prodigal in his self-servitude was sent into the field to feed the swine. The Father in His Love's garment put the " best robe " on him.

The prodigal in his self-longing would " fain have filled his belly with the husks that the swine did eat." The Father in His Love's bestowment put a ring on his hand.

The prodigal in his self-collapse exclaimed, " I perish." The Father in His Love's protection ordered shoes to be placed on his feet.

The prodigal in his self-misery found no one to help him, for " no man gave unto him." The Father in His Love's provision killed the fatted calf and feasted him.

The prodigal in his self-condemnation confessed he was unworthy, and was content with the place of a hired servant. The Father in His Love's satisfaction exclaimed, " This is My son."

The prodigal in his self-confession confessed, " I have sinned." The Father in His Love's defence, against the elder brother's criticism of His action for the prodigal, answers every charge.

Such love and such action makes us sing with Faber :

" That Thou shouldst be the God Thou art,
   And love me as Thou dost,
   Is darkness to my intellect,
   But sunshine to my heart."

This Lake is higher than God's throne. " Righteousness and judgment are the habitation of His throne." Righteousness and judgment are attributes of God, but Love is not an attribute, it is what God " is " in the essence of His being. We sing, " Love moved the mighty God." No, God, in His mighty love, moved. " God is Love." " In this was manifested the love of God towards us, because He sent His only

begotten Son into the world that we might live through Him.
Herein " (or, " In this ") " is Love, not that we loved God,
but that He loved us, and sent His Son to be a Propitiation "
(a Satisfaction) " for " (concerning) " our sins " (1 John
4 : 9, 10). This is how God in His love expressed Himself,
but that expression proves what He " is." David, long ago,
in his love for Absalom, when he knew he was slain, exclaimed,
" O my son Absalom : my son, my son Absalom ! Would
God I had died for thee, O Absalom, my son, my son !"
God did die for us ! God cannot die, but He Who died for
us is God ! For God, in the eternal value of His own Son
died for us. The Cross of God's love, the Lake of His grace,
reveals to us the heart of the One Who sits on the throne,
hence, He must be higher than the throne itself.

The Lake is broader than humanity's need. One of the
salient things in the life of Christ was He never met a need
but He supplied its necessity. When He saw the hungry
multitude He fed it. When He came against disease, He
banished it. When He beheld impotence, He energised it.
When He met death, He vivified it. When He saw a thirsty
soul, He satisfied it. When He beheld the eyes of sorrow
dripping with tears, He wiped them away. And when He
was appealed to for mercy and help, He always responded.

His very attitude on the Cross, as His form is extended
by the transfixing nails, is eloquent with loving appeal.
Those extended arms invite all to come to His saving
embrace. How true it is, the Cross reveals man at his worst,
and God at His best. " Where sin abounded, grace did
much more abound." These words are not general in their
statement, but particular in their application. At the Cross
the mountains of man's sin rose up to, and against heaven ;
but, thank God, the blood of Christ's atonement covered it
all. There is no sin but what that sacrifice has answered
for it.

This Lake is longer than eternity's chime. A boy once
said to the writer, as a Sunday School teacher, " When did
God have a beginning ?" Like a flash the answer came,
" There must have been someone without a beginning to
make a beginning." A deaf mute replied to the question

written on a blackboard, " What is eternity ?" " The life-time of God." The being of God is like a circle, without beginning or end. His love is like Himself, eternal. Hence, Love's givings are like Himself, eternal. The salvation He provides is eternal in its blessing. The life He gives is eternal in its holiness. The joy He bestows is eternal in its gladness. The redemption He affords is eternal in its issues. The relationship He effects is eternal in its outcome. The glory He brings is eternal in its satisfaction. And the love wherewith He loves is eternal in its affection.

> O Lake of God, so wide and boundless,
> O Love of God, so rich and free,
> I bathe my life in its abounding
> And I am satisfied in Thee.

II. The River

The Rockies feed the Lakes Superior, Huron and Michigan, in the United States, and these in turn make Lake Erie the sea it is. As Lake Erie nears the Niagara Falls it is confined by the nearing shores of Canada and the United States. Then as it comes closer to the Falls it speeds on with terrible onrush in the rapids above, and then drops with ominous sound over the Falls. Then on again for two miles, with whirling waters, till it reaches the whirlpool, and graduates down the last lap of rapids to the placid Lake Ontario. As the writer on one occasion stood on Goat Island, watching the tumultuous waters ere they went over the Falls, so as we watch the river of Christ's action, as He lived to die, we can see a correspondence between the waters of Erie's Falls and Himself.

Love leaped over the falls of man's sin. The legend of the " Maid of the Mist," and the many stories of those who lost their lives in the overwhelming waters of the Falls, are full of tragic interest, and not least among them is the love that prompted the maiden to leap into the waters where her lover had perished. That was a foolish act. But when the Lord would lift us out of our sin, it was essential He should identify Himself with us in it. The Gospel reveals not only Christ acting as our Substitute, but of His becoming so one with us in our sin that He speaks of our sin as His own, and therefore in Him we have answered for it. In the 38th Psalm, which is a Messianic one, we hear Christ speaking of " My sin," " Mine iniquities," " My wounds," " My sore," " My sorrow," " My sin," " Mine enemies," and " My salvation." Such sentences could not apply to Him personally for He had no sin, and knew no sin, therefore they must be understood representatively.

Love was confined in the gorge of human limitation. The cliffs that confine the whirling waters, after they have leaped the Falls, down to the placid waters of Lake Ontario, may be taken to illustrate how Christ placed Himself under human limitations by being Man. He was born in a manger, was thirsty and asked for a drink, was dependent upon others for His need to be met, preached from a loaned boat, slept in a tired body, buried in a borrowed tomb, and the only place He had to lay His head was on the Cross. The word for " lay," which occurs in the sentence " He had not where to lay His head," is the same as rendered " bowed " in referring to the fact that on the Cross " He bowed His head and gave up His spirit." How true it was. He emptied Himself of His glory that He might go to the gore of Calvary.

Love was whirled in the rapids and whirlpool of Calvary. The River Erie is illustrative again, for just as that river is whirled down the gorge, and swirled in the 400 feet of the whirlpool, so Christ in His sufferings on Calvary, exclaimed in prophecy, " Deep calleth unto deep at the noise of Thy waterspouts, all Thy waves and Thy billows have gone over Me " (Psa. 42 : 7). Jonah in the sea monster quotes this psalm when he exclaimed, " The floods compassed me about : all Thy waves and billows passed over me " (Jonah 2 : 3). Christ affirms Jonah's incarceration was a type of His death and resurrection, therefore, we are warranted in applying the words of the Psalmist to Him.

When Captain Webb risked his life, and lost it, in trying to swim through the rapids and the whirlpool, he took a chance of success or failure, but not so Christ. He deliberately and of His own choice laid down His life. His five-fold declaration in John 10 about His life was, " The Good Shepherd layeth down His life," and " I lay it down of Myself, no man taketh it from Me." " I have authority to lay it down and authority to take it again." His death was no accident. His star of destiny was His death on Calvary. " Deep" called " unto deep" on Calvary. The " deep" of man's sin, and Christ's answer for it. The " deep" of God's purpose, and the deep of Christ's fulfilment of it. The " deep" of God's justice, and the deep of His mercy. The " deep" of God's righteous requirement, and the deep of Christ's satisfaction in meeting it. The " deep" of God's being of Light called to the deep of His love in mutual action.

" If I were God," said a great German, " the sorrows of the world would break my heart." One, in referring to this saying, said : " He did not know what he said : the sorrows of the world did break the heart of God." Physically, the heart of Christ was not broken, but spiritually His spirit was anguished in death, His soul was poured out in love. His body was pierced with suffering. His brow was torn with thorns. His tongue was parched with the fire of hell. His hands were torn with the lacerating nails. His feet were transfixed with the spikes of perdition. His face was marred with the blast of sin's punishment. His body was racked on the rack of anguish.

Love's act leads to the placid Lake of peace. The whirlpool waters rush on in their rush to the town of Lewistown, but when those waters reach Niagara-on-the-Lake they are calm and placid as they merge into Lake Ontario. So the blood of Christ's spurting flood leads to the peace which He has made by His Cross, and what a peace that is ! It is calm as the throne of God, and bears on its bosom forgiveness of sins, eternal life, cleansing of the conscience, justification, holiness, purity, joy, and relationship with God as His children.

III. The Pitcher

God's provisions must be received by our takings if we are to have their benefits. It is said that a ship on one occasion was in Lake Ontario, and those on board were almost to the extreme point of dying of thirst. A passing ship was hailed, and fresh water requested, when, to the astonishment of those on board, in clarion notes through a megaphone the answer came, "Dip it up! Dip it up! The water around you is fresh." The remedy to their thirst was within their reach, but they did not know it. So men do not know the remedy for their thirst is within their reach in Him Who is the Water of Life. God's message is, "The Word is nigh thee, even in thy mouth and in thy heart. That if thou shalt confess Jesus as Lord (R.V.) and believe in thine heart that God hath raised Him from the dead, thou shalt be saved" (Rom. 10 : 8, 9). The full flood of God's provision is flowing past us, and unless we put into it the pitcher of faith, we shall not get the benefit of His love's giving.

The difference between salvation provided in the death of Christ, and the acceptance of the provision made, is very well illustrated in the following incident. In 1829 or 1830, George Wilson, in Pennsylvania, was sentenced to be hanged by a United States Court in Philadelphia for robbing the mails and murder. Andrew Jackson, as President of the United States, pardoned him, but Wilson refused the pardon, and insisted that it was not a pardon unless he accepted it. That was a point in law never before raised in the U.S.A. The Attorney-General said the law was silent on the point. The President was urged to call upon the Supreme Court to decide the point at once, as the Sheriff must know whether to hang Wilson or not. Chief Justice John Marshall, one of the ablest lawyers, gave the following decision : "A pardon is a paper, the value of which depends upon its acceptance by the person implicated. It is hardly to be supposed that one under sentence of death would refuse to accept a pardon, but if it is refused, it is no pardon. George Wilson must be hanged." And he was hanged. Who was responsible for his death ? No one but the man himself. The law said he must die. The President stepped in between him and the law, and the man refused the pardon.

Indirectly, the Supreme Court of the United States decided that the truth of the atonement of Christ, in making provision for the salvation of the whole world, is only beneficial to those who receive Him as their own personal Saviour. The righteousness of God is *unto* all in its *offer*, but it is *upon* them that believe in its *benefit* (Rom. 3 : 22).

IV. The Draught

" Eternal life " is the draught ! What a draught that is ! Who can estimate its contents and measure its wealth ? Westcott says, " Eternal life is not an endless duration of being in time, but being of which time is not a measure. It is beyond the limitations of time : it belongs to the being of God." Farrar has said something similar, " By qualifying the Divine life by the epithet ' eternal,' John meant not an endless life, but a spiritual life, the life which is in God, and which was manifest by Christ to us. By calling it eternal, he meant to imply . . . its ethical quality . . . its internal quality."

Keeping before us what Farrar says, that " Eternal life " is an " internal " and " ethical " quality, we may ask the question, " What is physical life ?" We read in the Epistle of James, " The body without the spirit is dead," so that we may say, physical life is the union of the spirit with the body, by means of the soul. What is spiritual life ? The union of the individual with God by means of the Lord Jesus. Christ Himself affirms this when He declares, " This is life eternal that they might know Thee, the only true God, and Jesus Christ, Whom Thou hast sent." The knowledge is more than knowing about, it is being personally acquainted with. " By means " of our Lord Jesus, this union is effected and effective.

Some years ago, when living in the West of England, in my garden there was a scabby, sour apple tree. The apples were so sour that they were hardly fit for cooking. One day I asked a gardener friend if he would not graft some good apple-grafts on the old stock. Having cut down the branches, he proceeded to graft two or three good grafts, and among them was a Peasgood-nonsuch and a Blenheim Orange. Within the compass of two or three years that old sour stock was producing some of the finest and most luscious apples ever eaten. The introduction of the new life overcame the old life. The same thing is true in the implantation of the spiritual life when we who believe in Christ are made alive unto God. That Life in its working counteracts the sour stock of our sinful nature, and produces the love of the

Spirit, for that Life in its manifestation is love. " We know we have passed from death unto life, because we love." Where love is wanting, life is lacking. What is love ? It is fulfilling life's mission with love's mercies. It is meeting the need of others at the expense of our life. We cease to bless when we cease to bleed. The living hand of love is full of gifts in ministering to the need of others. The lavishing heart of love beats in unison with the Heart of Grace, which bestows its best upon those who are the worst. When a Godly clergyman in the East End of London died, it was found in his will he had left a sum of money which was to be given to the undeserving poor ! The Church is so unlike Christ because she knows so little of Him. If Christians knew Him better, they would be better. If we took more from Him, we would be better. The late A. B. Simpson, in the hearing of the writer, on one occasion said, " The Lord is not finding fault with us because we are not better, but because we don't take more." I said to him after his address, " If we took more, we would be better." He replied, " Exactly, that's what I was driving at." Let us take a deep, long, and constant draught of this eternal life, and then we shall become like it, for it is holy in its nature, powerful in its working, and satisfying in its contents.

JEHOVAH'S LOVING PLAN FOR ISRAEL

Plan and purpose are stamped on the works of God's hands. The cycles of the tree, the number three on the bee, the variegated glories of the flowers, the grasses in their variety, the vitalities of the birds, the stars in their movements, the sun and moon in their ministries, the insects in their make, yea, all nature uttereth His glory, and declares the skill of Him Who createth and sustaineth all things.

What we see in nature we behold in God's dealings with the nations of the earth, and in the providence of His actions. The living Spirit ever moves in the cherubim of His righteous administrators, and they in turn are the instruments to regulate the wheels of His providential dealings with men (Ezek. i).

Jehovah in His dealings with Israel is regulating all things along the rails of His plan. The late Adolph Saphir said, " How many have wept over Israel, for whose sorrow can be compared with the sorrow of Jerusalem as Jeremiah laments. Your poet has said, ' The wild dove hath a nest, the fox its cave, mankind its country, Israel its grave.' Oh, no, a thousand times, no. Israel has the Scriptures, and these Scriptures it is which have kept Israel alive. Different from all nations, Israel has the Scriptures, and whenever the Holy Spirit breathes upon them, they shall behold Jesus, for the future is still before them, and that future which is spoken of all the holy prophets." Yes, Israel has the Scriptures, and in the Scriptures there shines out amid the surrounding darkness the Southern Cross of God's precious promises, which point to a glorious future for Israel, for there is no uncertainty in the voice of their testimony. In Rome there is to be seen the triumphal arch of Titus, representing his victory over Israel in the past. On it the captive Jews are seen, and the seven-branched candlestick, with the table of shewbread. There is another triumphal arch to be seen, and that is found in Rom. 9 : 11, and on this is written, " All Israel shall be saved " (Rom. 11 : 26).

The Book of Ezekiel is full of prophetic fore-gleams and emphatic predictions regarding Jehovah's future plans for Israel. One peculiar thing about these predictions is the certainty of their utterance. There are over three hundred " I Wills " in the book of Ezekiel. Some have been fulfilled, others, the majority of them, are yet to be fulfilled. In pondering those " I wills " in their setting, we find there are at least seven phases of Jehovah's plan in relation to Israel.

1. Israel and the Promised Land.

2. Israel and the Great Tribulation.

3. Israel and their Spiritual Restoration.

4. Israel and their Permanent Establishment in the Land.

5. Israel and the Throne of David.

6. Israel and their Blessing to Others.

7. Israel and Jehovah's Assurance to the Nation.

I. Jehovah's Plan Regarding Israel and the Promised Land

In Ezek. 11 : 16, 17, we read, " Therefore say," in spite of what Judah might say about their exclusive right to the land and the ten tribes (Israel), " Thus saith the Lord God, although I have cast them far off among the nations " (R.V.), " and although I have scattered them among the countries, yet will I be a little sanctuary in the countries where they shall come. Therefore, thus saith the Lord God, I will even gather you from among the people " (R.V., " peoples," i.e., nations), " and assemble you out of the countries where ye have been scattered, and I will give you the land of Israel."

There are three things to notice here. First, the fact of the dispersion of the nation of Israel. They are a people without a land. Scattered about like the feathers of a downy pillow, that has been rent and blown hither and thither by a fierce wind. Second, the promise of the Lord to be " a little sanctuary " to the people of His choice, assuring them of His love, care, and protection, in spite of all their distress and disloyalty ; and third, He pledges Himself to recover His people, and gather them back to their own land, even as the mother bird gathers her brood under her protecting wings. Mark how emphatic is His promise, " I will gather," " I will be," " I will give you the land of Israel." And He further pledges Himself by the way He speaks of Himself, " Thus saith the Lord God," that is, " Adonahy Jehovah." " Adonahy " signifies the One Who has proprietary rights : and " GOD " in small capitals declares God as Jehovah, that is, the Immutable One, Who will cause to be all He has promised. He will claim what are His rights, and He can do what He says, for He has the power.

In Ezek. 20 : 34, 40, 41, Jehovah says, " I will bring you out from the people " (R.V., " peoples "—nations), " and will gather you out of the countries wherein ye are scattered with a mighty hand, and with a stretched-out arm, and with fury poured out. . . . For in Mine holy mountain, in the mountain of the height of Israel, saith the Lord GOD, there shall all the house of Israel, all them in the land, serve Me : there will I accept them, and there will I require your offerings and the firstfruits of your oblations, with all your holy things."

Jehovah's Doings in the Past are the Guarantee of what He will do in the Future. The reference to Jehovah's "mighty hand" and "stretched out arm" at once takes us back to what He did in delivering Israel from Egyptian bondage (Ex. 6:6; Deut. 5:15), and which He continually refers to in giving a pledge of His future actions (Jer. 32:21). God's "has-beens" are guarantees of what will be. "I will bring them out from the people" (R.V., "peoples"), "and gather them from the countries, and I will bring them to their own land, and feed them upon the mountains of Israel by the rivers, and in all the inhabited places of the country. . . . For I will take you from among the heathen (nations), and gather you out of all countries, and I will bring you into your own land . . . . and say unto them : Thus saith the Lord GOD, Behold, I will take the children of Israel from among the heathen (nations), whither they be gone, and I will gather them on every side, and bring them into their own land . . . . I will bring again the captivity of Judah."

THE PLACE to which He will bring them is "to their own land" . . . "The mountains of Israel" . . . "Your own land" . . . "In their land." HIS PERFORMANCE IS succinctly expressed by such words as "Bring them out" . . . "Gather" . . . "Feed" . . . "Take" . . . "Bring" . . . "Have mercy" . . . "Dwell safely."

His Pledge of Promise in His "I will," is His assurance that He will perform what He has promised. He cannot go back on His word, for in the long ago He entered into a covenant with Himself to Abraham. We read, "THE LORD made a covenant with Abraham, saying, Unto thy seed have I given this land, from the river of Egypt unto the great river Euphrates" (Gen. 15:18). The extent of the land possessed by Israel did not reach to these limits. The extent of the land actually possessed became a proverb, namely, "From Dan to Beersheba" (1. Sam. 3:20). From Dan to Beersheba only occupied about 28,000 or 30,000 square miles. According to Ezek. 48:13-21, the Promised Land is to extend far beyond the boundaries ever possessed by Israel

yet. According to Dr. Keith, the Promised Land extends to
Mount Cassius on the River Arontes, as the North-west
boundary—the true entering into Hamath—and to Bir or
Berothah, on the Upper Euphrates, on the North-east
boundary. That is about 100 miles across from West to
East, with the mountains of Amanus at the back, shutting in
the Promised Land like an enclosed garden. The South-
west boundary is the river of Egypt—the Nile—and the
South-east boundary is the River Euphrates, where it empties
itself into the Persian Gulf. The Southern breadth of the
land from the Nile to the Euphrates is 1,100 or 1,300 miles.
The Western boundary is the Mediterranean Sea, and the
River Euphrates the Eastern boundary. The length of the
land from North to South is about 600 miles : which makes
the Promised Land about 300,000 square miles. This is
twice and a half as large as Great Britain and Ireland."

When the Land of Promise is fully possessed, then shall
come to pass what Jehovah hath declared : " When I have
brought them again from the people " (nations), " and
gathered them out of the enemies' lands, and am sanctified
in them in the sight of many nations : then shall they know
I am the LORD their God, which caused them to be led into
captivity among the nations, but I have gathered them unto
their own land, and have left none of them any more there.
Neither will I hide My face any more from them : for I have
poured out My Spirit upon the house of Israel, saith the LORD
God " (Ezek. 39 : 27-29).

The gathering of Israel back to their own land, is one
of the most wonderful of Jehovah's promises. Mark its
contents, and ponder its comprehensiveness. Jehovah has
pledged the gathering shall be accomplished. He speaks of
it as an accomplished fact. He declares the nations shall see
what He has done. He affirms the nations shall know He is
Jehovah, the Proprietor of Israel. He asserts the nations
shall recognize He is the One Who scattered Israel, and
gathered too. He promises the gathering shall not be
partial, but complete, so that none are left among the nations.
He assures His people He will not " hide His face " from
them " any more." He says He will give them great spiritual

blessing, for He will and has " poured out " His Spirit upon the House of Israel; and He signs Himself as " the Lord " (Adonahy, the Owner), and GOD (Jehovah).

II. Jehovah's Plan is to Cause Tribulation Upon His People in the Land

This Tribulation is Predicted by Jeremiah. " For, lo, the days come, saith the Lord, that I will bring again the captivity of My people Israel and Judah, saith the Lord : and I will cause them to return to the land that I gave to their fathers, and they shall possess it. And these are the words of the Lord concerning Israel and Judah. For thus saith the Lord, we have heard a voice trembling, of fear, and not of peace. Ask ye now, and see whether a man doth travail with child ? Wherefore do I see every man with his hands on his loins, as a woman in travail, and all faces are turned into paleness ? Alas ! for the day is great, so that none is like it : it is even the time of Jacob's trouble, and he shall be saved out of it " (Jer. 30 : 3-7).

There are seven things which lie on the surface of this prophecy :

(1) *Prediction.* Three times attention is called to what Jehovah " saith," and " the words that Jehovah spake." When Jehovah predicts, He is under the necessity to fulfil what He proclaims. His utterance is like the dawn, it illuminates and arrests.

(2) *Exception.* This time of trouble is exceptional. There has never been anything " like it " before, nor will there be again. This is not ordinary suffering and tribulation. It is the " great one " (Rev. 7 : 14, R.V.).

(3) *Location.* The centre of the fierceness of this time of anguish is in the Land of Palestine, and in Jerusalem. Where the blood of Christ was shed there will the blood be shed upon that race who said, " His blood be upon us and our children " (Matt. 27 : 25). Their prayer will be answered. The supper of the great God will be enacted (Rev. 19 : 17), where the Lord's Supper was instituted (Matt. 26 : 26).

(4) *Description.* Fear haunts the people as they hear the " voice of trembling, fear " and unrest, and men have the

unusual experience of travail pain, like a woman in the time of her trial, hence Jehovah says, "Ask ye now, and see whether a man doth travail with child." Such a question indicates the time of anguish coming upon the nation.

(5) *Restoration.* "He shall be saved out of it," declares the Spirit, in calling attention to the time of Jacob's trouble. "None like it" in the fierceness of the tribulation, and none like it in the grace and love of the Lord's triumph.

(6) *Emancipation.* "I will bring." "I will cause." By His own "I will" He assures His people of their deliverance. He cannot go back from the covenant He made with Abraham long ago (Gen. 17 : 1-19). He would not if He could, and could not if He would.

(7) *Affirmation.* When we read, "Thus saith the LORD," or Jehovah, He binds Himself to all He is as the Unchanging One to perform what He says. The name of Jehovah comes from the ancient form of the verb to be, which means, He will cause to be what He says, because of what is in Himself, for He is by Himself, in Himself, through Himself, and for Himself, therefore He cannot go back on Himself. We know this, but how gracious of Himself to tell us so.

Space will not permit us to pursue further the theme of the Tribulation through which Judah and Israel will pass, but we ask our readers to study Ezekiel's prophecy in Ezek. 22 : 17-22, the foregleam of the same theme in Dan. 12 : 1 ; the description given in Joel 2, Zech. 12 ; the prophetic word of our Lord in Matt. 24 : 21-24 ; the pictorial representation of the persecution of the woman in Rev. 12 ; and the details given under the fifth, sixth and seventh seals of the Book of the Revelation.

III. Jehovah's Plan is to Cause the Nation to be Restored to Him, and to Give Great Spiritual Blessing

Declension from God is always the cause of departure from Him. Again and again Jehovah declared, "Because ye have done all these works" of wickedness, "and have not heard My words" (Jer. 7 : 13 ; 25 : 8), therefore, punishment and disaster have followed. Yet in spite of all, He loved, and has mercy upon His people. But while He in

grace restores them to their land, yet He also quickens them
by His Spirit with a spiritual restoration to Himself. Let us
briefly note seven blessings He will give :

(1) *Life from Jehovah.* " Thus saith the Lord God . . .
Behold I will cause breath to enter into you, and ye shall
live " (Ezek. 37 : 5, 6). The vision of the condition of Israel
is likened to a valley of dry bones, very dead, and very dry.
In the graves of rationalism and unbelief the nation lies, till
the quickening breath of Jehovah vitalises it into faith in
Christ, and into newness of life. When men are dead to
God they are dead to everything that matters, and dead to
themselves. This Israel will find as a nation.

(2) *Cleansing by Jehovah.* When Israel is restored to
the Land, the Lord GOD (Adonahy, Jehovah) declares, " Then
will I sprinkle clean water upon you, and ye shall be clean
from all your filthiness, and from all your idols will I cleanse
you." The effectiveness of this cleansing is assured, for the
Lord will do it : and the thoroughness of it also is declared,
for it will be from " all " filthiness and idols. There are no
half measures with God. When He cleanses there are no
streaks of slime, no traces of crime, left behind.

(3) *Love to Jehovah.* When the generating power of life
is lacking, there is no " spontaneous " power to produce ;
but when Jehovah acts, He will cause to be what cannot be
otherwise. He affirms, " A new heart also will I give you,
and a new spirit will I put within you, and I will take away
the stony heart out of your flesh, and I will give you a heart
of flesh " (Ezek. 36 : 26). Mark the " also." To have the
cobwebs of sin removed, and not to clear out the spiders
would be fatal ; but when the Lord puts the spring of His
love to move, then the time of His truth shows itself on the
dial of life. His love moulds us and makes us like to Himself.

(4) *Sanctified in Jehovah.* Like the clarion note of the
jubilee trumpet which pealed forth liberation to Israel in the
long ago (Lev. 25 : 9, 10), so the Lord in the jubilant sound
of His grace declares as to His future action towards Israel.
" I will sanctify My great name " (the Name of Jehovah),
" which was profaned among the nations, which ye have
profaned in the midst of them, and the nations shall know

I am Jehovah, saith the Adonahy Jehovah, when I shall be sanctified in you before their eyes" (Ezek. 36 : 23). In many ways Jehovah will sanctify His people in the eyes of the nations, and especially when He shall make them a holy people to Himself. Like the sun in its shining, He will cause His consecrating power to be made known.

(5) *Identified with Jehovah.* "And ye shall dwell in the Land that I gave to your fathers, and ye shall be My people, and I will be your God" (Ezek. 36 : 28). Jehovah as the living God identifies Himself with His people, and makes them one with Himself. Many a person, brought up in lowly surroundings has been honoured by one who has lifted them from those surroundings by marriage. Jehovah will show Himself as the One Who will manifest Himself with Israel.

(6) *Power from Jehovah.* Deeper and larger grows Jehovah's blessing. There is no withholding in His givings, hence we read : " I will put My Spirit within you, and cause you to walk in My statutes, and ye shall keep My judgments, and do them " (Ezek. 36 : 27). Here is the motive power and the moving grace which will operate in the people. When the Holy Spirit is the Cause there must be results. When He is absent, all is wrong. When He is present all is clean within and mighty without.

(7) *Supplied through Jehovah.* Literally, in food supplies, and spiritually, in gracious giving, shall it be true, for He says, " I will call for the corn and will increase it, and lay no famine upon you " (Ezek. 36 : 29). Grace and godliness are the twin sisters of God's benedictions. Where the one goes, the other follows. When spiritual supplies are coming in, the famine of depletion is not present. Meanness of soul will soon empty the cupboard, but largeness of reception from the supply of heaven's resources dissipates all want.

IV. Jehovah's Plan is that the Next Restoration of Israel shall be a Final One

The following assuring and clear statements need no comment. In speaking of Israel as His flock, Jehovah says, " I will make with them a covenant of peace, and will cause the evil beasts to cease out of the land : and they shall dwell safely in the wilderness, and sleep in the woods. And I will make them and the places round about My hill a blessing : and I will cause the shower to come down in his season : and there shall be showers of blessing. And the tree of the field shall yield her fruit, and the earth shall yield her increase, and they shall be safe in their land, and shall know I am Jehovah when I have broken the bonds of their yoke, and delivered them out of the hand of those that served themselves of them, and they shall no more be a prey to the nations, neither shall the beast of the field devour them, but they shall dwell safely, and none shall make them afraid " (Ezek. 34 : 25-28). Such sentences in the above verses, proclaim the completeness and continuity of blessing, namely, " I will cause the evil beast to cease out of the land." " They shall be safe in the land." " They shall no more be a prey to the nations." " They shall dwell safely," and He further adds, " I will dwell in the midst of the children of Israel forever " (Ezek. 43 : 7), and " Judah shall dwell " (" abide ") " forever, and Jerusalem from one generation to another " (Joel 3 : 20) ; and yet one other climaxing passage, where Jehovah exclaims in triumphal language : " And I will plant them upon their land, and they shall no more be pulled out of their land, which I have given them, saith the Lord thy God " (Amos 9 : 15). Let the clarion note be rung out again and again, " No more be pulled out of their land."

V. Jehovah's Plan is to Make One King over all Israel

There are two great trunk lines of prophecy in the prophetic Word. One associated with Abraham and the Land, and the other connected with David and the Throne. As to the latter, if the reader will ponder 2 Sam. 7 : 4-29, he will find the covenant that Jehovah made with David had to do with Great David's Greater Son, and not merely with Solomon. Solomon's throne has crumbled to the dust, and his sun waned under the clouds of disgrace. But the future dynasty shall " move no more," " the throne of His kingdom " shall be " forever," the " mercy of " Jehovah " shall not depart from Him," and it shall be established.

Ezekiel focuses the same covenant with David, when Jehovah through him declares "David, My servant, shall be king over them, and they shall have one shepherd, they shall also walk in My judgments, and observe My statutes, and do them. And they shall dwell in the land that I have given unto Jacob My servant, wherein your fathers have dwelt, and they shall dwell therein, even they, and their children, and their children's children: and My servant David shall be their prince forever" (Ezek. 37:24, 25). When that comes to pass then shall be fulfilled the prediction which was given to Mary, relating to David's Lord, "He shall be great, and shall be called the Son of the Highest, and the Lord God shall give unto Him the throne of His Father David, and He shall reign over the house of Jacob forever, and of His kingdom there shall be no end" (Luke 1:32, 33).

When the King reigns over Israel, they will not want to say, as the Jews said to Pilate, when they wanted to reverse the inscription on the cross, "Jesus of Nazareth, the King of the Jews,"—"Write not, The King of the Jews, but that He said, 'I am the King of the Jews'"; for then they will exclaim, "O clap your hands, all ye people, shout unto God with the shout of triumph. For the Lord most high is terrible, He is a great King over all the earth. He shall subdue the people under us, and the nations under our feet. He shall choose our inheritance for us, the excellency of Jacob, whom He loved—Selah. God is gone up with a shout, Jehovah, with the sound of a trumpet. Sing praises to God, sing praises, sing praises unto our King, sing praises. For God is the King of all the earth: sing ye praises with understanding. God reigneth over all the nations. God sitteth on the throne of His holiness. The princes of the people are gathered together, even the people of the God of Abraham, for the shields of the earth belong unto God, He is greatly exalted" (Psa. 47:1-9).

VI. Jehovah's Plan is to Make Israel a Medium of Blessing to the World

A pamphlet on Zionism, issued by the authorities of the movement, affirms in speaking of the "mission of Israel," it was " not in his developing his own full national life on the ancient soil, but in his being scattered among the peoples, there to teach the unity of God, and His demands for a righteous life." This quotation recognizes that the nation will have a mission in being a blessing to others. The same pamphlet affirms, " The Jewish people have a spiritual history, as well as a material history, and they hope, therefore, for a spiritual future, as well as for mere existence as a separate unit."

This is according to the first promise given to Abraham, which was, " In thee shall all the families of the earth be blessed " (Gen. 12 : 3). Apart from many passages of Scripture in the Old Testament (Ezek. 34 : 26 ; 39 : 21 ; Zeph. 3 : 19, 20), we have the Spirit's utterance through the Apostle Paul, when he says : " For if the casting away of them be the reconciling of the world, what shall the receiving of them be but life from the dead ?" (Rom. 11 : 15). Israel's rejection for the time being has allowed Gentiles, who have no covenant of promise, to come in, but when the Lord's purpose is completed in relation to His Church, then Israel will be blest again, and their blessing will mean salvation to the world.

The late beloved John Wilkinson, in comparing the purpose of God to a railway track, used to say there were two trains on the track. The Jewish train, and the train of the Church. The Jewish train was shunted on to a siding to let the express train of the Church pass through, and when it was passed, then the Jewish train would come on to the main track again. That's another way of saying what the Apostle declared, when he said the Lord would bring in Israel again after the Church was completed, for His purpose is " All Israel shall be saved."

VII. The Jewish Plan, as Stated in Holy Scripture, will Surely be Carried Through, for Jehovah has Assured His People, by His Own Immutability, He Will Do It

Jehovah refers to the past scattering of the nation, for did He not predict through Jeremiah what He would do, and has He not done it ? His word was : " They shall know I am Jehovah, when I shall scatter them among the nations. and disperse them in the countries"; and He affirmed, "The word that I speak shall come to pass," and "the word which I have spoken shall be done" (Ezek. 12 : 15, 25, 28). The word of the future shall equally be fulfilled, and the nations will have to acknowledge the truth of His prophetic Word, for the Lord says, "Then the nations shall know that I, Jehovah, will build the ruined places, and plant that that was desolate, I, Jehovah, hath spoken it, and I will do it" (Ezek. 36 : 36).

There is a Jewish legend which represents two venerable rabbis musing among the ruins of Jerusalem, after its destruction. One laments, as he views the situation, "Alas! Alas! This is the end of all. Our beautiful city is no more, the holy temple is laid waste, and our brethren are driven away."

The other is animated with hope, and has a brighter outlook, and replies cheerfully, "True, but let us learn from the verities of God's judgments, the certainty of His mercies. He hath said, 'I will destroy,' and we have seen He has done it ; but He has also said, 'I will rebuild Jerusalem,' and shall we not believe Him?"

Seven times in the book of Deuteronomy He declared His love for Israel, which may be taken in a predictive sense :

Jehovah's Love is *Sovereign in its choice.* "Because He loved thy fathers, therefore He chose their seed" (Deut. 4 : 37) ; and in Jer. 31, in a series of "I wills" of promise, He pledges to bless them because He has "Loved them with an everlasting love" (Jer. 31 : 3).

Jehovah's Love is *Selective in its object.* "The Lord did not set His love upon you, nor choose you, because ye were more in number than any people, for ye were the fewest of all people" (Deut. 7 : 7). He speaks in a similar strain when He says His people shall see evil no more, for He "will rest in His love" (Zeph. 3 : 17).

Jehovah's Love is *Sacred in its remembrance.* The double reason for His choice was "Because the LORD loved, and because He would keep the oath which He had sworn to your fathers" (Deut. 7 : 8). The same note is heard when Israel recounts the "compassion" of Jehovah in blessing, and says, " Thou wilt perform the truth to Jacob, and the mercy to Abraham " (Micah 7 : 20).

Jehovah's Love is *Sanctifying in its outcome.* " The Lord had a delight in thy fathers to love them . . . circumcise therefore the foreskin of your hearts " (Deut. 10 : 15, 16). Love will captivate and consecrate when all else will fail. Israel's testimony is again to the point, for in speaking of Him, Who " delighteth in mercy," the remnant says, " He will subdue our iniquities " (Micah 7 : 18, 19).

His Love is *Supplying in its bestowment.* " He loveth the stranger " (Deut. 10 : 18), and this is found in His love for Israel, therefore they are to do the same. This again is in keeping with His love for the nation, for the ancient promise is, " I will bless thee . . . and in thee shall the families of the earth be blessed " (Gen. 12 : 1-3). Love appreciates God's love in loving others.

Jehovah's Love is *Strong in its determination.* Balaam's curse was turned into a blessing, and the reason " Because the Lord thy GOD loved thee " (Deut. 23 : 5). In a chapter which speaks of the Lord's judgments, we find coupled " with the day of vengeance," the " year of the redeemed," and based upon His deliverances for Israel is the " Lovingkindness " and " Love of the LORD " (Isa. 63 : 1-9). The love of God, like the rolling tide of the sea, submerges all that stands in the way of its purpose.

Jehovah's Love is *Singular in its benediction.* " Yea, He loved the people," is the statement which is the crystal sentence in the midst of a cluster of blessings upon Israel (Deut. 33 : 3). Jehovah's love in blessing Israel is the object lesson which commands our attention, stirs our love, animates our faith, and feeds our devotion.

THE EPISTLE TO THE EPHESIANS, AN ILLUSTRATION OF GOD'S GENERAL PURPOSE FOR THE CHURCH

Johnson once said to his friend Boswell : " Sir, you have two subjects—yourself and myself,—and I am sick of both." The best of men soon tire of the best in man. Not so with

Christ. He is the same, yesterday, to-day and forever, without any sameness. He is always fresh. There are infinite resources in Him, therefore, He can ever satisfy the need of the finite. This is brought out in this wonderful Epistle of Divine riches. Everything is summarized and summed up " in Christ " Himself.

Renan calls this Epistle " a third-rate composition!" Of such a statement we say, " It is low-rate impudence." We agree with Samuel Taylor Coleridge when he calls the Epistle " one of the Divinest compositions of men." Even this commendation is deficient : I would rather speak of the Epistle as the Divine unfolding of God Himself in the Man of men. Huxley, on one occasion, in looking at the evolution of a minute form of life under the microscope, spoke of " The Unseen Worker." As we take this Epistle and ponder it in its Divine unfolding, we see the perfect plan of the Divine Worker, God Himself, for it is essentially and distinctly a revelation of the Divine. The sweep of the Epistle contains seven Divine things, namely :

    I.   The Divine Purpose (1 : 3-14).

    II.   The Divine Power (1 : 15-2).

    III.   The Divine Proclamation (3 : 1-13).

    IV.   The Divine Presence (3 : 14-21).

    V.   The Divine Provision (4 : 1-16).

    VI.   The Divine Pattern (4 : 17—6 : 9).

    VII.   The Divine Panoply (6 : 10-20).

I. The Divine Purpose (1 : 3-14)

The first two verses of the Epistle embody the salutation, then comes the unfolding of the counsels relating to the Divine purpose in Christ in connection with the redeemed.

There are three points to ponder—the Centralizer, the Centralization, and the Centralized.

The Centralizer is " the God and Father of our Lord Jesus " (verse 3), hence we read of—

    1. His blessing us with all spiritual blessing (verse 3).

    2. His choice of us before Creation (verse 4).

3. His placing us before Himself "without blemish" (verse 4, R.V.).

4. His foreordination of us to Himself in adoption as His children (verse 5). This refers to place, and not to nature.

5. His sovereign act in doing all according to His good pleasure (verse 5).

6. His enhancing of His glory through His grace (verses 6, 12).

7. His bestowment of grace "in the Beloved" (verse 6, R.V.).

8. His redemptive act by means of Christ's blood (verse 7).

9. His wisdom made known in His actions (verse 8).

10. His will unfolded in His revealed secret (verse 9).

11. His goal in summing all up in the Christ (verse 10, R.V.).

12. His mind revealed in our association with Christ (verse 11).

13. His sealing with the Spirit in claiming us as His own (verse 13).

14. His possession of the redeemed and their glory (verse 14).

The Centralization is in the Christ. Not in the national blessing of Israel, not in the doom of the world, not in the many-headed monster of mystified twentieth century development, but " in Christ."

In the Christ of Deity—" Lord " (verse 2).

In the Christ of Calvary—" His Blood " (verse 7).

In the Christ of Sonship—" by Jesus Christ " (verse 5).

In the Christ of the heavenly places (verse 3).

In the Christ of God's Purpose (verse 10).

In the Christ of the Holy Spirit (verse 13).

In the Christ of the coming glory (verse 14).

All blessing is in Him, and in no one else beside.

The Centralized are spoken of as being—

" Saints " as to standing (verse 1).

" Faithful " as to service (verse 1).

" Blessed " as to enrichment (verse 3).

" Children " as to relationship (verse 5).

" Accepted " as to position (verse 6).

" Redeemed " as to liberty (verse 7).

" Sealed " as to possession (verse 13).

All this makes known to us the sovereignty of God's grace in blessing us. A lady once objected to the truth of election, to a servant of God. He advised her to read the 5th, 6th, and 17th chapters of John, where the words " elect " and " election " do not occur. He said to her, " And have you chosen Him, or do you think Christ has chosen you ?"

" Yes, He has chosen me, and I have chosen Him."

" If you chose Him first," he rejoined, " you make yourself to differ, and salvation is of works : if the Divine choice was first, your choice of Christ was the effect of it, and salvation is of grace."

II. The Divine Power (1 : 15-2)

The Divine power is demonstrated in two ways : First, in the resurrection of Christ from the dead ; and, second, in the salvation of the believer.

Christ's Resurrection (1 : 18-20). There are three " whats " of meanful importance which the Spirit's illumination enables us to see :

" *What* is the hope of His calling."

" *What* is the riches of the glory of His inheritance."

" *What* is the greatness of His power."

" *The Hope of His calling* " is what He will have when the Lord has accomplished all His purpose.

" The riches of *His inheritance* " is what the Lord has in His people.

And " the greatness of *His power* " is what He demonstrated in Christ's resurrection on our behalf, and what He can do for us, and in us.

The sweep and substance of that power is apprehended as we ponder the seven words— " Power," " Greatness," " Exceeding," " Power," " Mighty," " Working," " Wrought."

" *Power.*" The first word rendered " power " in verse 19 signifies power as an inherent quality, and then the manifestation of power in action. Power is latent in the inactive dynamite, but its power is patent when it explodes and rends the massive rock. Power was latent in Christ before the woman touched the hem of His garment, but it was patent in her, when it flowed from Him into her, and healed her of her disease. The word " virtue " in Luke 8 : 46 is the same as rendered " power " in Eph. 1 : 19.

" *Greatness.*" This word only occurs here, but it is derived from a word which signifies magnitude and magnificence, hence we read of " The Great God," " The Great High Priest," and " The Great Shepherd."

" *Exceeding.*" This is a compound word, one part meaning that which is over and above something else, and the other part meaning to throw, hence the word means to go beyond a given point.

" *Power.*" The second word in verse 19 denotes the manifestation of power, as when we read, " He shewed strength with His arm."

" *Mighty* " expresses inherent power. We speak of a statesman as being " wise," a soldier as being " valiant," and a powerful person as being " strong." Personal force and ability is meant.

" *Working* " and " *Wrought.*" These words come from one and the same source. They denote right and might, with the added thought of efficiency.

The Divine power which raised Christ from the dead is the same which operates in the believer's salvation, for no other power can meet the case. Chapter 2 opens with the significant words, " And you." If the italicised words are left out—" hath He quickened "—it will give clearness to the thought, that as the dead body of Christ was quickened by the powerful act of God, so that same power is needed to quicken from the death of sin. Rotherham renders it, " Unto you also." What the Lord has wrought for us is brought out or suggested in chapter 2 if we ponder what we were and what we are.

What we were.	*What we are.*
Separated from God—" dead."	Quickened.
Walking after the world.	Walking in Love.
Dominated by Satan.	United to Christ.
Children of disobedience.	Children of God.
Living after the flesh.	Indwelt by the Spirit.
Children of wrath.	Saved by Grace.
Without Christ.	In Christ.
Aliens.	Joint Heirs.
Hopeless.	Habitation of God.
Godless.	Access to the Father.
Far off.	Made nigh.
Enemies.	Reconciled.
Strangers.	Fellow Citizens.
Foreigners.	Household of Faith.

III. The Divine Proclamation (3 : 1-13)

The Apostle was in no doubt as to his message and the power which was behind him to make it effectual. His topic was Christ. The best kind of preacher is the one who preaches Christ, and the one through whom Christ preaches. One friend once asked another, " Where can I hear a good sermon ?" The friend in reply said, " There are two preachers whom you might hear. The first will give you an eloquent sermon, and will make you conscious of his ability ; and the second will put himself in the background, and you will see his Master alone." " Let us go and hear the latter," was the immediate reply.

There are seven things in relation to the Divine Proclamation :

1. *Commission, or Divine Appointment* (verse 2). The word " dispensation " should be " stewardship." It is so rendered in Luke 16 : 2-4. A steward is one who is put in trust, and stewardship is the designation of his office.

2. *Revelation, or Divine Communication* (verses 3-6). The words " revelation " and " revealed " indicate the making known of what could not be apprehended by any research of man. Revelation takes us beyond the realm of natural reason, and shuts out all human speculation.

3. *Construction, or Divine Creation* (verse 7). The word is rendered "made" and "become" in John 1 : 3, 12, in referring to Christ's creative acts and God's acts of grace in constituting believers His children. The minister who is made is the minister who makes.

4. *Proclamation, or Divine riches* (verse 8). The theme of the preacher is the "unsearchable riches" of Christ. The word "unsearchable" is rendered "past finding out" in Rom. 11 : 33, and points to the labyrinthine wealth and the untrackable and boundless resources there are in Christ. He is richer than the richest, higher than the highest, greater than the greatest, deeper than the deepest, and better than the best.

5. *Illumination, or Divine Light* (verse 9). The word translated "to make see" means to shed rays, to shine all around, thus to illuminate. The word is rendered "light" in speaking of a lighted candle in Luke 11 : 36, and "enlightened" in Eph. 1 : 18. The natural man is blinded by sin and unbelief, and it is the business of the spiritual man to give spiritual light through the operation of the Illuminator acting in and through him.

6. *Demonstration, or Divine Reflection* (verses 10-13). The Church (God's called out assembly—called out from the world to Himself) is the object of Heaven's " principalities and powers." They find their attention arrested and their admiration excited as they study " the manifold wisdom of God " displayed in the redeemed. The word " manifold " means many and varied, and much variegated, multifarious.

7. *Exhibition, or Divine Working* (verse 7). The man who is made is the man who makes, hence we read of the " effectual working " of God's power through him, for that power is the effectiveness of his making. The words rendered " worketh " and " effectual working " occur seven times in Ephesians, and is translated "worketh" in 1 : 11, 2 : 2, 3 : 20 ; " working " in 1 : 19 ; " wrought " in 1 : 20 ; and " effectual working " in 3 : 7 and 4 : 16.

IV. The Divine Presence (3 : 14-21)

There are seven things about the presence of the Holy One :

1. *It is Profound in its Nature.* The three persons of the Godhead are seen in the activities of grace, hence the " Father " is granting His grace ; the Spirit is strengthening in His power (verse 16) ; and the Christ is dwelling in the heart of His love.

2. This Presence is *Permanent in its Dwelling* (verse 17). The meaning of the word to " dwell " is to make one's home. Christ is no lodger, He is the Permanent Occupier of the house of the believer's inner nature.

3. This Presence is *Definite in its Purpose.* Christ's indwelling is " that we may be rooted and grounded in love." Rooted like a tree, firmly ; and grounded like a building, securely. The soil in which we are to grow, and the base on which we ground, is the love of God in Christ.

4. This Presence is *Centralising in its Attraction* (verse 18). The centre around which believers gather is Christ Himself when He indwells them, for they have a mutuality of interest in seeking to apprehend Him in the " breadth " of His love, in the " length " of His service, in the " depth " of His suffering, and in the " height " of His glory.

5. This Presence is *Satisfying in its Knowledge.* To know the love of Christ means to have an anchor to hold, a joy to thrill, a power to move, a sap to fructify, a foundation to uphold, a rule to guide, and a fulness to satisfy. To be " filled *with* the fulness of God " is an impossibility, but to be filled " unto " or into it, as an empty vessel may be dropped into a tub of water, is what is meant, then we are filled full to our satisfaction, and filled all around for our protection.

6. This Presence is *Unlimited in its Blessing* (verse 20). There is a pyramid of thought in this verse on answered prayer :

" *Ask.*"
" *Think.*"
" *All* we ask."
" *All* we think."
" *Above* all we ask or think."
" *Abundantly* above all we ask."
" *Exceeding* abundantly above all we," etc.

The words " exceeding abundantly above " are worthy of careful analysis. The word " abundantly " means " beyond measure " and " overmuch," and is so rendered in Mark 6 : 5 and 2 Cor. 2 : 7. " Exceeding " means what is " beyond measure " and beyond measure ; and " above " means what is beyond what is beyond measure and what is beyond what is beyond measure. And this is not all, for this passage is an elliptical one, that is, there is something wanting yet, so God is able to do beyond what is beyond measure, and what is beyond what is beyond what is beyond measure, and what is beyond what is beyond what is beyond measure, yea, what is beyond what is beyond what is beyond what is beyond of beyond measure.

We must not forget the two " accordings " : what He can do for us is according to what we allow Him to do in us. If we allow Him to work unhindered in us, He can work unlimited for us (verses 16, 20).

7. His Presence is *Marvellous in its Display* (verse 21). All God's acts of grace to and in us are leading up to the display of His glory through us. Grace never acts with the intent of bringing glory to itself. Grace is its own glory. There is no glory so glorious as grace acting in its disinterestedness. The beauty of grace is, it loves to beautify others to its own loss and displacement, but therein its beauty and glory are enhanced.

V. The Divine Provision (4 : 1-16)

Grace is the Source of the Divine Provision. God's giving is based upon His love to give. Such expressions illustrate, as " Given grace according to the measure of the gift of Christ," " He gave gifts unto men," " He gave," etc. (verses 7, 8, 11). Grace is Love blessing the undeserving, Mercy helping the needy, Power lifting the down-trodden, Fulness filling the empty, Compassion loving the hopeless, Beauty clothing the naked, Help saving the lost, Strength empowering the weak, Cleansing purifying the defiled, Tenderness melting the hardened, and Joy gladdening the miserable. Grace meets the sin of the sinner, and removes it. Grace answers for the sinner by dying for him. Grace lives to empower the saint, and to live in him. Grace equips the soldier, and conquers through him. Grace leads the child of God, and cheers him. Grace employs the servant, and for service fits him. And grace undertakes for the believer, and supplies all his need, hence verse 6 is the keynote of grace's action—" Father of all," for all come from Him. " Above all," for He alone is in the place of authority. " Through all," for He alone is the life of all. And " in all," for He alone can sanctify and qualify for all things in life and labour.

Christ is the Substance of the Divine Provision. Christ is the effulgence of God's glory, the express image of His Person, and the Reservoir of His fulness (Heb. 1 : 3). God has nothing to give apart from Him, and there is no more when He is given (Rom. 8 : 32). As the diamond flashes forth its excellence in the gold ring of its setting, so in the ring of this Scripture Christ's glory is revealed. The personal pronouns, His names and His titles enshrine and illustrate.

The " Lord " in the strength of His support (verse 1).

The " One Lord " in the supremacy of His glory (verse 5).

The " Christ " in the grace of His bestowment (verse 7).

The " He saith " in the authority of His Word (verse 8).

The " He ascended " of His acceptance (verse 8).

The " He led " of His splendid triumph (verse 8).

The " He descended " of His loving abasement (verse 9).

The " He might fill " of wonderful accomplishments (verse 10).

The " He gave " of His gracious endowments (verse 11).

The " Christ " of the oneness of the mystical body (verse 12).

The " Son of God " in the glory of His inspiring knowledge (verse 13).

The " Christ " in " the fulness " of His supply (verse 13).

The " Head " in its compacting and controlling ministry (verse 15).

The Spirit is the Strength of the Divine Provision. The Holy Spirit is spoken of in His Sovereignty as " the One Spirit." He is One in equality with the Father and Son. He is One in the fellowship of the co-operation of the Godhead in all things. He is One in the enhancing of the glory of Christ. And He is One as the Supplier of the believer in His need, hence He is the Spirit of Life to quicken, the Spirit of Grace to strengthen, the Spirit of Love to cheer, the Spirit of Truth to sanctify, the Spirit of Power to qualify, the Spirit of Christ to unify, the Spirit of Wisdom to instruct, and the Spirit of Joy to gladden.

Growth is the outcome of the Divine Provision. The expressions, " walk worthy " (verse 1), " perfect man " (verse 13), " no more children " (verse 14), " grow up " (verse 15), and " maketh increase " (verse 16), indicate progress, advancement, and care. To walk worthy of the Lord in the " lowliness of " humility, in the evenness of " meekness," in the " longsuffering " of endurance, and in the love of " forbearance," we need the worthy Lord Himself. To walk well for the Lord we need the Lord to walk in us. " The perfect man " of God's ideal is consummated in the ideal of His Son. The baby state of spiritual experience is characteristic of instability and inefficiency, while the man of grace is known by the Spirit's efficiency and steadiness. The outward growth in usefulness, and the downward growth in stedfastness, are the outcome of growing upward into Christ through His dominance over us. The success of the body's growth is forwarded by the individual member's advancement.

Ministry is the operation of the Divine Provision. " Perfecting," " work," " edifying," and " supplieth," are the keywords which indicate the work of the Head through the members in their mutual relations to each other. The end of all ministry is the adjustment to the saints in the will of God. The " work " of the ministry is the loving labour which each member expends on the other. The " edifying " outcome of the ministry is expressed in the building up of character. And the " dependence " of the ministry is manifested in each member's recognition of the dependence of all on each other in their supply from the Head.

VI. The Divine Pattern (4 : 17—6 : 9)

There are many things suggested in imitating a pattern. Among them are instruction, imitation, illumination, submission, union, responsibility, and appreciation. All these are illustrated in the section before us.

Instructed by Christ (4 : 17-31).   Key sentence, " Ye have not so learned Christ " (verse 20).   Instructed by Christ—

About the life of the walk (verse 17).

About the old man of past habit (verse 22).

About the new man of holy living (verse 24).

About the mastery of the wayward tongue (verses 25, 26).

About the obtrusiveness of the devil (verse 27).

About the commendableness of honest labour (verse 28).

About the helpfulness of helping others (verse 29).

About the sensitiveness of the Holy Spirit (verse 30).

About the blight and bitterness of unholy temper (verse 31).

Imitation of Christ (4 : 32 ;   5 : 1, 2).   Key sentence is " As Christ loved," etc. (verse 2).   Imitate Christ—

In kindness.

In forgiving grace.

In holy love.

In self sacrifice.

In God glorifying.

Illuminated in Christ (verses 3-20).   Key sentence, " Now light in the Lord " (verse 8).

Out of the darkness of sin (verses 3-8).

Into the relationship of light (verse 8).

Swayed by the Spirit of light (verses 9, 18).

Acting to the God of Light (verse 10).

Keeping from what is not light (verses 11-13).

Walking as children of light (verses 11, 15).

Worshipping in the light (verses 19, 20).

Submission to Christ (verses 21-28).

Evidence of being Spirit filled (verse 21).

Evidence of being under Christ's authority (verse 24).

All the relationships of life are to be fulfilled towards each other by recognizing our responsibility to Him. See " unto the Lord " in verse 22, and " ought " of verse 28.

Union with Christ (verses 29-33). Key sentence, " Members of His body " (verse 30). This union is—

Loving in its care—" nourisheth " (verse 29).

Attentive in its regard—" cherisheth " (verse 29).

Vital in its action—" members," etc. (verse 30).

Separating in its attraction (verse 31).

Mystical in its nature (verse 32).

Responsible to Christ (6 : 1-7, 9). Key sentence, " In the Lord " (6 : 1). Those who are subordinate, as children and servants, recognize they take the place of submission to Christ, and do all for Him in obeying them : and those who are over, as parents and masters, are responsible to the Father and Lord of all to act towards the subordinates with consideration.

Reward from Christ (6 : 8). Key sentence, " Receive the Lord." Everything done for love's sake for the Lord will bring recognition at the judgment seat in the glad day of the Lord's return.

VII. The Divine Panoply (6 : 10-20)

The key sentence is " The Armour of God " (verse 11). There are seven star words which shine out in the sky of this section.

The " Be strong " of the Lord's Empowerment (verse 10)·

The " Take " of the Lord's Equipment (verses 13, 16, 17).

The " Stand " of the Soldier's Endurement (verses 11, 13, 14).

The " Shod " of the Feet's Protectment (verse 15).

The " Above All " of Faith's Encasement (verse 16).

The " Praying " of the Spirit's Environment (verse 18).

The " Watching " of the Patrol's Alertment (verse 18).

The condition of heart that can commune with the Lord in order to understand and experience the grace and truth embedded in this mine of wealth is found in the last verse and in the sentence, " Grace be with all them that love our Lord Jesus Christ in sincerity " (margin, " Incorruption "). The word " sincerity " is rendered " incorruption " and " immortality " in 1 Cor. 15 : 42, 50, 53, 54 ; Rom. 2 : 7 ; 2 Tim. 1 : 10. When the heart of the believer is free from the corruption of sin, and has in it the love of incorruption, then there is the obedience of faith and the love of sacrifice.

6

THE HANDS OF AN ARTISTIC DESIGN

THE hand represents that member of the body, by means of which we are able to do things. We are exhorted, " Whatsoever thy hand findeth to do, do it with thy might ; for there is no work, nor device . . . in the grave where thou goest " (Eccles. 9 : 10). Christ, using the simile of the ploughman at his work, says : " No man having put his hand to the plough and looking back, is fit for the Kingdom of Heaven " (Luke 9 : 62). In speaking of the Spirit working with the Apostle, we read : " The hand of the Lord was with them " (Acts 11 : 21). The Psalmist, gazing upon the Heaven, declared : " The firmament sheweth His handiwork " (Psa. 19 : 1). God recognises what man does in his labour ; He speaks of the " works of thine hands " (Deut. 16 : 15). The hands are referred to in calling attention to spiritual ministry in the Acts, therefore we read : " By the hands of the apostles," " by the hands of Barnabas and Saul," and " wonders done by their hands " (Acts 5 : 12 ; 11 : 30 ; 14 : 3). Instances might be multiplied of the hands being indicative of work done.

When the Lord said to Moses, " Make Me a tabernacle that I may dwell among you," He did not leave His servant to follow his own ideas. He first of all commanded him into His presence—" Come up unto the Lord " (Exod. 24 : 1). Then in the forty days of communing He gave His servant full and detailed instructions, and according to those instructions he acted as may be seen in the thirty times the expressions, " All I have commanded thee " and " The Lord commanded," occur (Exod. 31 : 6, 11 ; 34 : 4, 18, 34 ; 35 : 1, 4, 10, 29 ; 36 : 1, 5 ; 38 : 22 ; 39 : 1, 5, 7, 21, 26, 29, 31, 32, 42, 43 ; 40 : 16, 19, 21, 23, 25, 27, 29, 32).

The Spirit of God in the Old and New Testaments has emphasized the fact that a pattern was given to Moses by Jehovah, and that he did everything according to that plan (Exod. 25 : 40 ; 26 : 30 ; 27 : 8 ; Lev. 7 : 38 ; Num. 8 : 4 ; Acts 7 : 44 ; Heb. 8 : 5).

As the tabernacle was constructed according to God's plan, so we see the Divine Architect's hand in all the structure of God's Word. If we take the dimensions of the tabernacle, we find that the number five is stamped on all measurements. The following sketch will illustrate. We only give the measurement of the Outer Court:

South Side

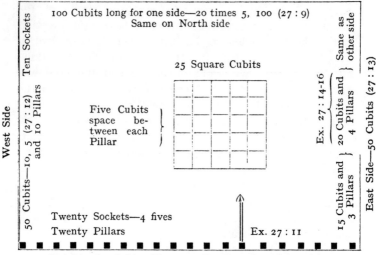

West Side

Ten Sockets
50 Cubits—10, 5 (27 : 12) and 10 Pillars

100 Cubits long for one side—20 times 5, 100 (27 : 9)
Same on North side

25 Square Cubits

Five Cubits space between each Pillar

Twenty Sockets—4 fives
Twenty Pillars

Ex. 27 : 11

Ex. 27 : 14-16
20 Cubits and 4 Pillars } Same as other side
15 Cubits and 3 Pillars }

East Side—50 Cubits (27 : 13)

Height of 5 Cubits (Ex. 27 : 18). Length and breadth repeated (27 : 18)

The number five, as used in Scripture, is full of spiritual suggestion. Five, as associated with God, is the number of His grace. This is made known in the five sections of the Name of our Lord—"His Name shall be called Wonderful, Counsellor, Mighty God, Everlasting Father, Prince of Peace." And the number five, when found in connection with man, indicates his weakness; hence, we read God uses five classes of workers—"Foolish things, weak things, base things, despised things, and things that are not" (1 Cor. 1 : 28).

F. W. Grant, in his Numerical Bible, maintains that the whole of the Scriptures is divided into five, as the following table illustrates:

The Books of the Law

1. Genesis
2. Exodus
3. Leviticus
4. Numbers
5. Deuteronomy

The Covenant-History

1. Joshua
2. Judges, Ruth
3. Kings
   First Book (Samuel)
   Second Book (Kings)
4. Captivity Books
   Ezra
   Nehemiah
   Esther
5. Chronicles

The Prophets

1. Isaiah
2. Jeremiah, Lamentations
3. Ezekiel
4. Daniel
5. The Book of Minor Prophets

The Psalm Books

1. The Psalms
2. Job
3. Solomon's Song
4. Ecclesiastes
5. Proverbs

The Gospels

1. Matthew
2. Mark
3. Luke
4. John
5. The Acts

The Pauline Epistles

1. {
   Romans
   Galatians
   Ephesians
   Colossians, Philemon
   Philippians
   }

2. {
   Thessalonians
   First Epistle
   Second Epistle
   Corinthians
   First Epistle
   Second Epistle
   Hebrews
   Timothy
   First Epistle
   Second Epistle
   Titus
   }

The Catholic Epistles and Revelation

1. Peter
   First Epistle
   Second Epistle
2. James
3. John
   First Epistle
   Second Epistle
   Third Epistle
4. Jude
5. Revelation

The Law of First Mention

The first time a word occurs in the Scriptures gives the key to understand its meaning in every other place.

The late Benjamin Wills Newton says: "I find in Scripture a principle of interpretation, which I believe if conscientiously adopted will serve as an unfailing guide as to the mind of God as contained therein. The first mention of a thing, the very first words of any subject of which the Holy Spirit is going to treat, are the keystone of the whole matter."

"Sanctified" (Gen. 2 : 3). The seventh day was set apart as a day of rest, hence the meaning of sanctification is, as Parkhurst says, "To separate, or set apart from a common and ordinary to some higher use or other purpose." The word is used to describe prostitutes, male and female, who were sacred to their idol, and practised their abominable impurities as acts of religion (1 Kings 14 : 24; 15 : 12; 2 Kings 23 : 7). The word is translated "Consecrate," "Holy," "Defiled," "Appointed," "Wholly," "Purified," "Dedicate," "Proclaim," "Kept," "Prepare," and "Bid." Moses is told "to consecrate," or set apart, Aaron and his sons for the priesthood (Exod. 30 : 30). The altar of burnt-offering became "holy" after its setting apart, and being set apart it set apart or made holy everything which touched it (Exod. 29 : 37). The first-born of Israel was "hallowed," or set apart, as the Lord's portion (Num. 3 : 13); the land of Israel was not to be sown with mixed seed lest it became "defiled," that is, set apart as something profane (Deut. 22 : 9); certain cities were "appointed," or set apart, in the land to which the inadvertent man-slayer might flee for safety (Josh. 20 : 7); the mother of Micah told him she had "wholly" dedicated, or set apart, to the Lord the eleven hundred shekels he had given (Jud. 17 : 3); "purified," or set apart, from uncleanness, is said of the wife of Uriah (2 Sam. 11 : 4); David did "dedicate," or set apart to the Lord, all the silver and gold he had taken from the nations (2 Sam. 8 : 11); Jehu, in his stratagem to slay the worshippers of Baal, said, "Proclaim" (or "sanctify," as margin) "a solemn assembly for Baal" (2 Kings 10 : 20); "Ye shall have a song in the night as when a solemn solemnity is kept " (Isa. 30 : 29), is Jehovah's promise to Israel as He gives the nation millennial blessing, it shall be a time set apart for special gladness ; " I will prepare destroyers against thee " (Jer. 22 : 7), is God's word of judgment through the prophet ; He will set apart those who shall fulfil His will ; and in describing His judgments in the latter day we read, " Hold thy peace at the presence of the Lord God, for the day of the Lord is at hand, for the Lord hath prepared a sacrifice, He hath bid (margin, 'sanctified') His guests " (Zeph. 1 : 7). Abundant evidence from text and context is thus gathered that the Hebrew word " Kadesh " means to set apart. Read in the light of the Gospel, its significance is separation to the Lord. The New Testament word is, " The God of Peace sanctify you wholly " (1 Thess. 5 : 23). Reading the different words into the call of the New Testament, we see how comprehensive the Lord's call is : Separation from an aimless life; " consecrated " to the Lord's worship ; separation from a hurtful influence ; " holy " in influencing to the Lord Himself ; separation from the Egypt of the world ; " hallowed " to the Lord's company ; separation from the defilement of sin ; " devoted " to the Lord's possession ; separated from the evil of self ; " appointed " to the Lord's service ; separated from the brokenness of a double life ; " wholly " given to the Lord's glory ; separated from the pollution of the flesh; " purified " to the Lord's ideal; separated from the selfishness of covetousness ; " dedicated " to the Lord's sacrifice ; separated from the enervation of the world ; " sanctified " to the Lord's joy ; separated from the grip of evil ; " kept " for the Lord's Christ ; separated from the world ; " prepared " for the Lord's return ; separated from the failure of a self-centred life ; and " bid " to the Lord's reward.

The Law of Centralizing Thought

One of the greatest words in the sacred pages is " Salvation," from the simple fact, God Himself is its centre and circumference, for as the late George Macdonald said, " Any salvation short of God Himself is no salvation at all." Jacob

in blessing his sons on his death-bed says, when he comes to
Dan, "Dan shall judge his people, as one of the tribes of
Israel. Dan shall be a serpent by the way, an adder in the
path that biteth the horse's heels, so that his rider shall fall
backward. I have waited for Thy salvation, O Jehovah"
(Gen. 49 : 16-18). The prophecy about Dan is wrapped up
in the meaning of his name. Dan means judgment. He was
predicted to be the judge of his people, and that he would
be treacherous in his dealings, hence, he is compared to a
serpent and to an adder, which bites the heels of the horse,
and causes the rider to be thrown to his hurt. Then the
patriarch immediately exclaims, "I have waited for Thy
salvation, O Lord." As if he said, "By Thy salvation I am
saved from judgment, and from the evil of the old serpent
acting through Dan."

Salvation! There is no word which is so large in its
meaning, lofty in its conception, and lasting in its blessing,
as this word "Salvation." As the New Jerusalem will have
twelve foundations, so the city of God's salvation has twelve
foundations to it.

God in His grace is its Author (Titus 2 : 11).

The Cross in the vicariousness of its atonement is its
Basis (1 Pet. 1 : 9-11).

Man in his need as a sinner is its object (Acts 13 : 26).

Faith in its reception of Christ is its inception (Rom. 1 : 16).

Deliverance in the many-sidedness of its blessing is its
meaning; hence, the word "Salvation" in the Old Testament is translated "help" in 2 Sam. 10 : 11; "welfare" in
Job 30 : 15; "health" in Psa. 42 : 11; and "deliverance"
in Psa. 18 : 50.

God's Word in the witness of its promise is its assurance
(2 Tim. 3 : 15).

Joy in the secret of its gladness by obedience is its exultation (1 Sam. 2 : 1).

The Spirit in the grace of His strength is its power (Phil.
2 : 12, 13).

Holiness of heart and life in their correspondence to
Christ is its fruit (2 Thess. 2 : 13).

Christ in the beauty of His character is its embodiment (Luke 19 : 10 ; Isa. 12 : 2).

Fellowship with the Lord in all the partnership of His love is its privilege (2 Cor. 1 : 5-7).

Glory in its likeness to Christ is its consummation (Heb. 9 : 28).

The Law of a Reliant Faith

Faith is the grace that receives from the Lord what He has to offer, and rests in the will of His Word.

The verb to believe denotes the steady resting of the heart upon an object outside of itself ; hence, for one person to rely, to trust, to depend upon another. Faith depends upon the living God. It has no reliance upon itself. The same word as rendered " believed " in Gen. 15 : 6 is rendered " nursed " in Isa. 60 : 4, where it says, " Thy daughters shall be nursed at thy side," referring to the Eastern custom of the mother carrying her child astride upon the hip and with her arm around the body. What better picture could we have of the act and attitude of faith than the child resting on the mother's hip and being supported by her ? Abram believed the Lord and Jehovah undertook all the responsibilities of his salvation and need.

The word rendered " believed " is translated " brought up " in Lam. 4 : 5 ; " sure " in Psa. 93 : 5 ; " verified " in Gen. 42 : 20 ; " established " in 2 Chron. 1 : 9 ; " faithful " in Num. 12 : 7 ; " stand fast " in Psa. 89 : 28 ; " assurance " in Deut. 28 : 66 ; " steadfast " in Psa. 78 : 8 ; and " trust " in Job 4 : 18. Reading these words into the meaning and association of faith, we may say of the man of faith, He is " brought up " by the Lord's ministry ; " sure " of the Lord's love ; " verified " in the Lord's truth ; " established " in the Lord's grace ; " faithful " in the Lord's service ; " stands fast " in temptation for the Lord's glory ; " assured " by the Lord's promise ; " steadfast " in the Lord's ways, and " trusts " in the Lord Himself.

The Law of Revealed Difference

There is no greater difference than that which is found between Law and Grace. The following alphabet will illustrate :

LAW	GRACE
A Dividing Veil (Ex. 26 : 33).	A Rent Veil (Heb. 10 : 19, 22).
Blots out the sinner (Ex. 32 : 33).	Blots out the sin (Col. 2 : 14).
Curses the offender (Gal. 3 : 10).	Covers the offender (Rom. 4 : 7).
Do and live (Deut. 8 : 1).	Done for the sinner (John 19 : 30).
" Every mouth stopped " (Rom. 3 : 19).	Every mouth opened (Rom. 10 : 9).
Favour to the good (Prov. 12 : 2).	Favour to the bad (Eph. 2 : 1-6).
Graven on stone—outward (2 Cor. 3 : 3).	Graven on the heart (2 Cor. 3 : 3).
" He added no more " (Deut. 5 : 22).	" Hath spoken by His Son " (Heb. 1 : 2).
Inexorable in its demand (Josh. 23 : 15).	Inspirational in its blessing (2 Cor. 5 : 14).
Judgment (Rom. 5 : 18).	Justification (Rom. 3 : 24).
Keep (Jas. 2 : 10).	Kept (1 Pet. 1 : 5).
Love demanded (Deut. 6 : 5).	Love exhibited (John 3 : 16).
Moves the sinner to sin (Rom. 7 : 8).	Moves the sin from the sinner (Matt. 1 : 21).
Nearness impossible (Ex. 20 : 21).	Nearness certain (Eph. 2 : 13).
Obedience necessary to blessing (Deut. 28 : 1, 2).	Obedience from blessing (1 John 4 : 19).
Prodigal stoned to death (Deut. 21 : 20, 21).	Prodigal robed and feasted (Luke 15 : 20, 22).
Quietus of death (Deut. 21 : 22, 23).	Quietness of Peace (Rom. 5 : 1).
Retaliates (Ex. 21 : 24).	Redeems (Gal. 3 : 13).
Sanctification demanded (Lev. 11 : 44).	Sanctification bestowed (1 Cor. 1 : 30).
Three thousand slain (Ex. 32 : 28).	Three thousand saved (Acts 2 : 41).
Unsatisfying to the conscience (Heb. 10 : 1, 2).	Unfailing in its remedy (Heb. 9 : 12-14 ; 10 : 10-14).
Voice of consternation (Heb. 12 : 18-21).	Voice of covenant and blessing (Heb. 12 : 22-24).
When Moses' face shone the people feared (Ex. 34 : 30).	When Christ's face shone people were attracted (Mark 9 : 15).
'Xcellent glory of righteousness (2 Cor. 3 : 7).	'Xcelling glory of grace (2 Cor. 3 : 8-11).
Yoked with a burdensome weight (Gal. 5 : 1).	Yoked with a loving Christ (Matt. 11 : 29, 30).
Zeal inspired and no salvation (Phil. 3 : 6).	Zeal imparted because saved (Titus 2 : 14).

The Law of Standing and State

Standing indicates what God in His grace has given to us, made us, and what we are in Christ. Standing is perfect, complete, and nothing wanting. State refers to experience, what we should be, and what God expects from us as His children in the Spirit. Faith in Christ is the condition for grace to place in Christ, our Standing. Faithfulness to Christ by obedience places in the state of well-pleasing to the Lord.

STANDING	STATE
" Accepted in the Beloved " (Eph. 1 : 6).	Accepted of Him—" well-pleasing " (2 Cor. 5 : 9).
" Blessed with all spiritual blessings " (Eph. 1 : 3).	" Blessed in his deed "—Doing the Word (Jas. 1 : 25).
" Called the sons of God " (1 John 3 : 1).	" Called you "—walk worthy of God (1 Thess. 2 : 12).
" Delivered from the wrath to come " (1 Thess. 1 : 10).	" Delivered always to death " (2 Cor. 4 : 11).
" Elected of God " (1 Thess. 1 : 4).	Election made sure (2 Pet. 1 : 10).
Forgiven by God (Eph. 1 : 7).	Forgiving like God (Eph. 4 : 32).
Grace, Saved by (Eph. 2 : 5).	Growing in grace (2 Pet. 3 : 18).
Holy Priesthood (1 Pet. 2 : 5).	Holy in all manner of living (1 Pet. 1 : 15, R.V.).
In Christ hidden (Col. 3 : 3).	In Christ abiding (John 15 : 4).
Justified without works (Rom. 3 : 28).	Justifying faith by works (Jas. 2 : 24).
Kept for Jesus Christ (Jude 1, R.V.).	Keep yourselves from idols (1 John 5 : 21).
Life eternal given (John 10 : 28).	Life eternal gripped (1 Tim. 6 : 12).
Meetness for the inheritance (Col. 1 : 12).	Meetness for service (2 Tim. 2 : 21).
Nearness by the blood (Eph. 2 : 13).	Nearness by consecration (Heb. 10 : 22).
Ordained to eternal life (Acts 13 : 48).	Ordained to good works (Eph. 2 : 10).
Peace with God secured (Rom. 5 : 1).	Peace of God enjoyed (Phil. 4 : 6, 7).
Quickened together with Christ (Eph. 2 : 5).	Quickened according to God's Word (Psa. 119 : 154).
Redeemed to God by Christ's blood (Rev. 5 : 9).	Redeemed from all iniquity (Titus 2 : 14).

STANDING	STATE
Sanctified in Christ (1 Cor. 1 : 2).	Sanctified wholly (1 Thess. 5 : 23).
Translated (Col. 1 : 13).	Transformed (Rom. 12 : 2).
Unspeakable gift (2 Cor. 9 : 15).	Unspeakable joy (1 Pet. 1 : 8).
Victory secured (Heb. 2 : 14, 15).	Victory experienced (1 John 5 : 4).
Washed in the blood (Rev. 1 : 5).	Washed for worship (Heb. 10 : 22).
Yielded up to death for us (Matt. 27 : 50).	Yielding our members (Rom. 6 : 13, 16).

The Law of Association or Context

There is a near context of chapter and book in which a verse or portion of God's Word is found, like one room in its relation to the whole house ; and there is the remote context of the whole Bible, which is like one star in its association with the planetry system in which it revolves.

Remote Context. Read Gen. 37 : 25-28, 36 ; 39 : 1. Charges have been brought by the higher critics that there are undoubted discrepancies in these verses, because in one verse it says " Ishmaelites " (verses 25, 27, 28) and in another " Midianites " (verses 28, 36). Undoubtedly the same company is meant, for Joseph was sold to the Ishmaelites, brought down to Egypt by the Midianites who sold him to Potiphar (37 : 36), and that these Midianites were called Ishmaelites (39 : 1). How could the Ishmaelites be Midianites and the Midianites be Ishmaelites ? How indeed ! We have no solution to the apparent discrepancy in the near context, but we have one in the remote context. In Jud. 8 : 24, where Gideon referring to the Midianites, that his followers had slain, says : " I would desire a request from you, that ye would give every man the earrings of his prey " (for they had golden earrings because they were Ishmaelites). Thus all Ishmaelites were Midianites as viewed in Judges 8, but all Midianites were not Ishmaelites, any more than all Britishers are Canadians, although all Canadians are Britishers because under British rule.

Besides there is another thing we may learn from the remote context. Ishmael and Midian were by the same father, but by different mothers. Abraham was the father of both, but Hagar was the mother of Ishmael (Gen. 16 : 11, 12), and Keturah was the mother of Midian (Gen. 25 : 2). And undoubtedly they shared the same country and life, the only difference being the Ishmaelites were distinguished by their nose or earrings.

Near Context. Most of the writers of the books of the Bible indicate the purport of their writing. Thus the ruling principle in the Book of Ecclesiastes is to show that everything " under the sun " is " vanity of vanities." Husks of earth cannot feed hearts intended for Heaven. Everything in the book is coloured and connected by this dominating note.

The purpose of John in the writing of his Gospel is that we might believe that Jesus is the Christ the Son of God, and that believing we might have life in His Name (John 20 : 31).

The blessing which comes to the believer is " life." Life is the one thing that throbs through the whole of the Gospel, so that the whole telegraphy of thought runs along this wire of connection. Some phase of life is seen in each chapter :

1. Life shining (1 : 4). 2. Acting (2 : 11). 3. Loving (3 : 16). 4. Giving (4 : 14). 5. Communicating (5 : 24, 26). 6. Feeding (6 : 35). 7. Satisfying (7 : 37-39). 8. Instructing (8 : 12). 9. Illuminating (9 : 25, 35-38). 10. Abounding (10 : 10). 11. Quickening (11 : 25). 12. Communing (12 : 2). 13. Serving (13 : 1). 14. Comforting (14 : 16). 15. Producing (15 : 4). 16. Guiding (16 : 13). 17. Interceding (17 : 9). 18. Rejected (18 : 40). 19. Accomplishing (19 : 30). 20. Assuring (20 : 31). 21. Commissioning (21 : 15-19).

The Law of Correspondence

Take the words of 1 Cor. 15 : 22, " As in Adam all die, even so in Christ shall He make alive." There are two interpretations to these words. First the Universalists' one, which declares, " All men will be saved, for as the ' as ' of death applies to all men, so the ' so ' equally applies to all mankind." The other interpretation is " All died in Adam," and only those " in Christ " will be " made alive " ; which means the first " all " means *all*, but the second " all " means

some. The "as" and the "so" will not permit of this
interpretation. The "as" and "so" in other places imply
an exact correspondence. For instance, "As Moses lifted
up the serpent in the wilderness, even so must the Son of
man be lifted up." "As My Father loveth Me, so have I
loved you." "As My Father hath sent Me, even so send I
you" (John 3:14; 15:9; 20:21). The only exegesis
which is fair and permissible is the "all" in each case
denotes all mankind. The main thing to observe is "What
is the *topic?*" The resurrection of the dead. Up to the
twenty-third verse three sections of the topic are treated.

First, the fact of Christ's resurrection (4-8).

Second, the sevenfold result if there be no resurrection of
the dead :

1. Christ is not risen.
2. The preaching of the Gospel is useless.
3. Faith in Christ is unavailing.
4. The Apostles were false witnesses.
5. Believers are yet in their sins.
6. The beloved dead have perished.
7. The most miserable of all people are the
saints.

12-19

Third, the emphatic statement about the resurrection of
the dead, given in three particulars.

The First-fruits. When the resurrection *from* the dead
is stated, Christ is the First-fruits of them that sleep (ver. 20) ;
but when it is the resurrection *of* the dead, Christ the First-
fruits includes the Head and members, the complete Body,
as stated in 1 Cor. 12:12. The details of this resurrection
are given in 1 Thess. 4:13-18. This is not therefore the
"*first* resurrection" of John 5:29 and Rev. 20:6, but a
*pre-*resurrection. For as *Christ personally* is the First-fruits
of the sleeping saints ; so *Christ mystically* is the First-fruits
of those who shall be raised afterwards.

The Saints at Christ's Coming. "Each in his own order,
Christ the First-fruits, then they that are Christ's, at His
coming" (ver. 23, R.V.). The Greek word "Tagma"
means anything arranged in order, as a body of troops which

is marshalled in ranks. The adverb of time "*then*" indicates the next rank, which includes all who participate in the "first resurrection" (Rev. 20 : 4, 5, 6), of which there are several parties (see Rev. 6 : 9 ; 11 : 3-11). When Christ comes with His Church to set up His Kingdom, the participators of the first resurrection are raised to His presence.

The Rest of the Dead. The reading of the text is unfortunate. It is not "Then *cometh* the end." "*Cometh*" is a gloss and is not in the original, as is indicated by the italicised word. Then the other words are, "Afterwards the last." The word "*end*" is rendered "*finally*" in 1 Pet. 3 : 8. The last of what ? We are not told, the context must say, and the context says, "the rest of the dead," and therefore corresponds to Rev. 20 : 5, 11-13. The last rank in the resurrection of the dead is "the dead."

The first-fruits are raised before the Great Tribulation. The next in order are the Tribulation saints before the Millennium, and the last rank is the wicked dead, who are raised at the end of the thousand years.

The Law of Emphasis

The word to "abide" will illustrate. The command of Christ to abide in Him is fruitful, and is one of the things He emphasises. Let us see how the following questions are answered.

First. What does the Greek word "*Meno*" mean ?

The word "*meno*" means to be in one place all the time. It is used to describe where a person dwells, as when the disciples asked Christ, "Where dwellest Thou ?" (John 1 : 38) ; for a person tarrying in a certain place, as when the Samaritans "besought" Christ to "tarry with them" (John 4 : 40) ; to represent something which lasts, hence, the Lord exhorts us to labour for the meat which "endureth unto everlasting life" (John 6 : 27) ; and Christ also uses the word when He speaks of "the sin which remaineth" (John 9 : 41). The continued presence of one person with another finds its explanation when Christ says, "These things have I spoken being yet present with you" (John 14 : 25). The word is used when a ship is stuck fast on the rocks, as when the vessel in which Paul was being conveyed to Rome " stuck fast, and remained unmoveable " (Acts 27 : 41). The word is translated " might stand " in speaking of the " fixed purpose of God " (Rom. 9 : 11) ; and Christ states that those who " continue in His word, are His disciples indeed " (John 8 : 31). The word is translated " dwellest," " tarry," " endureth," " remaineth," " present," " might stand," and " continue."

Second. *How does Christ use the word " abide " ?*

The word " *meno* " is mentioned by Christ in John 15 twelve times, and is translated " abide," " continue " and " remain."

1. Command to abide—" Abide in Me " (ver. 4). This is a call to obedience, and not an option in choice.

2. Christ's abiding in us depends on our abiding in Him. " Abide in Me and I in you " (ver. 4). The order of our obedience secures the Omnipotence of His presence.

3. Necessity of abiding. The branch is useless and helpless in itself (Ezek. 15 : 1-6). Its fruitfulness depends upon being united to the Vine. So union and communion with Christ are essential for fruitfulness (ver. 4).

4. Result of abiding (ver. 5). The " much fruit " of His dying (12 : 24) finds its counterpart in the " much fruit " of His living in us by our abiding in Him.

5. Consequence of not abiding (ver. 6). Want of fruit proves we are professors and not partakers. There may be a fruitless vine, but there cannot be a fruitless Christ, for union with Him proves itself by fruit from Him (Hosea 14 : 8).

6. Blessing of abiding (ver. 7). As we answer to the Lord in our obedience, He answers to our prayers with His blessing.

7. Sphere of abiding—" Continue ye in My love " (ver. 9). As we live in the element of God's love, we inbreathe His affection to our comfort, and we outbreathe it to others' help.

8. How to abide—" If ye keep My commandments ye shall abide in My love " (ver. 10). The royal road of God's benediction is the loyal road of our faithfulness.

9. Fellowship of abiding (ver. 10). Christ does not ask us to do anything He has done to God for us, and which He promises to do in us to God's glory.

10. Joy of abiding (ver. 11). The things of the world pass away, but the joy of the Lord comes to stay.

11. Reward of abiding (ver. 16). Abiding in the Son, we as abiding sons find the abiding fruit, for He not only gives the " fruit of union " (ver. 4), and the " more fruit " of discipline (ver. 2), and the " much fruit " of His indwelling and abundant life to God's glory (verses 5, 8), but the fruit that remains (ver. 16), which puts us in the place of prevailing prayer.

Third. *What is abiding ?* (See 1 John 3 : 24, R.V.)

The Spirit tells us what abiding in Christ means when He says : " He that keepeth His commandments abideth in Him and He in him : and hereby we know He abideth in us by the Spirit which He hath given us."

Fourth. *What does abiding involve ?*

Walking as Christ walked (1 John 2 : 6).

Loving our brethren (1 John 2 : 10 ; 3 : 14, 17).

Abiding with God (1 John 2 : 17).

Fellowship with God (1 John 2 : 19, R.V.).

Truth abiding in us (1 John 2 : 24).

Continuance in the Father and Son (1 John 2 : 24).

Teaching of the Spirit (1 John 2 : 27).

Preparation for the Lord's return (1 John 2 : 28).

Not sinning (1 John 3 : 6).

Recognition of the new nature (1 John 3 : 9).

Eternal life abiding in us (1 John 3 : 15).

Spirit remaining in power (1 John 3 : 24 ; 4 : 13).

Confessing Christ (1 John 4 : 15).

Living in love and ⎫ (1 John 4 : 16).
Love living in us ⎭

Faithfulness to the truth (2 John 2, 9).

The Law of Proportion

By comparing one Scripture with another we get a full meaning. The statement, " The just shall live by faith," occurs four times. By observing the context in each case it will be found the Spirit emphasises a word in the sentence which is in keeping with the character of the book where it occurs (Hab. 2 : 4 ; Rom. 1 : 17 ; Gal. 3 : 11 ; Heb. 10 : 38).

Let us emphasise and then explain each sentence.

" The just *shall* live by *his* faith " (Hab. 2 : 4).

" The *just* shall live by faith " (Rom. 1 : 17).

" The just shall live by *faith* " (Gal. 3 : 11).

" Now the just shall *live* by faith " (Heb. 10 : 38).

Habakkuk states the fact, that the man who humbles himself *before* God, trusts *in* Him, looks *to* Him, and lives *upon* Him, is the one who is blest by Him. Woes around, judgments without, vexation within, fears beside, famine before, and disaster ahead, but amid all, the man who lives with God, lives through all (see Hab. 3 : 17-19).

Paul in his letter to Rome emphasises again and again that the Gospel reveals the righteousness of faith, that is, the righteousness which God imputes to faith. Christ, the Righteousness of God, is put to the account of faith (see Rom. 4 : 3, 5, 6, 9, 11, 13, 22 ; 10 : 6, 10 ; Gal. 3 : 6). As Holsten says : " Righteousness is an *objective* state in which man is placed by a Divine act." And as Godet remarks : " The righteousness of God, according to Paul, embraces two bestowals of grace : man treated (1) as if he had never committed any evil, and (2) as if he had always accomplished all the good God could expect from him."

Then the Apostle goes on to say of the Gospel, " Therein is the righteousness of God revealed from faith to faith, as it is written, " the just shall live by faith."

The meaning of the sentence, " from faith to faith," is not from one degree of faith to another, as stating the progressiveness of faith, but God blesses on the principle of faith, so the words might read, " out of faith unto faith." God offers justification on the ground of faith and not of works, and we meet by our faith what He proffers (see Rom. 3 : 22 ; Phil. 3 : 9 ; Gal. 3 : 22). Therefore the word to emphasise in Romans is " *Just*," that is, the justified shall live on the principle of faith.

To the saints in Galatia the emphatic word is " faith " and Christ in contrast to " works " and law. The words for faith occur 27 times in the Epistle. Five times " the faith " is spoken of, which signifies the truth of the Gospel (1 : 23 ; 3 : 23, R.V.M. ; 3 : 25 ; 6 : 10, R.V.) ; and 22 times faith denotes the act and attitude of faith. Faith expresses itself in *confidence towards God*, hence, it looks away from self to Him ; *committal to God*, hence, it is separation to Himself ; and *communion with God*, hence, it is content in Him.

How this life of faith simplifies everything. The Jews in the Talmud have the saying, " The whole law was given to Moses at Sinai in 613 precepts." David in the 50th Psalm brings them all in the compass of 11. Isaiah beings them to 6 (Isa. 33 : 15) ; Micah to 3 (Micah 6 : 8) ; Isaiah again to 2 (Isa. 56 : 1, 2) ; and Habakkuk to this one, The Just.

When we turn to Hebrews and ponder the context of the sentence before us, the emphasis is on the word " *live.*" Trials and difficulties pressed the saints sore, but the secret power which carried them through was God in answer to their faith ; hence, the Spirit goes on in the next chapter to illustrate and demonstrate what faith in God has done in the past.

The Law of Interpretation

The best interpreter of the Bible is the Bible itself. When the Spirit works He always interprets. The words, " being interpreted," or " by interpretation," are frequently given by way of explanation.

1. A Present God. " Emmanuel, being interpreted, God with us " (Matt. 1 : 23).

2. A Significant Place—" Golgotha . . . being interpreted, the . . . place of a skull " (Mark 15 : 22).

3. A Meanful Cry—" Eloi, Eloi, lama sabachthani ? which is being interpreted, My God, My God, why hast Thou forsaken Me ?" (Mark 15 : 34).

4. A Glorious Teacher—" Rabbi, being interpreted, Master " (John 1 : 38).

5. The Anointed Saviour—" Messias, being interpreted, the Christ " (John 1 : 41).

6. A Changed Sinner—" Thou shalt be called Cephas, which is by interpretation, a stone " (John 1 : 42).

7. A Devoted Saint—" Barnabas, which is being interpreted, the son of consolation " (Acts 4 : 36).

8. A Royal Priest—"Melchizedek, King of Salem . . . being first, by interpretation, King of Righteousness, and then King of Salem, which is King of Peace" (Heb. 7 : 1, 2).

Other examples might be given, such as are found in John 9 : 7, Mark 5 : 41, and Acts 13 : 8. All this goes to show, the Spirit is a God of order, and that He makes things clear to those who are taught of God (1 Cor. 14 : 33).

The Law of Comparison

The careful comparison of one Scripture with another will generally explain a seeming contradiction. " He hath made us accepted in the Beloved," says the Apostle (Eph. 1 : 6), and yet he seems to contradict himself when he says, " We labour, that . . . we may be accepted of Him " (2 Cor. 5 : 9). In the one place he says the believer is " accepted," and in the other he is labouring to be accepted ! The explanation is found in the two different words rendered " accepted." To be " accepted in the Beloved " means to be an object of God's favour. The Greek word " *Charitoo* " comes from " *Charis*," to be gracious ; hence, its meaning is to grace, namely, to endue with honour, to highly favour. The word " *Charitoo* " only occurs in one other place, and that is in Luke 1 : 28. The angel said to Mary, " Thou art highly favoured," or " much graced " as the word might be rendered. The word " *Charis* " occurs 12 times in Ephesians. Read in the light of God's gracious act in making us accepted the word is like a beautiful necklace which adorns the wearer.

The salutation of grace blesses us (1 : 2).

The glory of grace adorns us (1 : 6).

The riches of grace endow us (1 : 7).

The power of grace saves us (2 : 5, 8).

The exceeding riches of grace elevate us (2 : 7).

The dispensation of grace enlightens us (3 : 2).

The gift of grace qualifies us (3 : 7).

The call of grace sends us (3 : 8).

The Christ of grace places us (4 : 7).

The holiness of grace separates us (4 : 29).

The benediction of grace companions us (6 : 24).

To be " accepted of the Lord " means to be well-pleasing to Him. The Greek word " *euarestos* " is a compound word. " *Eu* " means that which is well, and is translated "well done " in Matt. 25 : 21, 23 ; " good " in Mark 14 : 7 ; and " well " in Eph. 6 : 3. " *Arestos* " signifies that which is fit, agreeable, pleasing, and is rendered " pleasing " in 1 John 3 : 22. The compound word " *eu-arestos* " is rendered " well-pleasing " in Phil. 4 : 18, Col. 3 : 20, and Heb. 13 : 21 ; " acceptable " in Rom. 12 : 1, 2 and Eph. 5 : 10 ; " please well " in Titus 2 : 9 ; and " accepted " in 2 Cor. 5 : 9. The more correct rendering in each of the above verses would be " well-pleasing." To be accepted in the Beloved and to be well-pleasing to the Lord are different.

The Law of Similarity in Difference

Difference, or the law of diversability in the use of the same word and expressions. We all know how one word may be used in association with several things. Take the word " board." Primarily it meant a piece of wood, sawn into a thin wide plank. It is applied to the table upon which food is set, hence, you ask, " What's on the board ?" And it is applied to the food on the table, hence, men are said to pay for, or work for, their board. The word is not only applied to the table and what's on it, but also to the people who sit around it, hence, we speak of a board of trustees. When a man goes on a ship, he is said to be on board, and should he fall out of the ship, he is overboard. The conductor of the train cries out, " All aboard," and you say you are going to board up a window. The leather merchant talks about boarding the leather, that is, making it supple. The builder down South declares he is going to board a house, meaning to roof it. A person who selects the theatre as a profession, is said to be on the boards. The cook makes her pastry on a pie-board. The teacher sketches on the black-board. The housekeeper irons on the ironing-board. The mayor puts a notice on the bill-board. The tailor cuts the cloth on a tailor's board. The player plays on the chess-board. A book-binder binds the sheets of a book in boards, and you envelope an article in cardboards.

The English graduate wants to keep on the board. The sailor likes to make a board. The gambler endeavours to sweep the board. We also find one word in the Bible used in different ways.

The word "righteousness," in Romans, is used in seven different ways, and while its primary meaning is to be right, the context suggests the sense in which it is to be understood.

1. Personally, what God is, or His acts consistent with His nature, hence, that which is right (3 : 5, 9, 25).

2. Righteousness of the law, or what God demands from man (10 : 5 ; 9 : 31).

3. Righteousness displayed in the Gospel, that is, God's grace consistent with His character (1 : 17 ; 3 : 21-26 ; 5 : 17, 21 ; 8 : 10).

4. The Righteousness of God personified in Christ, that is, He is all God wishes, and has fulfilled all He required (Rom. 10 : 3, 4).

5. The righteousness of faith, or what God puts to our account, when we believe in Christ, namely, we are made the righteousness of God in Christ (4 : 3-22 ; 9 : 30 ; 10 : 6, 10).

6. The righteousness of the Spirit, or what He produces in the life of the believer (14 : 17).

7. The righteousness of the believer, or the practical outcome of union with Christ (Rom. 6 : 13, 16, 18, 19, 20).

The Law of Completion

To take one side of a truth, and not to recognise the others, is to be guilty of error. The Church in its different aspects will illustrate.

1. The Christship of Jesus is the foundation of the Church—"Thou art the Christ. . . . Upon this rock I will build My Church" (Matt. 16 : 18).

2. The blood of Christ is the atoning price of the Church—"The Church . . . which He purchased with His own blood" (Acts 20 : 28).

3. The Holy Spirit is the Administrator of the Church, hence, He sets "in the Church" His gifts, "severally as He will" (1 Cor. 12 : 28).

4. The ascended Lord is the Head of the Church, His mystical body (Eph. 1 : 22 ; 5 : 23).

5. Love is the motive and moving power of the Church, hence, the members are to love each other "as Christ loved the Church " (Eph. 5 : 2, 25).

6. Prayer is the life of the Church, the power that brings release, even as it did to imprisoned Peter, when prayer was "made without ceasing of the Church unto God " (Acts 12 : 5).

7. Worship of the Lord is the privilege of the Church, and Christ is ever the One Who in the midst of the Church leads her in praise to God (Heb. 2 : 12) ; and the Church is responsible, as well as privileged, to "come together " to remember the Lord's death (1 Cor. 11 : 18-26).

8. Edification, or building each other up, is the rule of the Church, hence, the keynote of all ministry in the Church (1 Cor. 14 : 5, 12, 19).

9. Unity of action is the responsibility of the Church, hence, there is to be no schism in the body, but each member is to tarry one for another, and hold the Head by recognising the members in mutual help and assemblage (1 Cor. 11 : 18-22 ; Eph. 4 : 16).

10. The truth of God is in the custody of the Church, hence, the Church of God is the pillar and ground of the truth (1 Tim. 3 : 15).

11. God Himself is the Centre and Circumference of the Church. The Church is called " the Church of God," and is said to be " in God the Father, and in the Lord Jesus Christ," and it is also " the Church of the Firstborn " (1 Cor. 1 : 2 ; 1 Thess. 1 : 1 ; Heb. 12 : 23).

12. The glory of God is the end of the Church, hence, it displays His manifold wisdom, and is to be to His manifested glory (Eph. 3 : 10, 21 ; 5 : 27).

The Law of Typology

When we say a certain thing is a type we should be perfectly clear of our ground, for a type is something which is used as a symbol by God to foreshadow the thing or person stated. What is a type ? Van Mildert says : " It is essential

242 / Major Bible Truths

to a type in the Scripture adaptation of that term, that there
should be competent evidence of the Divine intention in the
correspondence between it and the antitype." Types may
be divided under seven divisions—Persons, Institutions,
Events, Things, Offices, Places, Actions.

Persons

Adam, the Life-giving Lord (1 Cor. 15 : 45).

Isaac, the offered son (Gen. 22 : 13 ; Rom. 8 : 32).

Jacob, the working shepherd (Gen. 31 : 38 ; John
10 : 11).

Joseph, the rejected brother (Gen. 37 : 24 ; Isa. 53 : 3).

Melchisedek, the kingly priest (Gen. 14 : 18 ; Heb.
7 : 7-10).

Jonah, the incarcerated prophet (Jonah 1 : 17 ; Matt.
12 : 40).

Eliakim, the mighty opener (Isa. 22 : 20-22 ; Rev.
3 : 7).

Events

The flood of coming judgment (Matt. 24 : 37-39).

Creation's light and the Gospel (2 Cor. 4 : 6).

The Passover of Christ's death (1 Cor. 5 : 7).

The lifted serpent and Christ (Num. 21 : 8 ; John
3 : 14).

The manna and the Bread of Life (Exod. 16 : 16 ;
John 6 : 32).

The supply of water from the Rock and Christ (Exod.
17 : 6 ; 1 Cor. 10 : 4).

The priest and the great day of atonement (Lev. 16 ;
Heb. 2 : 17).

Things

The anointing oil and the Spirit (Lev. 7 : 35 ; 1 John
2 : 27).

The Mercy Seat and Christ (Exod. 25 : 17-22 ; Rom.
3 : 25).

Jacob's ladder and Christ (Gen. 28 : 12 ; John 1 : 51).

Laver of brass and God's Word (Exod. 30 : 18-20 ;
Eph. 5 : 26).

Firstfruits and Resurrection (Exod. 22 : 29 ; 1 Cor. 15 : 20).

Ark and salvation (Gen. 7 : 16 ; 1 Pet. 3 : 20, 21).

Golden candlestick and Christ (Exod. 25 : 31 ; John 8 : 12).

Actions

Killing of animal and Christ's death for sin (Lev. 4 : 15 ; Rev. 5 : 9).

Living bird and with blood of slain one on it (Lev. 14 : 4-7 ; Rom. 4 : 25).

Sprinkling of blood and cleansing (Lev. 14 : 7 ; Heb. 9 : 13).

Laying hands on sacrifice and identification (Lev. 16 : 21 ; 1 Tim. 4 : 14).

Banishment of scapegoat and Christ taking away sins (Lev. 16 : 22 ; Isa. 53 : 6, 12).

Placing blood on members of body and sanctification (Exod. 29 : 20 ; 1 Cor. 6 : 20).

Placing blood on doorposts and faith (Exod. 12 : 7 ; Heb. 11 : 28).

Offices

Moses the prophet and Christ (Deut. 18 : 15 ; Acts 3 : 22).

Aaron the priest and Christ the Offerer (Exod. 28 : 1 ; Heb. 10 : 11).

David the king and Christ (2 Sam. 7 ; Luke 1 : 32).

Joshua the captain and Christ (Josh. 5 : 14 ; Heb. 2 : 10).

Abel the shepherd and Christ (Gen. 4 : 2 ; John 10 : 1-18).

Joseph the saviour and Christ (Gen. 50 : 19, 20 ; Heb. 7 : 25).

Samson the conqueror and Christ (Jud. 16 : 9 ; Col. 2 : 14, 15).

Places

The Egypt of the world (Exod. 1 : 1 ; Rev. 11 : 8).

The wilderness of unbelief (Psa. 78 : 40 ; Heb. 3 : 8-11).

The curse of Sinai (Deut. 28 : 19 ; Gal. 3 : 13).

The Bethel of God's presence (Gen. 28 : 19 ; Matt. 28 : 20).

The tabernacle of God's indwelling (Exod. 25 : 8 ; John 1 : 14 ; 2 Cor. 6 : 16).

The safety of God's refuge (Num. 35 : 6 ; Heb. 6 : 18).

The Zion of blessing (2 Sam. 5 : 7 ; Heb. 12 : 22).

Institutions.

The Sabbath of rest (Gen. 2 : 2 ; Heb. 4 : 9).

The Passover of Deliverance (Exod. 12 : 11-28 ; 1 Cor. 5 : 7).

The firstfruits of resurrection (Lev. 23 : 10 ; 1 Cor. 15 : 23).

The trumpet of Christ's coming (Lev. 23 : 24 ; 1 Cor. 15 : 52 ; 1 Thess. 4 : 16).

The Pentecost of the Spirit (Lev. 23 : 15-21 ; Acts 2 : 1).

The Tabernacle of the Millennium (Lev. 23 : 33-36 ; Zech. 14 : 16 ; Matt. 17 : 4).

The Jubilee of Israel (Lev. 25 ; Isa. 60 : 1-3 ; Luke 4 : 18, 19).

The Law of Consequence

We find again and again in explaining the reason or ground of God's action, a " Therefore " or a " Wherefore."

1. Incarnation. "*Therefore* also that Holy Thing which shall be born of thee shall be called the Son of God " (Luke 1 : 35). The Producer of the Wonderful Producement of the Greatest Production, as evidenced in Christ, was the Holy Spirit.

2. Inspiration. "*Wherefore* He saith . . . Thou shalt not suffer Thine Holy One to see corruption " (Acts 13 : 35). The records about the Son of God, are the revelation of God Himself to us in His Son.

3. Justification. "*Therefore* it was imputed to him for righteousness " (Rom. 4 : 22). Abraham's faith credited God's faithfulness, and God put to His credit what Christ is and has done (Rom. 4 : 23-25, R.V.).

4. Ascension. "*Wherefore* He saith, when He ascended on high, He led captivity captive, and gave gifts unto men "

(Eph. 4 : 8). He has gained rights for us, and therefore we have a right to them.

5. Exaltation. " *Wherefore* God hath highly exalted Him " (Phil. 2 : 9). Because He took the seven downward steps to the Cross (2 : 5-8), God has given to Jesus the seven upward steps to the glory.

6. Intention. " *Wherefore* when He cometh into the world, He saith . . . a body hast Thou prepared Me " (Heb. 10 : 5). He was identified with us sinners that He might answer for our sins in His death.

7. Sanctification. " *Wherefore*, Jesus also, that He might sanctify the people with His own blood, suffered without the gate " (Heb. 13 : 12, 13). He went to the place of death that we might be separated to Him.

The Law of Initiation

The cause of the believer's initiation into God's secrets is because God makes them known by His Spirit in His Word.

There are several mysteries made known in the New Testament. The place where each is mentioned must determine the application. To mix up these mysteries is to make confusion worse confounded.

1. *The Mystery of Israel's Blindness* is no mystery regarding the blindness of Israel ; but its duration is made known in the fact that it is until the fulness, or the number, of the Gentiles be gathered in (Rom. 11 : 25).

2. *The Mystery of Godliness* is that God was made manifest in the flesh, hence its greatness and glory (1 Tim. 3 : 16).

3. *The Mystery of the Church* is that God, in His electing grace, is blessing those who receive Christ, and making them, whether Jew or Gentile, one in Him (Rom. 16 : 25 ; Eph. 3 : 3, 4, 9 ; 5 : 32 ; 6 : 19 ; Col. 1 : 26, 27 ; 4 : 3 ; 1 Tim. 3 : 9). Hence it is called the " mystery " of what was kept secret since the world began.

4. *The Mystery of Lawlessness* is the end of hell's working in the self-will of man, which will develop the production of the lawless one (2 Thess. 2 : 7).

5. *The Mystery of God* and of the Father and of Christ is the centralisation of everything, whether in grace or

government, in Christ, and that in Him dwells all the fulness of the Godhead bodily (Eph. 1 : 9 ; Col. 2 : 2 ; Rev. 10 : 7).

6. *The Mystery of the Seven Stars* is that Christ holds all those who are in places of responsibility, in God's assembly, by His almighty power (Rev. 1 : 20).

7. *The Mystery of Babylon* is that behind all the abominable mixture of the world's religions, and its commercial spirit, there is the Satanic spirit that governs it (Rev. 17 : 5).

8. *The Mystery about the Glorified Saints* is that we shall not all sleep, but that we shall all be changed, and be made like to our glorified Lord (1 Cor. 15 : 51).

9. *The Mystery of the Kingdom of Heaven*, in a general sense, is that behind the body of the outward meaning of revealed truth there is a soul of secret explanation (Matt. 13 : 11).

The Law of Definiteness

The Lord is always definite in His truth and teaching. When the Lord speaks, it is for us to bow and obey, but when He speaks in a specific character and in a special way, it is for us to listen attentively and intently.

This law could be illustrated from many Scriptures. We refer to Christ's messages to the Seven Churches as found in connection with the word, " These Things."

1. The Holder of the Stars. " These things saith He that holdeth the seven stars in His right hand " (Rev. 2 : 1). The stars represent the ministers whom the Lord uses in His ministry to the churches. When they are held by Him, and used in His service, He serves and speaks through them to purpose.

2. The First and the Last. " These things saith the First and the Last, which was dead and is alive " (2 : 8). Between Him Who is First in creation, and Last in consummation, is His death and resurrection. He can be to us the Genesis and Revelation, because He died for us, and lives for us.

3. The Possessor of the Two-edged Sword. " These things saith He which hath the sharp sword with two edges " (Rev. 2 : 12). His Word cuts both ways, as His message to

the church at Pergamos illustrates ; it cuts into the inner life as well as the outward. He lays bare the heart of purpose, and discovers where the life is barren and wanting.

4. The Eyes of Fire. " These things saith the Son of God, Who hath His eyes like unto a flame of fire " (Rev. 2 : 18). The flame will not burn unless it has fuel on which to feed, but when there is the combustibility of sin, it will scorch and burn to the hurt of the sinner.

5. The Possessor of the Spirit. " These things saith He that hath the seven spirits " (Rev. 3 : 1). Isa. 11 : 2, 3, reveals the Holy Spirit in His sevenfold character. The Lamb and the Spirit are always associated. The Bible begins with a Brooding Dove, and ends with the Bleeding Lamb.

6. The Holy One. " These things saith He that is holy," etc. (Rev. 3 : 7). He is Holy and True. Holiness and Truth are not merely attributes with Him, they express what He is in the essence of His being.

7. The Faithful Witness. " These things saith the Amen, the Faithful and True Witness, the Beginning of the creation of God " (Rev. 3 : 14). The " Amen " comes first, and the " Beginning " last, and between the two He is revealed as " The Faithful and True Witness." Does this not reveal to us Christ in His life and ministry, as the Revelation of God ? And as such He is the Amen, so let it be, and as the " Beginning " He can make it to be, as He did in the beginning.

The Law of the Spirit

" The Law of the Spirit of Life in Christ Jesus, makes us free from the law of sin and death " (Rom. 8 : 2).

A Spirit-filled life is extensive in its meaning. There are several phases and phrases which have to do with a Spirit-filled life.

" Baptism " is the Immersing Word, and denotes the Spirit's Power (Acts 1 : 5).

" Anointing " is the Qualifying Word, and speaks of His Consecrating Grace (2 Cor. 1 : 21).

" Sealing " is the Claiming Word, and avows His proprietary Rights (Eph. 1 : 13, R.V. ; 4 : 30).

"Enduement" is the Endowing Word, and proclaims His Empowering Ability (Luke 24 : 49).

"Earnest" is the Assuring Word, and guarantees the Coming Glory (2 Cor. 5 : 5, R.V.).

"Full" is the Sufficient Word, and tells of His Satisfying Efficiency (Acts 6 : 5).

"Filled" is the Overflowing Word, and represents His constant inflow and outflow in life and service (Acts 2 : 4).

"Filled in the Spirit," not "with," is the most extensive word which is used of His ministry. The preposition "en" should read "in," and not "with." The Spirit is in every believer as the Spirit of Adoption, but it is not every believer that is in the Spirit. It is one thing to possess the Spirit, and it is another thing to be possessed by Him. When the Spirit lives in us in absolute possession, we live in Him in the many-sidedness of His grace. When we live and walk in the extensiveness of His sphere, He is with us as our Friend to help, upon us as the Power to qualify, under us in His Might to sustain, before us in Leadership to guide, behind us in His Protection to shield, and around us in His Love to encompass.

There are three things we must never confound, and these are : The implantation of the life of the Spirit, the indwelling of the Spirit in the life He has implanted, and the infilling of the Spirit. In the first the Spirit is the Giver and Worker ; in the second the Father is the Sealer and Claimer ; and in the third the Son is the Promiser and Baptiser.

The Law of Obedience

The whole of the Christian life is summed up in the word "obey." If we read through the Book of Deuteronomy alone, we see how the Spirit of God emphasises the importance and influence of obedience.

1. Obedience is the Proof of Repentance. "If thou return unto the Lord, and shalt be obedient unto His voice" (4 : 30). The evidence of having returned to the Lord is response to Him in obedience.

2. Obedience is the Procurer of Blessing. "A blessing if ye obey the commandments of the Lord thy God" (11 : 27,

28). We command the Lord's blessings when we respond to the Lord's Word.

3. Obedience is the Preventor of Contamination. " Ye shall . . . obey His voice. . . . So shalt thou put the evil away " (13 : 1-5). Obedience is the circle which encloses us and separates from the evil around.

4. Obedience is the Evidence of Relationship. " Thou art become the people of the Lord thy God, thou shalt therefore obey the voice of the Lord thy God " (27 : 9, 10). Because the Lord is " Thy God," we are under obligation to do His will.

5. Obedience is the Secret of Victory. " Obey His voice . . . then the Lord thy God will turn thy captivity " (30 : 2, 3). Obedience is the hand that knocks off the fetters of bondage, and the cause of freedom in the Lord's service.

6. Obedience is the Soul of Prosperity. " Obey the voice of the Lord thy God . . . the Lord thy God will make thee plenteous in every work " (30 : 8, 9). The prosperity of the soul is the soul of all prosperity.

7. Obedience is the Means of Longevity. " Obey His voice . . . for He is thy life, and the length of thy days " (30 : 20). Length of days, and loyalty to the Lord, are bound together as cause and effect.

The Law of Comprehension

The little words of the Bible are large in their claim and revelation.

The magnificence, munificence, and the manifoldness of God's grace and love are seen in the use of the word " All " in Ephesians.

1. " All Spiritual Blessing " is the totality of His bestowment in Christ (1 : 3).

2. " All Wisdom " is revealed in the giving of His love " according to the riches of His grace " (1 : 7, 8).

3. " All Things " God will in the end gather together in the Christ (1 : 10).

4. " All Things " are made subservient to the " counsel of His will " (1 : 11).

5. " All the Saints " are in the plan of His love, and the purpose of His grace (1 : 15 ; 3 : 8, 18).

6. " All Principality, and power, and might, and dominion," are under Christ, for He is " above all " and " all " are " under His feet " (1 : 21, 22).

7. " All in All " is the descriptive word which proclaims the compass of His fulness (1 : 23).

8. " All Things were Created by Jesus Christ " (3 : 9), remind us Who is the Organiser and Originator, and by what means they were made to be.

9. " All the Fulness of God " (3 : 19) is the sphere into which believers are to find themselves in being supplied.

10. " All we Ask or Think," yea, " exceeding abundantly above," is the arresting word in declaring God's grace in bestowment (3 : 20).

11. " All Ages " are to witness to the glory and power of Christ (3 : 21).

12. " All Lowliness " with the sisters of " meekness, long-suffering, and forbearance in love," are to be the character-istics of the walk of the believer (4 : 1-3).

13. " All " ... " All " ... " All " ... " All." Four " alls " in one verse ! " One God and Father of all, Who is above all, and through all, and in you all " (4 : 6). He is sufficient for all His children, under all conditions.

14. " All Heavens." He is " above." He went to the lowest place, and now occupies the highest (4 : 10).

15. " All Things " He " fills " or " fulfils," no matter what the calls are which are made upon Him (4 : 10).

16. " All Come in the Unity of the Faith " (4 : 13), is the goal to which He is leading.

17. " All Things," and in them all He leads His saints to grow up into Christ (4 : 15).

18. " All Uncleanness with Greediness " (4 : 19), is the reminder of what was once the trend and tendency of the past life.

19. " All Bitterness . . . and All Malice," and all the kindred crop of ill growths, are to be put away (4 : 31 ; 5 : 3-6).

20. " All Goodness, and Righteousness, and Truth," are the trinity of the Spirit's fruit, which are to be seen (5 : 9).

21. " All Things that are Reproved are Made Manifest by the Light " (5 : 13). Light reveals the wrong, and points to the right.

22. " All Things " call for the Giving of Thanks (5 : 20).

23. " All " Having " Done," we are called not to trust in our victories, but to " stand " prepared for other assaults (6 : 13).

24. " All, Above All," Christ as the Shield of faith, covers all the armour, so that no part is unprotected (6 : 16).

25. " All the Fiery Darts of the Wicked " can be quenched by the Lord (6 : 16).

26. " All Prayer and Supplication." Praying at every point and in every time (6 : 18).

27. " All Perseverance and Supplication for All Saints " (6 : 18). Always, with all the soul, and for all the souls.

The Law of Enclosure

So many of God's thoughts enclose a world of meaning in the contents of their significance. Christ is called " The Word." This Title occurs four times in John 1, verses 1, 14.

The word rendered " Word " is " Logos," and signifies the thought of God expressed in action ; hence, we must remember that its significance covers the whole of Christ's personality,—His life, His work, and His message.

Christ, as the Word, proclaims :

1. The glory of His personality (John 1 : 14).
2. The glory of His miracles (John 2 : 11).
3. The glory of His love (John 3 : 16).
4. The glory of His life (John 4 : 14).
5. The glory of His revelation (John 5 : 39).
6. The glory of His supply (John 6 : 58).
7. The glory of His death and resurrection (John 19 : 30 ; 20 : 19-31).

The Law of Recompence

We should not give to get, but we get in giving. This is one of the fundamental principles which Christ enunciates. The following Scripture incidents illustrate.

Isaac gave the jewels to Rebekah, and Rebekah gave herself to Isaac (Gen. 24 : 22, 58).

Ruth clave to Naomi in her affection, and Naomi clave to Ruth in her service (Ruth 1 : 18 ; 4 : 16).

David received the men in the hold when they were in distress, and David was helped by them when he was distressed (1 Sam. 22 : 2 ; 1 Chron. 11 : 15-19).

Abigail ministered to David in his need, and David honoured her in her widowhood (1 Sam. 25 : 18-27, 39).

The widow of Zarephath gave out of her penury to Elijah, and Elijah was the means of bringing her the Lord's plenty (1 Kings 17 : 12-16).

The Shunammite woman entertained Elisha to his comfort, and the prophet obtained a child for her to her consolation (2 Kings 4 : 8-17).

The lad gave five cakes and the few fishes to the Lord and was rewarded by seeing twelve baskets full of broken and unhandled pieces after the multitude was fed (John 6 : 9-13).

And the greatest Example of all is He Who came not to be ministered unto, but to minister, and Who obtains by His love a willing and loving ministry in return (Matt. 20 : 28 ; 2 Cor. 12 : 15).

The Law of " According To."

The preposition " Kata " speaks of definite design in the Lord giving us a standing by which we estimate His grace and authority. This " according to " is of frequent occurrence in the Epistle to the Ephesians. (See 1 : 5, 7, 11, 19 ; 2 : 2 ; 3 : 7, 11, 16, 20 ; 4 : 7, 16, 22 ; 6 : 5 ; also rendered " after," 1 : 11, 15 ; " by," 3 : 3 ; " concerning," 4 : 22 ; and " with," 6 : 6.)

Taking this " according to " as it applies to the believer in a few places we find seven standards :

1. Standard of Authority—" According to the Scriptures " (1 Cor. 15 : 3, 4).

2. Standard of Salvation—" According to God's mercy " (Titus 3 : 5).

3. Standard of Blessing—"According to the riches of God's grace" (Eph. 1 : 7).

4. Standard of Power—"According to God's power in Christ's resurrection" (Eph. 1 : 19).

5. Standard of Giving—"According to the riches of His glory" (Eph. 3 : 16).

6. Standard of Effectiveness—"According to the effectual working of His power" (Eph. 3 : 20).

7. Standard of Supply—"According to God's riches in glory in Christ Jesus" (Phil. 4 : 19).

The Law of Reference

The Scriptures are like the many levers in a signal box in their interlocking connections. There are over 200 references to the Scriptures in the Book of The Revelation. There will be found fifty points of correspondence with the narrative of the journey of Israel from Egypt to the Jordan, and what is found in Peter's Epistles. We should expect to find these when we recall his letters were addressed to those of his brethren "scattered abroad" (1 Pet. 1 : 1).

This law if used will illustrate the truth that the best commentary on the Bible is the Bible itself.

Some references are direct, as when we read in Matthew's Gospel regarding what the Lord definitely spoke* " through " or " by the prophets" (1 : 22 ; 2 : 5, 15, 23 ; 4 : 4, 14 ; 8 : 17 ; 13 : 35 ; 21 : 4 ; 24 : 15 ; 27 : 9). Other references are indirect, such as God not sparing His own Son, while He spared Abraham the pain of killing Isaac (Rom. 8 : 32).

" In the midst of our Lord's hour of betrayal and the agonies of the passion week, He reminded the impetuous Peter that He had infinite resources of power had He chosen to draw upon them. ' Thinkest thou not that I could pray to My Father, and He should presently give Me more than twelve legions of angels ?' (Matt. 26 : 53). We have but to turn back to 1 Chron. 27 : 1-15 to find a hint of why He referred thus to ' twelve legions,' and get an illuminative illustration of His meaning : for there we read how David, His kingly type, surrounded himself with twelve legions of

---

* " Dia " with the genitive indicates an active agent.

servant-soldiers, each legion numbering 24,000, and all together therefore 288,000, or, including the 12,000 officers that naturally waited on the chief princes, an immense body-guard of 300,000 ! How beautifully our Lord thus taught His disciple, who was eager to draw a sword to smite His foes, that David's greater Son had at command resources far greater than Judea's King ; and if in one night one angel of the Lord had smitten with death a hundred and eighty-five thousand Assyrians, what might not twelve legions have done in that hour of distress ! Such a host could depopulate thirty-seven worlds like ours !"

The Law of Perspective

" The point of view must be found, before the relation of truth can be known." So many fail to give a true picture of truth because their perspective is at fault. What is the Church's standpoint ? Is it the Old Testament ? No, for it reveals Christ in relation to Israel. Is it the Gospels ? No, for the Church being built is yet future. Is it from the standpoint of the Acts ? Not exclusively, for there the Church is largely Jewish. Is it the standpoint of the Revelation ? No, for after the fourth chapter the Church is not mentioned. What is the Church's standpoint ? The Pauline Epistles, which make known the Church of God as the mystery hid in Him (see Rom. 16 : 25, 26 ; Eph. 3 : 4-12).

The Law of Order

We have often been told we should " put first things first." Some things are first in the order of time ; others are first in the place of importance. The mounted policemen are first in the order of a Lord Mayor's show, but they are not first in the order of importance. The Lord Mayor is the first in the order of importance. Paul says in speaking of the soul of the Gospel, " I declared unto you first of all, how that Christ died and rose again according to the Scriptures " (1 Cor. 15 : 3, 4) ; and Peter, in speaking of the character-istics of the last days, says, " Knowing this first, that there shall come in the last days, scoffers, walking after their own lusts, and saying, Where is the promise of His coming ?" (2 Pet. 3 : 3, 4). These are first in importance.

Christ uses the word "first" twice in the Sermon on the Mount, and in both of these instances the reference is to the first thing in the order of time. When one brings his gift to the altar and remembers his brother has something against him, he is to leave his gift and "first to be reconciled to his brother" (Matt. 5 : 23, 24). When the things of life are contemplated they are to be subordinated to the kingdom of God, hence Christ says, "Seek ye first the kingdom of God, and His righteousness : and all these things shall be added unto you" (Matt. 6 : 33).

The Law of Variation

The change from the singular to the plural pronoun in the prophecy about Tyre in Ezek. 26 is of Divine intent, and is confirmed by the facts of history. The verses seven to eleven refer to Nebuchadnezzar's exploits against Tyre, hence, we are told what "he shall do," but from verses twelve to fourteen we are told what "they" shall accomplish, referring to Alexander and his generals in their subsequent invasion against Tyre.

Another instance is found in what is known as one of the imprecatory Psalms. One has said, "In Psalm 109 there is a most noticeable change of number and person. In verses 1-5 the plural ' they ' is prominent ; and again, after verse 20. But from verse 6 to 19, the singular ' he ' and ' his ' and ' him ' are found thirty times. Here again this divides the psalm into three parts, and if the word ' saying ' be understood, at the close of verse 5, the whole imprecation that follows, down to verse 19, becomes not the psalmist's prayer for vengeance on his adversaries, but their imprecation of curses upon him, and renders the whole psalm luminous."

The Law of Discrimination

A critic, who observed to Michael Angelo that he seemed in his work to be careful about trifles, was answered, " Trifles make perfection, and perfection is no trifle." Take two facts about Christ. He is called "The only Begotten" (John 3 : 16) and "The First Begotten" (Heb. 1 : 6). As the only Begotten He was the only One of God Who could meet our need, and He stands alone in His Deity and Majesty; but as "The First Begotten" He rose from the dead as the One Who was the Pledge of all the redeemed who should be raised and glorified. God made His Son like to all that He might make all sons like to One.

Christ is called the Son of God, but the word for Son is used in an adoptive sense. He is not a descendant of God nor of man. He is eternally the Son of God, God the Son, Who was sent by the Father. As the Son of Man His humanity was the product of the Holy Spirit (Luke 1 : 35). Adam was born without a mother, and Christ was begotten without a human father.

The Law of Exhortation

Exhortation means an appeal to the heart and conscience of the individual to do something that is worthy and of importance and leads to a practical end. We frequently find the Apostles exhorting those to whom they write to do certain things in connection with the words, " Let us." The following outline in connection with the coming of Christ will illustrate.

1. *Separation.* Seeing "the night is far spent," and " the day is at hand, *let us* cast off the works of darkness and put on the armour of light " (Rom. 13 : 12). The clothes of the old man of sin are to be cast away as useless and worn out, and the armour of Him Who is Light is to panoply us.

2. *Walk.* " *Let us* walk honestly, and put on the Lord Jesus Christ " (Rom. 13 : 13, 14). To walk in the realm of honesty means to be open to the light, and free from any ulterior motives, namely, to be transparent. To be clothed with Christ signifies He is seen and heard.

3. *Following.* " *Let us* therefore follow after peace " (Rom. 14 : 19). The association of these words is in relation to our conduct towards each other. Our conduct will be reviewed at the judgment seat of Christ, when we shall each have " to give account of himself to God " (12), hence we are not to judge or despise each other, but to " follow after peace."

4. *Reaping.* " Let *us* not be weary in well-doing, for in due season we shall reap, if we faint not " (Gal. 6 : 9). We shall reap in kind what we sow.

5. *Alertness.* " Let *us* not sleep " (1 Thess. 5 : 6). To be in a state of spiritual slumber, as the word " sleep " means, is to evidence we are in a wrong condition of soul. To be awake is to show we are alert to the Lord's will.

6. *Watchfulness.* " Let *us* watch and be sober " (1 Thess. 5 : 6). We need a watchful eye to see what the enemy is after, a watchful heart to keep the garden of our inner being, and a watchful spirit to be ready for our Lord.

7. *Sobriety.* " Let *us*, who are of the day, be sober " (1 Thess. 5 : 8). Because of what we are, we ought to be different from others.

The Law of Distinctiveness

This law is finely and tersely made known in the use of the word " this " in John's First Epistle, especially if we know that the same word is rendered " herein " and " hereby." If students will look up the associations of the following sentences they will see what a glorious unfolding of truth there is found in this distinctive word.

" In *this* was manifested the love of God " (4 : 19).

" *This* commandment have we from Him " (4 : 21).

" By *this* we know that we love the children of God " (5 : 2).

" For *this* is the love of God that we keep His commandments " (5 : 3).

" *This* is the victory that overcometh " (5 : 4).

" *This* is He that came by water and blood " (5 : 6).

" *This* is the witness of God " (5 : 9).

" *This* is the record " (5 : 11).

" *This* is the confidence that we have in Him " (5 : 14).

" *This* is the true God and eternal life " (5 : 20).

The Law of Concentration

What a difference we find in the thought of man and in the revelation of God when the nature of God is in question. With the Greek, God is Beauty ; with the Roman, God is

Force; with the Jew, God is Jehovah; with the scientist, God is the First Cause; with the man in the street, God is Providence; with the moralist, God is Righteousness; with the philosopher, God is Thought; but when we turn to the pages of the New Testament we find in profound and simple language that "God is Love."

This love is not an attribute of love such as righteousness, goodness and truth, but it is the very nature of God and the eternalness of His nature, for it does not say that "God was Love," or that He will be Love, but that He "is" what He ever will be in the eternal present.

To illustrate the concrete character of God's Word we find in the First Epistle of John how he plays upon the words Light, Love and Life. We may sum them up by saying, Life is the sum of all being; Light is the sum of all intelligence; and Love is the sum of all moral excellence. The whole of John's Epistle may be summarized under the following points:

Division I. 1:1-4. Introduction. The Logos. His eternity and identity with the Father. His revelation in the flesh.

Division II. 1:5—2:11. The message concerning Light.

Division III. 2:12—5:3. The message concerning Love.

Division IV. 5:4-21. The message concerning Life.

The Law of Climax

The Lord always has an end in view in calling attention to any given thing, hence, when the Spirit of God speaks of the Priesthood of our Lord in contrast to the Priesthood of the past, He ends the whole of His teaching by saying, "Now of the things which we have spoken this is the sum, we have such a High Priest" (Heb. 8:1). This is more definitely seen when we know that the word "sum" indicates a capital, or a specific outcome.

This may be further apprehended when we read such a sentence, as we find frequently in the Prophets, "In that day," meaning, of course, the time when Christ shall come in His power and glory to set up His millennial kingdom on the earth, and if the prophecy by Isaiah alone is read it makes known what will take place in that day.

The Law of Prominence

Another thing of importance to observe is the prominence given to any stated truth. When Paul speaks of the death and resurrection of Christ, and uses the words, "*first of all*" (I Cor. 15 : 3), he not only means first in the sense of coming first, but *first in importance;* as Godet says: "We need not give the word 'first' the temporal meaning, it is the fundamental importance of those one or two points which Paul wishes to characterise by the term." The soldiers in a royal procession come first in the *order* of the march, but the king is the first one as to the personage of importance. That is the sense in which we must ever view Christ's death and resurrection. They can never take a secondary place. They must always be foremost and first. We call attention to Christ's death, to the fact that "Christ died for our sins." This must ever be first in importance, because it is the most important truth of all. All truth is of importance, but there are certain truths that have a *relative* importance, and there are others which have an *essential* importance, even as the hub of the wheel is of essential importance to the wheel, because of the position it occupies, while the spokes are of importance because of their relative connection with the hub.

Christ's Death is the Key-stone to the Arch of Truth. The Holy Spirit recognises this when He says, "Christ died . . . according to the Scriptures." The jewel of Christ's atonement lies in the casket of Truth. The following seven facts of history, declared in the prophetic Scriptures, will illustrate.

We are told how He would die in Psalm 22 : 16. He was "pierced" according to the Roman law, and not stoned to death according to Jewish law.

He was to be betrayed by "a friend" (Psa. 41 : 9), and sold for thirty pieces of silver (Zech. 11 : 12).

He was, by His death, to restore that which He took not away (Psa. 69 : 4). " He bare the sin of many " (Isa. 53 : 12), and " was numbered with the transgressors " (Isa. 53 : 12).

There was no compulsion in His sacrifice. His readiness is finely expressed in His " I delight to do Thy will, O God " (Psa. 40 : 8).

The depth and intensity of His sufferings are heralded forth in the words of soul despair, " My God, My God, why hast Thou forsaken Me " (Psa. 22 : 1).

His absolute identity with the sins of His people is tersely put, when He speaks of their iniquity as His own—" My sin " (Psa. 38 : 3).

The Divine Actor behind all is beyond question, for it " pleased Jehovah to bruise Him " (Isa. 53 : 10).

The late Adolph Saphir says : " The cross of Christ is the substantiation of all prophecy," yea, we may say, " The fulfilment of all Scripture," for as Christ Himself reminded the two disciples as He journeyed to Emmaus, His sufferings and glory are the two river beds in which the streams of truth flow. He is the Promised Seed of Eden ; the Shelter-ing Ark of Noah ; the Ram offered in the stead of Isaac ; the Passover Lamb of Exodus ; the Perfect Sacrifices of Leviticus ; the Life-giving Serpent of Numbers ; the Acces-sible Refuge of Deuteronomy ; the Gracious Saviour of Joshua ; the Mighty Man of Valour of Judges ; the Kinsman Redeemer of Ruth ; the Dependent Conqueror of Samuel ; the Glorious King of Kings ; the Vigilant Administrator of Chronicles ; the Prayerful Builder of Nehemiah ; the Wise Leader of Ezra ; the Prevailing Intercessor of Esther ; the Delivering Daysman of Job ; the Patient Sufferer of the Psalms ; the Upright Son of Proverbs ; the Wise Man of Ecclesiastes ; the Attractive Beloved of Canticles ; the Beautiful Messenger of Isaiah ; the Weeping Prophet of Jeremiah ; the Glorious One of Ezekiel ; the Cut-off Prince of Daniel ; the Refreshing Dew of Hosea ; the Resolute Judge of Joel ; the Raiser-up of Amos ; the Satisfying Possession of Obadiah ; the Afflicted Substitute of Jonah ; the Caster-away of sins of Micah ; the Irresistible Stronghold of Nahum ; the Holy Searcher of Habakkuk ; the Glad Singer of

Zephaniah; the Faithful Blesser of Haggai; the Smitten Shepherd of Zechariah; and the Coming Refiner of Malachi.

The Law of Personal Appeal

Christ was continually calling attention to Himself, and yet self is never obtruded. In John 14 Christ used the personal pronoun over thirty times. Here is a summary:

1. The " Me " of Faith's object (verse 1).
2. The " My " of " Father's Home " (verse 2).
3. The " I would " of assurance (verse 2).
4. The " I go " of preparation (verse 3).
5. The " I will " of come again (verse 3).
6. The " where I am " of place (verse 3).
7. The " whither I go " of knowledge (verse 4).
8. The " I am " of Way, Truth, and Life (verse 6).
9. The " by Me " of mediation (verse 6).
10. The " known Me " of the Father (verse 7).
11. The " have I been " of presence (verse 9).
12. The " known Me " of reproof (verse 9).
13. The " hath seen Me " of revelation (verse 9).
14. The " I am " and " in Me " of union (verse 10).
15. The " I speak " and " in Me " of the Father's Word (verse 10).
16. The " believe Me " of recognition (verse 11).
17. The " I say " of authority (verse 12).
18. The " believeth on Me " of promise (verse 12).
19. The " I do " of co-workmanship (verse 12).
20. The " My Name " of prayer (verses 13, 14).
21. The " I will " of answered prayer (verses 13,14).
22. The " love Me " of obedience (verse 15).
23. The " I will pray " of intercession (verse 16).
24. The " I will " of comfort (verse 18).
25. The " see Me " of vision (verse 19).
26. The " I live " of life (verse 19).
27. The " in Me " of union (verse 20).
28. The " My commandments " of responsibility (ver. 21).

29. The " loveth Me " of affection (verse 24).

30. The " I will love " of reciprocity (verses 21, 23, 24).

31. The " I have spoken " and " said " of remembrance (verses 25, 26, 28).

32. The " I leave " and " I give " of peace (verse 27).

33. The " loved Me " of attraction (verse 28).

34. The " nothing in Me " of sin (verse 30).

35. The " I love " and " I do " of love (verse 31).

The Law of Repetition

Eight times in the Prophecy of Amos in connection with eight peoples, we have the peculiar sentence, " For three transgressions, and for four, I will not turn away the punishment thereof " (Amos 1 : 3, 6, 9, 11, 13 ; 2 : 1, 4, 6). Then follows a reason why God dealt in punishment with the several parties which are associated with the eight times God uses the word " because."

Christ in the Gospel of Matthew uses the pregnant and personal sentence, " Verily I say unto you," no less than thirty times (5 : 18, 26 ; 6 : 2, 5, 16 ; 8 : 10 ; 10 : 15, 23, 42 ; 11 : 11 ; 13 : 17 ; 16 : 28 ; 17 : 20 ; 18 : 3, 13, 18 ; 19 : 23, 28 ; 21 : 21, 31 ; 23 : 36 ; 24 : 2, 34, 47 ; 25 : 12, 40, 45 ; 26 : 13, 21, 34).

His fiat is final and His Word settles everything.

In the Prophecy of Isaiah the hand of the Lord is frequently said to be " stretched out " in judgment (Isa. 5 : 25 ; 9 : 12, 17, 21 ; 10 : 4 ; 14 : 26, 27), and five out of the eight times the words, " For all this His anger is not turned away, but His hand is stretched out still," occur. Sin calls for judgment, and the judgment is not abated until the purpose is accomplished.

Three times Christ uses the sentence, " Cannot be My disciple," in laying down the conditions of discipleship (Luke 14 : 26, 27, 33). Three times Christ reminded the Jews of the consequence of unbelief, namely, they would " die in their sins," and " whither I go ye cannot come " (John 8 : 21, 24) ; and three times Christ asked Peter the question, " Lovest thou Me ? " (John 21 : 15-17).

The Law of Simile

In our Lord's teaching He was continually using similes. Again and again He said, " The kingdom of heaven is like " this and that (see the eight Parables in Matt. 13). A simile is one thing said to be like to another.

1. Sinners in their stupidity and straying are said to be " like sheep going astray " (Isa. 53 : 6). Straying sinners get away from God because of the strain and wilfulness in their hearts.

2. The Saviour, in His submission in giving Himself over to die for our sins, is " brought as " (like) " a lamb to the slaughter," and " as (like) a sheep before her shearers is dumb " (Isa. 53 : 7).

3. The Lord's love for His people is " like a father " who " pitieth his children " (Psa. 103 : 13). His love is true, tender, providing, constant, and eternal.

4. The Lord's care and discipline is " as " (like) " an eagle stirreth up her nest, fluttereth over her young, spreadeth abroad her wings, taketh them, beareth them in her wings " (Deut. 32 : 11). What an appropriate and beautiful simile of the Lord's tender service.

5. The Lord's ministry and mindfulness is like a shepherd for his sheep, for " He shall feed His flock like a shepherd " (Isa. 40 : 11). He tends His own tenderly, watchfully, constantly, and well.

6. The Lord's ability to secure His saints is happily expressed in David's testimony when he says, " He maketh my feet like hinds' feet " (2 Sam. 22 : 34). When we trust Him He maketh our goings secure as we tread the difficult places in life.

7. The Psalmist uses the word " like " in expressing his loneliness, sadness, and trial—" My days are consumed like smoke, and my bones are burned as (like) an hearth. My heart is smitten and withered like grass. I am like a pelican of the wilderness. I am like an owl of the desert. . . . As (like) a sparrow alone. A shadow that declineth, and I am withered like grass " (Psa. 102 : 1-11). Could a more mournful dirge be composed !

The Law of Similarity

Two small words of large meaning illustrate this law, namely, the words " as " and " so."

The " as " and " so " of love—" As the Father hath loved Me, so have I loved you " (John 15 : 9). Who can fathom the unknowable, and measure the immeasurable love of God !

The " as " and " so " of strength—" As thy days, so shall thy strength be " (Deut. 33 : 25). The day may be long and dreary, sad and weary, but the key of His grace fits the lock of our need, and locks us into the chamber of His love, secluding us to Himself.

The " as " and " so " of service—" As My Father sent Me, so have I sent you " (John 20 : 21). That sending meant for Him, the humility of Bethlehem, the trial of temptation, the agony of Gethsemane, the suffering of Gabbatha, the shame of the Cross, the victory of the Resurrection, and the glory of the Father's right hand, and so it means to us.

The " as " and " so " of Substitution—" As Moses lifted up the serpent in the wilderness, even so must the Son of Man be lifted up " (John 3 : 14). The necessity of His death is summarised in the " must," and the nature of that sacrifice is suggested—the lifting up,—for as the uplifted serpent was like the serpent that caused the Israelites to be stung, so Christ was made sin for our sin.

The " as " and " so " of Identification—" As He is, so are we in this world " (1 John 4 : 17). The association of this pregnant sentence is, His love makes us one with Christ, hence we are identified with Him in the acceptance of His worth and the completeness of His atoning work.

The Book of Proverbs abounds in these correspondences, which may be found by the careful reader of that Book of wisdom. One we give, " As cold water to a thirsty soul, so is good news from a far country " (Prov. 25 : 25).

The Law of Triplication

As the Godhead is a Trinity, so there are a great many instances where we and three things are relatively connected.

The threefold references to the Father in John 17 ; when Christ speaks to Him as " Father " ; when He addresses His Father on behalf of His people, He says, " Holy Father," and when He refers to Him as " Righteous Father " (John 17 : 1, 11, 25).

Threefold Evil. Sin is often coupled with " transgression " and " iniquity," but they cannot be substituted the one for the other. Sin is the missing of the mark of God's requirement. Transgression is going beyond the boundary of God's law. And iniquity is twisting what is straight and making it crooked. See Psalm 32 : 1, which tells us what God does with these.

Threefold requirement of God's request. There are three things which He requires from His creature man. " What doth the Lord require of thee, but to do justly, and to love mercy, and to walk humbly with thy God " (Micah 6 : 8).

All the blessings of the Gospel are triplets. The three aspects of salvation, eternal life, etc. The three appearings of Christ in Heb. 9 : 24-28 cover all the service of Christ for us. Themes might be multiplied, but these must suffice.

The Law of Double

It is said of the wise woman that all her garments are double (Prov. 31 : 21, margin). There is always the Divine side and the human, God's sovereignty and man's responsibility (John 6 : 37). We are justified before God through faith in Christ without works (Rom. 3 : 28) ; but we justify our faith before men by our works (Jas. 2 : 14-26). Christ said that our union with Him is double, hence, He says, " Ye in Me and I in you " (John 14 : 20). Our privilege is to be " in Him," and the secret of power is He in us. The double of acceptance is seen when we recall that believers are " accepted in the Beloved through Divine grace " (Eph. 1 : 6) ; and we are acceptable to the Lord when we do those things that are well pleasing to Him (2 Cor. 5 : 9). The double of love is brought out in John 3 : 16 and 1 John 3 : 16. God proved His love to us by giving His Son, and we prove our love to one another by sympathetic help. We have the double of assurance when we confess our sins, for He is

faithful and just to forgive them (1 John 1 : 9). He is not
only " faithful," but He is also " just," that is, that He is
faithful in His love and righteous in His act. The importance
of recognising the two sides of any given thing is paramount,
for what God has joined together, let no man put asunder.

The Law of Contrast

Dr. A. T. Pierson calls attention to 2 Cor. 4 as illustrating
this principle. He says :

" 2 Cor. 4 : 7 to 5 : 9 is a paragraph of continuous contrasts between what is seen and unseen, temporal and
eternal, outward and inward, visible and invisible, material
and spiritual, earthly and heavenly ; between affliction and
glory, being at home in the body and at home with the
Lord, faith and sight, dying and living.

" Of all these ten contrasts, the former members of each
belong in one group and are akin ; the latter members
equally inseparable. What is seen, temporal, etc., belong to
the realm of death ; what is unseen and eternal to the realm
of Life, and sight and faith are the respective organs of
vision in the two realms ; only sight which rightly sees in
its own sphere, is blind to the other and cannot interpret the
relation of the two ; but faith not only sees its own realm,
but all that sight sees beside, and is a true interpretation of
both realms. Sight refuses what faith chooses and inversely,
and knows only the present, while faith foretastes the future."

The Law of Supplement

One truth flows out from another, as the root produces
the tree, and the trunk the branches, and the branches the
leaves, blossom, and fruit. Christ's atoning death is the
fact of the Gospel, but flowing out of that fact is the living
factor of our identification with Him, which causes the
believer to die to sin and self. The late Denham Smith has
said, " Romans 5 is the Gospel for the sinner, for he is justified by the Blood of Christ (Rom. 5 : 9) ; but Romans 6 is
the Gospel for the saint, for it proclaims we are baptized
into His death (Rom. 6 : 3-17)." The death of Christ's substitutionary sacrifice cuts off the old associations of sin and

self, and unites us to the vitality of Christ's risen and vitalizing life. Further examples may be found in the "alsos" of John 14 and 17, the "much mores" of Rom. 5, and the repeated, "Ye have heard . . . but I say unto you," of Christ's sermon on the mount.

The Law of Time

Frequently the adverb of time, "then," is used, and gives the sequence of what follows. The five "thens" of Isaiah 6 give the subsequent steps in the Prophet's experience. The sight of Jehovah's holiness made him realise his sinfulness. "Then said I, woe is me . . . for mine eyes have seen the King, the Lord of Hosts." After that confession, "Then flew one of the Seraphim" and placed a live coal upon the lips of Isaiah and said, "Thine iniquity is taken away and thy sin atoned for," when he had been cleansed by his sin being answered for. Then he heard the voice of Jehovah saying, "Whom shall I send, and who will go for Us?" Having heard the voice, he could respond and say, "Then said I, here am I, send me." Following the answer to the call, he could speak to the Lord about the message he had to deliver, "Then said I, Lord, how long?"

The adverb of time as found in Matt. 24 and 25 in connection with our Lord's return as the Son of Man, gives the steps and associations of His judicial action; and the "then" as found in relation to Christ's temptation in the wilderness as showing the time and testing is of telling importance (Matt. 4 : 1, 5, 10, 11).

The Law of Full Mention

We have been told the Bible does not give us a full revelation in any one section of any given truth. But we find it does. A full revelation of Love's traits is made known in seventeen particulars in 1 Cor. 13 : 4-13. It endures for it "suffereth long." It is benevolent in ministry for it is "kind." It is unsuspicious for it "envieth not." It is real for "it vaunteth not itself." It is humble for "it is not puffed up." It is thoughtful for "it doth not behave itself unseemly." It is unselfish for "it seeketh not her own." It is sweet tempered for " it is not provoked " (R.V.). It is guileless for " it thinketh no evil." It is holy for " it rejoiceth not in iniquity." It is true for " it rejoiceth with the truth " (R.V.). It is unbending for " it beareth all things." It is faithful for " it believeth all things." It is expectant for " it hopeth all things." It is lasting for " it endureth all things." It is unfailing for " it never faileth." And it excels for " the greatest " of the graces is Love. Why ? Because Love is not a thing, but a Person—" God is Love."

A full revelation of the characteristics of faith is found in Hebrews 11, where we are reminded of the nature of faith. It makes the unseen real ; the objective of faith and the basis of faith, the Word of God and the God of the Word ; the activities of faith, in the several persons mentioned and what they did ; and the excellencies of faith and its rewards, for faith honours God to His glory, and God honours faith to its benefit and reward.

A full revelation of the Spirit's gifts and administrations is unfolded and made known in 1 Cor. 12 in their ninefold bestowments (8-11), and the several particulars of those gifts in their working (27-30).

In 2 Cor. 8 and 9 there is unfolded the worth and wealth of Christian giving. Money as such is not mentioned, but it is described as " the riches of liberality " (2), " Power " (3), " the gift " and " the fellowship " (4), " this grace " (6, 7), " abundance " (14), " ministering " (9 : 1), " bounty " (5), " this ministration " (13), and " liberal distribution " (13).

The Ten Commandments in their summary of man's duty and love toward God and men is an unrivalled unfolding of God's requirement from His creature (Exod. 20 : 1-17).

Christ's Sermon on the Mount in its kingly and majestic " Verily I say unto you," gives a full and glorious demand of the King upon His subjects, and where its rule operates gives a millennium of blessing.

The prophecy of Christ's Passional Propitiation as detailed in Isaiah 53 gives a wonderful unfolding of the sufferings of the Saviour. Who can estimate such pregnant and richly laden sentences as " A Man of Sorrows," " acquainted with grief," "borne our griefs," "carried our sorrows," "wounded for our transgressions, bruised for our iniquities, with His stripes we are healed," "laid on Him the iniquity of us all," "Cut off out of the land of the living," "For the transgression of My people was He stricken," "Pleased Jehovah to bruise Him," "Put Him to grief," "Make His soul an offering for sin," "He shall bear iniquities," "Poured out His soul unto death," and "Bear the sin of many."

The above seven instances are but samples of what might be multiplied. Several others may be looked up by the student of the Sacred Page, such as the sufferings of Christ described in Psalm 22, the Good Shepherd giving His life for the sheep in John 10, the Person and Work of the Holy Spirit in John 14, 15 and 16, the nature of true repentance in 2 Cor. 7:8-12, the evidence of being born of God in John's First Epistle as found in the sentence, " Born of God " and " Born of Him," the new birth as recorded in John 3, and the eight rewards which come to the overcomers as made known in the Book of the Revelation.

The Law of Exegesis

Exegesis means the bringing out the meaning of the words employed. A true expositor of God's Word is an Exporter and not an Importer, that is, he does not import his own thoughts into the Scriptures, but seeks to know and bring out the mind of the Spirit. The following quotation is an apt illustration of true exegesis on sin as referred to in John's First Epistle.

"It is unfortunate that our Version has failed to reproduce the studious precision of the Apostle's language in dealing with the question of the relation between the believer and sin. Observe these distinctions.

1. Unless it be expressly limited as to where it is written (1:7) that "the blood of Jesus Christ cleanseth us from " not "all" but "every sin." The noun, "sin," in the singular denotes the sinful principle, the evil thing called sin, while "sins" in the plural are its specific manifestations.

2. As regards the verb, "to sin," there is, as everyone who knows Greek is aware, a significant difference between

the present tense on the one hand and the perfect or the aorist on the other. The perfect denotes the past commission of a sin or sins, as when it is written (1 : 10) : "If we say *we have not sinned*, we make Him a liar"; while the aorist refers to a definite act of sin whether actual or prospective. Thus it is the aorist or prospective. Thus it is the aorist that is employed where we read (2 : 1) : "These things write I unto you, *that ye sin not*. And *if any man sin*, we have an Advocate with the Father." And what of the present tense? It means properly "to be sinning," "to keep on sinning," and so it is written (3 : 6) : "Whosoever abideth in Him, *doth not keep on sinning*; whosoever *keepeth on sinning*, hath not seen Him"—an idea which the Apostle more explicitly expresses by the phrase, "committing sin," or rather, as it is literally, "doing sin," that is, "making sin one's business." See how he interchanges these phrases (3 : 9) : "Whosoever is begotten of God *doeth not sin*, because His seed abideth in him, and he cannot *keep on sinning*, because he is begotten of God.'"

The Law of Command

The Lord commands our obedience that we may enjoy His blessing. Precepts are coupled with God's promises that we may enjoy the latter through our practice. Christ says, "If ye love Me, ye will keep My commandments" (John 14 : 15, R.V.). In Phil. 4 : 1-6 eight commands are to be found. The "so stand fast" of fidelity, the "be of the same mind" of sympathy, the "Help" of energy, the "Rejoice" of joyfulness, the "Let your moderation" of testimony, the "be careful for nothing" of anxiety, the "Everything by prayer and supplication" of entreaty, and "Thanksgiving" of doxology.

Seven passages where we find the word "Be" occurring further illustrate. The "Be holy" of consecration (1 Pet. 1 : 15), the "Be perfect" of adjustment (2 Cor. 13 : 11), the "Be strong" of equipment (Eph. 6 : 10), the "Be patient" of endurance (Jas. 5 : 7), the "Be sober" of conduct (1 Pet. 1 : 13), the "Be vigilant" of watchfulness (1 Pet. 5 : 8), and the "Be ye separate" of holiness (2 Cor. 6 : 14-17).

The Law of Sequence

Sequence speaks of that which follows as a consequence. The Jehovah Psalm is a beautiful illustration of this law. " Lord " occurs no less than thirteen times in the 27th Psalm. Jehovah means the Unchanging One, Who will cause things to be. This thought of sequence, or what follows in recognising the Lord as the faithful One, is seen several times. First, we have faith's avowal, then faith's blessing. " Jehovah is my Light and Salvation," and the sequence is, " Whom shall I fear ?" " Jehovah is the Strength of my life," and the sequence is, " Of whom shall I be afraid ?" " I may dwell in the house of Jehovah," and the sequence is, " In the time of trouble He shall hide me in His pavilion." " When my father and mother forsake me," the sequence is, " Jehovah will take me up." If the Psalmist had not seen " the goodness of Jehovah " he would have " fainted," but the sequence of seeing that goodness was he did not faint. To " wait on Jehovah " is to find the sequence of " good courage " and to have the heart strengthened.

The Law of Conciseness

There is a soul of meaning in the great star words which shine out in the sky of the Scriptures. Take but three, namely, Ebenezer, Mizpah, and Maranatha. " Ebenezer " was the name which Samuel gave to the stone, which he set up as a memorial of the Lord's help against the Philistines, and of his victory over them, hence its meaning, " Hitherto hath the Lord helped us " (1 Sam. 7 : 12). What a Helper the Lord is ! All other helpers fail, but He is the Helper that meets every need and conquers every foe. " Mizpah " was the name of the heap of stones which Laban and Jacob erected as a witness and a watchword between them, as its meaning testifies, " The Lord watch between me and thee when we are absent the one from the other " (Gen. 31 : 49). When the Lord is the soul of a compact, how binding our obligations are the one to the other.

" Maranatha " is what Paul said in the close of his first letter to the Church in Corinth. Our version reads, " If any man love not the Lord Jesus Christ, let him be anathema,

Maran-atha" (1 Cor. 16 : 22). There are no punctuation marks in the original. It has been suggested that the verse should read, " If any man love not the Lord Jesus Christ, let him be anathema (accursed). Maran-atha (The Lord cometh)." The fate of those who do not love the Lord Jesus Christ is to be accursed. Then the Apostle in a jubilant note says, " The Lord cometh " (Maran-atha). " The Lord cometh " settles all questions, Paul seems to say, so we need not worry about anything.

The Law of Eclipse

An eclipse is one thing overshadowing another, and blotting it out of the line of vision. The Epistle to the Hebrews illustrates this law. The word " Better " is one of the key-words of this letter. Christ is better than the angels because of what He is and has obtained (1 : 4, 8). Christ is better than Moses, because the Son is higher than the servant (3 : 1-6). Christ's priesthood is better than that of Aaron because it is not passed on to another, but is concentrated and consolidated in Himself (5 : 1-10). Christ brings in a better hope than the Law could give (7 : 7), also a better covenant (7 : 22 ; 8 : 6), and better promises and better sacrifices (8 : 6 ; 9 : 23), and grace bestows a better substance than can be obtained on earth (10 : 34), and we also find in the Christian regime a better country and a better resurrection (11 : 16, 35, 40).

The Law of Ellipsis

Ellipsis signifies a breaking off, hence, something wanting. We are told God is able to do exceeding abundantly above all we ask or think (Eph. 3 : 20). The word " abundantly " means a super-abundance, as when a vessel is filled to over-flowing. " Exceeding " signifies an abundance beyond an abundance, as when a constant supply is poured into a vessel so that the water drenches the carpet as well as the table-cloth. " Above " goes beyond the other two descriptions, so that the water poured into the vessel which drenches the cloth and the carpet flows out of the house and into the street. The word " abundantly " is rendered " enough and to spare" (Luke 15 : 17), "beyond measure" (Mark 6 : 51), "superfluous" (2 Cor. 9 : 1), and "overmuch" (2 Cor. 2 : 7), so that the sentence, "exceedingly abundantly above," means that which is beyond measure which is beyond measure of beyond measure, and beyond measure beyond measure which is beyond what is beyond measure of a beyond measure. It is right after the Apostle had said, "Exceeding abundantly above," that we find the ellipsis. He seems to say, "He is able to go beyond the measure of all the beyond measures." No matter how great the gap and want, the Lord's answer is unlimited and unmeasurable.

The Law of Conjunction

A conjunction is that part of speech which connects two parts. If we do not mind our conjunctions we shall lose our associations, as the man found when he got into a railway carriage which was not connected with the train and was left behind. We are exhorted to be "Looking for the Blessed Hope, *and* the glorious appearing of the Blessed God our Saviour" (R.V., Titus 2 : 13). Believers are waiting for Christ's coming *for* His saints as the Blessed Hope, and also as the Great God when He comes *with* His saints in His manifested glory to the world.

There is a very significant connection between John 2 and 3 which is not seen in our ordinary version, but which is given in the Revised. In John 2 : 24 we are told, "Christ did not commit Himself" unto certain who only professed to believe on Him ; but John 3 says, "Now there was a man of the Pharisees named Nicodemus" to whom He did commit Himself, hence we have the wonderful unfolding of the weighty truths revealed in what Christ said to him.

The "*and*" in its frequent occurrence in Gen. 32 : 22-31 gives a series of connective sentences, which binds the incident recorded, in a simple sequence :

"*And* He rose up that night.
And he took his two wives,
And his two women servants,
And his eleven sons,
And passed over the ford Jabbok,

And he took them
And sent them over the brook,
And sent over that he had,
And Jacob was left alone.
And there wrestled a man with him,
And when he saw he prevailed not against him, he
    touched the hollow of his thigh,
And the hollow of his thigh was out of joint.
And he said unto him, Let me go,
And he said, I will not let thee go except thou bless me.
And he said unto him, What is thy name ?
And he said, Jacob.
And he said, Thy name shall no more be called Jacob.
And thou hast prevailed,
And Jacob asked him, etc.
And he blessed him there,
And Jacob called the place Peniel, for I have seen God
    face to face.
And my life is spared.
And as he passed over Peniel, the sun rose upon him,
And he halted upon his thigh."

Take but two sentences in their connection and sequence,
" *And* Jacob was left alone, *and* there wrestled a man with
him." What is the thought ? Jacob had to be alone before
the Lord could deal with him.

The Law of Fact and Factor

Every fact of the Gospel in its historic significance is
meant to be a living factor in the heart and life of our
experience. Pascal has finely remarked : " Everything
which happened to our Lord should come to pass in our
experience." He died for sin that we should die to it (1 Pet.
2 : 24). He suffered uncomplainingly that we should follow
in His steps (1 Pet. 2 : 21). He rose from the dead that we
should seek those things which are above (Col. 3 : 1, 2). He
was born for us that He might be born in us (Gal. 4 : 4, 19).
He went about doing good that we might do good to all men
too (Heb. 13 : 16). He loved us even unto death that we
might love one another (1 John 3 : 16). He intercedes for us

that we might make intercession for all men (I Tim. 2 : 1). He trusted in God in life and death that He might be the Prince and Pattern of faith within us (Heb. 12 : 1, 2). He lived and died in doing the Father's will that we might delight to do the same (Psa. 40 : 8). He gave up all He had to benefit us, and He expects the same mind to be in us (Phil. 2 : 4-8).

The Law of Setting

Of the onyx stones which were attached to the ephod of the garments of the High Priest it is said, " Thou shalt make them to be set in ouches of gold " (Exod. 28 : 11). The setting secured the onyx stones, and they were thus found. The precious stones of the holy words of God's truth are found in the ouches of their golden setting, and they must not be torn from their association.

Three persons are said to be " full of the Holy Spirit "— Christ, Stephen and Barnabas. Of Christ it is said, " And Jesus being full of the Holy Spirit returned from Jordan, and was led by the Spirit into the wilderness " (Luke 4 : 1, 2) " to be tempted of the devil " (Matt. 4 : 1). Does not the fact of our Lord being full of the Spirit tell us that was the reason why He returned from Jordan (the place of death) ; and further, that being " full of the Spirit " the Spirit could lead Him to the place of temptation and the subsequent victory ? Of Stephen we read, " But he being full of the Holy Spirit, looked up steadfastly into heaven, and saw the glory of God, and Jesus standing at the right hand of God " (Acts 7 : 55). He would not have had that steadfast gaze, and that vision of the glory of the glorified Lord if he had not been filled with the Holy Spirit. The other instance of one being " Full of the Holy Spirit " was that of Barnabas, when he visited Antioch, of whom we read, " Who, when he came, and had seen the grace of God, was glad, and exhorted them all, that with purpose of heart they would cleave unto the Lord. For he was a good man, and full of the Holy Ghost and of faith ; and much people was added unto the Lord " (Acts 11 : 23, 24). The reason why he was " glad " when he saw the grace of God demonstrated in the lives of

the believers, and exhorted them to cleave unto the Lord
with purpose of heart, was because he was " full of the Holy
Spirit and faith." It is the Spirit alone Who can give us
grace to appreciate the work of God in others, and who can
use us to add others to the Lord.

The Law of Detail

Little things are often of great moment. Christ emphasized the jots and tittles of the law (Matt. 5 : 18), which
correspond to the dot on the " i," and the stroke of the " t."
" The taches and loops " (Exod. 26 : 4-11) of the tabernacle,
which kept the curtains together, might seem to be unim-
portant, but they kept them from being bedraggled. We
are exhorted to yield our members in detail, as well as yielding our bodies as a whole (Rom. 6 : 13, 16), hence the Lord
calls for the eyes of our attention (Psa. 123 : 2), the ears of
our obedience (John 10 : 27), the feet of our walk (Eph.
4 : 1 ; 5 : 2, 8, 15), the hands of our business (Eccles. 9 : 10),
the lips of our testimony (Titus 2 : 1), the speech of our
tongue (Col. 4 : 6), the heart of our affection (Col. 3 : 12-14),
the soul of our desire (Cant. 1 : 7), the will of our purpose
(John 7 : 17, R.V.), and the spirit of our intelligence (1 Cor.
2 : 11).

The Law of Resemblance

If we compare the Vine and the Body we shall see a
striking resemblance between the two. Dr. A. T. Pierson
has given the following :

The Vine and Branches	The Body and Members
The Sap	The Blood
The Vegetable Life	The Animal Soul
The Leaves as Breathing Organs	The Lungs and Respiration
The Interlocking Fibres	The Interwoven Muscles
The Circulation of the Sap	The Circulation of the Blood
The Growth of the Vine	The Growth of the Body
The Reproductive Power	The Reproductive Power
The Excision of Dead Branches	The Excision of Diseased Limbs
The Vegetable Exudations	Animal Respiration
Branches Apart from the Vine	Limbs Sundered from Body

Further illustrations may be found in the resemblances
between the Living Word and the Written Word. Both are

said to be " Sure," " Living," " Eternal," " Wonderful,"
" Perfect."

The same law holds good in the resemblance between
Christ and Believers. He is the Son of God. We are the
sons of God. He is the Living Stone. We are living stones.
He is the Light of the world. We are lights to shine. He is
the Faithful and True Witness. We are witnesses. And He
is the Branch, we are branches.

The Law of Gravitation

This law is a power which causes objects to draw to a
centre, like the law of gravitation, which causes the falling
apple to fall to the earth. The bride in the Song of Solomon
prays to her Beloved, " Draw me and we will run after
Thee " (Song of Solomon 1 : 4). The drawn one draws
others. Mark the " me " and the " we." Of the early
disciples, when the authorities let them go, it is said, " they
went to their own company " (Acts 4 : 23). When Peter
was let out of prison, he went immediately to the company
who were " gathered together praying " (Acts 12 : 12). One
of the first things that Saul of Tarsus did, after his conversion, was, " He assayed to join himself to the disciples "
(Acts 9 : 26). When Ananias knew that Saul was converted,
and he was bidden by the Lord to help him, then the one
that he had called " This man " became to him " Brother
Saul " (Acts 9 : 13, 17). The very names of believers demonstrate how they gravitate the one to the other, such as
"Brethren," "Disciples," "Branches," "Members," "Saints,"
" Sheep," and " Children."

The Law of Discernment

The Bible is a spiritual Book, to be understood by a
spiritual people, who are under the spiritual instruction of
the Spiritual Teacher, the Holy Spirit. One way in which
the spiritual understanding can be exercised is to discriminate
the words which are used in the translation of the Scriptures.
The translators have put in words in italics to give the sense,
but sometimes the italicised words, instead of giving the
sense, mar it. We are exhorted to be " Looking unto Jesus,

the Author and Finisher of *our* faith." The "*our*" is in
italics, and mars the sense. If we leave it out the text reads,
" the Author and Finisher of faith." Christ is the Prince
and Pattern of Faith, and as the setting illustrates, He was
the One Whose life and ministry was begun, continued, and
ended in a life of absolute dependence upon God, hence we
are exhorted to consider Him (Heb. 12 : 2).

In Acts 2 : 41, 47, we are told how converts were
" added "—the translators have supplied " unto them " and
" to the Church," the latter is not authorised by the best
manuscripts. The inspired phrase found later on " added
to the Lord " (Acts 5 : 14), suggests that the meaning may be
in all cases—added to Himself as disciples—a possible hint
of the vast difference between Divine converts and human
proselytes.

" Somewhat " in Christ's message to the Church in
Ephesus, lessens the force of His solemn charge (Rev. 2 : 4).
The pronoun " He " blunts the avowal of Christ in the
Garden of Gethsemane, when He affirmed, He was the " I
AM " (John 18 : 8). The " Therewith " of Phil. 4 : 11 takes
the edge off the Apostle's " In whatsoever state I am to be
content."

The Law of Geological Intent

To study the strata of the earth and to understand its
formation is always of captivating interest ; and to study
the words of Scripture and to get to know the soul of their
meaning is of paramount importance. What a world of
clinging meaning is made known in " Followeth hard " of
Psa. 63 : 8, when the Psalmist exclaims, " My soul followeth
hard after Thee." John Trapp renders it in his quaint way,
" My soul is glued to Thee." That is the thought, not only
following close, but so close that nothing can come between.
The same word is used of the scales of the sea monster
Leviathan, of which it is said, " His scales are his pride,
shut up together as with a close seal, one is so near to
another, that no air can come between them, they are joined
one to another, they stick together, that they cannot be
sundered " (Job 41 : 15-17). When the soul is so joined to

the Lord, no blighting air of the world can contaminate, and nothing of self or sin can come between.

There are two words in the New Testament which are rendered " son," one meaning the kinship of the same nature, and the other the position of adoption. Believers are said to be " The children of God," because they are " Begotten of Him " (see R.V., John 1 : 12, 13 ; 1 John 5 : 1-3). They are akin to Him and owe their spiritual being to Him, even as the child owes his being to his parents ; but we are waiting for the adoption (Rom. 8 : 23), although we know we are " Predestinated unto the adoption of children " (Eph. 1 : 5). We are children of God now, but we have not the place of glory for which we are destinated.

Christ is called, " The Son of God " and " The Son of Man," but the word " Teknon," a descendant, is not used when He is so called. He is not a descendant of God, He is God. He is not a descendant of man, for His humanity was a product of the Spirit of God (Luke 1 : 35). The word " Whyos," used of Christ as the Son of God and the Son of Man, denotes adoption, and therefore refers to the place He filled as the " Only Begotten Son," and to the place He assumed as the Son of Man, Who came to seek and to save lost humanity.

The importance of understanding the meaning of the words of the Holy Spirit is to have the key to unlock their secrets.

The Law of Geographical Outline

The First Epistle of John illustrates the thought of geographical outline. The introduction presents Christ as The Life, because that is what we need, but before life can come to us, Light and Love must act for us. Light is the claim of Love. Love meets the claim of Light ; and Life imparts the Life of Love.

The purpose of the Epistle is pointed to in the mention of " These things." " These things write we unto you, that your joy may be full " ; and " These things have I written unto you that believe on the name of the Son of God, that ye may know that ye have eternal life " (1 John 1 : 4 ; 5 : 13).

The late A. B. Simpson, of New York, was essentially a geographical preacher. The writer once heard him outline the Book of Nehemiah. He took for his text, " So did not I " (Neh. 5 : 15). The most casual reader of the Book can see how those words can be used as a pivotal sentence, and how each chapter may be surveyed in its outlook of country.

We should treat the Word of God as we do a letter, and read a Book or an Epistle right through and get its general meaning.

The Law of Metaphor

A metaphor means one thing is used to explain another. Christ said, " I am the Door." He did not mean He was a door, but as a door is the means of entrance, so He is the One through Whom we enter into blessing. Our Lord said of the bread which He broke, " This is My body." He did not mean the bread was His actual body, but that it represented it. When Christ is called " The Lamb of God," it does not signify He is a lamb, but as the lamb of the Passover was the means of diverting the judgment of God, so He is the Means to take away sin. The Psalms, in speaking of God, are full of metaphors. He is a Sun and a Shield, a Refuge and a Fortress, and a Tower and a Defence. A metaphor is one thing contained in another.

The Law of Topic

One profitable study is to trace out in an Epistle, a Gospel, or a Book, how a theme is repeated, or a word used. The following are a few of many. " In that day," in Isaiah ; " Thus saith the Lord," in Ezekiel ; " The Kingdom of Heaven," in Matthew ; " Straightway," in Mark ; " The Son of Man," in Luke ; " Light " and " Love," in John ; " The Holy Spirit," in the Acts ; " Righteousness," in Romans ; " Things of God," in Corinthians ; " Crucified," in Galatians ; " Riches," in Ephesians ; " Joy " and " Rejoice," in Philippians ; " Christ," in Colossians ; " Christ's coming," in Thessalonians ; " Better " things, in Hebrews; " Precious " things, in Peter's Epistles ; " Know," in 1 John ; " Truth," in 2 and 3 John ; and " Blessed " and " Overcome," in The Revelation.

Not only topical words, but a topical theme is often

The Following Brief Outline on the

SEVEN JUDGMENTS IN RELATION TO BELIEVERS IN CHRIST

Will Illustrate Further the Definiteness and Clarity of the Scriptures.

	Topic.	Judge.	Judged.	Judgment.	Where?	When?	Result.
1.	God's Judgment upon sin, at the Cross. Isa. 53:6, 10.	God acting in Righteousness. Rom. 3:25, 26.	Christ as the Substitute of His People. Luke 12:50. Isa. 53:5.	God's wrath against sin. Rom. 8:3, margin. 2 Cor. 5:21.	Calvary. Outside the Gate. Heb. 13:11, 12.	Once in the end of the age. Heb. 9:26-28.	"No condemnation," "shall not come into condemnation," "Not condemned with the world." Rom. 8:1, R.V. John 5:24. 1 Cor. 11:31, 32.
2.	God's Judgment of His children in chastisement. 1 Cor. 11:32.	The Father acting in Grace and Loving Discipline. Heb. 12:6-9.	The Children of God as such. Heb. 12:7.	Chastisement by trial (1 Pet. 1:7), by earthly losses (Job 1:21), by loss of spiritual power and bodily weakness (1 Cor. 11:30), by Satan (Luke 22:31), and by premature death (1 John 5:16).	In the Body. 2 Cor. 5:10.	When disobedient and when the Lord wants to purify His people. Num. 20:12. Ruth 1:21. Psa. 105:19. Mal. 3:3.	Fruit-bearing. Heb. 12:11.
3.	The Believer's Judgment of Himself. 1 Cor. 11:31.	The Word of God. Heb. 4:12, 13.	The Believer's thoughts (2 Cor. 10:5), motives (Philemon 9), ways (Psa. 119:9), work (Gal. 6:4), words (Matt. 12:36).	Christ testing His own by His all-searching presence. Rev. 2 and 3.	In the heart and life. Heb. 3:12. Eph. 4:17; 5:2, 8, 15. Col. 4:5. 1 John 2:6.	Always, while in the body. Phil. 1:20. 1 Cor. 9:27.	Confidence, Communion and Joy. 1 John 1:3-7; 3:21.

No.	Judgment	Agent	Subjects	Basis / Action	Place	Time	Result
4.	Church's Judgment by Discipline. Matt. 18:15-18.	The Church acting in the Lord. 1 Cor. 5:3-5.	Members of the Church. "Ye judge them that are within." 1 Cor. 5:12.	Admonition (2 Thess. 3:12; Titus 3:10), expulsion (2 Thess. 3:6), adjustment of differences among saints (1 Cor. 6:4-7), and deliverance over to Satan (1 Cor. 5:5; 1 Tim. 1:20).	Before the Lord. "In the name of the Lord Jesus Christ," viz., in His presence and as He would act. 1 Cor. 5:4.	When evil or error are manifest. 2 John 9-11. Rev. 2:14-16.	Restoration. Gal 6:1.
5.	The Judgment Seat of Christ. 2 Cor. 5:10.	Christ as Lord. 1 Cor. 4:4. 2 Tim. 4:8.	Believers only. Heb. 10:30.	Review of the life (1 Cor. 4:5), testing the work of the servant (1 Cor. 3:13), conduct towards fellow believers (Rom. 14:10), and inspection of motives (2 Cor. 5:9, 10).	In the Lord's presence. 1 Cor. 4:5. 1 John 2:28.	After Christ comes for His saints, and before He comes with them. 1 Thess. 4:3-13. 1 Thess. 4:13-18. Rev. 19:11-16.	Rewards. 2 John 8.
6.	Believer's Judgment of the World and Angels. 1 Cor. 6:2, 3.	Believers with the Lord. Dan. 7:22. Jude 14.	The ungodly and wicked angels. Rev. 20:12. 2 Pet. 2:3-9. Jude 15.	According to their works. Rev. 20:12. Heb. 13:4.	At the Great White Throne. Rev. 20:11.	At the end of the Millennium. Rev. 20:5.	Lake of fire. Rev. 20:15.
7.	Judgment of the House of Christendom. 1 Pet. 4:17.	Christ as Lord and Master. Matt. 7:20-23. Matt. 25:11-13.	Professors and those who are nominally Christians. 2 Tim. 2:20.	Passing through the fire of the great tribulation. Rev. 3:10.	On the Earth under the Antichrist. Rev. 13:7.	After the body of Christ is removed, and before Christ comes with His saints. 1 Thess. 5:9. 2 Thess. 2:1-13.	A multitude saved, but seemingly not in the Church, and others cast out. Rev. 7:13-17. Rev. 20:15.

given. Christ's superiority in Col. 1 : 15-19, R.V., explains His pre-eminence. He is—

Superior to all, for He is " The Image of the invisible God."

Superior in order, " First-born before all creation."

Superior in creation, " In Him were all things created."

Superior in power, " In Him all things consist."

Superior in position, " Head of the Body."

Superior in resurrection, " First-begotten from the dead."

Superior in place, " Pre-eminent."

Superior in possessions, " All fulness " dwells in Him.

" No Subject so glorious as He : no Theme so affecting to us." We say of Him

Christ is the Fact of facts, the Bible's Theme,
Who stands alone, august, unique, supreme ;
The Bread of Life, Who meets the need of men,
Who comes to all, o'er field, and moor, and fen ;
The Man of Pain, Who feels all human pain,
And slakes the thirst, and turns all loss to gain,
He is the God, all light from Him doth gleam,
He is the Man of men, beyond all dream ;
He is the God of Love, all love Divine,
He is the Hand of Power, all strength sublime ;
From Him all things come forth, in Him consist,
To Him all tend, and all by Him subsist,
The Book, it speaks of Him, the Christ reveals,
The eyes that close to Him, all truth conceals ;
He is the Gospel's Theme—He died for all,
His Death alone can free from sin's enthrall ;
His Resurrection Life, the might of might,
His reign within the soul, the life of right ;
His peace within the heart, the calm of love,
His joy untold, the thrill from realms above
His love, the fire that burns within the Fane,
His promises, the word's refreshing rain ;
The Spirit came, the outcome of His death,
The power of God, His grace and living breath ;
He's All ! the Visibility of God,
And so I sing of Him, and onward plod.

There are many other Laws which could be mentioned, but as we have gone beyond what we contemplated under this section, we must refrain from proceeding further. The student will find other Laws suggested as he studies the sacred pages of God's Word.

7

THE MOUTH OF A SPECIFIC UTTERANCE

WITHOUT discussing the general subject of the in-spiration of the Scriptures, attention is called to three introductory remarks. First, A Divine Impossibility, that there should "proceed out of the mouth of the Most High evil and good" (Lam. 3 : 38). A holy utterance must ever proceed from Him Who is holy. Second, A Divine Statement, "The word that goeth forth, or proceedeth, out of the mouth of the Lord shall not return unto Him void," but it must accomplish the thing that He has determined (Isa. 55 : 11). And third, Christ has endorsed the fact that the Word which proceeds out of the mouth of Jehovah must be of benefit to those who receive it, for it is by means of it that man lives to purpose (Matt. 4 : 4 ; Deut. 8 : 3).

There are two lines of study we follow in thinking of the mouth of a specific utterance : What is said in a general way of the distinct voice and claim that God Himself has spoken in a definite way ; and the rules to observe, to find how the Lord specifically speaks in the Word.

GOD'S AFFIRMATION IN HIS WORD THAT HE HAS SPOKEN

There was no doubt in the minds of the prophets and apostles that God had "spoken" to and through them. Peter's declaration about Christ in His past advent and His future return was : "And He shall send Jesus Christ, which before was preached unto you ; Whom the heaven must receive until the times of restitution of all things, which God hath spoken by the mouth of all His holy prophets since the world began." And in his second Epistle Peter is equally emphatic, when he charges those to whom he wrote to "be mindful of the words which were spoken before by the holy prophets, and of the commandment of us the apostles of the Lord and Saviour" (Acts 3 : 21 ; 2 Pet. 3 : 2).

We therefore turn to the Word of God to see how it affirms the fact, that God has definitely spoken to us.

I. *God has spoken generally through the medium of the prophets*

There is a recurring sentence in Matthew's Gospel, and that is, " That which is spoken of the Lord by the prophet saying." The hinge which causes the door of the sentence to open up with definite meaning is the preposition " Dia," rendered " By," which when found with the genitive signifies, something which is accomplished by means of an active agent. The importance of recognising the meaning of this preposition is seen when we know it is rendered " Through " when Christ speaks of Himself as the Medium through Whom we can be saved (John 3 : 17 ; 10 : 9), and when He also says that no one can " come to the Father but by (dia) Me " (14 : 6). To revert to Matthew again, we find there are given detailed particulars of what was spoken by the Lord through the prophet. The following are some of the instances. Christ being born of a virgin (1 : 22, 23), Christ coming out of Egypt (2 : 15), His dwelling in Nazareth (2 : 23), the illuminating ministry of Christ in specified places (4 : 13-17), His healing of the sick by taking their infirmities upon Himself (8 : 17), the characteristics of Christ as a Servant of Jehovah (12 : 17-21), the failure of the multitude to understand His teaching (13 : 35), the claiming of the ass by Christ that He might ride in triumph to Jerusalem (21 : 4), Christ's predictive statement regarding the signs of the end of the age and in the manifestation of the Antichrist (24 : 15), and the action of Judas in the betrayal of Christ and His subsequent untimely end (27 : 9). We are sometimes told that the prophet made known certain things, but the use of this preposition, which means " by means of " (see Heb. 9 : 15, where it is thus translated), puts the prophet on one side and leads us to see that it is the Lord Who is the speaker and that the prophet is only the instrument through whom He conveys His mind. When we speak to a friend by means of the telephone, we do not say that the telephone speaks, but that the friend speaks by means of the telephone. The same is true when the Lord spake by means of the prophet.

II. *In particular God is affirmed to have revealed His mind
to and through Moses*

Christ endorsed this fact in His well-known words, when
He said, " Moses wrote of Me " (John 5 : 46). The Jews too
recognised that " God spake unto Moses," although they
repudiated Christ (John 9 : 29). " When we look back over
the Books of Exodus, Leviticus and Numbers, even the most
superficial reader must be immediately arrested by the
tremendous sentence prefacing nearly every chapter : ' Then
the Lord said unto Moses,' ' And the Lord said unto Moses '
(Deut. 18 : 17-20). Indeed, it is only necessary to hold the
Bible in your hand, and just let page after page flit by, and
as though by a panoramic effect, these words seem to stand
out as the root and essence, the heart and manifestation, the
centre and circumference of the whole Pentateuch, as indeed
they are, for while the five books are divided by men into
one hundred and eighty-seven chapters, which might, with
greater wisdom and continuity of thought, be easily reduced
to say one hundred and sixty-seven, we have in all, it is
computed, five hundred and one distinct assertions in them
of supernatural authority, being an average of three such
claims in every chapter."

To take only a few references from the Book of Exodus,
we come across the frequent formula, " The Lord had spoken."
When Aaron, as the mouthpiece of the Lord, met the elders
of the children of Israel, he " spake all the words which the
Lord had spoken unto Moses " (4 : 30). Jehovah's prevision
making known that Pharoah would harden his heart, he did
this " as the Lord had spoken by Moses " (9 : 12, 35) ; and
in a general way, as the law-giver to Israel, it is declared,
" he gave them in commandment all that the Lord had
spoken with him " (34 : 32).

We need not recount the frequent sentence, " The Lord
said unto Moses." It is sufficient to the mind of faith to
repeat what we read, " The law was given by (by means of)
Moses " (John 1 : 17). He shines with the light of God from
the pages of the Word, even as he did on the Mount of
Transfiguration.

III. *God is said to have specifically spoken in Christ*

The climax of revelation is Christ Himself, " for God hath in these last days spoken unto us by His Son " (Heb. 1 : 2). All those who preceded Him were but foregleams of Him, and all the modes and methods by which God revealed Himself in the past were but shadows of Him, the Living Substance. He is said to be " The Word " (John 1 : 1-3). The thought of God is resident in Him, and expressed by Him, hence to see Him is to see and understand the Father. The Word " Logos " (Word) makes known the fact that all that He is, did, and said, is doing, and will do, is the living thought of God in action. How important then to listen to Christ's word about His words. He says, " The words that I speak unto you are spirit and life," hence to feed on them is to find the true bread and drink (John 6 : 53, 63).

Christ claimed to be the Mouthpiece of God. There is no doubt about the sense and substance of the following words of our Lord, " He that seeth Me, seeth Him that sent Me. He that rejecteth Me, and receiveth not My words, hath one that judgeth him : the word that I have spoken. . . . For I have not spoken of Myself, but the Father that sent Me, He gave Me a commandment, what I should say, and what I should speak. And I know that His commandment is life everlasting : Whatsoever I speak therefore, even as the Father said unto Me, so I speak " (John 12 : 45-50). These words about the word Christ uttered are prefaced by His claim to be the Light of the world. He came as the Light to illuminate the darkness. The word " He hath spoken " is claimed to be " the One " through whom the message of God is expressed. We cannot therefore reject the words of Christ, without ignoring the thought of God, and excluding the light. The sun of God's being shines forth in the rays of His Son.

Christ declared He was the Alpha and Omega of Revelation. When He spake to the two disciples, as they journeyed to Emmaus, He chided them and said, " O fools and slow of heart to believe all the prophets have spoken " ; and then He asked the question and gave a subsequent answer, as follows : " Ought not Christ to have suffered these things,

and to enter into His glory? And beginning at Moses and
all the prophets, He expounded unto them in all the Scriptures the things concerning Himself " (Luke 24 : 26, 27). He
practically said the same thing to the disciples in the Upper
Room, " And He said unto them, These are the words which
I spake unto you, while I was yet with you, that all things
must be fulfilled, which were written in the law of Moses, and
in the Prophets, and in the Psalms, concerning Me. Then
opened He their understanding, that they might understand
the Scriptures " (Luke 24 : 44, 45). Around the double star
of Christ's sufferings and glory everything centres and is
circumscribed (1 Pet. 1 : 11). These are the Jachin and Boaz
of God's temple (2 Chron. 3 : 17). As those pillars upheld all
the temple of old, so every truth of the Bible is held together
and focused in the Christ it makes known. We do not
know anything worth knowing, if we do not know Him, but
knowing Him we have the Key to all knowledge.

IV. *God is said to speak through the medium of words*

A vivacious schoolmistress from Boston, U.S.A., in talking with the writer on the ill-fated steamer, the *Lusitania*,
said, in referring to the inspiration of the Scriptures, " I
believe God gave the ' concept ' to the writers of the Bible,
and that they clothed the thoughts with their own words."
I replied, " How am I to know what is the ' concept ' of your
thoughts, if you do not tell me in words ?" She said, " You
cannot." Then I asked the question, " Won't you give God
the same privilege ? How can I know what is in His mind,
if He does not express Himself in words ?"

Again and again in the Books of Isaiah, Jeremiah,
Ezekiel, and others, we have the explanatory sentence, " For
the Lord hath spoken." When the Prophet Isaiah gave his
solemn charge to Judah, he prefaced it by saying, " Hear, O
Heavens, and give ear, O earth, for Jehovah hath spoken,"
and when he closed his charge with a warning of the consequence if they " refuse and rebel," he said, " for the mouth
of Jehovah hath spoken it." At the declaration of the
uselessness of Moab to pray, the prophet announces, " This
is the word Jehovah hath spoken concerning Moab," and

further says, " But now Jehovah hath spoken, saying, within three years . . . the glory of Moab shall be contemned." The prediction, the " glory of Kedar shall fail " and their " mighty archers shall be diminished " is because " The Lord God of Israel hath spoken it." In a variety of ways, instances and occasions we find the same thing announced. Sometimes " As the Lord hath spoken," " For the Lord hath spoken," " The Lord hath spoken this word," " This is the word the Lord hath spoken concerning him," " The Lord will do this thing which He hath spoken," " I have spoken it, and I will also bring it to pass," " I, even I have spoken," " The mouth of the Lord hath spoken," " I have spoken unto thee in a book," " That which Thou hast spoken has come to pass," " Because I have spoken unto them," " I, the Lord, have spoken it," " The word which I have spoken shall be done, saith the Lord God," " This is the day whereof I have spoken," " The Lord of hosts hath spoken it " (Isa. 1 : 2, 20 ; 16 : 13, 14 ; 21 : 17 ; 22 : 25 ; 24 : 3 ; 31 : 4 ; 37 : 22 ; 38 : 7 ; 39 : 8 ; 40 : 5 ; 46 : 11 ; 48 : 15, 16 ; 58 : 14 ; Jer. 9 : 12 ; 13 : 15 ; 25 : 3 ; 27 : 13 ; 30 : 2 ; 32 : 24 ; 35 : 17 ; 36 : 2, 4 ; 48 : 8 ; 51 : 62 ; Ezek. 5 : 13, 15, 17 ; 12 : 28 ; 17 : 21, 24 ; 21 : 32 ; 22 : 14 ; 23 : 34 ; 24 : 14 ; 26 : 5, 14 ; 28 : 10 ; 30 : 12 ; 34 : 24 ; 36 : 5, 6, 36 ; 37 : 14 ; 38 : 19 ; 39 : 5, 8 ; Hos. 12 : 10 ; Joel 3 : 8 ; Amos 3 : 1, 8 ; Obad. 18 ; Micah 4 : 4).

Could anything be more explicit than these personal, pointed, prophetic, varied, and clear messages, and to all and each of which might be attached the following Divine Word : " I, Jehovah, have spoken it, it shall come to pass, and I will do it : I will not go back, neither will I repent." To understand the full value of this section, the suggestion is made, that each passage should be studied and examined in its setting.

There are equivalent sentences which declare God hath spoken, such as " Thus saith the Lord," and the fact that " He spake." Someone has counted them, and declares they occur 2,601 times—680 times in the Books of Moses, 196 times in the Poetical books, 418 times in the Historical books, and 1,307 times in the Prophetical books.

The Psalmist says, "Thou hast magnified Thy Word above all Thy name" (Psa. 138:2), therefore we do well to glorify it above everything else. So we say it is:

(1) Divine in its source. To take but one book, the Acts, we find the Word is referred to 35 times. As " the Word of God" (4:31; 6:2, 7; 8:14; 11:1; 12:24; 13:5, 7, 44, 46; 17:13; 18:11; 19:20), 13 times; as " the Word of the Lord," 8 times (8:25; 11:16; 13:48, 49; 15:35, 36; 16:32; 19:10); as " The Word," 13 times (4:4; 6:4; 8:4; 10:36, 44; 11:19; 13:26; 14:3, 25; 15:7; 16:6; 17:11; 20:32); and as " Thy Word," once (4:29).

(2) Dynamic in its operation. Notice what it says about His Word in the Epistle to the Hebrews (1:3; 2:2; 4:12; 6:5; 11:3; 13:7). There lieth in the dynamite of God's Word all the latent possibilities of the life of the Almighty.

(3) Definite in its claim. The Epistles to the Thessalonians illustrate the claims of the Word. It is " the Word " in its authority (1:6); " The Word of the Lord " in its message (1:8; 4:15; second, 3:1); and " The Word of God " in its power (2:13). The Word claims the faith of our obedience, the loyalty of our love, and the desire of our hope.

(4) Distinct in its prophecy. The Book of the Revelation may illustrate what is found in many places. Christ is the Key (19:13), to keep it is our responsibility (1:9; 3:8, 10; 6:9; 20:4), and to bear record of it is our privilege (1:2).

(5) Distinguishing in its message. The many qualifying words of the Word indicate its manifold message. It is a Word of Life to quicken (Phil. 2:16), the Word of Faith to beget faith (Rom. 10:8), the Word of reconciliation to assure (2 Cor. 5:19), the Word of God to slay (Eph. 6:17), the Word of Christ to indwell (Col. 3:16), the Word of the Lord to reveal (1 Thess. 4:15), the Word of Faithfulness to keep (Titus 1:9), the Word of Righteousness to adjust (Heb. 5:13), the Word of Incorruption to endure (1 Pet. 1:23, 25), and the Engrafted Word to fructify (Jas. 1:21).

(6) Devoted in its promises. The Word, as such, is coupled with what the Spirit calls, " The Word of all His goodness." Solomon confessed that not " one word " of

God's good promise " failed " (1 Kings 8 : 56). His promises and the performance of them are continually referred to (Psa. 105 : 42 ; Acts 13 : 23, 32 ; 26 : 6, 7 ; Rom. 4 : 20 ; Gal. 3 : 14-29 ; Heb. 6 : 13-17 ; 2 Pet. 3 : 4, 9, 13).

Another interesting Bible study might be worked out in connection with the words, " He," or " The Lord," " hath promised " (Exod. 12 : 15 ; Deut. 12 : 20 ; 26 : 18 ; Josh. 23 : 10 ; 2 Chron. 6 : 15 ; Rom. 1 : 2 ; Heb. 12 : 26 ; Jas. 1 : 12 ; 2 : 5 ; 1 John 2 : 25).

(7) Dedicating in its influence. When we call to mind what the Lord says He will do by means of His Word, we can see how beneficent and practical it is in its inworking and out-working. Let us confine our thought to Christ and His teaching. He taught the Word was a fruit-producer (Matt. 13 : 23), a victory gainer (Matt. 4 : 4), a disciple witnesser (John 8 : 31), a sanctifying obtainer (John 17 : 17), a love prover (John 14 : 23), a prayer answerer (John 15 : 7), and a heart assurer (John 5 : 24).

RULES TO FIND THE SPECIFIC UTTERANCE

When we ponder God's works, we see that He is a God of Detail. We read, " He telleth the number of the stars, but of His understanding there is no number " (Psa. 147 : 4, 5, margin). He can number, but He cannot be numbered. A cob of maize will demonstrate there is never an odd row : there are rows of 8, 10, 12, 14, 16, 24. A slave was once promised his liberty if he could find a cob with an odd row. His ingenious mind solved the problem by cutting a row out of a young cob, and thus gained his liberty. The same law of regularity is found in the stem of a plant. Some branches are placed alternately, some opposite, and some are arranged spirally. In each tree there is perfect order. The same law and order may be found in God's Word. Nothing is left to man's caprice and ingenuity. Everything reveals artistic design. The importance of observing the following seven rules is obvious.

I. Where a Scripture is Found

The Gospel of John ends with the twentieth chapter. The twenty-first chapter is an appendix, and reveals the

Divine intent by way of emphasis. What is emphasised ? The Lordship of Christ in contrast to the self-action of man. That self-action is specially brought out in connection with Peter and the disciples. Self-will is seen when Peter says " I go a-fishing." Self-labour is evidenced when the disciples toiled all night and caught nothing. Self-sight is revealed when the disciples " knew not " the Lord on the shore. Self-resource is manifest when the Lord asked them if they had caught anything, and they had to say, " No." Self-boasting is made known when Christ asked Peter if he loved Him more than " these," for he had boasted, " Though all should be offended because of Thee, I will never be offended " (Matt. 26 : 33). Self-sin is hinted at in Christ's calling Peter by his old name of " Simon," and the reference to him being the " Son of Jonas " (a silly dove). Self-grief is evident when Peter was " grieved " by the searching and personal questions which Christ put to him ; and self-questioning is asserted when Peter seems more concerned as to what John should " do," instead of following his Lord.

Eight times Christ is called " Lord " (Kurios) in the chapter. John was the first to recognise the Lord on the shore, hence, he said, " It is the Lord." Peter reverenced the Lord when he " saw it was the Lord," and covered up his nakedness. The disciples, " knowing that it was the Lord," did not need to put the enquiry, " Who art Thou ?" Peter responded twice to the Lord when he said, " Yea, Lord," and further remarked to Him, " Lord, Thou knowest all things." Reference is made to the question of John when he asked the Lord at the table, " Lord, Who is he that betrayeth Thee ?" And, lastly, Peter's enquiry as to what John was to do, is recorded in his, " Lord, and what shall this man do ?"

Three thoughts are wrapped up in the Lordship of Christ. Ownership—" Ye serve " (as slaves) " the Lord " (Col. 3 : 23). Authority, hence the Lord's Supper is to be kept (I Cor. 11 : 20). Power, therefore we read, " The hand of the Lord " was with the disciples (Acts 11 : 21). All these thoughts are brought out in John 21. Ownership is claimed when Christ speaks of " My sheep." Authority is heard in

Christ's commands to " cast," to " come," and to " follow " ; and His power is evidenced when He caused 153 great fishes to be caught in the net.

Peter learned his lesson to recognise Christ as Lord, for in his first epistle (3 : 15, R.V.), he urged those to whom he wrote to " sanctify Christ as Lord " in their hearts.

II. What a Scripture Contains

The contents of John 3 : 16 have been called " the Bible in miniature." Like the gates of the New Jerusalem, there are twelve entrances to this temple of Truth.

The greatest possible need is in the conjunction " For." It takes us back to the previous verses which speak of the necessity of Christ's death because of man's sin.

The greatest possible Being is made known in the second word of the verse—" God." The One Who is Love, Light and Spirit, and Who in His being is Holiness, Justice, Goodness, Righteousness, Mercy, Truth, and Wisdom.

The greatest possible word is found in the " So." " So loved." This is the shortest word in the Bible with the greatest meaning. There is no sounding to the depth of this ocean, and no possible attainment to its height.

The greatest possible love is reached in this " God so loved." Love is revealed in its highest form, in its greatest giving, in its broadest width, in its deepest depths, and in its unscaleable heights.

The greatest possible place—" The world." The world with its sins and sorrows, the world sanctified by the feet of Christ, Who walked upon it for our advantage, and where He shed His precious blood for its benefit.

The greatest possible gift—" He gave." We cannot estimate what it cost when He gave His Best. That giving pierced into the heart of His being, and into the pleasure of His purpose. This gift is the treasure trove in which all His gifts are found.

The greatest possible One—" His only begotten Son." The Object of His soul's delight, the Express Image of His

Deity, the Eternal Son of His partnership, the Visibility of His personality, and the One of His holy equality.

The greatest possible offer—" Whosoever." There is no stint in His offers, no limitation in His love, no barriers in the way of His invitations, and no favouritism in His willingness to bless the unloving and unlovely.

The greatest possible power—" Believeth." Faith is an act of the will putting us into touch with the Infinite. The electric power of God's energy flows into the grasp of faith's receiving.

The greatest possible union—" In " (into) " Him." The preposition " Eis," not only brings to the Lord, but into Him, and makes one with Him, even as the bud engrafted into the tree makes it one with it.

The greatest possible doom—" perish." Hell is in this word. The hell of a lost soul, an outer darkness of despair, the marring of the whole being, and the impossible helplessness by being held in the grasp of the sins, in which the individual died.

The greatest possible blessing—" Eternal Life." This is more than eternal existence. It is eternal felicity with Him Who is eternal in His love and holiness. For ever in the circle of His being, in Whom is all well-being.

The roots of all truth are found in this root of God's planting, for this verse reveals God in His giving love, Christ in His atoning sacrifice, the Spirit in His quickening life, the Grace of God in its saving work, the wisdom of God's eternal purpose, the energy of faith in its assimilating process, the eternalness of heaven's glory, and the throb of love's forming ministry.

III. What a Scripture Suggests

There are several sentences of auxiliary comment in John's Gospel. " It was winter " (10 : 22), the Spirit says when Christ was receiving a cold reception from the Jews. " It was night " (13 : 30), we read in association with the dark purpose in Judas Iscariot's deed of betrayal. " It was cold " (18 : 18), it is said as Peter warmed himself at the fire.

He was cold in his soul, and that is the reason it was winter in his body. "Judas, not Iscariot" (14 : 22), called Jesus "Lord," but Iscariot did not do so. How we address the Lord reveals the dress in which our inner life is clothed.

How suggestive is the "I Am," which occurs in John's Gospel. At least twenty times we find "I Am" occurring. Sometimes we read, "I am *He*," the "*He*" is in italics, and should therefore be omitted. Sometimes the "I am" is coupled with additional words, such as "I am the Way." The "I am" takes us back to what Jehovah said to Moses, "I Am that I Am" (Exod. 3 : 14). Pondering these suggestive I am's we can see how much they suggest and contain.

The Unparalleled Speaker—"I that speak unto thee Am" (4 : 26). The Unique Food—"I Am the Bread of Life" (6 : 35). The Heavenly Manna—"I Am the Bread from heaven" (6 : 41). The Bread of Life—"I Am that Bread of Life" (6 : 48). The Living Bread—"I Am the Living Bread" (6 : 51). The Wonderful Illuminator—"I Am the Light of the world" (8 : 12). The Revealing One—"I Am from above" (8 : 23). The Independent Lord—"If ye believe not, I Am" (8 : 24). The Dependent Son—"Ye shall know I Am, and that I do nothing of Myself" (8 : 28). The Eternal Lord—"Before Abraham was, I Am" (8 : 58). The Darkness Dispeller—"As long as I Am in the world, I Am the Light" (9 : 5). The Sheeps' Protector—"I Am the Door of the sheep" (10 : 7). The Saving Mediator—"I Am the Door . . . Saved" (10 : 9). The Good Shepherd—"I Am the Good Shepherd" (10 : 11, 14). The Pledging Resurrection—"I Am the Resurrection" (11 : 25). The Glorifying Life—"I Am the Life" (11 : 25). The Master and Lord—"Ye call Me Master and Lord . . . I Am" (13 : 13). The Self-Existing Jehovah—"When it is come to pass . . I Am" (13 : 19). "The Way, The Truth, and The Life"—"I Am" to each (14 : 6). The True Vine—"I Am the True Vine" (15 : 1). The I Am—"I Am" (18 : 5, 8).

If we meditate upon the setting of these sentences, muse upon their meaning, and think on their application, we shall have to say :

Without the Word, there is no Speaking.
Without the Bread, there is no Feeding.
Without the Light, there is no Shining.
Without the Door, there is no Keeping.
Without the Death, there is no Saving.
Without the Grave, there is no Rising.
Without the Life, there is no Living.
Without the Way, there is no Going.
Without the Truth, there is no Knowing.
Without the Vine, there is no Growing.
Without the Lord, there is no Serving.
With THE I AM, Eternal Glowing.

IV. When a Scripture was Written

One of the earliest of the Epistles, if not the earliest, is Paul's letter to the Church in Thessalonica. It is generally agreed that this Epistle was written A.D. 54 to 56. We are sometimes told that these earlier epistles do not give us the larger view that the later ones do, but is that so? We shall find in these letters the ten great truths of the Bible, namely, the doctrines of God, the Bible, Christ, the Holy Spirit, man, sin, salvation, the Church, Angels, and the last things. We can only hint at these, and must leave the Bible student to work them out.

Doctrine of God. " God the Father . . . God our Father " (1 : 1), " Election of God " (1 : 4), " Your faith to Godward " (1 : 8), " Turned to God . . . the Living and True God " (1 : 9), " The Gospel of God " (2 : 2, 8, 9), " Allowed of God " (2 : 4), " God trieth the hearts " (2 : 4), " God is witness " (2 : 5), " Walk worthy of God " (2 : 12), " Please not God " (2 : 15), " Minister of God " (3 : 2), " We render to God " (3 : 9), " Before our God " (3 : 9), " God Himself and our Father " (3 : 11), " In holiness before God " (3 : 13), " Please God " (4 : 1), " Will of God " (4 : 3), " Know not God " (4 : 5), " God hath not " (4 : 7), " But God " (4 : 8), " Taught of God " (4 : 9), " Will God " (4 : 14), " Trump of God " (4 : 16), " God hath not " (5 : 9), " The Will of God " (5 : 18), " God of peace " (5 : 23).

Doctrine of the Bible. " Our Gospel came not in word only " (1 : 5), " Received the Word " (1 : 6), " The Word of the Lord " (1 : 8), " The Gospel of God . . . The Gospel "

(2 : 2, 4, 8, 9), " The Word of God " (2 : 13), " The Gospel of Christ " (3 : 2), " The Word of the Lord " (4 : 15).

Doctrine of Christ. " The " and " Our Lord Jesus Christ " (1 : 1, 3 ; 2 : 19 ; 3 : 11, 13 ; 5 : 9, 23, 28), " The Lord " (1 : 6, 8 ; 3 : 8 ; 4 : 6, 15, 15, 16, 17, 17 ; 5 : 2, 12, 27), " His Son " (1 : 10), " Christ " (2 : 6 ; 3 : 2 ; 4 : 16), " In Christ Jesus " (2 : 14 ; 5 : 18), " The Lord Jesus " (2 : 15 ; 4 : 1, 2), " Jesus " (4 : 14).

Doctrine of the Holy Spirit. " In the Holy Spirit " (1 : 5), " Joy of the Holy Spirit " (1 : 6), " Given unto us His Holy Spirit " (4 : 8), " Quench not the Spirit " (5 : 19).

Doctrine of Man. " Manner of men " (1 : 5), " Man " (3 : 3), " Spirit " (self-consciousness), " Soul " (life-consciousness), " Body " (sense-consciousness) (5 : 23).

Doctrine of Sin. " Idols " (1 : 9), " Deceit, uncleanness, guile " (2 : 3), " Flattering words, coveteousness " (2 : 5), " Killed " (2 : 15), " Please not God " (2 : 15), " Sins " (2 : 16), " Fornication " (4 : 3), " Lust of concupiscence " (4 : 5), " Defraud " (4 : 6), " Uncleanness " (4 : 7), " In darkness " (5 : 4), " Evil " (5 : 15, 22).

Doctrine of Salvation. Salvation includes the things which accompany it (Heb. 6 : 9). " Grace, peace " (1 : 1), " Thanks, prayers " (1 : 2), " Work of faith, Labour of love, Patience of hope " (1 : 3), " Election " (1 : 4), " Assurance " (1 : 5), " Faith " (1 : 8 ; 3 : 2, 5, 6, 7, 10), " Serve " (1 : 9), " Delivered " (1 : 10), " Walk worthy " (2 : 12), " Effectually worketh " (2 : 13), " In Christ Jesus " (2 : 14), " Saved " (2 : 16), " Joy " (2 : 20), " Establish " (3 : 2), " Comfort " (3 : 2), " Afflictions " (3 : 3), " Live, stand fast " (3 : 8), " Praying " (3 : 10), " Love " (3 : 12), " Holiness " (3 : 13 ; 4 : 7), " Walk and please God " (4 : 1), " Commandments " (4 : 2) ; " Sanctification " (4 : 3, 4), " Brotherly love " (4 : 9), " Study to be quiet " (4 : 11), " Work " (4 : 11), " Walk " (4 : 12), " Comfort one another " (4 : 18), " Watch and be sober " (5 : 6), " Hope of salvation " (5 : 8, 9), " Edify " (5 : 11), " Be at peace " (5 : 13), " Support and be patient " (5 : 14), " Follow that which is good " (5 : 15), " Rejoice evermore " (5 : 16), " Pray without ceasing " (5 : 17), " Give thanks " (5 : 18), " Quench not the Spirit " (5 : 19), " Hold

fast, prove all things " (5 : 21), " Abstain " (5 : 22), " Sanctify " (5 : 23), " Blameless " (5 : 23).

Doctrine of the Church. " The Church " (1 : 1),
" Brethren " (1 : 4 ; 2 : 1, 9 14, 17 ; 3 : 7 ; 4 : 1, 10, 13 ;
5 : 1, 4, 12, 14, 25, 26, 27), " Ensamples " (1 : 7), " Your
Faith " (1 : 8), " Witnesses " (2 : 10), " Followers " (2 : 14).

Doctrine of Angels. " Satan hindered us " (2 : 18).

Doctrine of the Last Things. " Hope " (1 : 3), " Wait for
His Son from Heaven " (1 : 10), " Crown of rejoicing . . . at
His coming " (2 : 19), " The coming of the Lord Jesus Christ
with all His saints " (3 : 13), " Them that sleep will God
bring with Him " (4 : 14), " Unto the coming of the Lord "
(4 : 15), " The Lord Himself shall descend " (4 : 16), " Dead
in Christ shall rise " (4 : 16), " Caught up together " (4 : 17),
" For ever with the Lord " (4 : 17), " Day of the Lord "
(5 : 2), " Salvation " (5 : 9), " Be preserved blameless unto
the coming of the Lord " (5 : 23).

All these vital and vitalising truths were known in this
early Church, therefore, knowing when they were written
we can see their importance and significance.

V. To Whom a Scripture was Written

Paul's pastoral epistles to Timothy and Titus are wise and
weighty, and the Christian worker does well to give heed to
what he says to these younger fellow-labourers. His letter
to Titus may be divided into seven sections.

1. *Personal Salutation* (1 : 1-4). Paul's personal address
to his own son in the faith speaks of his personal responsibility
to the Lord as a servant of God, acting at the command of
God, reminding his friend of their common interest in God's
purpose in relation to them in the grace and mercy and peace
which come from the Father and the Lord Jesus.

2. *Personal Supervision* (1 : 5-9). A true bishop acting
under the authority of the Spirit has authority to adjust
matters which relate to the Lord's service, as " the steward
of God." First, he is to see that he is qualified in his personal life ; hence he is to be blameless in character, not self-
willed, of an even temper, free from intoxicants, not to
retaliate when injured, not to love money, and in relation

to others he is to be a lover of hospitality, of good men ; and as to his personal fitness for his office, he is to be sober, just, holy, and temperate, and to hold tenaciously to the Word which is committed to his care.

3. *Powerful Subjugation* (1 : 10-16). Titus is reminded that he will come against those that profess great things, but deny the Lord in their inconsistent character and conduct. He is not to allow these to question the truth of God, but to rebuke them sharply to the end that they may be " sound in the faith." Thus Paul reminds Titus that he is to set in order those who are vain talkers.

4. *Practical Shepherding* (2 : 1-10). Paul tells Titus what his attitude is to be to those to whom he ministers ; hence he is to speak those things which become " sound doctrine," and to shepherd the aged men, the aged women, the young men, the young women, servants, and masters, and in all things to be a pattern of good works himself, and thus pastor and people are to adorn the doctrine of God in all things.

5. *Precious Supplies* (2 : 11 ; 3 : 1-9). Titus is instructed by the apostle as to his teaching. He first reminds him of the seven golden links in the chain of grace which are sum- marized in the salvation which grace bestows ; the instruc- tion which grace gives ; the hope that grace begets ; the price which grace has paid ; the end which grace had in redeeming from all iniquity ; the acquirement which grace obtains in making God's people his own ; and the zeal which grace inspires. Paul charges Titus to see that he speaks and exhorts and rebukes with all authority, and ever to recog- nise the love of God and the renewing work of the Holy Spirit.

6. *Perverted Sinners* (3 : 10, 11). Titus is instructed how to deal with heretics. Toleration is not allowed when the truth of God and the ways of God are in question. Heretics are to be kindly admonished, but they are to be faithfully dealt with too.

7. *Partners Serving* (3 : 12-15). Titus is reminded what his conduct and thought is to be in relation to his fellow- labourers. Several of them are mentioned by name, and good works are to characterise one and all.

From this brief outline it will be seen how important it is to recognise the letter that Paul wrote to Titus, and how it illustrates the importance of recognising to whom a Scripture was written.

VI. Why a Scripture was Written

The Spirit tells us in John 20 : 31 why the Gospel of John was written. " But these are written, that ye may believe that Jesus is the Christ, the Son of God ; and that believing ye may have life in His Name." There are four things to ponder in these pregnant words, the root, the tree, the blossom, and the fruit.

The Root. " But these are written." The " signs " and things which are " written " in the Gospel of John are many. There are several fibrous roots found in what had been " written." The Revelation of Christ's Divine Personality as the Word (1 : 1-5) ; the Incarnation of Christ's Becoming-ness in dwelling in the tabernacle of His humanity (1 : 14) ; the Exhibition of His manifested glory as seen in what He did (2 : 11) ; what He revealed (3 : 16) and promised (14 : 3) ; The Instruction He gave as identified with the double " verilys " of His utterance (1 : 51 ; 3 : 3, 5, 11 ; 5 : 19, 24, 25 ; 6 : 26, 32, 47, 53 ; 8 : 34, 51, 58 ; 10 : 1, 7 ; 12 : 24 ; 13 : 16, 20, 21, 38 ; 14 : 12 ; 16 : 20, 23 ; 21 : 18) ; The impartation of the many gifts He bestowed as found in " My flesh " (6 : 51), " My peace " (14 : 27), " My glory " (17 : 22, 24) ; and the Expiation of His finished work on the Cross (3 : 14 ; 12 : 12-33) ; and the Might of His Resurrection (20 : 1-9). Here are roots from which the gigantic tree of Truth grows.

The Tree. What is said of Christ's personality is the tree. It is said, " That Jesus is the Christ, the Son of God." The " Jesus " of Nazareth is the Sent One, and the Saviour of the world (3 : 16-18). He is " The Christ," the Messiah of the Old Testament (4 : 42), the Anointed One with the Spirit (3 : 34), and the Sent One of the Father ; and He is also " The Son of God," God the Son, in His eternal existence, and as the Only Begotten One in His love, grace, power, the Embodiment of Deity.

The Blossom. The blossom is faith. The things were written that we might " believe " what is said about Christ. Faith embodies the assent of the mind, the consent of the will, and the accent of the life. Faith by the act of the will unites us to Christ, hence it is more than believing Christ, it believeth *into* Him. Faith in Him brings us to God, and God to us.

The Fruit. The fruit is life, Eternal Life. " His Name " stands for Himself, therefore, believing through His Name puts us in association with Him. The " life " of which the Apostle speaks, finds its Source in God, its Spring in Love, its Embodiment in Christ, its Power in the Holy Spirit, its Sustenance in the Word, its Sequence in Holiness, its Confession in Service, its Consummation in Glory, and its Channel in Faith.

How important it is to understand why the Word or any section was written. Pascal says, " There is light enough for those who wish to see." Denison Maurice, writing to Charles Kingsley in 1849, declared, " The Bible is the history of a Deliverer. . . . The Book brings us to the root of things, and there—is nothing, or there—is God."

VII. What the Scriptures Require

There are certain claims the Scriptures make, and requirements for which they call.

The first requirement is, *The Recognition of the Bible being Inspired.* The claim of the Book is, " All Scripture is given by inspiration of God " (2 Tim. 3 : 16). Scripture means sacred writing. When we claim the Scripture is inspired we do not mean translations. Translators have made mistakes. We mean the original Scripture was the product of the Holy Spirit, and not the evolution of man's thought. " Inspired of God " means " God breathed," or " God breathing." The late Dr. Bishop, of America, once said, in speaking of the Bible itself being the greatest proof of its Divine origin, " The Scriptures are their own self evidence. We take the ground, the sun needs no critic—truth no diving bell. When the sun shines, He shines the sun. When God speaks, His evidence is in the accent of His words."

Throwing overboard all theories about inspiration, we must accept the *fact* of it. The contents of the Book prove Him Who wrote it, and the words are "Words which the Holy Ghost teacheth" (I Cor. 2 : 13). Even those who have been tinged with modernism have to own there is that which is Divine. The late Archdeacon Farrer acknowledged "There are over a million and a quarter words in the New Testament and only about 1,300 of which are considered doubtful words. There are 17,000 in Matthew, and on a rough calculation only 17 of these are doubtful, leaving, 16,983 absolutely genuine words. In Matthew 24 there are 830 words in Greek, and only 5 of these are disputed words, thus leaving 825 words, respecting which there is little room for dispute or difference of opinion"; and the same writer affirms, "No disputed word is so vitally important, as to destroy the sense of Scripture." Another critic owned to his students, "Take all we can away, there still remains the fact, it is the only message that meets human need."

As the greatest evidence of Christianity is the Christ, so the greatest proof of the Bible is the Bible.

The second requirement is, *we must have spiritual life* to have the capacity to understand the Book. Illumination within is essential to comprehend the inspired Book without. We need eyes to see the sun, to see the sun that shines. Caroline Fry, out of her personal experience, was able to pen this testimony: "The Scriptures are good for me in sadness, for they are full of encouragement; good for me in doubt, for they are full of promise; good for me in carelessness, for they are full of warning; good for me in contrition, for they are full of mercy; nay, they are good for me in any case, for they are full of Jesus." When we know Him in faith, we receive spiritual life, and then we find we need His Word that the life may be nourished.

The third requirement is *a spiritual condition* in the saint to understand the spiritual Book. For that spiritual Book is for a spiritual people to develop their spiritual life. Paul had to say to the unspiritual Christians in Corinth, that they were carnal, hence he had to remind them, "Eye hath not seen, nor ear heard, neither have entered into the heart of man, the things which God hath prepared for them that love Him. But God hath revealed them unto us by His Spirit: for the Spirit searcheth all things, yea, the deep things of God " (1 Cor. 2 : 9, 10). There is a minute form of life, called a Rotifer, which cannot be seen with the naked eye, but when the drop of muddy water, which is the world in which it lives, is placed under a microscope and a powerful light is turned upon it, the Rotifer is seen to be a perfect form of life, and is so transparent that its heart can be seen beating. As that minute form of life can be seen by means of the illuminated microscope, so as we walk in fellowship with God, He reveals His secrets to us, as He did to Moses, " He made known His ways unto Moses, His acts unto the children of Israel " (Psa. 103 : 7). They only knew His ways by His acts, but Moses knew God's ways before He acted.

The fourth requirement is, we need *to see the Christ* in the Book, to understand the Book of which the Christ speaks. We read of the disciples more than once, that not knowing the Scriptures, they did not understand the words and acts of Christ (John 2 : 22 ; 20 : 9), and after His resurrection He explained to the two disciples and the eleven, that His death and resurrection were but the fulfilment of the Scriptures (Luke 24 : 27, 45), and John writing of the events associated with the death of Christ, again and again said of those events, they were that the Scripture might be fulfilled (John 19 : 24, 28, 30, 36, 37), and Christ's own testimony was, " They are they which testify of Me."

What the notes are to music, what the egg is to the shell, what the kernel is to the nut, what the diamond is to the ring, what the life is to the tree, what the heart is to the body, what the sun is to the moon, so Christ is to the Bible. If He is taken away we have nothing but an empty sepulchre.

There was once an artist who made a wonderful shield, and worked his own name so cleverly into it, that it could not be removed without destroying the shield. The Bible is like that shield, Christ is so identified with it, that the one cannot be taken away without destroying the other. The Living Word and the Written Word are so identified the one with the other that they cannot be separated. As we cannot have music without notes, eggs without shells, kernels without husks, diamond ring without ring, tree without life, body without heart, light of moon without sun, neither can we have the Christ apart from the Bible.

This is proved if we call to mind one fact, namely, that which is applied to Christ is designated of the Bible.

" His name is called the Word of God " (Rev. 19 : 13).

" Pressed upon Him to hear the Word of God" (Luke 5 : 1).

" I will be unto her a wall of fire " (Zech. 2 : 5).

" My word like as a fire " (Jer. 23 : 29).

" His name shall be called Wonderful " (Isa. 9 : 6).

" Thy testimonies are wonderful " (Psa. 119 : 129).

" Worship Him that liveth for ever " (Rev. 4 : 10).

" The Word of God liveth for ever " (1 Pet. 1 : 23).

" My Beloved is chiefest among ten thousand " (Cant. 5 : 10).

" The law of Thy mouth is better to me than thousands of gold and silver " (Psa. 119 : 72).

" A bone of Him shall not be broken " (John 19 : 36).

" The Scripture cannot be broken " (John 10 : 35).

The fifth requirement is *to be taught by Him Who inspired the Book*. Three essential things are connected with and supplementary the one to the other, namely, the Christ explains God, the Word explains Christ, and the Spirit explains the Word. Of the Scriptures, Christ, and the Prophets, we read, " Of which salvation the prophets have enquired and searched diligently, who prophesied of the grace that should come unto you ; searching what, or what manner of time the Spirit of Christ which was in them did signify, when it testified beforehand the sufferings of Christ, and the glory that should follow " (1 Pet. 1 : 10, 11). The prophets did not understand until they were taught, and when they were taught they knew. A personal acquaintance with the Author of the Book will give us to understand the contents of it. To know Him is to find them.

The sixth requirement is *to believe the Spirit resides in the Scriptures*. An old Puritan has said, "The Holy Spirit always rides in the chariot of His Word." Christ said of His words, "The words which I speak unto you they are spirit and life" (John 6 : 63). Professor Godet comments, "Christ's words are not merely the means of communicating life, but the Holy Spirit is resident in the words." The Word of God is living (Heb. 4 : 12), therefore if we would have the life of the Word, we must be in touch with the Word of Life.

The seventh requirement is *a wholehearted study and search* to know the meaning of the Scriptures. There are three words that have been translated "search" in the New Testament. The word "search" in John 5 : 39 and 7 : 52 means to seek out and is used of a lion which scours the country and traces the footsteps of the man who had robbed it ; and is associated with Him Who is the Searcher of hearts, and the Spirit Who "searcheth the deep things of God" (Rev. 2 : 23 ; 1 Cor. 2 : 10). The word "search" in Matt. 2 : 8, means to examine in order to verify, and is used of those who "enquire" to find out (Matt. 10 : 11), and also of one who wishes to "ask" about anything, that he may know (John 21 : 12). The third word is found in Acts 17 : 11, where there were Bereans who "searched the Scriptures daily," and means to divide, to make a distinction, to judge, to sift, and which results in a decision. This word is rendered "Examined" in Acts 28 : 18, "Discerned" in 1 Cor. 2 : 14, "Asking question" in 1 Cor. 10 : 25, and "Judge" in 1 Cor. 4 : 3. On the human side, it will therefore be seen, there has to be careful study, whole-hearted diligence, and spiritual discernment. A great leader of a religious organisation defined sin as follows : "Sin consists in doing that which we know to be wrong, inwardly or outwardly, or in not doing that which we know to be right." He could not have put man's consciousness of sin, if he had known that "sin is a missing of the mark of God's requirement, or any want of conformity to the will of God," and that the law said, "Though he wist it not, yet is he guilty."

The eighth requirement is *to count upon the Holy Spirit* to make true in our experience what is true for us in the

Word. Professor Bonney, in speaking of the study of Geology, says: " The study of Geology has added much to the happiness of my life; it has taught me to appreciate more fully the beauties and marvels of nature; it has often restored me, when weary and jaded, to bodily health; it has helped me to bear those trials which are the common lot."

In a deeper and more satisfying sense, the child of God can say: " The reception of the Sacred Word by the Holy Spirit, has been the medium of the joy of my life; it has revealed to me the beauty and satisfying perfection of my Lord; it has ever been the channel of blessing in every condition; and it has ministered comfort and power as I have received it from Him, Who is its Author."

The ninth requirement is *a consistent practice* of what we have been taught, to enjoy what we know. This must be if we remember, " The Word " is the Bestower of Life (1 Pet. 1 : 23), the Revealer of Christ (John 5 : 39), the Giver of Assurance (1 John 5 : 13), the Imparter of Joy (Jer. 15 : 16), the Inspirer of Prayer (John 15 : 7), the Sword of Victory (Eph. 6 : 17), the Sanctifier of the Heart (John 17 : 17), the Feeder of the Soul (1 Pet. 2 : 2), the Equipper of the Servant (Acts 8 : 4), and the Plan for Guidance (Exod. 40 : 16, 19, 21, 23, 25, 27, 29, 32).

> " When thou hast read what Heaven hath writ,
> Let thy best practice second it,
> Then twice the precept read shall be,
> First in the Book, and then in thee."

Lastly, the spiritual truths of the Book can only be *communicated by means of the Spiritual Power* of the Spirit. " Comparing spiritual things with spiritual " (1 Cor. 2 : 13) has been rendered, " communicating spiritual things by means of spiritual power." The live wire which communicates its power and moves the car, is only alive as it is connected with the power house. The same principle holds good in the Lord's service. Christ not only told His disciples to preach the Gospel, but to tarry till they were endued with power, that the Spirit might communicate it to others.

Labour must be " in the Lord " or else it will be " in vain," but it can never be " in vain " if it is " in the Lord." The Spirit needs the work and us, but He needs us for His work, even as the cog wheels need each other to move the train on the Swiss mountain railway.

What a different world there would be if we always followed the Inspired Scriptures and the Inspirer of them. What a different Church there would be if its behests were obeyed ; and what different individuals we should be if we knew the Scriptures experimentally.

We say of the Book what J. Cooke has done, " A nation would, indeed, be truly blessed, if it were governed by no other laws than those of this blessed Book. It is so complete a system that nothing can be added to it or taken from it. It contains everything needful to be known or done. It affords a copy for a king, and a rule for a subject ; and gives instruction and counsel for a senate, authority and direction for a magistrate. It cautions a witness, requires an impartial verdict of a jury, and furnishes the judge with his sentence. It sets the husband as lord of the household and the wife as mistress of the table ; tells him how to rule, and her how to manage. It entails honour to parents, and enjoins obedience to children. It prescribes and limits the sway of the sovereign, the rule of the ruler, and the authority of the master ; commands the subjects to honour, and the servants to obey ; and promises the blessing and protection of the Almighty to all that walk by its rules. It gives directions for weddings and for burials. It promises food and raiment, and limits the use of both. It points out a faithful and eternal guardian to the departing husband and father—tells him with whom to leave his fatherless children, and in whom his widow is to trust,—and promises a father to the former, and a husband to the latter. It teaches a man how to set his house in order, and how to make his will ; it appoints a dowry for his wife, and entails the right of the firstborn, and shows how the younger shall be left. It defends the right of all, and reveals vengeance to every defaulter, over-reacher and oppressor. It is the *first* Book, the *best* Book, and the *oldest* Book in the world. It contains the choicest matter—gives the best instruction ; affords the greatest pleasure and satisfaction that ever was enjoyed. It contains the best laws, and the most profound mysteries that were ever penned. It brings the best tidings, and affords the best of comfort, to the enquiring and disconsolate. It exhibits life and immortality from everlasting, and shows the way to glory. It is a brief recital of all that is past, and a certain prediction of all that is to come. It settles all matter in debate, resolves all doubts, and eases the mind and conscience of all their scruples. It reveals the only living and true God, and shows the way to Him, and sets aside all other gods, and describes the vanity of them, and all that trust in such. In short, it if a Book of laws, to show right and wrong ; a Book of wisdom, that condemns all folly, and makes the foolish wise ; a Book of truth, that detects all lies, and confutes all errors ; and a Book of life, that shows the way from everlasting death. It is the most compendious Book in the world—the most authentic, and the most entertaining history that ever was published. It contains the most ancient antiquities, strange events, wonderful occurrences, heroic deeds, unparalleled wars. It describes the celestial, terrestrial, and infernal worlds, and the origin of the angelic myriads, human tribes, and devilish legions. It will instruct the accomplished mechanic and the most profound artist. It teaches the best rhetorician, and exercises every power of the most skilful arithmetician ; puzzles the wisest anatomist, and exercises the nicest critic. It corrects the vain philosopher, and confutes the wise astronomer. It exposes the subtle sophist, and makes diviners mad. It is a complete code of laws, a perfect body of divinity, and unequalled narrative—a Book of lives—a Book of travels, and a Book of voyages. It is the best covenant that ever was agreed on—the best deed that ever was sealed—the best evidence that ever was produced—the best will that ever was made, and the best testament that ever was signed. To understand it, is to be wise indeed, to be ignorant of it, is to be destitute of wisdom. It is the king's best copy, the magistrate's best rule, the housewife's best guide, the servant's best directory, and the young man's best companion. It is the schoolboy's spelling book, and the learned man's masterpiece. It contains a choice grammar for a novice, and a profound mystery for a sage. It is the ignorant man's dictionary, and the wise man's directory. It affords knowledge of witty inventions for the humorous, and dark sayings for the grave, and is its own interpreter. It encourages the wise, the warrior, the swift, the overcomer ; and promises an eternal reward to the excellent, the conqueror, the winner and the prevalent. And that which crowns all, is that the Author is without partiality, and without hypocrisy, ' in Whom is no variableness, neither shadow of turning.' "

So we say of this wondrous Book,

> " Yes, 'tis a mine of precious jewelry,
>   The Book of God ; a well of streams divine !
>   But who would wish the riches of that mine
> To make his own ; his thirst to satisfy
> From that pure well ; must ear, eye, soul, apply ;
>   On precept, precept scan, and line on line ;
>   Search, ponder, sift, compare, divide, combine,
> For truths that oft beneath the surface lie.
> Yes ; there are things which he who runs may read,
>   Nor few there are, which yield a harder part,
> To mark, discern, and know. With cautious heed,
>   'Tis God's command, survey the safety's chart ;
> Lest arduous things, distorted, death-ward lead
>   The mind unlearn'd, and the unstable heart."

8

THE LUNGS OF A DOUBLE ACTION

A S the lungs in their functioning in-breathe and out-breathe, so we find there is a double aspect of every truth of the Gospel. We give three examples, namely, suggestive hints as to the doubles of God's blessings ; second, the two advents of Christ ; and third, the relative importance of the double of Christ's atonement and advent.

Almost every blessing which comes to us through our Lord Jesus Christ has a double meaning. There is that which God gives to us in His objective grace, and there is the result of that grace in a subjective sense operating in our hearts and lives. The field is too large to do more than hint at what we might call these double blessings of the Gospel.

Two-fold Meetness. The Father in His love and grace has "made us meet for the inheritance of the saints in light" (Col. 1 : 12) ; and we are responsible to see that we are vessels "meet for the Master's use" in being sanctified and prepared unto every good work (2 Tim. 2 : 21).

Two-fold Acceptance. God in His grace has made us "accepted in the Beloved" (Eph. 1 : 6) ; and because of this, we are to make it our aim and ambition " to be accepted of Him," that is, to be "well-pleasing to Him" (2 Cor. 5 : 9, R.V.).

Two-fold Justification. We are justified before God without works (Rom. 3 : 26, 28) ; but we justify our faith by our works (Jas. 2 : 14-26).

Two-fold Sanctification. Christ having met every claim of God on our behalf in answering for our sin, declares that the believer has been "sanctified through the offering of the body of Jesus Christ once for all," and " we are perfected forever" (Heb. 10 : 10, 14, R.V.) ; and because of this, we are " being sanctified by faith " as the Holy Spirit works within us (Rom. 15 : 16).

Two-fold Election. God has chosen us in Christ that we should " be holy and without blame before Him in love " (Eph. 1 : 4, 5) ; and we are responsible to make our calling and election sure by adding to our faith the graces of virtue, knowledge, temperance, patience, Godliness, brotherly-kindness, and love (2 Pet. 1 : 5-11).

Two-fold Possession. Those who are born of the Holy Spirit possess the Holy Spirit, as the seal of God marking them off as His property (Eph. 4 : 30) ; but it is not every believer who is possessed by the Spirit, hence the exhortation is to " be filled in the Spirit " (Eph. 5 : 18, R.V.).

Two-fold Rest. Christ promises the rest of salvation to those that come to Him, and thus they find rest of conscience from their sins ; but there is also a deeper rest—the rest of heart from anxiety as we take the yoke of God's will upon us, and keep in that yoke with our Lord (Matt. 11 : 28, 29).

Two-fold Righteousness. Because Christ has been " made sin for us " we are " made the righteousness of God in Him " (2 Cor. 5 : 21) ; but we are exhorted also as a consequence of our union with Christ to be righteous and thus evidencing our oneness with Him (1 John 2 : 29).

Two-fold Cleansing. The conscience is cleansed from guilt by the atoning blood of Christ, hence we are said to be " justified " (counted righteous) " by means of His blood " (Rom. 5 : 9) ; but the relative to this is, that we " cleanse ourselves of all filthiness of the flesh and of the spirit, perfecting holiness in the fear of the Lord " (2 Cor. 7 : 1).

Two-fold Redemption. We are redeemed to God by the blood of Christ, hence in Him " we have redemption " (Eph. 1 : 7) ; but the outcome of this means we are to be redeemed from all iniquity (Titus 2 : 14).

Two-fold Life. Believers in Christ have eternal life as God's gift (Rom. 6 : 23) ; but we are to lay hold on eternal life as an experience (1 Tim. 6 : 19).

Two-fold Work of Grace. The grace of God saves us from what we deserve as sinners ; but it also teaches us that we should deny ungodliness and worldly lust, and live soberly, righteously and Godly (Titus 2 : 11, 12).

Two-fold Forgiveness. God in His wondrous love graciously forgives us our sins (Eph. 1 : 7) ; and that is to be the incentive to forgive one another even as He has forgiven us (Eph. 4 : 32).

Two-fold Deliverance. God has delivered us from the power of darkness (Col. 1 : 13), that we should be delivered from this present evil world (Gal. 1 : 4).

The above will indicate a few of the many doubles that are found in connection with God's blessings. What God has joined together we must not put asunder. It is our privilege to recognise what is ours in Christ, but we are equally responsible to allow Christ to live in us that we may fulfil our responsibilities.

ADVENT AND ATONEMENT

The star of Christ's first coming, leading on to the goal of His atonement, is intimately associated with His return as the Bright and Morning Star. As the main pillars in Solomon's Temple, Jachin and Boaz were identified with the whole house of God ; so the prominent truths of the Temple of Truth are Christ's atonement for sin, and His advent to consummate the whole purpose of the Lord. The names of the two pillars are full of meaning. " Jachin " means " He shall establish," and " Boaz " signifies " In Him is strength." The Boaz of Christ's death is the strength of all He has and will become ; and in the end He will establish all things in His kingdom and glory, and that because of His death. The Lamb on the Throne is the Man Who was once on the Cross.

The late Dr. Saphir has given a concise and consecrated testimony of the importance of Christ's Cross of atonement, and His advent of glory. He says : " To know Jesus Christ and Him crucified is not the minimum of knowledge, but the maximum of knowledge ; that to thus know Him is not a descent from a loftier region, but an elevation into the highest sanctuary ; that in Jesus Christ and Him crucified, all doctrines, all God's teachings, and man's experiences culminate ; that from Jesus Christ and Him crucified, all duties, all works, all ministries, are to emanate and to be evolved.

Here is the hidden and perfect wisdom of God. No doctrine is seen clearly and truly unless it leads to the Cross; no work is God-pleasing, no experience or attainment genuine and vital, unless it has its source, root, and strength in the Cross; no waiting for the Second Coming is healthy and purifying unless it is called forth by the contemplation of the great God and Saviour, Who gave Himself for us, and redeemed us from all iniquity. O blessed concentration! Blessed simplicity of the Gospel! From this centre, from this Cross of Christ Jesus, as from the heart, are the issues of life."

TWO FEASTS

The feasts of the Passover and Trumpets show how the two truths are associated. These two feasts are closely allied in the Book of Zechariah. In Zech. 14 : 4-21 we have seven times what shall take place " in that day," that is, the day of Millennial glory, when the Lord shall tabernacle amongst us again.

1. Arrival of the Lord with His saints at the commencement of His tabernacling. " His feet shall stand in that day upon the Mount of Olives " (4).

2. Darkness leading to light will be the phenomenon " at that day." The American Revised Version of verses 6 and 7 reads : " In that day there shall not be light, the bright ones shall withdraw themselves (the stars) . . . but at evening time it shall be light," that is, Von Oreilli says, " The light of salvation will break its way through the night of judgment " (see Isa. 30 : 26).

3. Living waters blessing the earth. " It shall be in that day living waters will go out of Jerusalem " (8). The river described in Ezekiel 47 will bring blessing in its onward and deepening flow.

4. Christ's universal reign. " The Lord shall be King over all the earth in that day " (verse 9). All the nations will know the right and might of His reign.

5. Christ's might victorious over His enemies. The peoples that have warred against the Lord shall be brought under His judgment " in that day " (verses 12-15, A.R.V.).

6. " Holiness unto the Lord " shall characterise every-thing " in that day " (verse 20). Everything shall be sacred to Him.

7. Exclusion of the enemy. " In that day there shall no more be the Canaanite in the house of the Lord of hosts " (verse 21). The trafficker for self and sin will be excluded.

All this is preceded by Judah looking upon Him Whom they have pierced, and in knowing Him Who was smitten by the sword of Jehovah on their behalf (Zech. 12 : 10 ; 13 : 7).

" Decease " and " Glory."

The same combination of atonement and advent is made known in the scene on the Mount of Transfiguration, which scene is a picture, Peter declares, of Christ's " power and coming " in " His majesty " (2 Pet. 1 : 16). Of our Lord and those who were with Him we read : " There talked with Him two men . . . who appeared in glory, and spake of His decease " (Luke 9 : 30, 31). " His decease " refers to His death, to His exodus, to His going out of the body in death. The theme of these glorified ones was Christ's death. Saphir says : " The source of the glory is Jesus Christ crucified. When He said, ' It is finished,' two eternities met ; there was revealed and accomplished the counsel of God, and there was purchased and secured the glory of His people. Thus the preaching of Christ crucified is central and compre-hensive." The Spring of the Hope of Christ's glory ever flows from the smitten rock of Calvary. Those who " ap-peared in glory " with Christ were there because of His decease about which they were talking. The vantage point of Calvary gives us the vital place in the glory.

The Lord's Supper and the Kingdom

As Christ handed the cup to His disciples at the institu-tion of the Lord's Supper, He said : " This is My blood of the New Testament which is shed for many for the remission of sins ; but I say unto you, I will not drink henceforth of this fruit of the vine, until that day when I drink it new with you in My Father's kingdom " (Matt. 26 : 28, 29). The two phrases, " This is My blood " and " This fruit of the vine " take us back to the Cross and on to the kingdom. The first is a metaphor which signifies one thing represented or embodied in another, so that " My blood " stands for His atoning death. The words, " This fruit of the vine," come under the figure of speech " periphrasis," which means a description is given of a thing instead of naming it. So the " Fruit of the vine " and " My blood " stand for the death of Christ and the outcome. As the bunch of grapes has to be cut off the vine, and the grapes crushed to obtain the wine, so Christ had to be cut off in death, and crushed in the winepress of God's wrath before there could be any benefit to us. That blood was " shed (poured out) for many." The " for " (" peri ") signifies action towards an object, and means " concerning the many," that is, He was acting for them, and the end He had in view was " for the remission of sins." The other " for " is " eis," and embodies intention, and the intention is expressed, it was unto " remission of sins." And remission signifies not only the cancelling of guilt, but the removing of the sins which brought the guilt.

Will the Lord's Supper be in or after the Millennium ? Christ points on to the time, in His Father's kingdom, when He will again observe the Supper which He had inaugurated, for as Alford says : " These words carry on the meaning and continuance of this sacrificial ordinance, even into the new heavens and the new earth." Alford also gives a quotation from Thiersch : " The Lord's Supper points not only to the past, but the future also. It has not only a commemorative, but also a prophetic meaning. In it we have not only to show forth the Lord's death until He come, but we have also to think of the time when He shall come to celebrate His Holy Supper with His own, new, in His kingdom of glory. Every celebration of the Supper is a foretaste and prophetic anticipation of the great marriage supper which is prepared for the Church at the second appearing of Christ. This import of the sacrament is declared in the words of the Lord : ' I will not drink henceforth the fruit of the vine until I drink it new in My Father's kingdom.' "

We therefore see that the Lord's Supper not only shows forth His death until He comes, but when He has come we shall still proclaim that death to which we owe everything, even as in the Millennium there will be commemorative sacrifices to point back to that death of deaths, that sacrifice of sacrifices, and that only atonement for sin (see Ezek. 46).

Expiation and Expectation

Of Christ's atoning death in the past and His outlook in the future, it is declared: "But this Man, after He had offered one sacrifice for sins for ever, sat down on the right hand of God from henceforth expecting till His enemies be made His footstool" (Heb. 10:12, 13). Expiation means to make reparation for wrong done, or to give satisfaction for an evil committed. What the seraph said to Isaiah, "Thy sin is purged," might be rendered, "Thy sin is expiated, or atoned for." Christ's offering is said to be "for our sins," that is, on behalf of our sins, in answering for them; as Westcott says: "The offering of Christ, His perfect life crowned by a willing death, in which He fulfilled the destiny of man and bore the punishment of human sin, is that, and by, and in, which every human life finds its consummation." There is infinite value in that death, because of the value of His infinite worth, for it was in the eternal value of His eternal Spirit He offered Himself without spot to God, and so brought an eternal benefit to us.

To quote Westcott again: "It is significant that Christ is said to perfect by His offering; it is not said the offering perfects. His action is personal in the application of His own work." It is the Person Who gives value to His work. This is further elucidated if we omit the comma after the word "ever" and place it after the word "sins." Then the sentence reads, "After He had offered one sacrifice for sins, forever sat down." The work of His atoning death being finished, He will never rise up to open the question of atonement for sin again, for His one offering once for all offered is complete and eternal. The text read in the ordinary way from 1611-1630, but in 1638 the comma was removed, and placed after the word "sins," and it read, "forever sat down," thus going back to the punctuation of the Bishop's Bible of 1568. This is the punctuation in the Book of Common Prayer. Alford inclines to the reading, "forever sat down," for as he comments: "The words seem better to refer to an enduring state than to a past act." The words that follow confirm this: "For by one offering He hath perfected forever them that are sanctified." His perfect act brings unto a perfect state, therefore there is no need for Christ to rise again from His Father's throne, for since sin has been remitted on the ground of a perfect sacrifice, there is no more offering for sin (Heb. 10 : 18). "The virtue of Christ's work remains ever available as long as the need of man exists." That need is eternal, and that eternal need is met by the Eternal Offerer, Who offered a sacrifice eternal in its value, therefore He could not die again, and will not rise again to repeat His atoning work.

The Cross and the Throne

Flowing from Christ's perfect expiation for sin is an outlook of expectancy, of complete triumph over His enemies : "Henceforth expecting till His enemies be made His footstool." The word for "expecting" is used only of "one waiting" for another. It is translated "waiteth for : tarry, for : look for." The impotent folk were "waiting for" the moving of the water by the angel (John 5 : 3). Paul "waited for," and was content to "look for," certain brethren (Acts 17 : 16; 1 Cor. 16 : 11). Brethren were exhorted to "tarry one for another" when they remembered the Lord's death (1 Cor. 11 : 33). Abraham "looked for" a city whose Builder was God (Heb. 11 : 10). The husbandman "waiteth for" the fruit of his toil (Jas. 5 : 7). God "waited" in the days of Noah for the repentance of men (1 Pet. 3 : 20). And Christ is waiting till His enemies shall be subject to Him.

The Lamb Slain and Slaying

The one pre-dominating thought in the Book of the Revelation is, the Lamb, in all the livingness of His death, puts down His foes, and reigns over His enemies. The wounded One of Calvary is the Warrior conquering His enemies. The Book of the unveiling is the revelation that God's Little Lamb shall conquer the red dragon of hell, He

will put down the seven-headed and ten-horned beast of a
revived Roman Empire. He will blast the false prophet of
Antichrist by the brightness of His coming. He will cause
the corrupt woman of Christendom to be slaughtered by the
confederates. He will wipe out the sin-riddled and demon-
possessed City of Babylon. He will break the nations who
oppose Him with the rod of His power. And He will remove
all who stand in the way of His sway as He merges the kingdoms of the world to crown Him King of kings and Lord of
lords. The Lamb that was slain is the Conqueror. He was
once trodden in the winepress because of man's sin, and
because of this He shall conquer His enemies as He treads
them down in the fierceness of God's wrath.

The Double

This double truth of atonement and advent might be
multiplied. The following brief outline will emphasise:

1. Christ's sufferings and glory is the theme of the Scriptures. " The prophets . . . prophesied . . . of the sufferings
of Christ, and the glory that should follow " (1 Pet. 1 : 10, 11).

2. Christ's suffering and glory was the topic of Christ's
conversation with the two disciples as He journeyed with
them to Emmaus (Luke 24 : 26).

3. " Till He come " we observe the memorable feast
which proclaims His death (1 Cor. 11 : 26).

4. The assurance of the resurrection of our loved ones
who have fallen asleep, and the quickening of the living ones
is based on " Christ died " (1 Thess. 4 : 14).

5. " Who died for us " are the Spirit's words, as He
declares the ground why we are appointed (placed in) the
salvation of the future (1 Thess. 5 : 9, 10).

6. The Church will be set before the Lord without a spot
or wrinkle, or any such thing, because He loved her and gave
Himself for her (Eph. 5 : 25, 27).

7. We are exhorted to be looking for that Blessed Hope,
and the appearing of the glory of the great God and Saviour,
Who gave Himself for us (Titus 2 : 13).

The cords of God's love bind us to the altar of Christ's
sacrifice, and its flame fuses us into God's nature, and the

glory of Christ's coming attracts us to the heaven of His holiness. Since the Lord has such a claim upon us, and we have been called to such a glory, what manner of persons ought we to be? With such a past of His passion, and with such a prospect of His glory, we cannot, if we know Him, be anything else than wholly devoted to Him.

TWO ADVENTS

Christ's two advents are intimately connected the one with the other. There is a correspondence between the two, and yet there is a contrast. The first was in humiliation, the second will be in glory. Let us look at some resemblances between the two advents.

Christ's Own Statements

We are not left in any uncertainty about Christ's first coming. His Word is positive, peculiar, and emphatic. In relation to the law He says, " I am come to fulfil it " (Matt. 5 : 17). As to His mission He declares, " I am not come to call the righteous, but sinners to repentance " (Matt. 9 : 13). Reverting to the authority behind Him in all He said and did, He assures us, " I am come in My Father's Name " (John 5 : 43). In calling attention to two of the blessings He came to give, namely, Light and Life, His testimony is beyond all question—" I am come a Light into the world," and " I am come that ye might have life " (John 10 : 10 ; 12 : 46). Could anything be clearer?

When Christ, in the absence of Judas, speaks of His coming again He says, " I will come again and receive ye unto Myself " (John 14 : 3). His " I come " is in contrast to His " I go." And " again " cannot mean anything else than " again." " Palin," the word for " again," means a repetition. Peter not only denied his Lord once, but " again," and Christ in the garden not only prayed once, but He went " away again " and prayed the same words. The two pillars of the temple of truth are Christ's first coming to atone for sin, and His second coming to reign.

The Father's Two Sendings

Without referring to the forty-three times in John's Gospel which speak of Christ being sent by the Father, we recall the two sendings to which Peter refers in his second sermon after Pentecost. " God sent Him to bless you," and that in a specific way, " by turning away everyone of you from his iniquities," and this by means of the One Who died and rose again. But of that same One it is also declared, " He shall send Jesus Christ," and lest there should be any doubt that the sending is future, Peter further declares, " Whom the heavens must receive until the times of restitution " (Acts 3 : 20-26). The Father's first sending of Christ was that through (by means of) Him salvation might be provided for the world (John 3 : 17) ; but His second sending is that the covenant with Abraham about the land of Palestine might be fulfilled, and His covenant with David might be completed, and the other things of " the times of restoration," or " restitution," spoken by the prophets, might be consummated.

Two Visibilities

The fact of Christ being seen is one of the essentialities of the Gospel. The testimony of the Apostles is beyond doubt or question. John's witness is, " We have seen with our eyes," " We behold His glory " (I John I : I ; John I : 14). Simeon exclaimed, as he held the infant Christ in his arms, " Mine eyes have seen Thy salvation " (Luke 2 : 26, 30). The people saw " the mighty works which He did " (Luke 19 : 37) ; and, after His resurrection, " He showed Himself alive . . . by many infallible proofs, being seen of them forty days, and speaking of the things pertaining to the kingdom of God. Those who saw Him beheld an actual Person, and not an apparition.

> " The Word had breath, and wrought
> With human hands the creed of creeds
> In loveliest of perfect deeds."

The actuality of the Christ of the past is a prophecy of the Christ of the future. The exultant note of the blessed hope of Christ's return is buoyantly expressed in the soul-stirring words, " We shall see Him." Israel is reminded in the Sacred Word of prophetic outlook, " They shall look upon Him Whom they pierced " ; and in the universal light which shall come to all, the Divine declaration is, "Every eye shall see Him (Zech. 12 : 10 ; Rev. 1 : 7).

Two Ministries

"The Son of Man came not to be ministered unto, but to minister, and to give His life a ransom for many" (Matt. 20 : 28). The climax of His ministry was to give His life. There was no compulsion upon Him, He gave His life— willingly and lovingly He deliberately laid down His life ; and that vicariously, that is, instead of the "many." Thus did His last act show forth the ministry of all His ministry. That ministry was not a general serving, but refers to the specific act of His death. "This," as Alford comments, "is a plain declaration of the sacrificial nature of the death of our Lord." He gave Himself as a ransom, and this denotes a payment equivalent for a life destroyed (Exod. 21 : 30) ; the price of redemption for a slave (Exod. 21 : 26) ; and a propitiation for sin (Job 33 : 24).

One of the most wonderful promises of Christ is when He promises to "come forth and serve" those servants whom He finds faithfully watching for His return, and watching with girded loins and trimmed lamps (Luke 12 : 35-40). We would be content to kiss His feet in humble submission and adoration ; but that He should "come forth" and serve us, and that, as Alford suggests, "His coming in turn to each" is beyond our conception. When love is appreciated by whole-hearted devotion it commands the service of special regard. What an exceptional ministry that will be if our Lord should find us worthy of it. The fact He says He will do it, tells us He will come to perform it.

Two centuries ago the M'Cheyne of his time, and who, like him, was early called home, once said at a communion service, "Oh, when shall those blue heavens be rent, and we be admitted to the marriage supper of the Lamb ? I long for the day when all the language of heaven and earth shall be, 'Come, come Lord Jesus.'" Such an ardent longing is the outcome of a loving devotion to the Lord. Readiness for Him is the outcome of a full obedience to Him.

Twofold Life

"I am come that ye might have life" (John 10 : 10).
"When Christ Who is our Life shall appear, then shall ye
also appear with Him in glory" (Col. 3 : 4). The positive
message of the Gospel is "Eternal Life," and that is, as
Westcott says, "Beyond the limitations of time. It belongs
to the being of God, and finds its consummation in the
transforming vision of the Son seen as He is. . . . It cannot
be separated from Himself. Therefore His coming was
crowned by His passover and exaltation, whereby His life
was made available for others through death. . . . Eternal
life is not an endless duration of being in time, but being of
which time is not a measure. . . . Life for a finite creature is
union with God." These quotations from Westcott, inspired by Divine revelation, tell us that "Eternal life belongs
to the Being of God"; Christ is its Embodiment. Union
with God by means of Christ is its meaning, and what we
shall be when we are like Christ is its consummation.

Eternal life, the Life of God,
  The Life is God supreme ;
'Tis what He is, 'tis what He has,
  And is the Gospel's theme.

Eternal life ! Eternal life !
  What can with it compare ?
'Tis found in Christ, in Christ alone,
  In Christ Divine and fair.

The Life is like a Circle true,
  Including all within ;
God wanteth none, He giveth all,
  And all is found in Him.

But God did break the Circle rare,
  And by the Cross doth show,
That through the Christ that died thereon,
  We in the Circle go.

And now the Christ doth say to us,
  " I am the Way, the Life,
And he that comes to God by Me,
  He finds eternal life."

The essence of that Life is Love,
  And with it, too, is Light,
And Love and Light are Life expressed,
  For " God is Love " and " Light."

And as we take the Gift of Life,
    We Life in Christ possess,
And as the Life our lives enflame
    There is no care nor stress.
The goal of Life, the Life indeed,
    When Christ shall come again,
Will cause us like to Christ to be,
    And in His glory reign.

What a life this Life is! We cannot measure its infinitude, sound its depth, reach to its height, or comprehend its far-reachingness. But we can rejoice in Him Who says, " I am the Life " and be " Looking for the mercy of our God, unto Eternal Life."

Twofold Manifestation

Christ's incarnation is variously described. In regard to the Father, it is a " sending," a mission. In regard to the Son, it is a coming. In regard to the form, it is in flesh. In regard to men, it is a manifestation. In John's first epistle we find him frequently stating the fact of Christ's manifestation in the past, and its purpose (1 John 1 : 2 ; 3 : 5, 8 ; 4 : 9) ; and reference is also made to His future manifestation, when he says, " He shall be manifested " (1 John 2 : 28 , 3 : 2). The manifestation means an unveiling, so that that which was invisible shines forth. He was manifested in the past to take away our sins, and to destroy the works of the devil ; and He will be manifested in the future to make His own like Himself. The future shining forth will be the complement of the past. The one would not be perfect without the other.

Elizabeth Browning, in her " Drama of Exile," makes Christ say to Eve :

" I, wrapping round Me your humanity,
    Which, being sustained, shall neither break nor burn
    Beneath the fire of Godhead, will tread earth,
        And ransom you and it, and set strong peace
    Betwixt you and its creatures ; with My pangs
        I will confront your sins, and since your sins
    Have sunken to all Nature's heart from yours,
    The tears of My clean soul shall follow them,
        And set a holy passion to work clear,
    Absolute consecration. In My brow
    Of Kingly whiteness shall be crowned anew
    Your discrowned human nature. Look on Me !

> As I shall be uplifted on a Cross
> In darkness of eclipse and anguished dread,
> So shall I lift up in My pierced hands,
> Not into dark, but light—not unto death,
> But life—beyond the reach of guilt and grief,
> The whole creation."

How prophetic and significant are the words :

> " . . . In My brow
>   . . . shall be crowned anew
> Your discrowned human nature."

Yea, we may say our nature shall not only be " crowned anew," but we shall have a body like His, for the goal of the Lord's purpose is, we shall not only recover what is lost, but we shall have a body like to " His body of glory " (Phil. 3 : 20, 21, R.V.). It is His design to set us in His presence without spot, without wrinkle, or any such thing.

Twofold Purpose

" Once in the end of the ages " (R.V.), " hath He appeared to put away sin by the sacrifice of Himself. . . . He shall appear the second time without sin " (without a sin-offering) " unto salvation " (Heb. 9 : 27, 28). The one definite end He had in view when He first appeared was to put away sin, and the means whereby He put it away was by the sacrifice of Himself. Sin is viewed as a hindrance, keeping man from God, and God from man ; or if we take the word " put away " in its actual meaning, He disannulled sin (the same word is rendered " disannulling " in Heb. 7 : 18) by His sacrifice. Annulling its power and fact by the potency of His death, and thus rendering it naught. " The thought goes beyond the redemption from transgression. It is literally for the disannulling of sin." Sin is vanquished, shown in its weakness, set at naught. The death of Christ has settled the question of sin, and therefore the fact of sin is settled by the living Factor of Christ's death. Sin laid Him low in death, but by His death He has laid sin low.

A second time He will appear, and " unto salvation." The word " appear " denotes the Object seen, and not so much the act of seeing. It is rendered " seen " in referring to the fact that Christ was "seen" by many people after His resurrection (1 Cor. 15 : 5-8), and means to look in the face of another, hence it is often used in speaking of His return, when many will "see" HIM (Matt. 24 : 30 ; Mark 13 : 26 ; 14 : 62 ; Luke 21 : 27 ; John 16 : 16, 17, 19, 22 ; 1 John 3 : 2 ; Rev. 1 : 7 ; 22 : 4). He will be "seen unto salvation." "Salvation" points to what we shall be saved to, although it takes in from what we shall be saved. Westcott comments : " To accomplish, consummate salvation, which means not only the removal of sin, but also the attainment of the ideal of humanity."

Twofold Conquest

Christ's first coming had a distinct end in view in relation to the devil—" For this purpose the Son of God was manifested, that He might destroy the works of the devil " (1 John 3 : 8). He came to unloose all that the enemy had bound, for " destroy " means to unloose, as Lazarus was loosed from the grave-clothes ; and it also means to break down and melt (John 11 : 44 ; Eph. 2 : 14 ; 2 Pet. 3 : 10). And further, Christ is said to have taken our nature, that by means of death He might destroy him that had the power of death (Heb. 2 : 14), that is, to make him void, and bring to nought all the power and jurisdiction of the devil ; hence, Christ has now the keys of hades and of death.

In the Book of The Revelation our Lord, as the Lamb, is represented as marching on in His victorious way and in His mighty conquest. And that conquest over His enemies is revealed in several particulars. Mystical and actual Babylon are destroyed (Rev. 17 : 16 ; 18 : 21) ; the Beast of the revived Roman Empire, and also the False Prophet who supported him, are cast into the lake of fire (Rev. 19 : 20) ; the " ten kings " who act under the Beast are overcome by the Lamb (Rev. 17 : 12-14) ; Satan is placed in the abyss during the Millennium, and afterward cast into the lake of fire (Rev. 20 : 2, 3, 7-10) ; the nations which act under the devil after the Millennium are devoured with fire from heaven (Rev. 20 : 8, 9) ; and the wicked dead are judged according to their works (Rev. 20 : 12-15).

The Lord of Calvary must win through all His enemies, for none can stand before the weapons of His wounds. The Victim of the Cross is, and will be, the Victor in all conquests. This is the throbbing thought right through the Book of the Revelation. The seemingly conquered One on the tree is the sweeping Conqueror of the future.

Only Begotten and First Begotten

He was the Only Begotten when He first came. Dr. I. M. Haldeman, of New York, has well put this hallowed mystery. He says: "It is the pre-existent personality as the Only Begotten of the Father that must always define and defend the character of Incarnation as the act of God, and not at all as the act of man; for, as the woman could not conceive a personality even in nature (Heb. 7 : 10), and as a sinful man could not beget the sinless human nature which was born of her, then that nature could have been, and was, produced only by the interfering act of God; and as God the Father could not beget in her the personality of His already eternally begotten Son, and the Son is the outgoing and forthputting of the Father creatively, then the Son came into the world born of a woman, unbegotten of man and clothed with the created humanity produced by Himself in conjointure with the Father and the Spirit. The eternally pre-existent personality of the Son determines the atonement. Two things are necessary in an atonement manward and Godward. A man must die in the place of men. To do this he must be free from the law of sin and death. To be sinless and thus free from death he must have a humanity distinct from that of the First Man. Since a sinful man cannot beget a sinless human nature, and an angel cannot beget the nature of man, such a nature must be begotten of God."

" But something more is required than a sinless man. Only that which is equal can meet that which is equal. Atonement calls for the death of a victim. God, if He would atone, must die. God as God cannot die. If He would offer death as a sacrificial equivalent for sin, then He must have a human nature. It follows, therefore, that ' for the suffering of death,' and to ' taste death for every man,' God must become incarnate. Thus incarnation is in the nature of things. As the Son of God and God the Son has been from all eternity the " form," the visibility of God, and by His place and function in the Godhead alone could be, He only of all the persons of the Godhead could become incarnate, God manifest in the flesh ; and, therefore, both in fulfilment of His essential relationship to Godhead, and by the terms of the everlasting covenant, He did, indeed, become so, and on the Cross offered His perfect humanity as a sacrifice for sin. That sacrifice finds its value neither in the extent of time in which it was offered, nor in the degree of suffering of the offerer, but in the infinite value of the infinite personality of Him Who offered it."

When Christ is spoken of as " The Only Begotten," His eternal existence is before us, and His manifestation in time. But when He is declared to be " The First Begotten," His resurrection is before us, and His present existence as the Representative of those whom He has redeemed. The Only Begotten is the One Who was given *for* us (John 3 : 16). The First Begotten is the One Who is coming again in manifest glory ; hence, when His return is revealed, it is said, " When He bringeth His First Begotten into the world " (Heb. 1 : 6). The reason of His return to the inhabited earth is because the Father brings Him. He is behind Him, and with Him, and the cause of His return and all He does. Being the First Begotten, He is the Guarantee of those who are being glorified with Him. Dr. Haldeman well says : " By the term ' first born (begotten) from the dead,' we are to understand the grave as His mother, and out of that dark womb He was begotten by the Father as the first immortal Man. The words ' immortal ' and ' immortality ' are applied in Scripture only to the body, never to the soul ; but by this it is not intended to say the soul ceases to exist at death. The Son of God has settled that. He says you can kill the body ; you cannot kill the soul. Scripture teaches that the soul will exist for ever, whether saved or lost. ' Immortal ' is applied to a body that is incorruptible and deathless—such a body is the privilege alone of sons of God."

Twofold Taking

When Christ came and clad Himself with a human body, it is said of Him, " He took not on Him the nature of angels, but He took on Him the seed of Abraham " (Heb. 2 : 16). Under the law, only a kinsman could act for one who had lost an inheritance, as in the case of Ruth (Lev. 25 : 48 ; Ruth 4 : 3-10). It was essential that Christ should become one of us that He might have the right to act for us. As the Son of Man He had the right, and as the Son of God He had the power. Under the law sometimes the near kinsman, who had the right, had not the power, as in the case of Naomi's nearer kinsman than Boaz (Ruth 4 : 6). The forcefulness of Christ's taking hold of our nature when He first came is enhanced when we know the word to " take " is the one which is used of Peter when Christ " caught " him as he was sinking into the water (Matt. 14 : 31). Christ has caught hold of our humanity by becoming man, and thus making it possible for us to be saved, as Paul declares, " There is one God and one Mediator between God and man," or more correctly, " pertaining to God and man," " the Man Christ Jesus, Who gave Himself a ransom for all " (1 Tim. 2 : 5, 6). A procuring price, instead of all, is what the giving of Himself means. His incarnation was necessary to His ransom, but it is ransom which saves, and not His incarnation. There was only one Christian life that began at Bethlehem and ended at the Cross. Every other Christian life begins at the Cross and goes back to Bethlehem.

John, in the Spirit, describes a wonderful scene in heaven (Rev. 5). He sees in the right hand of the One sitting on the throne a seven-sealed roll ; and an angel asks the question, " Who is worthy to open the Book, and loose the seals thereof ?" " And no man in heaven, nor in earth, neither under the earth, was able to open the Book, neither to look thereon." And this fact filled the apostle with consternation; and caused him to " weep much." Whereupon one of the elders bids him not to weep, and the reason given is because the Lion of the tribe of Judah had prevailed to open the Book and to loose the seals. Then John described the Lamb coming and taking the Book out of the hand of Him Who sits upon the throne, and there followed a detailed account of the opening of the seven seals by the Lamb. Without going into the interpretation of the application of the seven seals, whether they have been opened, or will be opened, the one thing to recognise is the Lamb Who became Man, and was slain, has the right to govern, because of what He became, and because He was slain. The One Who was slain has the right to reign, and reign He will, for none can dispute His claim, and all will have to own Him, whether they will or not.

Twofold Knowledge

Writing to the saints in Corinth on the incentive to Christian giving, the apostle says : " Ye know the grace of our Lord Jesus Christ, that, though He was rich, yet for our sakes He became poor, that ye, through His poverty, might be rich " (2 Cor. 8 : 9). His grace of undeserved favour is manifest, in that He, Who was intrinsically rich (rich in Himself in every way) for our sakes (on our behalf) became a beggar (the word " poor " is the same as used in describing Lazarus as a " beggar "), that we out of His beggary might be enriched. It is not " through His poverty " as a medium, for the word is " ek," which means " out of." Out of His beggary comes our riches ! Wonderful statement indeed. Out of His death comes life. Out of His curse comes blessing. Out of His ignominy comes glory. Out of His judgment comes salvation. Out of His hell comes heaven. Out of His darkness comes light. Out of His emptying comes fulness. Do we know Him thus ? Hallowed knowledge ! Life-giving knowledge ! This is no knowledge of mere intellectualism, but the knowledge of heart experience, and heart culture.

Looking forward to the future bliss of God's children, the Spirit through the Apostle John says : " We know that when He shall appear we shall be like Him, for we shall see Him as He is " (1 John 3 : 2). " See Him as He *is*," not as He *was*. He was the Man of Sorrows, and shamed on the Cross ; but " as He is," He is honoured and glorified. A full description of Him as the glorified One is given us in Rev. 1.

We shall be "like Him." This we know, for we are assured it shall be so. Like Him, we shall be pure in nature, spotless in character, beautiful in form, clothed with light, perfect in body, incorruptible in being, and luminous in glory. What a prospect! What a Hope! What manner of persons ought we to be with such a glory before us!

Two Places

When Christ came into the world there was "no room" (the word "room" in other places is given "place") "for Him in the inn" (Luke 2:7). And as Christ was about to go out of the world His parting message and promise was, "I go to prepare a place for you, and if I go and prepare a place for you, I will come again and receive you unto Myself" (not to the "place," John 14:2, 3). Thus the two advents are related and connected again; and yet one other place cements them, and that is the place called Calvary. By an indissoluble and living bond these three places are united. There would have been no place for us in the glory of His presence if He had not been in the place of incarnate love and vicarious death. "No room for Him" means "room for us." "The place called Calvary" places us in the place of the many mansions.

Twofold Application

Every fact of the Gospel is meant to be a factor in us. Pascal remarks that everything that happened to Christ as a matter of history is meant to have a correspondent experience in our hearts and lives; hence, Christ was born for us that He might be born in us. Paul, in writing to the believers in Galatia, said, "My little children, of whom I travail in birth until Christ be formed in you" (Gal. 4:19). It is when Christ is within that the Christian life can be lived out, for the simple reason He is the Life, and lives. The violet has the fragrance because the fragrance is in the violet. They are inseparable. So the Christ, when He is in the heart, His fragrance perfumes the life.

What was it that attracted the wise men to come and worship the infant Christ? They themselves tell us. They said, " We have seen His star in the East, and have come to worship Him " (Matt. 2 : 1-12). And when they saw Him they worshipped Him, and " presented unto Him gifts, gold, frankincense, and myrrh." As we, too, are looking not for the Babe of Bethlehem, but the Bright and Morning Star, we shall bring to Him the gold of obedience, the frankincense of a holy life, and the myrrh of a glad fellowship in His death and resurrection.

The importance of recognising the double aspect of truth is essential to have an even balance in the mind of our thought and in the testimony of our utterance, for a false balance is " an abomination to the Lord," and on the other hand " a just weight and balance " is said to be His (Prov. 11 : 1 ; 16 : 11). Error is always a part of truth and is sometimes hard to distinguish from the truth itself, as Tennyson has said,

> " A lie which is all a lie
> May be met and fought outright,
> But a lie which is a part of truth
> Is a harder matter to fight."

Therefore we need to pray that we may be saved from an " untheological devotion, and an undevotional theology."

9

THE EARS OF A PERPETUAL ATTENTION

"HE that planted the ear, shall He not hear?" (Psa. 94 : 9). Everything that God made had a purpose in its creation. The ear is that organ of the body by means of which we are able to receive a communication from another, and through the mind we are able to understand its meaning (Job 12 : 11). Metaphorically the ear represents the power which knows the condition of another, as the little girl said, "God hears thoughts"; also hearing stands for the attention which results in action, as when Christ said, "My sheep hear My voice and they follow Me."

Prayer is the voice of need which appeals for aid to the One Who can give it. Frequently we read of one appealing for help, who cries, "Give ear to my prayer" (Psa. 17 : 1). The whole of God's Being is represented as being alert for our blessing. He has a heart to love us (Psa. 33 : 11), a hand to help us (Isa. 41 : 10), an eye to watch us (2 Chron. 16 : 9), feet to run to us (Luke 15 : 20), a mouth to speak to us (Deut. 8 : 8), a face to cheer us (Psa. 42 : 5, 11), a bosom to embrace us (Isa. 40 : 11), arms to enclose us (Deut. 33 : 27), a thought to encourage us (Psa. 40 : 5), a soul to delight in us (Isa. 42 : 1), and ears to listen to us (Psa. 116 : 2).

The general thought of prayer is, man's appeal to God for His intervention to aid, and is the most potent ministry that can be exercised, for it brings us to God and binds us to Him; and brings God to us in His power and grace. Tennyson has well expressed it in the well-known lines :

> "More things are wrought by prayer
> Than this world dreams of. Wherefore, let thy voice
> Rise like a fountain for me night and day.
> For what are men better than sheep or goats
> That nourish a blind life within the brain,
> If, knowing God, they lift not hands of prayer
> Both for themselves and those who call them friend?
> For so the whole round world is every way
> Bound by gold chains about the feet of God."

330

Man has been called "a praying animal." We would rather say, man has the capacity to pray, but, alas! in too many instances he is dumb. It is when the Spirit awakens man to his vocation in life, that it is said of him, " Behold he prayeth" (Acts 9:11). Happy are we, if we "Pray without ceasing" (1 Thess. 5:17), for prayer is the open sluice through which the water of life comes and feeds us, and it is the last act in the drama of life as we say with Stephen, "Lord Jesus, receive my spirit " (Acts 7:59).

"Pray" and "Prayer" occur about 350 times in God's Word. There are twelve Hebrew words and seven Greek words; and in them we have a wonderful revelation of what true prayer is. If we neglect the grace of prayer, we shall be wanting in the grace to live. We cannot fulfil the responsibilities of life, if we do not enjoy the privilege of prayer.

The words for prayer have a touch and tension in their varied meanings, which reveal its many-sidedness and potency.

The Request of Prayer

" *Shaal.*" Prayer does not always articulate its request. Sometimes its silent attitude is most expressive, as when the Psalmist said, "I am prayer" (Psa. 109:4). The blind beggar, with an open hand, is a speaking petition! The word " Pray " in Psa. 122:6 is " Shaal," and is the simplest form of prayer. It means to ask, to make request for something. The word is variously given, and it generally means to make an enquiry, and is so given in the following passages: "Ask" (Deut. 4:32; 32:7; 1 Sam. 25:8; 1 Kings 3:5; 2 Kings 2:9; 2 Chron. 1:7; Job 12:7; Psa. 2:8; Isa. 7:11; Jer. 48:19; Hag. 2:11) "Ask counsel" (Jud. 18:5). "Ask on" (1 Kings 2:20). "Ask also" (1 Kings 2:22). "Ask me" (Isa. 45:11). "And ask" (Jer. 6:16). "Ask ye" (Jer. 18:13; 30:6; Zech. 10:1). "Enquire" (1 Sam. 17:56; Job 8:8). "Pray" (Psa. 122:6). "Pray for the peace of Jerusalem " indicates the directness of prayer. The same word is rendered " Borrow " in Exod. 12:35, but does not mean to " borrow," but to make a request. The children of Israel did not " borrow " from the Egyptians, but they asked for what they received.

Directness in petition is essential for success in prayer. When we want something for which we ask, we are sure to obtain the something for which we pray.

The Entreaty of Prayer

"*Ana*" and "*Na*" Girdlestone says are interjections, the former of which is found in Gen. 50 : 17 ; and the latter in Gen. 12 : 13 ; 18 : 4 ; and Judg. 9 : 38. "*Ana*" is rendered "I pray thee" in Gen. 50 : 17 and Jonah 4 : 2. When Joseph's brethren feared that he might deal hardly with them, because of their dealing with him, they made up their minds they would quote the words of their father, by saying, "Thy father did command before he died, saying . . . Forgive, I pray thee, the trespass of thy brethren." Their plea was more than a request, it was a heart entreaty, the deep feeling of the soul in its conscious need and conviction. Jonah appealed to the Lord ; he not only "Prayed unto the Lord," but he said, "I pray Thee . . . take my life from me," that is, he entreated Him. There is urgency in the prayer that is an appeal. It suggests a weeping and clinging Jacob appealing for blessing. When our prayers are marked by urgency, there is a soul of entreaty, a heart of feeling, a grasp of reality, a cling of faith, a longing of desire, a pleading of supplication, and a cry of extremity.

The Attitude of Prayer

"*Chanan*." Solomon in his dedicatory prayer of the Temple uses the word "pray," when he pleads that if any of those who got into captivity shall "bethink" themselves and confess their sins, that the Lord shall deal graciously with them (2 Chron. 6 : 37)   This thought is embodied in the word "Chanan." It means to seek the favour of another, that he may stoop in kindness, and exercise grace towards the suppliant. The word is rendered "make supplication" in 1 Kings 8 : 33, 47, 59 ; 9 : 3. This aspect of prayer suggests the applicant looks to the exercise of God's mercy, like the publican when he prayed to the Lord to be "merciful" to him. It is not the merit of the suppliant which is seen, but the mercy of the One Who is supplicated. The picture is that of a criminal who is doomed to die for his offence, and who appeals for favour from the Sovereign of the Realm. There is no merit in our praying, but there is in the One Who answers. When we leave ourselves in the Lord's hands, we find His hands on our hearts to our benefit.

The Fragrance of Prayer

Prayer is often represented as incense. The Psalmist says, " Let my prayer be set before Thee as incense, and the lifting up of my hands as the evening sacrifice " (Psa. 141 : 2). When John saw the four and twenty elders and the four living creatures who fell down before the Lamb, they had in their hands " golden vials full of odours, which are the prayers of saints " (Rev. 5 : 8). Both of these passages are directly or indirectly associated with the burnt offering, and the incense burnt on the golden altar, which are typical of Christ in the fragrance of His atoning sacrifice (Eph. 5 : 2), and priestly service for us (Heb. 7 : 24-27).

When Elihu speaks of the one who is delivered from " going down to the pit," because an " atonement " has been found for him, he not only recounts the freshness of youth which comes to him, but he says, " He shall pray unto God, and He shall be favourable unto him, and he shall see His face with joy " (Job 33 : 24-26, margin). See again how atonement is connected with prayer. When we plead the fragrance of Christ's atoning death, we have a plea which is always effective in its pleading.

" *Athar*." The word " *Athar*," which is rendered " Pray " in Elihu's statement, has wrapped up in the thought of its meaning not only entreaty, but also that of fragrance, like the aroma of the violet with the plant. Wilson says of the word, " To entreat, to make earnest and fervent prayer, which ascends like incense before God. Others think the primary meaning of the word implies power and abundance, as well as sweet odour." The word is rendered " Intreated " four times (Gen. 25 : 21 ; Exod. 8 : 30 ; 10 : 18 ; Judg. 13 : 8) ; " Be intreated " eight times (Gen. 25 : 21 ; 2 Sam. 21 : 14 ; 24 : 25 ; 1 Chron. 5 : 20 ; 2 Chron. 33 : 13, 19 ; Ezra 8 : 23 ; Isa. 19 : 22). The intreaty of a heart expressed need is always a fragrance to the Lord. When our prayers ascend to the Lord perfumed with the wealth and worth of Christ's fragrance, He can do no other than answer whatsoever is asked for in His Name. Christ has said that whatsoever we shall ask in His Name, shall be granted. To ask in His Name is to pray as He would pray, for His Name stands for His Nature. To pray in Him is to be perfumed by Him, and the aroma of His fragrance is ever pleasing to Himself.

The Insistence of Prayer

Christ has taught us there is an insistent importunity of prayer in the parables of the friend at midnight knocking up his friend (Luke 11 : 5-10), and in the importunity of the supplicating widow (Luke 18 : 1-8). He has also taught us this in the threefold and progressive sentences, "Ask and ye shall receive," "Seek and ye shall find," "Knock and it shall be opened unto you." Sometimes the Lord keeps us waiting before He answers, that He may test the reality of our prayer, the tenacity of our faith, and the soul of our petition. Waiting time is never wasted time.

" *Paga*." The insistence of prayer is taught in the word " Paga." One long ago asked the question, " What is the Almighty that we should serve Him ? And what profit should we have, if we pray to Him ?" (Job 21 : 15). Was he thinking of something he might gain if he prayed, for the word " profit " means to make a profit ? If we plead for profit, there will be no profit in our pleading.

" Paga " is variously rendered—" Come," " Fall upon," " Intreat," " Make intercession." Strong says of this primary verb, " To impinge by accident or violence, or figuratively by importunity." It is used of one falling upon another to his hurt (1 Kings 2 : 29), to intervene between two parties as coming " betwixt " them (Job 36 : 32). The triple thought of intervention, urgency, and persistence is brought out in this word for prayer. Meaningless phrases, idle requests, prefunctory petitions, and formal intercessions are in vain, and do not accomplish anything, nor get anywhere. When we are insistent and persistent in our pleading we pierce the heart of God to His attention, and lay hold and keep hold to our blessing.

The Habit of Prayer

" *Palal.*" Young says of " Palal," " To judge self, to pray habitually." These two thoughts are demonstrated in its use. It is rendered, " Be judged " and " Execute Judgment " (Ezek. 28 : 23 ; Psa. 106 : 30), to " judge " (1 Sam. 2 : 25 ; Ezek. 16 : 52), " Thought " (Gen. 48 : 11), " Intreat " (1 Sam. 2 : 25), " Make supplication " (Isa. 45 : 14), and to make prayer. This word is one of the most frequently used to express the act of prayer, and denotes the habit of prayer, as the result of self-judgment and the revolving in the mind of what is needed, and therefore embodies the thoughtfulness of prayer, which focuses itself in some definite request. This thought is found in the following cases where prayer is cited.

In bitterness of soul, Hannah " prayed unto the Lord," " continued praying," " praying unto the Lord," " for this child I prayed," " and Hannah prayed " (1 Sam. 1 : 10, 12, 26, 27 ; 2 : 1). She was exercised in soul, so continued to pray.

Solomon in his dedicatory prayer of the Temple continually refers to those who are in conscious need, who plead in pointed prayer. He says, " Hearken unto the cry and to the prayer, which thy servant prayeth." Then he cites the conditions of urgency in which the children of Israel are found, such as when they " pray " to be forgiven, when they " pray " because smitten by an enemy, when they " pray " for rain which had been withholden because of sin, and when others shall " pray " because of what they shall find out about Jehovah's " Great Name " (1 Kings 8 : 28, 30, 33, 42, 44, 48).

When Hezekiah knew there were those among the people who " had not cleansed themselves, yet they did eat the passover otherwise than it was written. . . . Hezekiah prayed for them . . . and the Lord hearkened " (2 Chron. 30 : 18, 20). He judged the sin committed, and prayed to the Lord about it, and was answered.

Nehemiah was exercised when he heard about the condition of Jerusalem, and wept and " prayed " and fasted many days, and when he stood before the King and was

questioned by him, and he was not sure of the issue, before
he answered him, " He prayed to the God of Heaven " (Neh.
1 : 4, 6 ; 2 : 4). His attitude of soul is delightfully summed
up in " So I prayed " !

Job gained what he had lost and the Lord turned his
captivity when he " prayed for his friends " (Job 42 : 10).
His judgment of himself in his confession, " I am vile," and
" abhor myself," was the precursor to the benediction which
came upon himself and his friends.

Daniel in the confession of his sins, as he identified himself with the nation in its sore need and captivity, " prayed "
and said, " I prayed and made my confession " (Dan. 9 : 4, 20).
Like His Lord, he took the place of judgment, as he made the
nation's sins his own.

Jonah went on his self-willed way, till the Lord arrested
him by the great fish, " Then he prayed unto the Lord his
God out of the fish's belly " ; and he also " prayed " against
himself when he asked that his life might be taken, but he
did it when he was " angry " and " displeased " with Him,
which suggests he prayed in a wrong manner (Jonah 2 : 1 ;
4 : 2).

All the above illustrations reveal, as one has said, " the
primary idea of rolling, revolving (as in the mind), there it is
judging, levelling, placating, and interceding."

The Humility of Prayer

" *Tsela* " only occurs twice, and in each case is rendered
" Pray." Cyrus made a decree of certain supplies which
were to be granted to the Elders of the Jews that the priests
might fulfil their priestly office, and also that they might
" pray for the life of the king and his sons " (Ezra 6 : 10) ;
and of Daniel it is recorded, " He kneeled upon his knees
three times a day, and prayed " (Dan. 6 : 10). " Tsela "
means to bend low in adoring worship. Humility of spirit
and lowliness of heart are requisites in praying. The grace
of humility is always greeted by the grace of God. When we
obey the command of the Lord to be humble, we command
His attention to our uplifting. Those who bend low in true
humility, find the Lord bends low in answering their petitions.

" Let us worship and bow down : let us kneel before the Lord our Maker " (Psa. 95 : 6).

The Meditation of Prayer

" *Siach*." We say of one who is thinking deeply, " He is in a brown study." To ponder what we pray is the preventative to rashness in prayer. " Be not rash, and let not thy heart be hasty to utter anything before God " (Eccles. 5 : 2). The word " Siach " means to meditate and commune. The Psalmist uses this word when he determines to " pray,"— " Evening and morning and at night, will I pray and cry aloud, and He shall hear my voice " (Psa. 55 : 17). " Siach " is rendered " commune " in Psa. 77 : 6, " Meditate " in Psa. 119 : 15, " Complain " in Job 7 : 11, " Speak " in Psa. 69 : 12, " Talk " in Psa. 119 : 27, " Declare " in Isa. 53 : 8, and " Muse " in Psa. 143 : 5. One of the greatest feeders to prayer is meditation on God's Word. When we feed our prayer life with the fuel of God's Word, we shall never lack a burning fire of ardent petition. George Müller confessed, that he at one time prayed and then read God's Word, but in the after days he read the Word and then prayed that Word into his heart and life. That is the better way in every way.

The Individualism of Prayer

" *Tephillah*." We are happy if we have friends to pray for us, but we are happier when we go direct to Headquarters for ourselves. We are independent of others when we are dependent upon the Lord. " Tephillah " means to make supplication. It occurs 76 times, and 31 of these are in the Psalms. The individualism is seen in the fact, that the Psalmist says again and again, " Hear my prayer " (4 : 1 ; 39 : 12 ; 54 : 2 ; 84 : 8 ; 102 : 1 ; 143 : 1), " Receive my prayer " (6 : 9), " Give ear to my prayer " (17 : 1 ; 55 : 1 ; 86 : 6), and " Attend unto my prayer " (61 : 1).

The individualism of prayer is illustrated in the individuals named, who prayed in their personal need, namely, David (2 Sam. 7 : 27 ; Psa. 17, Title ; 72 : 20 ; 86, Title ; 142, Title) ; Moses (Psa. 90, Title) ; Solomon (1 Kings 8 : 28, 29, 54 ; 2 Chron. 6 : 19, 20) ; Daniel (Dan. 9 : 3, 17, 21) ;

Manasseh (2 Chron. 33 : 18, 19) ; Nehemiah (Neh. 1 : 6, 11) ; Mattaniah (Neh. 11 : 17) ; Job (Job 16 : 17) ; Habakkuk (Hab. 3 : 1).

Individualism is suggested in the following : " I have heard thy prayer " (Solomon—1 Kings 9 : 3 ; 2 Chron. 7 : 12) ; " Lift up thy prayer " (Isaiah—2 Kings 19 : 4 ; Isa. 37 : 4) ; " I have heard thy prayer " (Hezekiah—2 Kings 20 : 5 ; Isa. 38 : 5) ; " My prayer " (David—Psa. 35 : 13 ; 42 : 8 ; 66 : 19, 20 ; 69 : 13 ; 88 : 2 ; 102 : 1 ; 141 : 2, 5,; Jonah 2 : 7). " Thy people Israel " (1 Kings 8 : 38, 45, 49 ; 2 Chron. 6 : 29, 35, 39 ; 30 : 27) ; Thy people (Psa. 80 : 4) ; This people (Jer. 7 : 16 ; 11 : 14) ; The destitute (Psa. 102 : 17) ; The wicked (Psa. 109 : 7) ; The upright (Prov. 15 : 8) ; The righteous (Prov. 15 : 29). The Climax of Individualism is surely reached when the Psalmist exclaims, " I, prayer "—omitting the words in italics (Psa. 109 : 4).

Miss Ada R. Habershon has beautifully expressed it in the following lines :

" I am a prayer, O Lord, a constant prayer,
I cannot tell Thee all my wants in words ;
I have no eloquence with which to plead,
But 'tis enough—I am myself a prayer.
Like beggar, whose outstretched hand appeals,
Or fledgling in the nest with open beak,
My case to Thee is mutely eloquent ;
And seeing me Thou seest all my need,
For Thou Who mad'st my frame can always read
The language of desire it doth speak.
Thou art the Answer, Lord, Thyself alone !
For every need Thou art the rich supply,
Thou art the " Yea " to all God's promises,
The sure " Amen " to every one I claim.
' Is it for me ?' my heart with longing cries,
One sight of Thee proclaims a gladsome ' Yea ' ;
' Oh, make it mine,' the yearning stronger grows,
' Amen, it shall be so,' and it is done ;
And as each promise is to me made good,
Thou, Lord, in me art freshly glorified.
'Tis at the mercy-seat that heaven and earth
In presence of the blood communion hold,
And at the Throne the prayer and Answer meet—
The Answer waits before the prayer begins,
For Thou art first at every trysting place.

As iron filings to the magnet fly,
My wants all spring to Thee and gladly rest.
I've found the reason why Thou canst bestow
Exceedingly abundant, far above
What I can ask or even think! It is
Because Thou art the Answer—I the prayer.
I am an answered prayer, but still I plead,
For as each want is met new ones arise,
And every day I crave the Answer still.
My very being is a constant prayer,
Each member adding words of mute request :
These empty hands need filling from Thyself,
And ask for strength to do their work for Thee ;
The feet would fain be guided in the way
That they, with oil anointed, may speed on,
And run the race which Thou hast run before ;
Mine eyes need Thine illuminating beams,
That they may see Thy footprints and Thy face,
And gaze upon the wonders of Thy Word ;
Mine ears need opening to Thy still, small voice,
My lips need touching with the living coal,
My tongue inflaming with Thy wondrous love,
That it may speak with glowing words of Thee ;
My mouth fresh filling with the heavenly food,
And satisfying with the latter rain ;
My brow needs daily sealing with Thy peace ;
My heart with every beat proclaims its need,
And every breath I take repeats the tale.
So I would fain for evermore abide
Within the secret place of the Most High
Like an empty vessel in the flowing stream,
That thus the prayer may in the answer dwell."

The Pleading of Prayer

" *Chalah* " is rendered " Pray " three times, and all three
are found in Zechariah (7 : 2 ; 8 : 21, 22), and in each
instance in the uniform sentence, " Pray before the Lord."
If the passages are pondered, it will be found that those who
prayed, pray, or will pray in a time of stress and pain, and
cry out as a woman cries out in travail till her strength is
nearly worn out. The word is rendered " Intreat " (Prov.
19 : 6), " Besought " (1 Kings 13 : 6), " Make prayer " (Dan.
9 : 13), " Make supplication " (1 Sam. 13 : 12), " Make suit "
(Job 11 : 19), " Travail " (Jer. 4 : 31), and to become weak
(Judg. 16 : 7, 17).

There are occasions when the stress of circumstances, the heaviness of trial, the pressure of some burden of sorrow, the conflict of fierce temptation, the agony of oppressing persecution, and the horror of some haunting ordeal, causes us to be in an agony, like our Lord in Gethsemane, and we pray in agonised entreaty for the cup to pass from us.

The Whisper of Prayer

" Lachash." The Spirit's promptings are not always articulated in words, they are read in the inner desires of the heart (Rom. 8 : 26). " Lachash " is the word used in Isa. 26 : 16, where the prophet speaks of the nations, and says, " Lord, in trouble have they visited Thee, they poured out a prayer when thy chastening was upon them." The margin gives the word " prayer," " secret speech." The condition of those who prayed was so grievous that only a whisper could be expressed. This gives the meaning of " Lachash." It is used of one who seeks to charm another by charming (Ps. 58 : 5), of a woman who attracts by her earrings and other ornamentations (Isa. 3 : 20), of an " enchantment " (Eccles. 10 : 11), and of an eloquent " orator " (Isa. 3 : 3). There is a charm in the Lord's estimation in the " soul's sincere desire." He, who heard the sigh of the groaning Israelites in bondage (Exod. 2 : 24), and saw the moving lips of Hannah (1 Sam. 1 : 9-13), and felt the touch of the diseased woman (Luke 8 : 44), and marked the beggar in his need (Luke 16 : 20, 21), and beheld Zacchæus in his desire (Luke 19 : 3), and appreciated the widow in her giving (Luke 21 : 2), and beheld the man's withered hand in its helplessness (Matt. 12 : 10), and the bowed woman in her extreme condition (Luke 13 : 11), will surely hear and answer the devoted and devout heart, although the voice is not heard by another.

The Fervency of Prayer

" Beah." Daniel was found at prayer, by those who were opposed to him in Babylon. Doubtless they heard him in the fervency of his earnest praying and making supplication before his God (Dan. 6 : 11). The word " praying " is " Beah," which Strong says corresponds to " Baah." " Beah " means to seek, ask, desire, make petition, pray, request ; and " Baah " means to gush over, to swell, to desire earnestly. " Baah " is rendered " Boil " in Isa. 64 : 2, where we read, " The fire causeth the waters to boil." We have only to recall the character of Daniel's recorded petitions and ponder the concern he felt for the nation to be assured that there was the fire of earnest pleading, and the gushing over of a boiling utterance, as he voiced himself in holy request. When there is the fire of a holy desire, the concern of a loving intensity, the zeal of an ardent purpose, and the emotion of an intensified interest, then we have a burning request throbbing the words of prayer, and the ensuing answer. Elijah would never have had the responding fire on Carmel if he had not had first the fire of earnest petition. When the earnest desire of fervent prayer ascends to God, He will respond in consuming fire and consecrating grace.

When we approach the Holy of Holies of the New Testament we have revealed to us a wonderful array of furniture in the words which express to us the mind of the Spirit in relation to prayer, each of which has its own phase of revelation.

The Supplication of Prayer

The word " *Deesis* " means to make a request, hence to petition another, to supplicate a favour, to pray. It is often rendered " supplication " and sometimes coupled with prayer as intensifying it. The word is rendered " Prayer," in calling attention to the " prayer" that Zacharias prayed (Luke 1 : 13), and " supplication " in recording the fact that the early Christians were found in this attitude (Acts 1 : 14). Paul uses this word when urging the saints in Ephesus to be " Praying always with all prayer and supplication in the Spirit, and watching thereunto with all perseverance and supplication for all saints " (Eph. 6 : 18). Here the " supplication " of prayer is found in a wonderful combine, namely, praying with prayer and supplication in the sphere of the Spirit, and being alert with diligence and persistency. " Prayer " again is coupled with " supplication " when the apostle urges the believers in Philippi to pray, and is also associated with thanksgiving and making known their requests to God (Phil. 4 : 6). Another combine is found in

Paul's letter to Timothy when he pleads that " prayers " and " intercessions " should be with " supplications " (1 Tim. 2 : 1), and in the same letter when he refers to the widow who trusts in God is a " widow indeed " and one who is well-pleasing to God, for she " continueth in supplications and prayers night and day " (1 Tim. 5 : 5). As the juice of a ripe peach is luscious and refreshing to the one who eats it, so as we have the juice of a holy petition in our praying, there is a luscious flavour which is appreciated by the Lord.

The Matter of Prayer

While the former suggests the manner of praying, " *Deomai* " embodies the matter of our petition, as denoting a definite request. It means to beg, to bind one's self to something, to beseech a favour. It is variously rendered, namely, " Beseech," " Besought," " Make request," and " Pray." The following out of the many instances will illustrate the thought, that in each case something is requested. " Pray " that the Lord of the Harvest may send forth labourers (Matt. 9 : 38). " I have prayed for thee," said Christ to Peter, " that thy faith may not fail " (Luke 22 : 32). Peter urged Simon the sorcerer to " pray to God " that his wickedness might be forgiven, and Simon asked that Peter would " pray to the Lord " for him (Acts 8 : 22, 24). The Eunuch said to Philip, as he read the Scriptures, " I pray thee, of Whom speaketh the prophet ? " (Acts 8 : 34). The Demoniac " besought " Christ that he might be with him (Luke 8 : 38). When the father came to Christ about his demon-possessed son, he said, " I beseech Thee look upon my son " (Luke 9 : 38), and the apostle, in writing to the saints in Rome about his contemplated journey, asked them to be " making request " that it might be a " prosperous " one (Rom. 1 : 10). Each of these instances illustrate that " Deomai " means to make a definite request. Many prayers have no end in view. They are like a man who shoots with a bow and arrow, but has no target to fire at. Whereas true prayer is like Esther, who came into the presence of the king with the definite request for the life of her people.

The Intercession of Prayer

The word "*Enteuxis*" only occurs twice, and in each instance in Paul's letter to Timothy, and is there rendered "Intercessions" and "Prayer" (1 Tim. 2 : 1 ; 4 : 5), and in each case is used relatively, when Timothy is requested "to make intercession for all men," and what we eat is to be received with thanksgiving and not be refused if it is "sanctified by the word of God and prayer." To pray beyond our personal need in holy petition for others is to ally ourselves with Christ, Who ever liveth to make intercession for us. Some prayers are warped by the heat of selfishness, and twisted by the limitations of personal desire. The loving entreaty of a ministry of prayer for others is the highest art of service. When we plead the cause of others, we plead our own need, and receive for them what we requested, and find ourselves receiving benefits too.

The Benefit of Prayer

"*Erotao*" means to speak, to call, to request, to ask, to desire, to pray, and is rendered "Pray," "Ask," "Besought," "Intreat," "Desired," and "Beseech." The underlying thought in the use of this word is not only the making of a request, but that some benefit should accrue. Christ said, "I will pray," when He promised to plead for the benefit of the Comforter's presence (John 14 : 16). Three times in John 17 : 9, 15, 20, Christ is found pleading for His own, when He says, "I pray for them," that they may have the benefit He desired for them, and that they should be specially kept from the evil in the world. The Samaritans came, and "besought" Christ that He would "tarry with them" that they might have the benefit of His presence and teaching (John 4 : 40). Paul asked the brethren at Philippi, in his loving plea, that those women who helped him in the Gospel might have the benefit of their help, hence, he says, "I intreat thee help those women who laboured with me in the Gospel" (Phil. 4 : 3). When Paul was in Ephesus, the believers "desired him to tarry long with them that they might have the benefit of his ministry" (Acts 18 : 20) ; and the Apostle John used the same word when he wrote to the

elect lady and said, " I beseech thee, lady " (2 John 5),
that he might have the benefit of her true affection.

The benefit of prayer is beyond all expression. We
cannot estimate its worth, nor gauge its benedictions. It is
like the benefit which comes to the fruit orchards in Cali-
fornia from the life-giving water which is channeled to the
roots of the trees, but for this water from the conserved
heights there would be no growth nor fruit. The curse of
Christendom is the drought of listlessness, and dry rot of
unbelief, which are born of prayerlessness.

The Inness of Prayer

" *Euche* " is rendered " prayer " in Jas. 5 : 15, and
comes from " Euchomai," which means to wish, to ask,
to will, to how, to pray. " Euchomai " is rendered
" Pray " and " Wish." It is the word in Jas. 5 : 16, where
we are exhorted to " pray one for another," and is found in
2 Cor. 13 : 7, where the Apostle says, " I pray to God that ye
do no evil." The word is rendered " Wished " in Acts
27 : 29, where we read that those who were conscious of their
danger of being ship-wrecked and knew not their position in
the darkness " wished for the day," and the same word is
given " wish " in 2 Cor. 13 : 9, and 3 John 2, where Paul had
the inner " wish " for the saints' " perfection," and John
had the fervent desire for the well-beloved Gaius, which he
expressed in the following, " I wish above all things that
thou mayest prosper and be in health."

The inner flame of a holy desire is the warmth which
causes the life of prayer to glow with satisfaction to the
heart of God. The sun is incarnated in the beauty and
fragrance of the flowers and is glorified by them, so when the
heart of devotion is burning in the soul of our pleading, we
bring beauty and warmth to others as well as ourselves.

The Fire of Prayer

" *Proseuche* " and " *Proseuchomai* " will be recognised as
relative to the words in the above " Euche " and " Euchomai,"
and intensified with the prefix " Pros," which gives the
thought of intensity, hence, speaks of the fervency of
prayer.

" Proseuche " is found frequently in the Book of the Acts, and is used of the disciples who were found in " one accord in prayer " (1 : 14), of the young converts who continued " in prayers " (2 : 42), of Peter and John who went up to the temple at the hour of prayer " (3 : 1), of the purpose of the apostles to give themselves " continually to prayer " (6 : 4), of the assurance given to Cornelius that his " prayers " had " come up to God as a memorial " (10 : 4, 31), of the Christians who made " prayer " without ceasing for Peter's deliverance from prison (12 : 5), and of the act of Paul and Silas who " went " to a place " where prayer was wont to be made " (Acts 16 : 13, 16). Behind all these instances there is the fire of desire which moved those who were found in the act of prayer.

" Proseuchomai " is rendered " Prayed earnestly " in Jas. 5 : 17, in calling attention to Elijah's pleading, and in association with " the effectual fervent prayer of a righteous man availeth much." This word is used of Christ in His prayer life, of whom it is written, " He went into a mountain to pray," " I go and pray," " He went and prayed," " He went away again and prayed," " and prayed the third time " (Matt. 14 : 23 ; 26 : 36, 39, 42, 44). Also the word is employed in the frequent request found in the Epistles when the urgent desire is expressed in the sentence, " Pray for us " (see Rom. 8 : 26 ; 1 Cor. 14 : 13 ; 14 : 14, 15 ; Col. 4 : 3 ; 1 Thess. 5 : 25 ; 2 Thess. 3 : 1 ; Heb. 13 : 18).

" Prayers ardent open heaven," one has said, and Tennyson speaks of " Battering the gates of heaven with storms of prayer."

The Help of Prayer

" *Parakaleo* " is a compound word—" Kaleo " to call, and " Para " to be near. To call another near to oneself that help may be given is the embodied thought. The word is rendered " Prayed," " Besought," " Beseech," " Exhort," " Desired," " Intreat," and " Be comforted." The Demoniac " prayed " that he might be with Christ, that he might have the help of His presence (Mark 5 : 18). The ruler " besought " Christ to come to his daughter that she might have the help of His healing power (Mark 5 : 23). Paul indicates the help of a true ministry, which " beseeches " men to be reconciled to God (2 Cor. 5 : 20). Peter's ministry on the Day of Pentecost is summarised in that, "with many other words did he testify and exhort" (intreat), and thus helped those who heard him (Acts 2 : 40). When Peter was in Joppa the disciples " desired " him to exercise the help of his life-giving power in raising Dorcas, which he did after he had prayed (Acts 9 : 38). Paul declared that the purpose in his service was to "intreat" and not to hinder, although he was often " defamed " (1 Cor. 4 : 13) ; and Paul uses the same word when he speaks of the Lord as the One Who " comforteth " those who need His consoling presence (2 Cor. 1 : 4).

We cannot over-estimate the helpfulness of prayer. If our prayer life is slack everything is slack. Prayer to the Lord is the buckler to brace our spiritual energies. Prayer is the electric wire to keep us in touch with the power-house of the Holy Spirit. Prayer is the empty hand of need taking the supplies from the larder of God's bounty. Prayer is the hedge of protection which hedges us in the realm of the Lord's keeping. Prayer is the fructifying soil which gives us the rootage in God's truth, and the fruitage of the Spirit's life. Prayer is the life's blood which circulates in the realm of our spiritual being, giving life and vigour to all. Prayer is the expression of faith which believes in, and brings God's ability to enable us to fulfil our responsibilities. Prayer is the disinfectant which will kill the dry rot of unbelief, to counteract the blight of worldliness, and everything contrary to the will of God.

If we truly pray we become like Him to Whom we pray. Hartley Coleridge has tersely summed up this thought :

> " So have I dreamed ! O, may the dream be true !
> That praying souls are purged from mortal hue,
> And grow as pure as He to Whom they pray."

Contact with God by means of prayer causes us to be conformed to Him, even as the graft of the rose bud makes the brier a rose tree.

Waiting on the Lord in Prayer

This study would not be complete if we did not make a brief reference to what expresses the deeper life of prayer, namely, waiting upon God.

Spurgeon says : " Wait at His door with prayer ; wait at His feet with humility ; wait at His table with service ; wait at His window with expectancy." Waiting on the Lord means at least three things :

I. *Dependence on the Lord.* " On Thee do I wait all the day " (Psa. 25 : 5)

Matthew Henry well says, " To wait on the Lord is to live a life of dependence on God, as the child waits on his father in whom he has confidence, and on whom he casts all his care." To wait on God is to expect all good to come to us from Him as the Worker of all good for us and in us, and the Protector of us from all evil. Thus David explains himself, " My soul wait thou only upon God," and continue to do so, " for my expectation is from Him " (Psa. 62 : 5). There are three ways in which this dependence will manifest itself.

(1) By allowing the Lord to have the management of the life. It is possible to get into a fretful mood in relation to our spiritual life. One wrote a friend, " I do sincerely and earnestly want to give everything to the Lord, my whole self and everything that He has given me in trust. But I do wish He would show me more definitely what He wants me to do. I do not feel at all certain that my life up to the present time has been what He would have it to be. How much easier it would be if He would only say to me each day, ' Elsie, do this.' " If whatsoever we do, we do as to the Lord, and in His Name, and because He tells us to do it, we shall have the consciousness of a life that is pleasing to Him.

(2) By doing the common round of duties as to Himself. Three " whatsoevers " in Col. 3 : 23, 1 Cor. 10 : 31, and John 2 : 5 emphasise this.

(3) By receiving everything as from the Lord. Francis Xavier's direction to his servant was, " I must have sleep, or I shall die. No matter who comes, do not disturb me. I

must sleep." Hastening to his tent he left his faithful servant to watch. In a little while, however, the servant saw Xavier's white face at the tent door. Answering his call, he saw on his countenance a look of awe as if he had seen a vision. "I have made a mistake. If a little child comes, waken me."

II. *Humility before the Lord.* The Psalmist expresses the thought of Humility's absolute resources in Him when he says: "My soul, wait thou only upon God" (Psa. 62 : 5). "A God that worketh for him that waiteth for Him" (Isa. 64 : 4, R.V.).

Freda Hanbury sums up this aspect of waiting on God:

"'Wait only upon God': my soul, be still,
And let thy God unfold His perfect will.
Thou fain would'st follow Him throughout thy year,
Thou fain with listening heart His voice would'st hear,
Thou fain would'st be a passive instrument
Possessed by God, and ever Spirit sent
Upon His service sweet—then be thou still,
For only thus can He in thee fulfil
His heart's desire. Oh, hinder not His hand
From fashioning the vessel He hath planned.
' Be silent unto God,' and thou shalt know
The quiet, holy calm He doth bestow
On those who wait on Him ; so shalt thou bear
His presence, and His life and light e'en where
The night is darkest, and thine earthly days
Shall show His love, and sound His glorious praise.
And He will work with hand unfettered, free,
His high and holy purposes through thee.
First on thee must that hand of power be turned,
Till in His love's strong fire thy dross is burned,
And then come forth a vessel for thy Lord,
So frail and empty, yet, since He hath poured
Into thy emptiness His life, His love,
Henceforth through thee the power of God shall move
And He will work for thee. Stand still and see
The victories thy God shall gain for thee ;
So silent, yet so irresistible,
Thy God shall do the thing impossible.
Oh, question not henceforth what thou canst do ;
Thou canst do *nought*. But He will carry through
The work where human energy had failed,
Where all thy best endeavours had availed
Thee nothing. Then, my soul, wait and be still ;

Thy God shall work for thee His perfect will.
If thou wilt take no less, *His best* shall be
Thy portion now and through eternity."

III. *Blessing from the Lord.* Blessing of strength comes to those who wait on the Lord for the Word says, " But they that wait upon the Lord shall renew their strength ; they shall mount up with wings as eagles ; they shall run, and not be weary ; and they shall walk, and not faint " (Isa. 40 : 31).

The meaning of the word " *wait* " is to bind together by twisting, or to collect in one place. The term is rendered " *gathered together* " in speaking of the waters under heaven being gathered in one place (Gen. 1 : 9). When our weakness is bound together with God's strength, His strength is made perfect in our weakness. His Omnipotence is displayed through our impotence. Before we meet the Goliaths of opposition we need to be like David who had learnt in secret to overcome the lion and bear.

The blessing of reproduction comes too to those who wait on the Lord. Things in nature grow like their surroundings. Polar bears are white because they live amid the snow. The tigers are striped like the sun glints which fall upon them through the trees of the jungle in which they move. Plaice living near the sand become like the sand upon which they move ; and caterpillars become like the green leaves upon which they feed. So those who wait on the Lord become like Him upon Whom they wait.

What encouragement we have to pray and wait upon the Lord when we remember, " His ears are open unto our cry," and that **when**" the righteous cry to Him, the Lord heareth, and delivereth them out of all their troubles " (Psa. 34 : 15-17). His vigilant and loving ears of attention are ever " open " to us. This should lead us to plead with holy diligence in supplication, intercession and prayer.

Andrew Murray says, " Wait on God till you know you have met Him. Prayer will then become so different. And when you are praying, let there be intervals of silence, reverent stillness of soul, in which you can yield yourself to God, in case He may have ought He wishes to teach you or work in you."

10

THE FEET OF A PROGRESSIVE MOVEMENT

THE feet are often used in Scripture in a metaphorical sense to indicate the life, power and movement, as well as the character. The following brief Scriptural sentences will indicate :

As indicating character it is said, " The wicked man speaketh with his feet " (Prov. 6 : 13). As pointing to movement, it is said that our first parents " Heard the voice of the Lord God walking in the garden in the cool of the day " (Gen. 3 : 8). As associated with power, God promises to those who are faithful to Him in a wholly separated life to Himself, " I will dwell in them and walk in them . . .and ye shall be My sons and daughters, saith the Lord God Almighty " (2 Cor. 6 : 16-18). As proclaiming a progressive movement, it is said of the Lord Jesus Christ in prophecy, in pointing to His mission in the world, and as the Herald of God's grace and love, " How beautiful are the feet of Him that bringeth good tidings of good, that publisheth salvation, that saith unto Zion, Thy God reigneth " (Isa. 52 : 7). And also the same thing is said of the messengers of the Gospel now, although the singular is changed to the plural, " How beautiful are the feet of them that preach the Gospel of peace and bring glad tidings of good things " (Rom. 10 : 15).

The Scriptures might be multiplied to indicate that the feet are associated with the progressive movement of God in His mercy and ministry towards us.

PROGRESSIVENESS OF PROPHECY, OR THE PROPHETIC DAYS OF SCRIPTURE

" Distinguish the Ages," said Augustine, " and the Scriptures will harmonize." If this is not done, the Scriptures will be a maze, but if it is done they will be a beautiful piece of mosaic work or music, full of harmony, colour, and interest. There is no want of perspective in the prophetic outlook of the Word of God. The clear and emphatic statement of the Holy Spirit, in speaking of Christ as the medium through Whom God acted in the past periods of time, is " Through Whom He made the Ages " (Heb. 1 : 2, R.V.M.). Mark the revised reading : not " Through Whom He made the worlds," but " the ages." The Greek word is " aions," not " kosmos." " Kosmos " refers to the world as God's creation in the present order of things, but " aions " denote periods of time.

Those " ages " may be summed up under ten distinct periods as we think of the past and future :

The Adamic Age, or the period of man's innocence, covering the time from his creation to his expulsion from the presence of God because of his sin.

The Noahic Age, or the period of man's lawlessness, beginning with man's fall, covering the judgment of the flood, and the life of Noah to Abram.

The Abramic Age, or the period of Israel's pilgrimage, commencing with the call of Abram and covering the lives of the twelve patriarchs, and reaching on to Israel's bondage in the land of Egypt.

The Mosaic Age, covering the period of Israel's redemption from Egypt, and reaching to the reign of David.

The Davidic Age, or the period of man's rule, covering David's reign and the dispersion of Israel and Judah, and their captivity in Assyria and Babylon.

The Gentilic Age, or the period of " The Times of the Gentiles," commencing with the Babylonish captivity and running on to the time of Christ.

The Gospelic Age, or the Dispensation of the Spirit, beginning with the death and resurrection of Christ, and running on to His coming for His saints.

The Messianic Age, or the period of Israel's supremacy during the Millennium, when that nation will be the great missionaries of the world.

The Goldenic Age, the period after the Millennium, when Christ will be supreme in love, and reign for an unlimited period, and all things will be summed up in Him.

The Jehovic Age, or eternity, when God will be All in all.

Sometimes these ages overlap each other, as one covering in joining another will do, but they can easily be distinguished, as they each have some distinct and distinguishing feature. The same is true of the prophetic days of Scripture. They stand out in the universe of Scripture like nine great luminaries, shining with unmistakeable light and distinctiveness. These days begin with the incarnation of Christ, and run on to eternity. The periods are the Day of Jesus, the Day of Man, the Day of the Son, the Day of Salvation, the Day of Christ, the Day of the Lord, the Day of Judgment, the Day of the Lamb, and the Day of God.

The following diagram will indicate the characteristics of these prophetic days :

COMMENCEMENT	CHARACTERISTICS	CONSUMMATION

DAY OF JESUS: JOHN 8:56

COMMENCEMENT	CHARACTERISTICS	CONSUMMATION
The Incarnation of the Son of Man. Matt. 1:21-25 Luke 1:31,32 1 Tim. 3:16	Revelation (John 17:6) Expiation (Heb. 9:26) Victory (1 John 3:8) Love (1 John 4:9) Life (1 John 1:2) Power (John 2:11) Glory (John 1:14)	Calvary, where atonement was made for sin, and salvation provided for all men. 1 Peter 1:18-20 1 Tim. 2:6 Rom. 5:6

DAY OF THE SON: PSALM 2:7

COMMENCEMENT	CHARACTERISTICS	CONSUMMATION
The Resurrection of Christ from the Dead. "God . . . raised up Jesus . . . as it is written in the second Psalm, 'Thou art My Son, this day have I begotten Thee.' " Acts 13:33	Covers Christ's present ministry for His saints, hence, twice in the Epistle to the Hebrews in relation to His Priesthood and His session at God's right hand, the quotation from the second Psalm is given. Heb. 1:5; 5:5	Christ's Advocacy and Priestly service will end when He comes for His own, and He presents us faultless to His Father, for there will be no need for such service when believers are glorified. Jude 24

DAY OF CHRIST: PHILIPPIANS 1:6, 10

COMMENCEMENT	CHARACTERISTICS	CONSUMMATION
When Christ comes for His people, hence, the Day is always in the Future. "In the Day of Christ." Phil. 2:16	Day of Redemption (Eph. 4:30) Day of Manifestation (1 Cor. 1:7,8) Day of Reckoning (2 Tim. 1:12, R.V.M.) Day of Testing (1 Cor. 3:13; 4:5) Day of Reward (2 Tim. 4:8) Day of Rejoicing (2 Cor. 1:14; Phil. 2:16) Day of Completion (Phil. 1:6) Day of Grace (1 Cor. 5:5; 2 Tim. 1:18) Day of Glory (2 Pet. 1:19)	The Day of Christ ends when the Day of the Lord begins, viz., when Christ comes with His saints. 2 Thess. 1:8-10; 2:1-8, R.V.

DAY OF THE LORD: 2 THESSALONIANS 2:2, 3 R.V.

COMMENCEMENT	CHARACTERISTICS	CONSUMMATION
Begins when Christ comes with His saints. Zech. 14:1-5	The Day of the Lord is ushered in by fearful judgments (Joel 2:1-11), then there comes a time of great blessing (Isa. 10:20-25), universal peace (Micah 4:3), Israel's restoration (Zeph. 3:11-17; Joel 2:25-29).	The Day of the Lord is for a 1,000 years. Rev. 20:4

DAY OF THE LAMB: PSALM 8, R.V.

COMMENCEMENT	CHARACTERISTICS	CONSUMMATION
After the Millennium, and Satan's last revolt. Rev. 20:7-10	All things summed up in Christ. Eph. 1:21 When He will reign as the Lamb, and all will yield glad homage to Him. Rev. 21 to 22:1-6	An indefinite period, when "all things will be put under Him." 1 Cor. 15:27,28

COMMENCEMENT	CHARACTERISTICS	CONSUMMATION

DAY OF GOD: 2 Peter 3:12

Eternity.	"God all in all." 1 Cor. 15:28	"God...unto Him be glory in the Church in Jesus Christ througnout all ages, world without end." Eph. 3:19-21

DAY OF MAN: 1 CORINTHIANS 4:3

The Day of Man reached its highest point of iniquity when "sin" did "much more abound" in the slaying of Christ on the Cross. This present time of man's revolt is called "night" by the Spirit. Rom. 13:12	Man apart from God, dead in sin, walking after the course of this world, and according to the prince of the power of the air. Eph. 2:1,2	The Day of man's mis-rule will culminate with the over-throw of the man of sin, the false prophet and Satan, when Christ comes with His saints in judgment. 2 Thess. 1 and 2

DAY OF SALVATION: 2 CORINTHIANS 6:2

Provisionally it began as soon as man fell, hence, on the ground of the atonement to be made by Christ, sins done "aforetime" were "passed over" by virtue of the ransom to be paid. Rom. 3:25, R.V.	Offer of God's grace in Christ, and specifically offered since Christ died for our sins and rose again for our justification. Rom. 4:25 Acts 13:39	Runs parallel with man's day, till Christ returns in judgment. Jude 15

DAY OF JUDGMENT: MATTHEW 10:15; 11:22, 24; 12:36

When Christ sits on the Great White Throne. Rev. 20:11 John 5:22, 27	Christ will "judge in right-eousness" (Acts 17:31), and men will be judged "according to their works." Rev. 20:13	At the end of the millen-nium, before the time of Christ's perfect rule. Rev. 20:5

I. *These Prophetic Days Begin with the New Testament*
The most casual reader of the New Testament must be
convinced of the fact that it opens up a new and distinct
order of things. We recognise that there are certain great
principles running through both Old and New Testaments,
but there is also something in advance of the Old in the New,
even as the oak is in advance of the acorn, although coming
out of it. Let us ponder a few Scriptures by way of illustration.

Heb. 1 : 1, 2—" God, Who at sundry times and in divers
manners spake in time past unto the fathers by the prophets,
hath in these last days spoken unto us by His Son." These
words suggest a *process* which reaches a *climax*. The process
was that God spake in " divers portions " (R.V.) ; for instance,
He revealed to Adam the manner of Christ's coming, that He
should be " the Seed of the woman " (Gen. 3 : 15) ; to
Abraham He made known that Christ should be from the
nation of which he was the head (Gen. 12 : 3) ; to Jacob it
was declared that Christ should belong to the tribe of Judah
(Gen. 49 : 10) ; to David it was communicated that Christ
should be of the family of David (Psa. 132 : 11) ; to Micah
it was revealed that Christ should be born in the obscure
village of Bethlehem (Micah 5 : 2) ; to Malachi it was stated
that Christ should be preceded by a forerunner, who should
herald His approach (Mal. 3 : 1) ; to Daniel it was made
known the time Christ should appear to be " cut off " in
death, namely, at the end of the 69th week of the 70 weeks
of years (Dan. 9 : 26) ; to Zechariah it was shown that Christ
would be betrayed for thirty pieces of silver (Zech. 11 : 13) ;
to Isaiah it was unveiled that Christ should die for the sins
of the people, be numbered with transgressors, intercede for
His murderers, and be buried in a rich man's grave (Isa.
53 : 9-12) ; to the Psalmist it was revealed the manner of
Christ's death, that it would be by crucifixion (Psa. 22 : 16) ;
and that He should rise from the dead (Psa. 16 : 10, 11).
Thus in these, and in many other portions, God made known
His purpose regarding His Son ; but Christ, when He came,
was the culmination of His revelation. The Divine Word
has said all there is to be said as far as salvation, life, and

godliness are concerned; hence, God has been silent since Christ went back to His throne.

John 19 : 30—"It is finished," or more correctly, "It is accomplished." What was accomplished? The Scriptures were fulfilled which spoke of His coming and death. Law was magnified, justice satisfied, sin removed, heaven opened, hell defeated, and God glorified. Old Testament promises and types were accomplished. The shadows passed for the reality had come.

Matt. 11 : 11—"Among them that are born of women there hath not risen a greater than John the Baptist; notwithstanding, he that is least in the kingdom of heaven is greater than he." John was in the Old Dispensation. Those in the kingdom are in the New. The latter were not greater than the former in *character*, for he was the "greater," as Christ says; but those who are in the realm of grace are greater in privilege than John was in the realm of law. Grace brings on to higher ground, and into greater privilege.

Acts 13 : 38, 39—"Be it known unto you therefore, men and brethren, that through this Man is preached unto you the forgiveness of sins; and by Him all that believe are justified from all things, from which ye could not be justified by the law of Moses." There was no mercy to the lawbreaker under Moses. Take one contrast alone. Under the law the prodigal was put to death. No mercy was shown to him (Deut. 21 : 18-21); but under grace the prodigal is forgiven, clothed, fed, and joyed over (Luke 15 : 20). These things "could not be" under Moses, but they can be and are in Christ.

Rom. 3 : 25—"Passing over the sins done aforetime." The sins referred to are not those of the believer before he embraces Christ, but those committed by Old Testament saints before Christ came. God, on the ground of the prospective sacrifice of Christ, passed over their sins. The apostle does not use the word generally employed to signify "remission," but studiously and intentionally uses another word which means pretermission, or passing by. The sins of Old Testament believers were passed over by virtue of the atonement which was to be made ; ours are forgiven because it has been made.

John 7 : 39—" This spake He of the Spirit, which they that believe on Him should receive ; for the Holy Ghost was not yet *given ;* because that Christ was not yet glorified." The Holy Spirit in Old Testament times came and went ; He did not abide in believers as He does now. Christ must pass through the baptism of God's fiery judgment against sin before He can be the Baptizer with the Holy Spirit.

These and many other Scriptures go to prove that the New Testament reveals a new order of things, which grows out of the Old, and is subsequent to it, and which is far beyond it.

II. *These Prophetic Days are Distinct in Their Character*

Their character may be indicated by different colours. We have the crimson day of Christ's glory in the flesh— crimsoned by suffering, sorrow and sin, and yet full of the glory of grace, love and truth ; the black day of man's sin and iniquity, seething with rebellion, lawlessness and unbelief ; the variegated day of the Son in His many-sided present ministry at the right hand of God ; the green day of salvation in its testimony of God's love and grace ; the blue day of Christ's satisfaction in the splendour of His return for His own ; the yellow day of the Lord's kingly rule ; the brown day of the Judge's righteous judgment ; the purple day of the Son of Man's excelling glory ; and the golden day of God's perfect glory.

The Day of Jesus is inceptive of blessing. It began with Christ's incarnation and ended with His crucifixion. When He came, He brought in a new order of things. *A new wonder* was seen, God manifest in the flesh. He no longer hid Himself in thick darkness, but was seen and heard in Christ. *A new unfolding* was given. An unfolding of the love of God as seen in the compassion of Christ, which came to bless humanity, like the morning light which hallows with glory the hills lately shrouded in darkness. *A new attraction* was evidenced in the beautiful life of Christ, which, like an oasis in the desert, was felt in all He was, and said, and did. *A new Gift* was bestowed in the Good Shepherd giving His life, which given life was to be the mystic key to open heaven's storehouse of blessing, and to hush every cry of earth. *A new power* was realised in Christ's resurrection from the dead, which like a tornado was to sweep hell's power before it, and supply a force to move all the required machinery of the Church. *A new Bestowment* was supplied in the Holy Spirit, Who should be like the earth, sun, and rain to the sown corn, the Fertilizer of the spiritual life of the believer. *A new relationship* was inaugurated for those who would receive the Christ. They should henceforth know God as their Father, hence His first words to His disciples on the resurrection morn were, " My Father and your Father."

The Day of Man is Destructive in its Tendency. Slowly and surely the tremendous onrush of water which falls over Niagara is having its effect upon the stone and slate beneath. It is estimated by scientists that it has taken from 35,000 to 75,000 years for the water to have cut away the coraline limestone and other varieties of stone which are found in the Gorge, to have brought the Falls to their present location from Lewiston, seven miles ; and that the average recession along the whole contour of the Horse-shoe has been, since 1842, about 2.4 feet per year. In the centre of the channel, where the bulk of the water passes, the average yearly recession is 4.8. At the point where the acute angle is formed, the recession from 1842 to 1875 was about 100 feet, and from 1875 to 1886 more than 200 feet. As we trace the history of human sin, we find that man in his downward tendency gets worse and worse. God tried man in innocency and he failed. He left him to his conscience, and the result was the burning mass of sin which brought the flood of judgment. Man was placed under law, which he promised to keep, but the height of his promise only made his fall the greater. Man was next tried under government, but he only got on to a lower level, which culminated in his being placed under Gentile supremacy, as is evidenced in Israel's captivity under Assyria and Babylon. Last of all, God sent His Son, but this only gave man the opportunity to put the crowning act upon his previous deeds, for with wicked hands man took the Lord and nailed Him to the cross. Yet one other sin man can add to his cup of iniquity, and that is to turn a deaf ear to the Spirit's testimony regarding Christ. The sin of sins is not to believe in Him. God cannot, and will not, have anything to do with those who turn their back upon His Son. For those who wilfully and habitually reject the one sacrifice for sin, there remains nothing but judgment.

The Day of the Son is Respective in its Office. This day has to do with Christ's present ministry at the right hand of God. This ministry has to do with believers only. He appears in the presence of God "*for us.*" As our Representative He lives for us, as our High Priest He pleads for us, as our Advocate He answers for us, as our Succourer He aids us, as our Keeper He preserves us, as our Shepherd He tends us, as our Friend He cheers us, and as our Companion He has fellowship with us. We hear Him say, as He said of His own long since, "I pray for them." Thus His present service is respective to God's people.

The Day of Salvation is Elective in its Purpose. The Lord is taking out from the world a people to His name. These constitute the Church, which is His mystical Body; hence, in order to accomplish this, those who are saved go forth and proclaim the willingness of God to save to the uttermost. Those who are blessed by Him receive a seven-fold benediction—they are saved by His grace, secured in His power, sealed by His Spirit, supplied at His board, sanctified in His fellowship, satisfied with His favour, and sent forth to His service.

The Day of Christ is Restrictive to the Redeemed. This period covers the time between Christ coming for and with His saints. For that day believers are kept, and in that day they will be made like Christ. They will stand before His judgment seat that their work may be tested, their motives examined, their conduct reviewed, and rewards given for those services rendered for the sake of Christ.

The Day of the Lord is Distinctive in its Character. It covers that period known as the Millennium. It is ushered in with fearful judgments, and then, when everything which offends has been removed, there will be the time of universal blessedness. The Antichrist will be destroyed, the nations will be judged, Satan will be bound in the bottomless pit, war will cease, creation will be delivered, Israel will be blessed, and Christ will be acknowledged as Lord and King.

The Day of the Lamb is Ideal in its Perfection. There are many Scriptures which forecast a period when Christ's reign will be universally acknowledged with loving adoration. In the Millennium the Hand of Power will keep all men under the sway of Christ ; but in the ideal period, unlimited in duration, there will be loyal worship, and all things will be keyed up to Him, for then all things will be summed up in the Christ.

The Day of Judgment is Punitive in its Application. It takes place at the end of the Millennium. At this time the Great White Throne is set up. The books will be opened and the dead will be judged ; and hell will be opened to receive the lost.

The Day of God is Prospective in its Outlook. This points on to eternity, when God will sum up all things in Christ, and God will be All in all.

As we think of these prophetic days in all the sweep of their broad outline, it leads one to ask the practical question : " What is the effect upon the life ?" Coleridge says :

> " Work without hope draws nectar in a sieve,
> And hope without an object cannot live."

The child of God who is looking for the fulfilment of God's purposes and promises which relate to Christ's coming can never be "without an object." He rather says with Goldsmith :

> " Hope like the cheering taper's light,
> Adorns and cheers our way ;
> And still as darker grows the night,
> Emits a brighter ray."

AN ILLUSTRATIVE EXAMPLE

The progressiveness of Divine Revelation is further illustrated in the following study of the Secrets of the Kingdom of Heaven in relation to prophecy. The key to the mysteries of the Kingdom of Heaven is found in the Book of Daniel.

In that book "the God of Heaven," "the King of Heaven," and "the Lord of Heaven" are mentioned seven times (Dan. 2 : 18, 19, 28, 37, 44 ; 4 : 37 ; 5 : 23).

Heaven is constantly recognised, hence we read, "The heavens do rule" (Dan. 4 : 26) ; and things in relation to Heaven are mentioned thirty-two times. The predominating thought is embodied in Dan. 2 : 27-30—"Daniel answered in the presence of the king, and said, The secret which the king hath commanded cannot the wise men, the astrologers, the magicians, the soothsayers, show unto the king ; But there is a God in Heaven that revealeth secrets, and maketh known to the king Nebuchadnezzar what shall be in the latter days. Thy dream, and the visions of thy head upon thy bed, are these ; As for thee, O king, thy thoughts came into thy mind upon thy bed, what should come to pass hereafter : and He that revealeth secrets maketh known to thee what shall come to pass. But as for me, this secret is not revealed to me for any wisdom that I have more than any living, but for their sakes that shall make known the interpretation to the king, and that thou mightest know the thoughts of thy heart."

The above Scripture reveals to us the soul of our subject, namely, that there is a God in heaven that revealeth secrets, and overruleth all things. "The kingdom of heaven" is confined to the prophecies which relate to the Nations and to Israel. Remembering this limitation we must look for the secrets as revealed concerning them.

The Secret of Double Fulfilment. A fundamental principle to recognise in the study of prophecy is, that when prophecy becomes history, history again becomes prophecy. We have many examples of this principle. The outpouring of the Holy Spirit on the Day of Pentecost was a filment of the prophecy in Joel, but it did not exhaust it, hence we look for its fulfilment in the "afterwards" of which the prophet speaks (Joel 2 : 28).

The prophecy about Tyre has a double application. The first part of Ezekiel 26 predicts the invasion of the kingdom by Babylon, while the latter part of the chapter found its fulfilment in the invasion under Alexander the Great, as can be easily gathered in noticing that the pronoun is changed from the singular to the plural.

The prophecy again about the Little Horn in the 8th of Daniel has an application to Antiochus Epiphanes. This Assyrian monarch lived 150 years before Christ, and yet did not fill to the full the prophecy which, according to Christ, has reference to the abominator who will arise in the time of the end.

The prophecy in relation to the destruction of Jerusalem was " a time of trouble " to the Jewish nation, but that limited destruction is a prophecy of the Great Tribulation that shall come in the near future, and which shall try all the inhabitants of the earth.

Not to recognise the double application of prophetic truth is to miss a great deal of its significance and suggestion, hence the safer plan for all prophetic students to follow is, to be a Harmonist rather than only to be a Preterist, or a Futurist. Thus, we say with the late Dr. J. Anderson, of Brighton : " The acknowledged double fulfilment of certain prophecies is an argument in favour of the possibility of a double fulfilment of other prophecies." And he also says, in reference to Matt. 24 : " It will be found that the interpretation regarding the siege and destruction of Jerusalem will be simplified if we recognise that destruction as the background, and the second advent of our Lord with its preliminary events, judgment upon the Jewish nation, as a more complete and exhaustive fulfilment."

The Secret of Significant Break. We can only refer to three illustrations. The first is the well known one of Christ's omission in His statement in the synagogue of Nazareth. He quotes Isa. 61 : 1, 2, and yet while He emphasises the benevolent ministry that was inaugurated at His first coming, He leaves out the sentence, " The day of vengeance of our God " (Luke 4 : 18, 19). This, as well as the omission, is most speaking, and confirms the thought that in His first coming He came to bless ; but in His return to the world, He will come in judgment.

The wonderful chapter which Luther calls " The Passional," namely, Isa. 53, predicts the advent of Christ in such a way that the prophecy seems to be continuous, and yet we know there is a break of nearly two thousand years in such a couplet as : " It pleased Jehovah to bruise Him " and " He shall see His seed, He shall prolong His days, and the pleasure of the Lord shall prosper in His hand."

The third instance that we cite as to a significant break is with regard to the prophecies which relate to Babylon. The overthrow of that city in the past was most minutely fulfilled, but reading the predictions of Isaiah, of Jeremiah, and John the Apostle, we cannot come to any other conclusion but that that city will be rebuilt, and will suddenly be overthrown as it never was before by the direct act of God, for the figure that is used is that of a stone that is dropped into the water (Rev. 18 : 21).

The Secret of Holy Enshrinement. There is a soul or inner meaning to the word of prophecy. As there was a Holiest of All in the Tabernacle, and this was relative to the Holy Place and the Outer Court, so there is the outer court of the body of Scripture which leads to the soul of inspiration, and thence to the spirit of inner meaning. This is brought out in the Parables of Matt. 13. The people did not understand the parabolical language of Christ ; but He revealed the spirit of their meaning and application to His disciples, and said to them, " To you is given to know the mysteries of the kingdom." But even to them He did not explain the parables of " The Treasure " and " The Pearl." The Treasure is undoubtedly the Israelitish people, of whom He said, " Ye shall be a peculiar treasure unto Me." He found the treasure hid in a field of the world of nations, and separated that one nation to be a people to Himself who should not be reckoned among the nations.

The Secret of Over-ruling Adjustment. Behind all the acts of men we behold the over-ruling of God. God's permissions are often spoken of as His givings. Daniel, in his address to Nebuchadnezzar, confirms this, for he said to him, " Thou art a king of kings, for the God of heaven hath given thee a kingdom, power, strength, and glory " (Dan. 2 : 37).

Cyrus, King of Persia, recognised the same prerogative, for in his declaration to his subjects regarding the building of the Lord's house, he proclaimed : " The Lord God of heaven hath given me all the kingdoms of the earth ; and He charged me to build Him a house at Jerusalem, which is in Judah " (Ezra 1 : 1, 2). Doubtless Daniel would explain the words of Jeremiah to Cyrus, such as are found in Jer. 25 : 12, 13, where we read : " And it shall come to pass when the seventy years are accomplished, that I will punish the king of Babylon . . . and I will bring upon that land all My words which I have pronounced against it, even all that is written in this book, which Jeremiah hath prophesied against all the nations."

All this goes to prove that God moves the chessmen on the board of history. They think in their pride and self-will they are carrying out their plans, but all the while Jehovah is, (to change the figure) like the mono-typist touching the keyboard as he sets up the author's manuscript in type, setting up the record of His purpose, and in the after history is demonstrating He is the Accomplisher in the affairs of nations.

The Secret of Undermining Cause. The undermining power of sin is always the cause of decay and destruction of earthly kingdoms. With repeated emphasis, like the tolling of the bell, which proclaims the passing of the dead, the prophet Jeremiah asserts as he proclaims the word of Jehovah, that the reason of Jehovah's judgments is, " Because of the evil doings." Again and again He explains the cause of His acts, as because of sin. Let the following black list speak for itself : " Because of the evil of your doings " (4 : 4) ; " Because their transgressions are many " (5 : 6) ; " Because they have not hearkened unto My words " (6 : 19) ; " Because ye have done all these works " (7 : 13) ; " Because ye have sinned against the Lord " (8 : 14) ; " Because ye have forsaken My law " (9 : 13) ; " Because ye have forsaken the land " (9 : 19) ; " Because they have hardened their necks " (19 : 15) ; " Because their sins were increased " (30 : 14) ; " Because thou hast taught rebellion against the Lord " (28 : 16) ; " Because ye have sinned against the

Lord " (40 : 3) ; " Because of their wickedness " (44 : 3) ;
" Because of the evil of your doings " (44 : 22) ; " Because
of the abominations which ye have committed " (44 : 22) ;
" Because ye have burned incense " (44 : 23) ; " Because ye
have sinned against the Lord " (4 : 23).

Following these reasons of God's judgments, is the
announcement of doom, in such and similar words as, " Therefore this evil is come upon you." If Jer. 25 is carefully read
with Matt. 25 : 31-46, it will be seen the judgment of the
nations means to be cut out of existence, for the word
" punishment " in Matt. 25 : 46 is " Kolasis," which means
" a cutting off." God judges nations in time, but individuals
in eternity.

The Secret of Drifting Declension. " There are certain
uniform dispensational features which distinguish every new
period. Each dispensation is marked by seven features, in
the following order : (*a*) Increased light ; (*b*) Decline of
spiritual life ; (*c*) Union between disciples and the world ;
(*d*) A gigantic civilization worldly in type ; (*e*) Parallel
development of good and evil ; (*f*) Apostasy on the part of
God's people ; (*g*) Concluding judgment. We are now in the
seventh dispensation, and the same seven marks have been
upon all alike, showing one controlling power.—*Deus in
Historia.*"

The history of the world's powers is always from bad to
worse, and not from worse to better.

> " Here is the moral of all human tales,
>   'Tis but the rehearsal of the past.
>   First freedom, then glory—
>   When that fails
>   Wealth, vice, corruption, barbarism at last ;
>   And history with all her volume vast
>   Hath but one page."

The visions of Daniel portraying the Times of the Gentiles
illustrate this drifting declension. The golden kingdom of
Babylon with its absolute autocracy is followed by the silver
kingdom of Medo-Persia with its parliament of princes. The
brass kingdom of Greece with its sweeping conquests, under
Alexander the Great and his four generals, is followed by

the iron rule of Rome with its many senators ; and, lastly, we have the brittle clay of the powers in the time of the end. If we look at the weight of these several materials in their specific gravity, we see how there is a declension :

Gold is equivalent to 19·3.
Silver   ,,   ,,   10·51.
Brass   ,,   ,,   8·5.
Iron   ,,   ,,   7·6.
Clay   ,,   ,,   1·9.

Thus we see that the Image is top heavy, and we are not surprised at its overthrow.

The same principle is illustrated in the vision that Daniel saw as recorded in Dan. 7. The kingly and majestic lion is followed by the strong and brutal bear, and the bear is followed by the cunning and sleek leopard, and the leopard is followed by the hybrid and horned monstrosity.

The Secret of Judicial Method. We find certain great principles illustrated and enunciated, namely, (1) That Jehovah uses one nation to punish another, as in the case of Judah being overcome by Babylon ; and (2) God punishes the nation that He had used to punish another, so Babylon in turn is crushed by the Medo-Persian. (3) God deals with nations in their corporate capacity in time, and not in the hereafter. Nations have no hereafter, the individual has. Individuals are forgiven, but nations are not. God deals with them in righteousness when they go on in unrepentant sin.

Nations as nations have been cut out in the past. " Multitudes, multitudes in the valley of decision " (Joel 3 : 14). These words describe the gathering of the nations ; but the word " decision " does not convey the thought ; the sentence should read, " Multitudes, multitudes in the valley of excision." " Excision " means a cutting off, or a cutting out. The Hebrew word is used in describing the mining of gold, in separating the gold from the refuse (Prov. 16 : 16), and the word is also used in speaking of a sharp threshing instrument, which is used to separate the chaff from the corn (Isa. 41 : 15). Under another figure Christ gives the same thought, when He speaks of a shepherd separating the sheep from the goats (Matt. 25 : 32).

The above unmistakably shows the judgment of the nations will be one of the things Christ will perform when He comes in His glory, and that the judgment will be the annihilation of nations, as nations, in their being cut out of being.

The Secret of Loving Purpose. There are two great and wonderful lines of prophecy in relation to Abraham and David. God promised to Abraham the land which is called "The Land of Promise," the dimensions of which are given in Gen. 15 : 18. Another line of prophecy is in connection with the throne of David and the promises which relate to the occupancy of it by one of his seed. These are clearly stated in 2 Sam. 7 : 8-17 and expounded in Psa. 72.

We call these promises "The Secret of Loving Purpose" for the simple reason that God has covenanted with Himself, and thus placed Himself under obligation to fulfil His word and oath. He cannot do any other, and He would not if He could. In spite of all the sin and iniquity of Israel, which as a nation has been ruthlessly sifted among the nations, Jehovah has pledged Himself in His love and grace that not a grain of the nation of Israel shall be lost. His word of Promise is : "I will sift the house of Israel among all nations, like as corn is sifted in a sieve, yet shall not the least grain fall upon the earth." "In that day will I raise up the tabernacle of David that is fallen, and close up the breaches thereof ; and I will raise up his ruins, and I will build it as in the days of old : . . . And I will bring again the captivity of My people of Israel, and they shall build the waste cities, and inhabit them ; and they shall plant vineyards, and drink the wine thereof ; they shall also make gardens, and eat the fruit of them. And I will plant them upon their land, and they shall no more be pulled up out of their land which I have given them, saith the Lord thy God." Could any promise be more full, explicit, than that which is found in the seven golden "I will's" in the above words ? (Amos 9 : 9-15).

How important it is, therefore, to recognise that "Israel is the true key to prophecy, and the Divine dealings with

Israel are an important clue to the right understanding of
the purposes of God as regards the world at large, and multitudes of the human race generally. The Bible is mainly a
record of Israel's history. Gentile nations are brought into
prominence only as they help to elucidate Israel's position
and career."

The Secret of Focusing Goal. " There are some 666
general prophecies in the Old Testament ; 333 of which
refer particularly to the coming Messiah and meet only in
Him." We are not surprised, therefore, that the goal of
God's purpose in which all things are to be focused is the
coming of Christ to take up the reins of government. No
more explicit word could be given than we find in Paul's
address to the Athenians, when he declared that God hath
appointed the day, that is, a period of time, in which He
will judge, or rule, the civilised world in righteousness by
that Man Whom He hath ordained whereof He hath giveth
assurance unto all men, in that He hath raised Him from
the dead (Acts 17 : 31).

Talking with two leading business men in the City of
Chicago recently, one of whom was the Vice-Chairman of the
great Santa Fe Railroad, and the other the President of one
of the leading and great Insurance Companies, on separate
occasions, each of them said to me, " The only cure for all
the ills of humanity and the disorders that are found in the
world, is the personal coming and intervention of the Lord
Jesus Christ."

When we turn to the pages of the Book we find by
prophetic vision, by clear statement, by predicted utterance,
by many types, in the fore-shadowing by individuals, by the
clear teaching of Christ, by the Spirit's inspired word,—that
it is God's purpose to sum up all things in the Son of His
love. Since this is so, how important it is that we should
have fellowship with God about the future glory of His Son.

" The study of prophecy promotes present and abiding
communion with God, giving reality to the eternal state and
throwing marvellous light on the future of man. Prophetic
truth reveals very fully the mind and will of the Lord, and

the more the purposes of God are apprehended and His wondrous plans understood, the more real does everything become in reference to man's true relationship to the Divine. Abiding in Christ, walking with God and hearing His voice, the interest deepens, the spirit is quickened, expectancy is aroused, the things of earth recede, Heavenly things brighten and intensify, and life becomes a reality. In abiding communion with God, the Lord Jesus as the coming King is earnestly looked for, the love to Him is increased, the loyalty to Him is intensified, the blessed hope and appearing of the glory of our great God and Saviour Jesus Christ shines brighter and brighter, until at last, He, the long-expected One, comes, and in a moment, in the twinkling of an eye, we are changed, we are caught up to meet Him in the air, ' and so shall we ever be with the Lord.' " So writes Dr. J. Anderson.

THE PROGRESSIVENESS OF OUR LORD'S CHRISTSHIP

We have already seen that there is a distinct progressiveness in the revelation which God has given of Himself, in chapter 3, in the four great trunk names which are given, as Jehovah, Adonahy, Elohim, and the Father. The same progressive revelation is made known in the truth concerning our Lord as " The Christ."

1. *Personally.* The Gospels reveal our Lord Jesus as the Christ, Who came to do a work for us ; hence, they are written that we might " believe Jesus is the Christ, the Son of God, and that believing we might have life through His Name " (John 20 : 31). Also it is upon His personal worth and work as the Christ that His Church is built, as Christ Himself declared when Peter confessed, " Thou art the Christ " (Mark 8 : 29 ; Matt. 16 : 13-16).

2. *Positionally.* Jesus is exalted to the right hand of God in the place of authority and power, and as the Giver of the Holy Spirit, hence, Peter under Divine inspiration said on the Day of Pentecost, " God hath made that same Jesus both Lord and Christ," or as the Revised Version more emphatically states, " God hath made Him both Lord and

Christ, this Jesus Whom ye crucified " (Acts 2 : 36). The despised Man is in the place of absolute authority as " Lord," and as " Christ " is the Giver of the Holy Spirit, hence all through the Book of the Acts the testimony is to " The Christ " (2 : 31 ; 3 : 20 ; 9 : 22).

3. *Mystically*. Christ is made known as " The Christ," which in a mystical sense signifies Christ and the members of His body. The Head is the complement of the members, and the members are the complement of the Head, hence, the two are summed up " as the Christ " (1 Cor. 12 : 12). Christ is the Fulness of the Church (Col. 2 : 9, 10), and the Church is the fulness of the Head (Eph. 1 : 23).

4. *Representatively*. Christ is the One in Whom believers are found, and with Whom they are identified, hence, we are " found in Him " (Phil. 3 : 8, 9), " Dead with Christ," " Risen with Christ " (Col. 2 : 20 ; 3 : 1) ; " Quickened together with Christ," and seated in heavenly places " in Christ Jesus " (Eph. 2 : 6, 7).

5. *Provisionally*. Christ is God's Reservoir in Whom is found " all spiritual blessings," for the Father has given to all believers all blessings in Him (Eph. 1 : 3). He has nothing to give us apart from Him, but there are no withholdings with Him.

6. *Potentially*. Christ as the Christ is the secret of the Christian life. Christ alone can reproduce the Christ-life, hence, we need the strengthening of the Spirit to cause Christ to take up His permanent abode in us, that we may know what the Apostle knew, when he declared " Christ liveth in me " (Eph. 3 : 16 ; Gal. 2 : 20), not Christ *and* me, but " Christ *in* me."

7. *Prophetically*. Christ is the Guarantee that those who have fallen asleep in Him will be raised from the dead, for the " dead in Christ shall rise first " (1 Thess. 4 : 16) ; and then they and the living saints will be together in the glory, for " Christ the Firstfruits " (not the " Firstfruit " but " Firstfruits ") includes all who are in the Body (1 Cor. 15 : 23), and that when " Christ Who is our Life shall appear we shall appear with Him in glory " (Col. 3 : 4).

11

THE FINGER OF A DISTINCT DIRECTION

THE Finger is often used as a metaphor of the distinct and definite act of God. The magicians of Egypt recognised that the plagues of Egypt were the act of God when they exclaimed, " This is the Finger of God " (Exod. 8 : 19). The Law is declared to have been " written with the finger of God " (Exod. 31 : 18 ; Deut. 9 : 10). Christ announced that it was by " the Finger of God " He cast out demons (Luke 11 : 20). And the Psalmist said to the Lord that " The heavens were the work of Thy fingers " (Psa. 8 : 3).

With His master-hand the Spirit is constantly arresting our attention by some glowing sentence, startling truth, pointed declaration, soul-stirring exhortation, unequalled revelation, uplifting promise, or apprehending word. One such word with its associates is " Behold." Let us muse upon this golden word of Revelation.

" **Behold Your God** " (Isa. 60 : 9). The one Person whom men seem to forget is God. The fact of God throbbing through the universe, the righteousness of God insistent in His law, the truth of God revealed in His Word, the wisdom of God made known in His works, the love of God unfolded in the Cross, the mystery of God speaking in His providence, and the Christ of God made known in the Gospel, is seen if men have eyes to see. The world is walking on its careless way without God.

The same lack is found in those who profess to believe in Christianity. The Editor of " The British Weekly " has said : " When we meditate on present day Christianity, of which we ourselves form part, we may recognise that it often suffers not so much from a lack of zeal as from an error in emphasis and direction. To put the point quite bluntly, many religious people are being diverted and distracted from the chief end of religion—which must be nothing short of God Himself." It is sad that ever such a

statement should have to be made, for it reveals the very
fundamental fact of Christianity is not known, namely, that
Christ suffered, the Just for the unjust, to bring us to God
(I Pet. 3 : 18) ; and the vitals of its meaning consist in
being " alive unto God " (Rom. 6 : 11).

There is also a grave danger to which believers in Christ
are exposed, and that is, lest we be occupied with the things
of God, and forget the God of the things.

One has said, " Some men still miss their God in discussing Him and defining Him. They attend more to the
process than to the result. They analyse their own faith
and trust to their own conviction, instead of forgetting
themselves in faith's living Object.

" Or they rely on some inward experience of redemption
in place of adoring their Redeemer. Whereas it is characteristic of the Gospel that it points us to One Who is far
above and beyond ourselves, Who does for us all that we
ourselves can never do.

" Salvation comes from without ; and the watchword of
salvation is not ' Behold your creed, your theology, your
experience,' but ' Behold your God.' "

The true aim, and attitude, and acknowledgment of a
believer in Christ is expressed in the following lines :

" My goal is God Himself, not joy or peace,
Not even blessing, but Himself, my God."

" **Behold The Man** " (John 19 : 5). The proof of
Christianity is Christ Himself. No other evidence is needed.
He is the Evidence of all evidence. Let any honest person read
the Gospels without prejudice or preconceived notions, and
he must be convinced that the Jesus therein revealed is not
the product of human thought. The fact of Christ is the
fact that is indisputable.

There is one Scripture which is often misquoted. Nine
ministers out of ten misquote it. The misquotation is, " The
truth as it is in Jesus." The quotation is, " As the truth is
in Jesus " (Eph. 4 : 21). There is no " it." To put " it "
in, is to make the statement to be a comparative one, namely,
that truth is to be found somewhere else, as well as in Jesus ;

whereas to declare, " As the truth is in Jesus," is to make a positive and exclusive claim, and that is, truth is only to be found in Him ; and mark, in Him, " as Jesus," that is, in the Man of Nazareth. Think of a few statements that are made of Him as the Man. " Never man spake like this Man " (John 7 : 46) ; " This Man receiveth sinners " (Luke 15 : 2) ; " I find no fault in this Man " (Luke 23 : 4) ; " Truly this Man was the Son of God " (Mark 15 : 39) ; " This Jesus hath God raised . . . hath made . . . both Lord and Christ " (Acts 2 : 32, 36) ; " Through this Man is preached the forgiveness of sins " (Acts 13 : 38) ; " This . . . Man offered one sacrifice for sins " (Heb. 10 : 12) ; " He hath appointed a day in which He will judge the world in righteousness by that Man Whom He hath ordained " (Acts 17 : 31). Now what does the Spirit claim for " This MAN ?" He has spoken a message none other has given ; He does what none other does ; He is what none other is—faultless ; He evidenced a personality none other can reveal—He is the Son of God ; God has honoured Him, in giving Him the highest place ; through Him is offered what no man can bestow—forgiveness of sins ; He has performed a work in His death that no other can accomplish ; and through Him God is going to administer a judgment, or rule, that no one could carry out.

" **Behold The Lamb of God** " (John 1 : 36). Christ, as the Lamb, reveals Him in the eternal fact of His death. He suffered in the body of His humanity. He suffered in the soul of His feelings, and He suffered in the spirit of His personality. The supernaturalness of His death is the essential thing to ponder. God cannot die, and yet there is the eternal fact, that He Who died for us is God. We are exhorted to be " Looking unto Jesus Who endured the Cross." The " unto " might be rendered " into." To be looking " into " that Holy One Who endured the Cross, is something more than a surface look. It means painstaking research, constant meditation, holy gazing, prayerful observation, soul communion, consecrated attention, and spiritual insight. To gaze at a minute form of life in the evolution of its being is to see the hand of a mystic worker, so as we ponder the death-agony, the soul-suffering, and the atoning work of our Lord, we behold more than the actuality of His death, we see there :

> An infinitude in His sacrifice,
> An eternal value in His blood,
> A holy satisfaction in His offering,
> A substitutionary fact in His act,
> A God-glorifying work in His death.

Yes, a Deity of Divine Personality acting in the limitations of human nature. In that death of deaths we have a fathomless depth beyond human sounding, a height beyond man's reach, a wealth exceeding the financier's calculation, a sky of stars no astronomer can discover, and a heaven of benefit that none can estimate. Behold the Lamb, and see Him of Calvary's Love—how, in His death, God is glorified, justice is satisfied, law is magnified, hell is stultified, man is justified, angels are edified, believers are sanctified, service is intensified, creation is beautified, sinners are vivified, covenants are ratified, and Christ Himself is gratified.

" Behold a King." " Behold, a King shall reign in righteousness " (Isa. 32 : 1). Christ was rejected as King when He came the first time. In derision Pilate said to the Jews, as he pointed to Jesus, " Behold, your King !" (John 19 : 14). And he placed upon the Cross, " The King of the Jews." Christ, having been rejected as the King, has gone into the " far country to receive unto Himself a kingdom, and to return " (Luke 19 : 12). When He returns He will be manifested as the King. No one can imagine that our Lord is acknowledged as King at present. His Kingly rule is flouted, not followed. His beneficent sway is not received in our day. The condition of things as now operating is depicted in Psa. 2, where the nations are said to be raging, and if not openly, yet actually by their ignoring His claims and commandments, setting themselves against the Lord and His Christ. Men think, in their proud arrogance, that Jehovah takes no notice of their actions ; but He that sitteth in the heavens, in the calm of His majestic might and absolute sway, laughs at the pelting peashooters they point at Him, for He hath set His King on His holy hill, and soon

He will give to His Son " the nations for His inheritance, and the uttermost parts of the earth for His possession."

Meantime faith, with its insight and long-sight, can see the time when the King shall reign with the hand of righteous grace, with the might of loving power, with the heart of tender pity, with the ear of responsive regard, with the truth of absolute equity, with the peace of calm enactment, and with the special consideration of helpful service. The state of things then—as described in Psa. 72—shall be fulfilled in every detail.

" Behold Thy Saviour." " Behold, thy salvation cometh," or, as it might be translated, " See, thy Saviour cometh " (Isa. 62 : 11). The announcement has special reference to the restoration of Israel. If Isa. 61 and 62 are pondered it will be apprehended what the Lord will do for His people in the frequent " I will " of His promise ; and the effect of His operation is summarised in the repeated, " Thou shalt " : " Thou shalt be called by a new name," " Thou shalt be a crown of glory," " Thou shalt no more be called Forsaken," " Thou shalt be called Hephzibah," " Thou shalt be called Sought Out."

All the fulfilment of the promises, and the experiences declared, shall come to pass when the Saviour of Israel shall return. When He comes as the Saviour, then a seven-fold salvation shall be known. Jehovah will save Israel from the desolations and disasters of their wandering state, as a scattered nation, for He says, " I will take you from the nations " ; He will save Israel to Himself, for He affirms, " I will be your God " ; He will save Israel from all their uncleanness, for He declares, " I will save you from all your uncleanness " ; He will save them from their unbelief, for He pledges to " take away the stony heart " ; He will save Israel from their disobedience, for He assures them, " I will cause you to walk in My statutes " ; He will save to the possession and power of the Holy Spirit, for He promises " to put His Spirit " within them ; and He will save Israel to be a praise among the nations, whereas before they profaned His holy Name among them (Ezek. 36 : 23-29).

" Behold The Lion of The Tribe of Judah." The Lion and the Lamb are the notes upon which the Spirit plays, as the music of heaven sounds forth the glory of our Lord. The Lamb in His gentleness, and the Lion in His powerfulness. As the Lion, Christ has prevailed to open the Book of God's purpose, and to unloose the seals thereof, hence, He is worthy because of what He is, and has done, to adjudicate in overthrowing the wrong, and to establishing the right. When men try to get rights, they seek to acquire them by the force of might ; but Christ obtained His by the conquest of right. Not without meaning are the Lion and the Lamb found together in Rev. 5 : 5, 6. One of the elders told John the Lion had " prevailed to open the books," and yet, in response to the elder's direction to " Behold," he saw not a " Lion " but a " Lamb," and " a Lamb as it had been slain " in all the livingness of His death. The slain Lamb becomes the slaying Lion. The Bruised One becomes the Bruising One. The record of the Revelation of Christ's future is that He goes forth conquering and to conquer. The word " prevailed " is translated " overcome " and " conquering " (Rev. 3 : 21 ; 6 : 2), and in the afterwards it is said when the confederated kings act under the leadership of the beast against the Lamb, that " the Lamb shall overcome them," and the reason given is, " He is Lord of lords, and King of kings." So again we find the combination of the Lamb in His sacrifice, and the Lord in His sovereignty. The cross and the crown are the crest of heaven. By His sacrifice He sways the sceptre. Well did Dr. Denney say : " It is on the ground of His death, and the redemption effected by it, that all praise is ascribed to the Lamb, and the knowledge and control of all put into His hands."

" Behold The Lord Cometh." Enoch long ago prophesied : " Behold, the Lord cometh with ten thousand of His saints to execute judgment " (Jude 14, 15). Three things are of moment in the prophecy of Enoch. First, the Person Who is coming—" The Lord." " Kurios " speaks of ownership, authority, and power. The Lord as Owner has a right to exact an account from His creatures ; as Lord He has authority to demand a statement, and also has the power to see it is given. Second, the purpose of His coming is to execute judgment upon those who have misused His gifts, and who have sinned against Him; and, third, the partners who are said to come with Him are His "saints." God's holy ones, made so by His grace in Christ, and by His Spirit in His truth, will exercise judgment with Him.

We must distinguish between the Lord's coming for His saints in grace, and His coming with them in judgment. We are "looking for the Blessed Hope, and the glorious appearing of our great God and Saviour" (Titus 2 : 13). Mark the "kai" ("and"), for it points to something in addition to the "Blessed Hope." It connects it with "the glorious appearing." Christ's coming for His saints is described in 1. Thess. 4 : 13-18, and His coming with them in 2 Thess. 1. There is all the difference in the world in the scene in the upper room, when Christ promised to come and receive His own to Himself, and the scene depicted in Rev. 19 : 11-16, where the white horse riders are seen accompanying the white horse Rider.

How Should we Behold Him ? We should behold Him with the clean heart of unsullied purity. Purity of heart is essential to see Him. The unveiled face is necessary to behold His unsurpassed countenance. As the fogs without, or a cataract on the eye, will obscure the sun, so the impure heart within and the fogs of the world will hinder us from seeing the Lord.

We should behold Him with the intense love of an ardent affection. It was after Isaiah had seen the King, that he ardently responded to the Lord's call, "Who will go for us," by saying, "Here am I, send me." Love never counts the cost; it is a delight to give whatever the cost may be.

We should behold the Lord with the full faith of absolute confidence. Abraham's vision of the Lord enabled him to fulfil his vocation as a pilgrim and a stranger. He did not know where He was going, but he knew with whom he was travelling. Faith does not look at its confidence, but it looks to the Lord with unswerving joy.

We should behold the Lord with the loyal hands of right action. The turning point in the life of Zacchæus was when he saw the Lord, and His look of love drew out the response of the tax-gatherer's avowal that he would restore aught he had wrongly taken, and give to others in pressing need. When the heart is beating healthily it will cause the hands to act righteously.

We should behold the Lord with the warm glow of devoted service. A creaking wheel proclaims an obvious want, but a well-oiled machine works effectively without noise. The reason why Mary gave her devoted service to the Lord was because she had looked into His face so often that its image was stamped upon her heart.

We should behold Him with the earnest lips of a pure intercession. When the heart of a fire is a flaming force, how easily the added fuel is consumed ; so when the fire of an earnest cause moves us, how fervidly our lips plead ! The secret of the endurance of Moses amid Egypt's attractions and Israel's faithlessness was because he saw Him Who was invisible. The visible things of earth pale in the light of heaven's splendour.

We should behold the Lord with the earnest gaze of hope's expectancy. Enoch was the man who looked beyond death, and through the Lord's removal of him he never saw it. It is the privilege of the child of God to be looking for the coming of Christ Himself. Not for signs, not for death, but Himself.

" Behold, I Make All Things New " (Rev. 21 : 5). When we look out on the world it is like a cauldron of boiling metal ! The fire of hell beneath it is being stirred by the devil with the poker of hate. There is only One Who can remedy matters, and that One is the One Who says, " Behold, I make all things new." The nailed Hand of Calvary is the only Hand that can arrest the hard hand of might. The love of Christ is the only power that can fuse the mass of mankind into the common interest of brotherhood. The selfless Lord, Who emptied Himself, is the only One Who can give the disinterestedness of mutual good. When He begins to remake, the iron hand of anarchy will be broken, the wilful mind of lawlessness will be ended, the lusting heart of greed will be suppressed, the harmful fist of cruelty will be crushed, the covetous eyes of selfishness will be put out, the stinging tongue of blasphemy will be rebuked, and the order of get-all-you-can-for-yourself will give place to give-all-you-have-for-others'-benefit.

This is no delusive hope, but a promise of Divine Revelation. Three times in Rev. 21 : 5, 6 we have the declaration of " He said." His promise : " He said . . . I make all things new." His assurance : " He said . . . these words are faithful and true " ; and His accomplishment : " He said, It is done."

" Behold, I Come Quickly." Three times in the Revelation He makes this announcement, and once, " Surely I come quickly," and in each case with a different association. First, with the exhortation to " hold fast," lest the crown of reward should be lost ; second, with the promise of blessing to those who keep the sayings of the Book ; and third, with the promise of reward for work done ; and fourth, with the assurance, " Surely I come quickly " (Rev. 3 : 11 ; 22 : 7, 12, 20).

" Quickly " may be taken in three ways : (1) Meaning *at once*, as when the servants were told to go on their Master's mission " quickly," and as Mary rose up " hastily " (Luke 14 : 21 ; John 11 : 31). " Hastily " and " quickly " are the same word. (2) " Quickly " also means " suddenly," as the word is given in 1 Tim. 5 : 22. (3) The word also describes the way a person does a thing, as the women who " departed quickly " to tell that Christ was risen (Matt. 28 : 8), that is, with speed. " Quickly " does not seem to mean " *at once* " from the time Christ gave the word (unless the faithlessness of the Church has hindered His starting) ; therefore, the suggestion is, when He rises to come, He will do it suddenly, and His method in coming will be with speed.

THE MANIFESTATION OF CHRIST

The Spirit of God travels along many lines in His distinctive ministry to bring us to the terminus of God's revelation about His Son, and one such line is found in what He says regarding the purpose of Christ's manifestation.

378 / Major Bible Truths

The Greek words, " Phaino," " Phaneros," and " Pha-
neroo," rendered " appear " and " manifest," signify to show,
to lighten, to shine upon, to disclose, to exhibit, and to
reveal.   The words are used to describe " a light that
shineth " (2 Pet. 1 : 19) ; to give a reward " openly " (Matt.
6 : 4) for what has been done in secret ; to come " abroad "
Mark 4 : 22) ; to make a person " known " by announcing
his presence (Mark 3 : 12) ; to exhibit anything to another
so that it can be said it has been " shewed " unto him (Rom.
1 : 19) ; to reveal, as when the Apostle said, " The life of
Jesus was made manifest in our mortal flesh " (2 Cor. 4 : 10) ;
and to appear before another, as when Christ " appeared "
unto the eleven disciples in the Upper Room (Mark 16 : 14).

There are, at least, fourteen truths brought before us,
covering a complete course of Biblical study, in connection
with Christ's manifestation.

1. **God,** or Christ the Manifestation of God's Person—
" God manifest in the flesh " (1 Tim. 3 : 16).   Christ is God
expressed in living characters.   God is not fully known apart
from Christ, but He is well known if we know Him.   He is
the visibility of God.

2. **Sin,** or Christ the Revealer of sin's iniquity—" The
Light shineth in darkness and the darkness comprehended
it not " (John 1 : 5).   The Light revealed the sightless eyes
of man's ignorance, the evil of his nature, and the plague
spots of his wickedness.

3. **Love,** or Christ the Manifestation of God's love—" In
this was manifested the love of God toward us," etc. (1 John
4 : 9).   Love is seen in three stages in 1 John 4 : 9-17 :
Love for us, answering for our sins in the past (verse 9) ;
Love in us, moving us to love in the present (verse 12) ; and
Love with us, giving us a bright outlook as to the future
(verse 17, margin).

4. **Atonement,** or Christ the Satisfaction for sin—" Once
in the end of the world He appeared to put away sin by the
sacrifice of Himself " (Heb. 9 : 26).   Provisionally He puts
away sin by giving satisfaction for it in His death, and thus
removes it as a hindrance.   Substitutionally He removes sin

as a penalty, as we believe in Him (1 Pet. 2 : 24). Effectively
He puts away sin as a power, as we identify ourselves with
Him, by reckoning we are dead to it (Rom. 6 : 8-11). Pro-
phetically He will remove sin as a presence, for He is the
Lamb of God, Who takes away the sin of the world.

5. **Substitution,** or Christ suffering in our stead—" He
was manifested in these last times for you " (1 Pet. 1 : 20).
" For you " may be read, " On your behalf," and thus in
your stead. We must distinguish between Provision, Substitution, and Identification. Provision is for the needy
world, for Christ has made it possible for all to be saved.
Substitution is for the believing sinner, for Christ has borne
his sin and he will not have to bear it. Identification is the
Gospel for the saint, for we have died with Christ in His
death.

6. **Resurrection,** or Christ the Manifestation of God's
power—" He shewed Himself " (John 20 : 1-14). The fact
of Christ's resurrection is the living flame which ever burns
on the altar of Christianity, and it is also a living factor in
the life of the believer which lifts him from the realm of self
to the fellowship of Him Who lives in the power of an endless
life.

7. **Salvation**—" The grace of God which bringeth salva-
vation to all men hath appeared " (Titus 2 : 11, margin).
Provisionally, salvation is a blessing offered to all. Personally, salvation is a benefit to the individual believer.
Practically, salvation is a force to mould us like to Christ.
In the first, Christ is offered to us (Acts 13 : 26) ; in the
second, Christ is accepted by us (Eph. 2 : 8) ; and in the
third, Christ by the Spirit lives in us (Eph. 3 : 16, 17).

8. **Life,** or Christ the Communicator of Life—" The life
was manifested " (1 John 1 : 2). Sin brings death, which means
separation from God. Christ brings life, which means union
with God in Christ (John 17 : 3). As natural life is the union
of the spirit and body (Jas. 2 : 26), so spiritual life is the
union of the believer with Christ (Col. 3 : 3). Christ is
revealed to us as the Quickener from sin's death (Eph. 2 : 1) ;
He is revealed in us as the Sanctifier of heart and life (Gal.

1 : 16), and He is revealed through us to others by a consecrated testimony (1 Thess. 1 : 8-10).

9. **Power**—" Manifested forth His glory " (John 2 : 11). Glory is the excellence of anything in display. Christ's first miracle displayed the excellence of His power. It is fitting that His first miracle should display His power to change things. By the cleansing of His blood and the conformation of His Spirit He can change the sinner into a saint. Translation, transfiguration, and transformation cover the ground of God's Gospel of grace, godliness and glory. Translated into His Kingdom, as to place (Col. 1 : 13) ; transfigured by His Spirit, as to character (2 Cor. 3 : 18, R.V.) ; and transformed by His coming as to the glorified body (Phil. 3 : 20, 21 ; 1 John 3 : 2).

10. **Satan.** Christ was the Victor over the Evil One—" The Son of God was manifested to destroy the works of the devil " (1 John 3 : 8). The works of Satan are mighty and manifold, but Christ has met him upon his own ground and conquered and routed him. Take but one chapter out of the Gospels, and in it we have a record of how Satan raised a storm, demonized an individual, tormented a woman, and caused the death of a child. But Christ raised the dead to life, healed the woman, delivered the man, and stilled the tempest (Luke 8).

11. **Emancipation.** Christ is the Remover of sins—" He was manifested to take away sins " (1 John 3 : 5). The word for " take away " is rendered " removed " in Matt. 21 : 21, " loosing " in Acts 27 : 13, " lifted up " in John 11 : 41, and " take away " in John 11 : 39. The word signifies to take away, by taking up upon one's self, and is so indicated in John 1 : 29, where the margin reads, " beareth away." Christ removes the sins from us by His propitiation and power, by bearing their consequence in His death, and by severing us from their control by His presence.

12. **The Holy Spirit.** Christ is the One, Who endowed and who is endowing with the Spirit—" He was manifest " (John 1 : 31). John knew Christ when he saw the Spirit resting upon Him, and knew that He was also the Baptizer

with the Spirit. Christ was anointed to do a definite work (Acts 10 : 38 ; Heb. 9 : 14), and when He accomplished that work, became the Anointer with the Spirit as a reward (Acts 2 : 33).

13. **The Father.** Christ the Revealer of the Father—"I have manifested Thy name" (John 17 : 6). John 17 reveals what that manifestation means : A work done for us to the Father (verse 4), The blessing of eternal life from the Father (verse 2), Confidence in the Father (verse 8), Possessed by the Father (verses 9, 10), Kept through the Father (verse 11), Message from the Father (verse 14), Sanctified in the Father's truth (verse 17), Oneness with the Father (verse 21), and Seeing the glory of the Father (verse 22).

14. **Immortality.** Christ is the Bringer of life and immortality to light (2 Tim. 1 : 10). Life is more than perpetuity of existence—immortality is more than deathlessness. The latter is a state of holiness and bliss, in an incorruptible and glorified body, from which it is impossible to fall, and this life is holy in its nature and joyous in its bliss.

The Revelation which God makes *to us* in the Scriptures, is meant to be revealed *in us* by the Spirit through faith, and revealed *through us* by His effective working in our testimony.

DISTINCTIVE WORDS OF THE SPIRIT

There are certain luminous words which have a distinct and definite meaning in their use and application. We call attention to eight of these by way of suggestion : Atonement, Blood, Reconciliation, Purchase, Redemption, Believed, " Beginning," and " Lord."

Atonement

There is a mass of meaning in the great words of Scripture as they operate in our life and testimony. One such word is atonement.

I have found seven vitalizing principles which govern all these great words.

1. The first time a word occurs explains its meaning in other places.

2. There is one verse which embodies the truth.

3. There is one book which covers the many-sidedness of a word.

4. There is one chapter in which a full revelation is given.

5. There is one word in the New Testament which corresponds to the Old Testament word.

6. The derivations from a root word are coloured by the original meaning.

7. The specific revelation given in a word and its practical bearing.

1. **First Occurrence.** The first time a word occurs explains its meaning in other places. It comes under the law of first mention. The first time the word atonement occurs is in Gen. 6 : 14, and is rendered " pitch." " Thou shalt pitch the ark within and without with pitch," was God's direction to Noah. Both the verb and the noun occur. The meaning of the word atonement here is obvious, namely, to cover The verb kaphar means to cover and the noun kopher signifies a covering.

In a general sense the words mean that which covers, or the act of covering. In a particular sense to make an atonement signifies that which answers for the offender and hides him from view. Canon Girdlestone says : " The prevailing idea set forth, both in the Septuagint and in other translations, is that atonement is the doing away with a charge against a person by means of expiation, propitiation, or otherwise, so that the accused may be received into divine favour and be freed from the consequences of wrong-doing.

" Pacification, propitiation, and such words, are by no means adequate for the purpose of conveying the doctrine of atonement ; they savour too much of heathenism and superstition, and lead to the supposition that man pacifies God, instead of teaching that God shelters man ; but whatever word is used, the more carefully the Scripture is studied, so much the more will the unity, the beauty, and the grandeur of God's way of mercy commend itself to the soul."

2. **Embodying Truth.** There is one verse which embodies the truth of atonement. "For the life of the flesh is in the blood, and I have given it to you upon the altar to make an atonement for your souls: for it is the blood that maketh an atonement for the soul . . . by reason of the life" (Lev. 17 : 11, R.V.).

The words life and soul (nephesh) are the same. Life is in the blood. Man's life is forfeited on account of sin, therefore the life of another must be given to save the life forfeited. The one thing that Christ emphasized was that He would give His life, and it is in that substitutionary death that our salvation is found, for without shedding of blood is no remission ; but since the blood has been shed every sin of the believer has been answered for.

3. **Covering Book.** There is one book which covers the many-sidedness of atonement and that is Leviticus. There are seven aspects of atonement in Leviticus.

(1) The necessity for atonement. "Make an atonement . . . concerning his sin" (4 : 26). If there had been no sin there would have been no necessity to make an atonement for it. The Cross is meaningless apart from the fact of sin.

(2) The authority for atonement. "As the Lord hath commanded" (8 : 34 ; 9 : 7). The Lord knew all the facts of the case and the requirement that was essential to meet them, and He has met every requirement in the atoning death of Christ, and so there is no other requirement to meet.

(3) The person who could make an atonement. "The priest" (4 : 20, 26, 31, 35 ; 5 : 6, 10, 13, 16, 18 ; 6 : 7 ; 7 : 7 ; 12 : 7, 8 ; 14 : 18, 19, 20, 21, 29, 31, 53 ; 15 : 15, 30 ; 16 : 6, 10, 11, 16, 17, 18, 20, 24, 27, 30, 32, 33, 34 ; 19 : 22). The priest acted in a twofold capacity : he represented God to the people, and he represented the people to God. Christ did the same, He offered Himself without spot to God, and He made reconciliation or atonement for the people (Heb. 2 : 17 ; 9 : 14).

(4) The means by which atonement was made. "The blood that maketh atonement" (10 : 17 ; 16 : 10, 11 ; 17 : 11). We must always remember that the blood shed indicates the

life given. Christ Himself emphasized this in one of His
parting messages to His disciples, when He said, " Even as
the Son of Man came not to be ministered unto, but to
minister, and to give His life a ransom for many " (Matt.
20 : 28).

(5) The Person to whom atonement was made. " Before
the Lord " (14 : 18, 31 ; 15 : 15, 30 ; 16 : 10). Sin is against
the Lord, therefore atonement for it must be to Him. He
alone can estimate the sinfulness of sin, and He it is Who
says, " Deliver him from going down to the pit, for I have
found an atonement " (Job 33 : 24, margin).

(6) The blessings which come because of the atonement :

Forgiveness. The outcome of the atonement is tersely
expressed, " Make an atonement for his sin which he hath
sinned and it shall be forgiven him " (4 : 20, 26, 31, 35 ;
5 : 10, 13, 16, 18 ; 6 : 7 ; 19 : 22).

Cleansing. Here again the word is specific and clear, for
the divine record proclaims, " Make an atonement . . . to
cleanse you, that ye may be clean from all your sins before
Jehovah " (16 : 16, 30).

Rest. In connection with the Feast of Trumpets, the
tenth day of the seventh month was to be a day of atonement, and identified with that holy convocation " no work "
was to be done (23 : 27-29) ; therefore there is the thought of
rest associated with atonement. Since Christ has entered
into " His rest " from the work of atonement, we are rested
in the rest He enjoys (Heb. 4 : 10), and we are seated with
Him in heavenly places because He has sat down as the Sin-
offerer at the right hand of God (Heb. 10 : 12).

Release. Lev. 25 gives us the benefits which accrue in
the year of jubilee, and some of those benefits were, release
to the debtor, freedom to the slave, and rest to the land. All
this is typical of the fact that Christ came, as He Himself
states, to give deliverance to the captives, etc. (Luke 4 : 18,
19).

(7) There was only one way by which the benefit of
atonement could be received and that was by faith. This is
suggested by the offerer placing his hand on the victim which

had been offered up to make an atonement for his sin (1 : 4). The same principle holds good in the New Testament, for it is through Christ that we receive the atonement or reconciliation (Rom. 5 : 11).

4. **Illustrative Chapter.** There is one chapter in which a full revelation is given on atonement. We find that the verb " to make an atonement " occurs sixteen times in Lev. 16. Fifteen times kaphar is rendered " make an atonement," and once " make reconciliation " (verse 20). It is an interesting study to see the different places and things for which atonement was made, for it emphasizes the fact that everything is based on atonement whether it be the salvation of the sinner or the work and worship of the priest.

5. **Corresponding Word.** There will be found a corresponding word in the other Testament. The corresponding word to atonement in the New Testament is propitiation. The word propitiation is found in Rom. 3 : 25 ; 1 John 2 : 2 ; 4 : 10. In these passages God sets forth Christ to be " a propitiation for our sins."

6. **Coloured Words.** The derivations from the root word are coloured by its original meaning.

Kaphar (verb). This is a primary root which is rendered " pitch " in Gen. 6 : 14 ; " make an atonement " in Lev. 16 ; " purged " in Isa. 6 : 7 ; " disannulled " in Isa. 28 : 18 ; " pacified " in Ezek. 16 : 63 ; " put off " in Isa. 47 : 11 ; " appease " in Gen. 32 : 20 ; " make reconciliation " in Ezek. 45 : 15 ; " cleansed " in Num. 35 : 33 ; " forgive " and " pardon " in Jer. 18 : 23, and 2 Chron. 30 : 18.

Kopher (noun). From kaphar is derived kopher, which is rendered " pitch " in Gen. 6 : 14 ; " sum of money " in Exod. 21 : 30 ; " ransom " in Exod. 30 : 12 ; " satisfaction " in Num. 35 : 31, 32 ; " villages " in 1 Sam. 6 : 18 ; " bribe " in 1 Sam. 12 : 3 ; " camphire " in Cant. 1 : 14 ; " atonement " in margin of Job 33 : 24. All the above have the thought of a covering. For instance, a bribe covers the face of the judge, so that he cannot see the offence ; and camphire denotes the henna flower, from which the women got a rouge to beautify themselves (see margin of Cant. 1 : 14, R.V.).

Kapporeth. From kopher is derived kapporeth, which is rendered " mercy-seat " seven times in Exod. 25 : 17, 18, 19, 20, 20, 21, 22. The mercy-seat was the covering of the ark.

Kephir. This is derived from kopher, and is rendered " young lion " in Amos 3 : 4, and " village " in Neh. 6 : 2. A village is a place of covered dwellings ; and a young lion is called a kephir because he keeps in his lair.

Kephor. This is also derived from kopher, and is translated " hoarfrost " in Exod. 16 : 14, and " bason " in I Chron. 28 : 17. We know that the hoarfrost is the beautiful rime which hides the blackness of the trees ; and the bason referred to was a covering for a vessel in the Temple service.

7. **Specific Revelation.** The specific revelation which the Lord has given in this great word is that the atonement is a work done for us by the death of Christ. It expresses what Christ has given to God on our behalf, and is the ground of our acceptance with Him, and also proclaims that all blessing comes to us by means of Him—" by means of His blood." Therefore to say that atonement means " at-one-ment " is to misunderstand its meaning. Reconciliation is an outcome of the atonement. Atonement is not a blessing which comes to us, but a work—Christ's work—done for us.

This work secures all blessing, " at-one-ment " or reconciliation included. Christ's atonement did not placate God, that is, get God into a mind to save us ; it was because God had a mind to save us that Christ came ; yea, God meets His own claim in Christ. Christ did not come to reconcile God to us, but God was in Christ reconciling the world to Himself.

" THE BLOOD."

1. **The first time** " blood " is mentioned in the Bible is Gen. 4 : 10—" The voice of thy brother's blood crieth unto Me." The law of first mention, as indicating the meaning of the use of a word, is strikingly demonstrated in the shed blood of Abel by Cain. The blood shed never means the life as lived, but always the life given, poured out, or taken. Christ's blood was " shed," poured out (Matt. 26 : 28).

2. **The key verse** of " the blood " is found in Christ's own words—" This cup is the New Testament in My blood

which is shed for you " (Luke 22 : 20), " for (unto) the remission of sins " (Matt. 26 : 28). The wine in the cup at the Lord's Supper is typical of the poured out life of the Saviour as the atoning sacrifice, and the end in view is the cancelling of the guilt of sin, and the removal of it from the sinner's conscience.

3. **The pivot chapter** on "the blood" is Heb. 9. If that chapter is carefully pondered in the reflected light of chapter 10, it will be found that the blood is the atoning blood of satisfaction to God (9 : 7), the obtaining blood of access (9 : 12 ; 10 : 19), the cleansing blood of purification (9 : 13, 14), the dedicating blood of consecration (9 : 18 ; 10 : 29), the covenanting blood of obligation (9 : 19, 20), the loosing blood of deliverance (9 : 22), and the perfect blood of accomplished atonement for sin (9 : 25 ; 10 : 4, 19). Four things are paramount and prominent, namely, the Perfect Saviour Who did the work, the perfect work accomplished by the Saviour,—(The one offering " once " offered. Note the seven times " once " occurs in the chapters),—the perfect provision found in the perfect Saviour through His perfect work, and the perfect outcome in the Person of Christ as we have it applied in power to the heart and life by the Spirit.

4. **The embodying Book** on " the blood " is Leviticus. Over seventy times blood is used in an atoning and purifying sense. The outstanding verse which shines like a star of the first magnitude is, " For the life of the flesh is in the blood, and I have given it to you upon the altar to make an atonement for your souls ; for it is the blood that maketh an atonement for the soul " (Lev. 17 : 11). The life is in the blood, but it is not the life while it remains in the blood which atones, but the life's blood poured out.

5. **The corresponding truth** in the Old Testament, linking by God's scarlet line the New to it, is Exod. 12, where we read of the blood of the Paschal Lamb. The blood was found in four different places, namely, upon the lintel, upon the two side-posts of the door, and upon the doorstep. The word " basin " (verse 22) should be " threshold," and is so rendered in other places. The threshold of the door was the

place where the lamb was slain. There was more blood therefore on the doorstep than in any other place ; and that blood kept the destroyer outside, and kept the sheltered ones safe inside the houses.

6. **The relative words** which emphasize the truth are many. Think of the many Calvary words which proclaim the fact of atonement and sacrifice ! Sometimes—generally— words are derived from the root word which colours and elucidates and illustrates the truth ; but in this instance there are many different words which shine with the ruddy colour of Calvary. One of the many words is " died." Take the six occurrences in Romans : " Christ died for the un- godly," " Christ died for us," " He died unto sin once," " It is Christ that died," " To this end Christ both died," etc., " For whom Christ died" (Rom. 5 : 6, 8 ; 6 : 10 , 8 . 34 ; 14 : 9, 15). Mark, it does not say, " Christ lived for us," but " died for us."

7. **The practical application,** in its revelation, of this solemn topic is found everywhere. The blood is the basis of sin's forgiveness (Eph. 1 : 7), the breaker of sin's bondage (Rev. 1 : 5, R.V.), the bringer of untold blessing (Lev. 4 : 20, 26, 31, 35 ; 5 : 10, 13, 16, 18 ; 6 : 7), the banisher of sin's judgment (Ex. 12 : 13), the bond of the saints' communion (1 Cor. 10 : 16), the blighter of Satan's power (Rev. 12 : 11). and the beautifier of heaven's glory (Rev. 21 : 23).

Perhaps the most significant words relative to our subject are those of Christ's, when He speaks of eating His flesh and drinking His Blood (John 6 : 53-56). Participation with Christ in His death not only brings untold benefits, but it results in the kindling of a fire in the soul which expresses itself in holy living, pure devotion, consecrated service, generous giving, ardent faith, sacrificial love, and Christly compassion.

RECONCILIATION

Reconciliation is not an Old Testament word. It is a New Testament revelation. The word rendered " recon- ciliation " in the Old Testament should be " make an atone- ment," especially in Lev. 6 : 30 ; 8 : 15 ; 16 : 20 ; Ezek.

45 : 15, 17, 20 ; Dan. 9 : 24. Expiation and not reconcilia-tion is the thought in these passages. Reconciliation is the outcome of expiation or atonement.

God is never said to be reconciled, but He is said to be propitiated or satisfied. Christ did not come to make God love us, but He did come to meet God's requirement, or better, God in Christ met His own requirement.

Atonement is the Godward aspect of Christ's mission : what He gave to God on our behalf in dying for our sins. Reconciliation is the outcome of Christ's atonement, hence it is said we are " reconciled to God by the death of His Son."

1. **The first time** the Greek word for " reconciliation " (katallasso) occurs is in Rom. 5 : 10—" For if when we were enemies, we were reconciled to God by " (" dia " rendered " by " with the genitive means " by means of ") " the death of His Son, much more, being reconciled we shall be saved in " (not " by " but " en "—" in ") " His life " (Rom. 5 : 10). Here we have four explicit thoughts : (1) The persons recon-ciled—" enemies." (2) The means by which the reconcilia-tion is effected—" by the death of His Son." (3) The Person to Whom the rebels were reconciled—" to God." (4) The power into which reconciliation brings—" saved in His life."

2. **The key verse** on reconciliation is Rom. 5 : 11—" And not only so, but also glorying (margin) in God, through our Lord Jesus Christ, through Whom we have now received the reconciliation " (R.V.). " Atonement," as given in the A.V., is wrong ; it should be, as elsewhere rendered, " reconcilia-tion." One of the blunders of translation is that where the word should be " reconciliation " we have given to us " atonement," and where the word should be " atonement," as in Heb. 2 : 17, we have " reconciliation." The key verse emphasizes that reconciliation is " through " Christ, which " we have now received " (Mark the " now " and the " we have "), and because of this we enjoy the high privilege of " joy in God," or boast in Him, and thus cease from self and others, and find our home in God Himself.

3. **The embodying Book** on reconciliation is Colossians, as epitomized in chapter 1 and verses 19-23. In repudiating the error of many angelic mediations, the Spirit emphasizes the fact that Christ is " The Firstborn of all creation," and therefore the Cause of all things. He is the Medium of all creation and of all things in the Church, and therefore " by means of Him " and His Cross all things are adjusted, or reconciled ; not only believers, but " things " as well.

4. **The pivot chapter** in which reconciliation is emphasized is 2 Cor. 5 : 18-20. Reconciliation is mentioned five times : (1) Cause, end and means of reconciliation—" God, Who hath reconciled us unto Himself by Jesus Christ." (2) Co-workers in the ministry of reconciliation—" Hath given unto us the ministry of reconciliation." (3) Contents of the gospel of reconciliation—" To wit, that God was in Christ, reconciling the world unto Himself." (4) Committal of the word of reconciliation—" Hath committed unto us the word of reconciliation." (5) Call to reconciliation—" We pray you in Christ's stead, be ye reconciled to God."

5. **Corresponding Truth.** There is no word in the Old Testament which answers to the New Testament one for reconciliation. It is a New Testament Revelation.

6. **The relative words** to reconciliation are full of suggestion and significance. " Allos," a primary word, signifies that which is different and is rendered " otherwise " in Gal. 5 : 10. From " allos " is derived " allasso," which, means to make different, hence a change. " Katallasso " comes from " lasso " and " kata," which denotes a mutual change, hence to come to an agreement, and is rendered " reconciled." From " katallasso " comes " katallage," which is the word for " reconciliation," and means an adjustment. " Diallasso " means to change throughly, to conciliate. And " apokatallasso " signifies to reconcile fully, and is the word for " reconcile " in Eph. 2 : 16 and Col. 1 : 20, 21.

7. **The Spirit's teaching** regarding reconciliation is, that God effects in us, not in Himself, a thorough change from enmity and unbelief to faith and love ; hence God's

purpose in the death of Christ was to bring men to each other, as well as bring men to Himself. Therefore we read the effect of faith in Christ is to break down the middle wall of partition between Jews and Gentiles—" That He might reconcile both unto God in one body by the Cross, having slain the enmity thereby" (Eph. 2 : 16). When men are right with God they want to be right with each other, and they prove they are right with God by being right with each other. Hence Christ most emphatically says, " If thou bring thy gift to the altar, and there rememberest that thy brother hath ought against thee : leave there thy gift before the altar, and go thy way ; first " (mark the " first ") " be reconciled " (" diallasso ") " to thy brother, and then come and offer thy gift " (Matt. 5 : 23, 24).

PURCHASE

There are two principal words in the New Testament conveying the thought of redemption, and these are " agorazo " and " lutroo." The former signifies to buy something in the market, hence to acquire something for one's self ; and " lutroo " means to release anything by virtue of a price which has been paid for it. There are also in the Old Testament two principal words for redemption, namely, " gaal " and " padah." We must limit our study to " agorazo."

One of the most important things to keep before us is the difference between purchase and redemption. The whole world has been purchased by Christ, but it is only believers who are said to be redeemed, therefore to sing, " He hath redeemed a world from sin," is singing something which is not correct.

1. **The first time** " agorazo " occurs is in Matt. 13 : 44, where we are told the man buys the field to get the treasure out of it. The word there is rendered " buyeth " and " bought " (verse 46). Some would make the sinner give up all he has in order to buy Christ or salvation, but surely in the light of Revelation the correct thought is, Christ is the One Who gave up all He had, that He might buy the field

(Matt. 13 : 38) of the world, to get the treasure of His people out of it. He found the Church in the eternity of the past (Rom. 8 : 29), in time He gave up all the glory He had (Phil. 2 : 7, R.V.), He purchased the world by His blood (2 Pet. 2 : 1) to take out from it a people for Himself (Acts 15 : 14).

2. **The key verse** of purchase, or where " agorazo " is found, is Rev. 5 : 9, where we read of those who are said to be " Redeemed to God by Thy blood," or more correctly as R.V., " Didst purchase unto God." There are four thoughts here : (1) The Person Who redeems, the Lamb ; (2) How He redeems, " By His blood " ; (3) To Whom the redeemed are redeemed, " to God " ; and (4) the identity of the Purchaser with the price of the purchase, with those who are purchased, and the permanent value of all, as suggested by the preposition " en " (" in ") rendered " by."

3. **The central chapter** where " agorazo " is emphasized is 1 Cor. 6 : 20, where believers are exhorted to remember that they have been " bought (agorazo) with a price." The apostle is talking about the excesses of the saints at Corinth by means of the body (there are seven references to the body in 1 Cor. 6 : 15-20), and forbids the same, and gives in the " for " and " therefore " the reason of their obedience— " For ye were bought with a price, glorify God therefore in your body " (R.V.).

4. **The embodying Book** where " agorazo " is found, with the prefix " ex," is the Epistle to the Galatians. " Exagorazo " means to buy out of the market, hence we are reminded that " Christ hath redeemed us from the curse of the law," and that His purpose too was " to redeem them that were under the law " (Gal. 3 : 13 ; 4 : 5). To place ourselves under the yoke of the law is to find ourselves in an irksome bondage and an intolerable curse, and to repudiate the redeeming work of Christ. This is the burden of the apostle's message to the saints in Galatia.

5. **The Old Testament words** which correspond to the New Testament " agorazo " are " padah " and " gaal."

6. **The relative word** " agorazo " is derived from " agora," which signifies a market, hence " agorazo " means

to go to market for a purchase ; but when the prefix " ex "
is added to " agorazo " (" exagorazo ") it signifies to buy out
of the market, that is, to buy in order to release. " Agorazo "
is applied in three ways: (1) To buy in a general sense, and is
rendered " buy " and " bought " in Matt. 14 : 15 ; 21 : 12 ;
25 : 9, 10. (2) To buy mankind as denoting God's pro-
prietory right, and is applied to wicked men who " deny the
Lord Who bought " them (2 Pet. 2 : 1). And (3) " agorazo "
is used in a peculiar sense in referring to believers as being
the purchase of Christ, and is rendered " redeemed " (R.V.,
" purchased ") and " bought " (1 Cor. 6 : 20 ; 7 : 23 ; Rev.
5 : 9 ; 14 : 3, 4). " Exagorazo " gives the thought of release
because of a price which has been paid, and is applied to
believers in Christ alone. This word only occurs four times.
Twice in Galatians (3 : 13 ; 4 : 5), where we are reminded
what Christ has redeemed us from ; and twice in two epistles
where believers are urged to be " redeeming the time " (Eph.
5 : 16 ; Col. 4 : 5).

7. **The Divine Revelation.** Purchase, as applied to
believers, reminds us of the price which has been paid for us
and that as a consequence we do not belong to ourselves, but
to Him Who has purchased us. And further, since we have
been set at liberty from the bondage which once held us, we
are to stand fast in the liberty wherewith Christ has made
us free. And yet once again we are to buy up the oppor-
tunities in holy living and consecrated service, and thus to
be redeeming the time. We have only one life to live, and
only the present opportunity to serve the Lord, so let us fill
up the time, that no chance may be lost to do something for
Him, Whose we are and Whom we serve.

" REDEMPTION."

The word " apolutrosis," rendered " redemption," is a
compound one. " Lutrosis " means to release, and with the
profix " apo," which means away from, signifies being set
free by virtue of a price which is paid.

1. **The first occurrence** of " redemption " is in Luke
21 : 28, where our Lord told His disciples to " lift up " their

heads for their " redemption draweth nigh." A time would come when they would be freed from earth's conditions and woes, that is, at His return. The word in its meaning and usage covers the whole blessing of salvation. Believers are freed from the condemnation and control of sin, self and Satan, by virtue of the atoning death of Christ, and by virtue of His expiation, they will be emancipated from the body of sin and death.

2. **The Book** in which redemption is embodied is the Epistle to the Ephesians. Three times the word is found. The blessing of redemption—" In Whom we have redemption, through His blood, the forgiveness of sins, according to the riches of His grace " (Eph. 1 : 7). Here are seven things worthy of notice. The means of redemption is " through His blood " ; the measure of redemption is " according to the riches of His grace " ; the meaning of redemption is being set free ; the accompaniment of redemption is " the forgiveness of sins " ; the certainty of redemption is expressed in the " we have " ; the treasury of redemption—" in Whom " ; and the basis of redemption is " His grace." The completion of redemption. The Holy Spirit is the Earnest " unto the redemption of God's own possession " (Eph. 1 : 14, R.V.). The completion of our redemption, when we are freed from all that is associated with our present earth's conditions, will be when Christ returns ; for this we are marked by God and for Him " unto the day of redemption " (Eph. 4 : 30).

3. **The chapter** in which redemption is embodied is Rom. 3, focusing in verse 24—" Being justified freely by His grace through the redemption that is in Christ Jesus." These pregnant words tell us " Grace " is the provider of redemption ; Christ is the conserver of it, for it is " in Christ Jesus ;" His blood of atonement is the implied means of redemption, for it is " through " Him it is given ; those who receive the blessing of redemption are " justified freely " (the word " freely " is rendered " without a cause " in John 15 : 25, that is " without a cause " of merit in themselves) ; and the outcome of redemption is " being justified," that is being accounted righteous in the Righteous One.

4. **The verse** in which redemption is expressed is 1 Cor. 1 : 30, where we read, " But of Him are ye in Christ Jesus, Who of God is made unto us wisdom, and righteousness, and sanctification, and redemption." The general sense of these words in the light of their setting is, God makes Christ to be to those who believe in Him, righteousness, holiness and redemption in its comprehensive meaning. Righteousness is conformity to God's law, holiness is conformity to God's nature, and redemption is conformity to God's Son.

5. The Old Testament **corresponding word** is found in Exod. 8 : 23, where Jehovah says, " I will put a division, or redemption between My people and thy people." A redeeming act of deliverance was what God put between His people and the Egyptians. The redemption was threefold, a redemption by protection in Egypt, a redemption by blood from judgment, and a redemption by power in deliverance from Egyptian bondage.

6. The **association** of the word " apolutrosis " is as follows. The stem of the word is " luo," which means to loosen—" The string of his tongue was ' loosed ' " (Mark 7 : 35).

" Lutron " comes from " luo," which signifies something which loosens, namely, a redemption price, and is rendered " ransom " (Matt. 20 : 28 ; Mark 10 : 45).

" Lutron " occurs once with the prefix " anti." " Antilutron " signifies a substituted ransom, or an equivalent price ; hence we read of Christ, " Who gave Himself a ransom for all " (1 Tim. 2 : 6).

" Lutroo " is derived from " lutron," and means to redeem, to set at liberty, and is rendered " redeem " and " redeemed " (Luke 24 : 21 ; Titus 2 : 14 ; 1 Pet. 1 : 18).

" Lutrosis " is derived from " lutroo," and denotes the blessing of redemption, and is translated " redeemed " and redemption in Luke 1 : 68 ; 2 : 38 ; Heb. 9 : 15.

" Apolutrosis " denotes redemption in full. The word is rendered " redemption " nine times (Luke 21 : 28 : Rom. 3 : 24 ; 8 : 23 ; 1 Cor. 1 : 30 ; Eph. 1 : 7, 14 ; 4 : 30 ; Col. 1 : 14 ; Heb. 9 : 15) and once " deliverance " (Heb. 11 : 35).

" Lutrotes " from " lutroo " denotes a redeemer, and is rendered " deliverer " in Acts 7 : 35 (margin, " redeemer "), namely, one who has the right and power to loose from bondage.

7. The **practical outcome** of the Redeemer's delivering grace is that we might be loosed from every contaminating thing—" Redeem us from all iniquity " on the one hand ; and " purify a people for His own possession " on the other hand. The pierced hand of Calvary is the providing hand of Pentecost. Grace always leads to godliness. Every fact of the Gospel is a factor in the life.

Having studied this great word of redemption, without any great mental effort we can see what the Holy Spirit suggests through the following outline.

First. The subjects of redemption. Those who were in bondage to a " vain manner of living " (1 Pet. 1 : 18, R.V.).

Second. The Source of redemption. Of God it is said that " His grace " operates " through the redemption that is in Christ Jesus," and that the redemption comes to us " according to the riches of His grace " (Rom. 3 : 24 ; Eph. 1 : 7).

Third. The price of redemption. The price is " His blood " (Eph. 1 : 7), which Christ gave as " a ransom " (Matt. 20 : 28), and is the equivalent for all demands (" antilutron," 1 Tim. 2 : 6).

Fourth. The substance of redemption. Christ is its Substance and Embodiment ; hence, " He is made unto us Redemption " (1 Cor. 1 : 30). There is no blessing apart from Him, and there is no withholding in Him.

Fifth. The receiver of redemption. Faith, like Anna who " looked for redemption " (Luke 2 : 38), finds what it looks for in the Redeemer.

Sixth. The meaning of redemption is " deliverance." The Lion of the tribe of Judah breaks every chain.

Seventh. The consummation of redemption is when our Lord returns. Hence, we are waiting for " the redemption of our body " (Rom. 8 : 23).

BELIEVED

Faith is a self-abasing grace and a god-reliant one. It detaches itself from earthly supports and attaches itself to God by resting in Him. Generally speaking, faith has God for its Object, the Word of God for its Warrant, Prayer as its Outlet, Obedience as its Expression, Love as its Accompaniment, the Spirit as its Life, and Christ as its Model.

1. **The first time** the word "believed" occurs is in Gen. 15 : 6, where we read, Abram "believed in the Lord, and he counted it to him for righteousness." The Hebrew word means to build up or support, hence it is used of a nursing mother carrying her child on the hip, as the mother does in the East. The word is rendered "nursed" in Isa. 60 : 4. How beautiful is the picture of Abram's faith. As the child rests upon its mother's hip with the parent's arm around it and is thus supported, so Abram resting in God's Word had Jehovah's protecting arm to keep him.

2. **The key verse** on believing is Acts 16 : 31—" Believe on the Lord Jesus Christ." To believe on Christ as Lord Jesus Christ, signifies to believe on Him as Jesus and thus be saved, to believe on Him as Christ and thus be sanctified, and to believe on Him as Lord and thus be swayed by Him. This is not one act merely, but a life's attitude. This is implied in the preposition "on" ("epi"), and as it occurs with the accusative case signifies direction towards, and thus motion is implied ; hence, it denotes pressing upon as when one is letting one's self go in order to trust absolutely in the object of its faith.

3. **The Book** in the Bible where believing God is emphasized is the Gospel of John. The word "pisteuo" occurs ninety-nine times. Once rendered "commit" (John 2 : 24). The whole subject focuses round seven pivotal points.

(1) The Object of Faith—God in the Person of His Son. "Believe on Him Whom He hath sent" (6 : 29 ; 14 : 1). (2) The Warrant of Faith—God in the authority of His Word. "They believed the Scripture" (2 : 22 ; 4 : 50 ; 5 : 46, 47). (3) The Call to Faith—Christ in the substitutionary work of the Cross. "All men through Him might believe" (1 : 7 ;

3 : 16, 18). (4) The Outcome of Faith—Blessings of God's Grace in Christ. Sonship (1 : 12), Salvation (3 : 15), Not condemned (3 : 18), Life (3 : 36), Satisfaction (6 : 35), Blessing to others (7 : 38), Mightier Works (14 : 12). (5) The practical Power of Faith—" Whosoever believeth on Me shall not abide in darkness " (12 : 46). (6) The Confession of Faith—" We believe that Thou art the Christ, the Son of the Living God " (6 : 69). (7) The sin and condemnation of not believing in Christ—" He that believeth not is condemned " (3 : 18 ; 16 : 9).

4. **The chapter** in which a full revelation of what believing in God means is John 3, where we have Christ's own teaching about it, and where He emphasizes the essentiality of believing what He says (3 · 12) ; the result of believing in Him as the uplifted One Who atones for us, and as the gift of God's love (3 : 15, 16, 19) ; and the positive blessing of Eternal life (3 : 36).

5. **The word** in the New Testament which corresponds to the one in the Old Testament is undoubtedly the one we have been considering, for there is implied within not only confidence in God's Word, but also committal to the Lord Himself, for it is rendered " committed " and " put in trust " (Gal. 2 : 7 ; 1 Thess. 2 : 4). The following correspondences between Old and New Testaments will be of interest.

" Achish believed David " (1 Sam. 27 : 12). " I believe God " (Acts 27 : 25).

" Nursed at thy side " (Isa. 60 : 4). " Put in trust " (1 Thess. 2 : 4).

" His heart faithful " (Neh. 9 : 8). " Committed unto me " (Titus 1 : 3).

6. **The derived word** " pisteuo " is derived from " pistis," and this comes from a primary verb " peitho," which means, as Strong says, " To convince (by argument true or false) ; by analogy to pacify or conciliate (by other fair means) ; passively to assent (to evidence) ; to rely (by inward certainty)."

The word is rendered : " Agreed "—" To him they agreed " (Acts 5 : 40). " Assure "—" Assure our hearts "

(1 John 3 : 19). " Believe "—" Some believed " (Acts 17 : 4). " Have confidence "—" We have confidence " (2 Thess. 3 : 4). " Obey "—" Obey the truth " (Gal. 3 : 1). " Persuaded "— " I am persuaded " (Rom. 8 : 38). " Trust "—" I trust in the Lord " (Phil. 2 : 24). " Yield "—" Do thou not yield unto them " (Acts 23 : 21).

7. **The practical outcome** of faith in the Lord is evident when we recall the many applications and associations of believing in Him. John's Gospel illustrates this. Believing in Christ expresses itself in appreciation of Him (4 : 41, 42), satisfaction with Him (6 : 35), confession to Him (11 : 36-38), manifestation of Him (14 : 12), acknowledgment of Him (20 : 8), walking with Him (12 : 46), and blessing from Him (20 : 31).

BEGINNING

The word arche, rendered " beginning," indicates commencement, or chief and is used in a variety of associations. The word is translated, " beginning," " first," " principalities," " power," " rule," " principles," " magistrates," and " corners." The " beginning " of all things (Rev. 21 : 6), the angels who " kept not their ' first ' estate " (Jude 6), the " principalities " that Christ spoiled (Col. 2 : 15), the " power " that is in the hands of a governor (Luke 20 : 20), the " rule " that Christ will put down (1 Cor. 15 : 24), the elementary stage of the " principles " which are identified with the Christian life (Heb. 6 : 1), the " magistrates " because of the chief place they occupy (Luke 12 : 11), and the " corners " in referring to the beginnings of a sheet (Acts 10 : 11). God's beginnings are always of primary importance. Unless we begin with God, like the Book of Genesis, we shall never get anywhere. The Genesis of the New Birth leads to the Exodus of redemption, the Exodus of redemption introduces to the Leviticus of worship, the Leviticus of worship is essential to the Numbers of a pilgrim life, the Numbers of pilgrimage prepares us for the Deuteronomy of instruction, and then we are qualified for the Joshua of Canaan and the Judges of the Spirit's power, which in its turn brings us to the rest of Ruth.

The first grace of the Christian life is faith, its chief grace is love, its essential walk is holiness, its dominating power is obedience, its inherent greatness is humility, its regulating rule is prayer, its highest delight is God's will, and its secret fellowship is joy.

1. **The first mention** of arche is in Matt. 19 : 4, where we read, in speaking of man and woman's creation, that " He which made them at the ' beginning,' made them male and female." This statement explodes the theory that man and woman are an evolution. At the " beginning" they were " made" what they are. The Spirit has anticipated the theories and errors of man by the declaration of His Word.

2. **The key verse** of arche is Rev. 1 : 8, where Christ declares, " I am Alpha and Omega, the Beginning and the Ending, saith the Lord, which is, and which was, and which is to come, the Almighty." Here is *multum in parvo* indeed ! Christ declares Himself to be seven things—He is the " Alpha " of origination, the " Omega " of finality, the " Beginning " of all things and the Head and Chief in all, the " Ending," the sum and substance, and consummation of everything, the " Lord " as the Owner of all things, Jehovah (Who is, Who was, and Who is to come) as the " I am " of self-existence and unchanging immutability, and " the Almighty " of complete satisfaction. Could we have Deity more completely expressed or God more tersely revealed ?

3. **The Book** where arche is unfolded is Colossians, where we find that Christ is not only said to be " the Beginning," but the thought is also expressed by other suggestive words. The word occurs four times, three times rendered " principalities " and once " beginning." Christ is the " Beginning " of those who will be raised from the dead (Col. 1 : 18), and the " Head of all principality and power " (Col. 2 : 20), and He is the Creator of all " beginnings " (" principalities ") and the One Who spoiled the " principalities " of evil (Col. 1 : 16 ; 2 : 15).

The thought of Christ as the Source, Substance and Chief

is expressed in many ways. Take but the first chapter, and He is said to be—

" The Image of the invisible God."

" Firstborn of every creature."

" All things were created by Him and for Him."

" He is before all things."

" In Him all things consist " (held together).

" Head of the body, the Church."

" Firstborn from the dead."

" In all things He might have the pre-eminence."

" In Him should all fulness dwell."

" Christ in you the Hope of glory."

" Present every man perfect in Christ Jesus."

4. **The chapter** in which the word " beginning " is focused with significant meaning is John 1, where we read, " In the beginning was the Word." " The same was in the beginning with God " (John 1 : 1, 2).* Before the beginning, the Word was, and He is the beginning of all that was, is, and is to be. Only He Who was without a beginning could make a beginning. Being without a beginning, He is without an end. Four times He is said to be " the Beginning " in the Revelation, and in three out of the four He is said, as a correlative, to be " the Ending " and " the End " (Rev. 1 : 8 ; 3 : 14 ; 21 : 6 ; 22 : 13). Those who know Him as " the Beginning will find Him unending in their experience.

5. **The corresponding word** in the Old Testament to arche is that which is found in Gen. 1. " In the beginning God created," or as we might read, " God, in beginning, created," etc. All things that ever were, are, and will be, owe their being to God. He is the Cause, Origin, and Source of all things. How essential in the spiritual realm to recognise we have no spiritual being or well-being until we own the hand of creative skill, and the heart of consecrating love !

6. There are many **derivations and associations** of the word arche, all of which have the thought of commencement and chief position.

---

* There are three chapters of John's writings in which Christ is referred to as " The Beginning " (see John 1 : 1 ; 1 John 1 : 1 ; Rev. 1 : 8).

Without giving the associations, the following will speak for themselves, and one illustrative passage will confirm :

Archegos. A chief leader. Used four times of Christ and rendered " Prince," " Captain," and " Author " (Acts 3 : 15 ; 5 : 31 ; Heb. 2 : 10 ; 12 : 2).

Archiereus. Used of Christ as the " High Priest " many times in the Epistle to the Hebrews and is also rendered " Chief Priest " (Matt. 2 : 4).

Archipoimen. A head shepherd, and used of Christ as " the Chief Shepherd " (1 Pet. 5 : 4).

Archaggelos. A chief angel (1 Thess. 4 : 16 ; Jude 9).

Archisunagogos. A director of the synagogue, services, and rendered " chief ruler of the synagogue " (Acts 18 : 17).

Architekton. A chief constructor, and rendered " master builder " (1 Cor. 3 : 10).

Architriklinos. A director of the entertainment, and rendered " governor of the feast " (John 2 : 8).

7. **The definite revelation** and the practical application of the use of this word as used of Christ is, that He should have the chief place in our lives, and should be the director of all our conduct. The associated words under point six may be used by way of illustration. Let us in the light of these words ask ourselves the following practical questions. Is Christ the Prince of our life, the Captain of our salvation, and the Author of our faith ? Is Christ the One Who leads us in devotion and consecration ? Will Christ have a reward for us when He returns as " the Chief Shepherd " ? Shall we be among the number that Christ will call to glory when He returns ? Does Christ dominate us in any service we may be doing in a religious sense ? Is Christ the Master Builder to form the temple of our character ? And does Christ direct us in all our pleasures ?

LORD

There are three prominent thoughts found in all references to Christ as Lord, and these are Ownership, especially where the title is used in the possessive case, as the " Lord's Table " (1 Cor. 10 : 21) : Authority, hence Paul said, " Lord, what wilt Thou have me to do ?" ; and Power, hence, when the Lord works with His people or through them, " the hand of the Lord " is said to be " with them " (Acts 11 : 21).

1. **The first time** that Kurios (Lord) occurs in the New Testament is Matt. 1 : 20, where we read that " the angel of the Lord appeared " unto Joseph about taking Mary, the mother of Jesus, to wife. Under the circumstances we can quite understand the hesitancy of Joseph, and in his quandary of thought we have the principle that should govern our actions ; namely, that when we are in uncertainty about anything, we should seek the Lord's will and act according to His instructions.

2. **The key verse** of Kurios is 1 Pet. 3 : 15, where we are exhorted to " sanctify " in our hearts " Christ as Lord " (R.V.). We naturally would read, " Sanctify your hearts to the Lord " ; but instead of that we are charged to set apart the Lord for our hearts. As King George was set apart to the throne of the British Empire by the Coronation Act, so Christ is to be crowned over the dominion of our being. It has been well said, " We do not crown Him Lord at all if we do not crown Him Lord of all."

3. **The central chapter** of the use of Kurios is Acts 9. The following outline covers nearly every phase of the subject : Opposition to the Lord (verse 1) ; Recognition of the Lord (verse 5) ; Claim of Jesus as Lord (verse 5) ; Question to the Lord (verse 6) ; Direction from the Lord (verse 6) ; Call of the Lord (verse 10) ; Response to the Lord (verse 10) ; Command from the Lord (verse 11) ; Hesitation before the Lord (verse 13) ; Choice of the Lord (verse 15) ; Sent from the Lord (verse 17) ; Testimony to the Lord (verse 27) ; Authority in the Lord (verse 29, R.V.) ; Walking in the fear of the Lord (verse 31) ; Conversion to the Lord (verse 35) ; Believing in the Lord (verse 42). A careful study of the chapter will reveal the following among other things : Submission to the Lord, Salvation by the Lord, Sanctification in the Lord, Service from the Lord, Sustainment by the Lord, Supremacy in the Lord, Sending by the Lord, and Supply through the Lord.

4. **The embodying Book** where Kurios is used is the Epistle to the Ephesians. The word is translated " Master " in chapter 6 : 9. Seven times the names of " Lord Jesus Christ " occur together (1 : 2, 3 ; 3 : 11, 14 ; 5 : 20 ; 6 : 23, 24). " Unto," or " to the Lord " as the One to Whom we are responsible, is mentioned four times (5 : 10, 19, 22 ; 6 : 7). " Of the Lord " is found five times (4 : 1 ; 5 : 17, 20 ; 6 : 4, 8 ; 4 : 1, should read as in the R.V., " In the Lord "). " In the Lord Jesus " occurs in chapter 1 : 15, and " In the Lord" seven times (2 : 21 ; 4 : 1, R.V. ; 4 : 17 ; 5 : 8 ; 6 : 1, 10, 21). Here again a prayerful study will repay. " From the Lord " are all our supplies ; " In the Lord " is the sphere of our movements ; " To the Lord " we are responsible for everything ; and knowing the will " of the Lord " is the secret of power and victory.

5. **The corresponding** word to Kurios in the Old Testament is Adonai. Girdlestone says : " The title indicates the truth that God is the owner of each member of the human family, and that He consequently claims the unrestricted obedience of all." Over 200 times in the Book of Ezekiel is Adonai used, and used in connection with the expression, " Saith the Lord God " (literally, Adonai-Jehovah). In Ezek. 16 the expression occurs eleven times (verses 3, 8, 14, 19, 23, 30, 36, 43, 48, 59, 63), and if the chapter is studied it will be seen that Adonai was the authority and power behind the messages of the prophet.

6. **The derivation.** Kurios is derived from Kuros, which means " supremacy," and therefore gives to Kurios the thought of one who is supreme in authority. Kurieuo, Kuriakos, Kuriotes, and Kuroo are all derived from the same root. Kurieuo means " to rule," and is rendered " exercise lordship over " (Luke 22 : 25), and " have dominion over " (Rom. 6 : 9, 14 ; 7 : 1 ; 2 Cor. 1 : 24). Kuriakos speaks of that which belongs to the Lord, as " the Lord's Supper " and " the Lord's Day " (1 Cor. 11 : 20 ; Rev. 1 : 10). Kuriotes signifies mastery, and is translated " dominion " and " government " (Eph. 1 : 21 ; Col. 1 : 16 ; 2 Pet. 2 : 10 ; Jude 8). Kuroo means to make authoritative or to ratify, and is rendered " confirm " (2 Cor. 2 : 8).

7. The practical application. No subject is more practical in its application than the Lordship of Jesus. Christ Himself enforces this when He says, " Ye call Me Master and Lord (Teacher and Owner) : and ye say well ; for so I am. If I then, your Lord and Master, have washed your feet, ye also ought to wash one another's feet " (John 13 : 13, 14). Notice that Christ puts the Lord first and then the Teacher. We cannot truly learn from Christ if we are not found in the place of obedience to Him.

It is not without significance that Judas Iscariot is never recorded to have called Jesus " Lord " (see Matt. 26 : 21-25), and that the other Judas when he called Christ " Lord " is said not to be Iscariot. If Judas had known Christ as Lord, he would never have acted as he did.

There are several duties that the Lord expects from us ; namely, to " call upon the name of the Lord," to " live unto the Lord " (Rom. 14 : 8), to " glory in the Lord " (1 Cor. 1 : 31), to be " faithful in the Lord " (1 Cor. 4 : 17), to " abound in the work of the Lord " (1 Cor. 15 : 58), to be " strong in the Lord " (Eph. 6 : 10), to " rejoice in the Lord " (Phil. 3 : 1), to " stand fast in the Lord " (Phil. 4 : 1), to " walk worthy of the Lord " (Col. 1 : 10), to " cleave unto the Lord " (Acts 11 : 23) ; and to remember that God has made " Jesus, Lord " (Phil. 2 : 11), that He is " Lord of all " (Acts 10 : 36), that " the same Lord is rich " (Rom. 10 : 12), and to depend upon the Holy Spirit that we may truly recognise that Jesus is the Lord (1 Cor. 12 : 3), for no one can truly call Him Lord but in the Spirit's power. Then we shall feel safe in His Ownership to act under His Authority, and we shall have the consciousness of His Power.

DISTINCTIVE STATEMENT

The conciseness of Scripture statement may be seen on almost every page of the Sacred Page. Ephesians 1 gives no less than 28 themes, each of which is pointed to with the index finger of the definite article in the Authorised Version.

" **The God** " (1 : 3, 17). " God," the Source of all things, is variously revealed. As " the God and Father of our Lord

Jesus Christ " He is made known as the Giver of all spiritual blessing, because of the intimate relationship existing between Him and Christ, and between Christ and the Believer, hence, the force and fulness of " our Lord Jesus Christ."

" **The Lord Jesus Christ** " (1 : 2, 15). All three names and title are given in verse 2, and " the Lord Jesus " in verse 15. " Grace and peace " come from " the Lord Jesus Christ," and " faith is in the Lord Jesus." As " Lord " He is the embodiment of peace, as " Jesus " He is the means of peace, and as " Christ " He is the centre of peace. Our faith is " in Jesus," for He is the One Who alone can save us ; and it is in " The Lord," for He alone can keep us.

" **The Spirit of Wisdom and Revelation** " (1 : 17). The Holy Spirit in His Supreme Personality is set forth in His perceptibility and penetration, hence, He alone can make us wise in " the knowledge of Him," Who is the Wisdom of God, and the apex of revelation. Inner illumination is requisite as well as outer revelation.

" **The Word of Truth** " (1 : 13). " The Word of Truth " has Christ for its Substance, the Holy Spirit as its Source, and " salvation " as its blessing. " Truth " is its principle, and " The Word " is its message.

" **The Will of God** " (1 : 1). There are four things said of " The Will." Paul is in his apostleship " by the will of God " (verse 1) ; the predestination of believers is " according to the good pleasure of His will " (verse 5) ; " The mystery," or the secret, " of His will " (verse 9) He has made known to us ; and " The counsel of His own will " (verse 11) is the basis of all His actions.

" **The Saints** " (1 : 1). " The Saints " is a title by which God calls His children. We are called " saints," and as " saints " we are to be saintly.

" **The Faithful** " (1 : 1). " The Faithful " are " in Christ Jesus." They cannot be faithful apart from Christ, but being " in " Him they are responsible to be faithful. Privilege brings responsibility.

" **The Foundation of the World** " (1 : 4). The Creator is the Producer of creation. The world is, because He is, but before it was, the saints were " chosen in Him." Redemption and the Church are no after-thought of God, but His pre-determination.

" **The Adoption of Children** " (1 : 5). Predestination is coupled with " adoption," and has reference to place and not to kinship. " The adoption " is " by " (by means of) " Jesus Christ," and is " unto Himself " as to end. Man finds everything and has all things when he finds God in Christ.

" **The Beloved** " (1 : 6). " The Beloved " is the Beloved Son. Believers are " made accepted in " Him. God made and God blessed, we are blessed indeed, for we are as He is. Grace blesses the graceless, and makes them as the Graced One of God.

" **The Glory of His Grace** " (1 : 6). The glory of grace is to give to the undeserving, the glory of grace and the grace of glory. " Bread enough and to spare," " the best robe," the ring and the shoes, as well as the fatted calf, are what the prodigal received from the Father when he came to Him.

" **The Forgiveness of Sins** " (1 : 7). " Forgiveness " in its meaning is more than pardon. Forgiveness is not only a cancelling of the sentence upon the guilty, but is a letting go from the sins which brought the guilt. This is by means of the blood of Christ.

" **The Riches of His Grace** " (1 : 7). The measure of God's bestowments is not " out of His riches," but " according to His riches " and " the riches of His grace." If a beggar is helped " out " of a millionaire's riches he is helped, but if he is helped " according to " the riches of the millionaire, he ceases to be a beggar.

" **The Fulness of Times** " (1 : 10). " The fulness of times " points on to the golden age beyond the millennium, when sin, curse, sorrow, and death will cease to exist, and " all things " will converge in Christ, and bow to Him in loving adoration and praise.

" **The Praise of His Glory** " (1 : 12, 14). Glory is the excellence of anything in display, like the flash of the facets of the diamond. What His grace has done, is doing, and will do will enhance His glory.

" The Gospel of Your Salvation " (1 : 13). The gospel is the good news that Christ died for our sins and rose again for our justification, hence, we are saved from sin's penalty, pollution, power, and presence.

" The Earnest " (1 : 13). " The Earnest " is a part of the whole. The whole is a glorified body in a glorious state from which it will be impossible to fall, hence, " The Spirit of Promise " is the seal to the contract.

" The Redemption of the Purchased Possession " (1 : 14). " The purchased possession " is the inheritance which the Lord has acquired for Himself, and which He has acquired for us. When He returns for His own, He will coo they get all He has determined to give them, and fully release them from every hindering thing.

" The Father of Glory " (1 : 17). Every qualifying sentence means He will qualify every qualification. The glory of the Father which Christ prayed His own might enjoy, will be given by the Father of Glory.

" The Knowledge of Him " (1 : 17). The knowledge indicated is the full knowledge of personal acquaintance. To know the Lord is the sum of all knowledge. The classic injunction of Greece was, " O man, know thyself." The substance and secret of Christianity is, " O man, know thy God."

" The Eyes of Your Understanding " (1 : 18). The mind that is darkened by sin and unbelief is in the gross darkness of condemnation and superstition, but the heart that is cleansed and illuminated is in the light of truth, and love, and grace.

" The Hope of His Calling " (1 : 18). To think God's thoughts after Him is to find how much He thinks of us. Low thoughts of God lead to low thoughts of life. " The Hope of His Calling " is what the Lord longs for us.

" The Riches of the Glory of His Inheritance in the Saints " (1 : 18). To know what the Lord has in His saints is to give them a lofty conception of what they are to Him. The Lord's portion is His people.

" **The Exceeding Greatness of His Power** " (1 : 19). Creation reveals the power of God's creative skill, but Christ's resurrection unfolds to us the effectiveness of His supernatural act.

" **The Working of His Mighty Power** " (1 : 19). "Resurrection" manifests "the might of His power" (margin). Christ, in rising from the dead, went through the swathing that enwrapped His body without disturbing a thread.

" **The Heavenly Places** " (1 : 20). "The Heavenlies" is used in contrast to the Earthlies. It denotes the sphere of the believer's oneness with Christ, hence, he is a pilgrim and a stranger on the earth.

" **The Church** " (1 : 22). The error of Christendom is "It is the Church which makes Christians," the truth of the Spirit is, Believers in Christ constitute the Church.

" **The Fulness of Him that Filleth all in all** " (1 : 23). The revelation of the Epistle to the Colossians is, Christ is God's fulness and the Church's fulness, but the unfolding of Ephesians is, the Church is Christ's fulness. The Body completes the Head, and the Head is the complement of the Body.

As we scan this brief summary of specific mention of Ephesians 1 we behold how vast is the country seen, and how many truths are made known. The following doctrines are indicated : The doctrine or teaching of God, the Lord Jesus Christ, the Holy Spirit, the Word of Truth, God's Will, the Saints, the Faithful, the World, Adoption, the Beloved, Grace, Forgiveness, Riches of Grace, Fulness of Times, Glory, the Gospel, the Earnest, Redemption, the Father, Knowledge, the Mind, Hope, Inheritance, Power, Resurrection, the Heavenlies, the Church, and Union.

Practically every doctrine of the Bible is mentioned, either specifically or inferentially, in the chapter. All Theology is covered by the following ten Doctrines : The Bible, God, Christ, the Holy Spirit, Sin, Salvation, Angels, the Church, Man, and the Last Things.

12

THE EYES OF A PROPHETIC OUTLOOK

IN the Christian life there are many outlooks. There is the outlook of faith, which counts upon the Lord to meet its need. There is the outlook of love, which sympathetically cares for others and supplies their wants. There is the outlook of carefulness, which by its forethought and service anticipates the emergency which may arise. There is the outlook of hope, which prepares itself for the future with the buoyancy of expectancy, and waits with ardent desire for the coming of the Lord ; and there is the outlook of interest, which watches the current course of events, and knows by their developments what issues are in their portent.

God's Outlook. Everything with God is an eternal Now, and known unto Him are all His ways from the beginning.

> " When heaven and earth were yet unmade,
>   When Time was yet unknown,
>   Thou in Thy bliss and majesty
>   Didst live and love alone !
>   Thou wert not born ; there was no fount
>   From which Thy Being flowed,
>   There is no end which Thou canst reach :
>   But Thou art simply God."

Yet we find God speaks after the manner of men, and anticipates what is, as though it were to be. Thoughts are many, like the flakes in a snowstorm, as we think of God's outlook. So let us haste away to that oasis of revelation, where God is associated with Christ in His suffering and glory. There is a two-fold pleasure spoken of in Isa. 53, namely, " Yet it pleased Jehovah to bruise Him ; He hath put Him to grief ; when Thou shalt make His soul an offering for sin, He shall see His seed, He shall prolong His days, and the pleasure of Jehovah shall prosper in His hand."

The " yet " with which this verse begins is important, for it connects with what goes before, and that which goes before speaks of the perfection of the Perfect Life of the Perfect Christ. " Yet it pleased Jehovah to bruise Him." Surely that pleasure was because of the pleasure of His purpose, for whom that pleasure was to bring pleasure ? And because of the pleasure which Jehovah had in bruising or crushing Christ, the pleasure of Jehovah shall prosper in the hands of the Bruised One. Thus a double pleasure is indicated.

The word " Pleasure " speaks of an inward pleasure and delight. It is rendered " Purpose " in Eccles. 3 : 1, " Delight " in Psa. 1 : 2, " Desire " in 1 Kings 10 : 13, " Willingly " in Prov. 31 : 13, " Pleasant " in Isa. 54 : 12, and " Acceptable " in Eccles. 12 : 10. Each of these words may be used to express the outlook of God, for He will fulfil the " purpose " of His grace to glorify those whom He has called (Rom. 8 : 30). He will " delight " to " rejoice " over a redeemed Israel " with joy " (Zeph. 3 : 17). His " desire " is expressed in the loving words of " I will betroth thee to Me . . . in lovingkindness and faithfulness, and thou shalt know Me as Jehovah " (Hos. 2 : 19, 20). His willingness to bless is stated in the loving words, " I will rejoice over them to do them good " (Jer. 32 : 41). And there is a time coming when " Judah and Jerusalem " will " be pleasant unto Jehovah," " as in former years " (Mal. 3 : 4).

Christ's Outlook   When Christ first came He had two things before Him, namely, " His sufferings and the glory that should follow " (Luke 24 : 26). The bitterness of the Cross lies behind, and the brightness of the Crown lies before Him. When Daniel saw the world-powers depicted in the Image and Four Wild Beasts (Dan. 2 and 7), he saw also the powers and their " dominion taken away," and further the Ancient of Days gave to the Son of Man " dominion and glory," and all nations are made to serve Him (Dan. 7 : 12-14). What that glory will be in its manifold splendour we cannot fully comprehend, but at least it will be sevenfold in its manifestation. He will have the glory of peculiar honour in having the Name which is above every name (Phil. 2 : 9). He will have position above every position, for He will be King of kings and Lord of lords (Rev. 19 : 16). He will have

the outshining of majestic power which will crush the
opposition of the Man of Sin (2 Thess. 2 : 8). He will have
the glory of unsurpassed victory for He will overthrow the
great usurper and consign him into the Lake of Fire (Rev.
20 : 2, 10). He will have the glory of a majestic reign as
given in detail in Psa. 72. He will have the glory of being
glorified in His saints (2 Thess. 1 : 10). And He will have
the glory of the glorified Lamb lighting up the New Heavens
and the New Earth (Rev. 21 : 23). What an outlook for
Him when He shall see the travail of His soul and be satisfied.

The Believer's Outlook   Briefly summarised, we may
say there is a sevenfold outlook of blessing before the believer.
We shall " meet " Christ (1 Thess. 4 : 17), and that means, as
the word " meet " suggests, we shall be caught up to meet
Him in the air, and come back with Him to the earth. We
shall " see Him as He is " (1 John 3 : 2), not as He was, in
humiliation and death, but as He is in glory and incorruptibility. We shall be received by Him (John 14 : 3), as
He promised, " I will receive you to Myself," which means
He will take us to His heart. We shall stand before Him
that our life and service may be tested, and our conduct
towards our fellow-believers scrutinised (Rom. 14 : 10 ;
1 Cor. 3 : 12-15 ; 4 : 5 ; 2 Cor. 5 : 10). We shall be rewarded
by Him, for when we stand before the judgment seat of
Christ it is that " each " may have his " praise from God "
(1 Cor. 4 : 5). We shall be " like " Him in all the beauty of
His manhood, and His body of glory (1 John 3 : 2 ; Phil.
3 : 20, 21) ; and we shall be with Him and have the joy of
His companionship forever (1 Thess. 4 : 17).

The World's Outlook   Long ago Jehovah asked the
question, " Why do the nations tumultuously assemble, and
the peoples meditate a vain thing ?" (Margin R.V., Psa. 2 : 1).
When the Great War was in progress we were told, " It was
a war to end war," but, alas ! the ideal has not become
actual ! Leagues, conferences, and representatives of the
Powers have met, and broken up ; but we are still wanting a
working and peaceful policy. The rulers " take counsel
together," or gather by appointment, as the sentence is ; but

how apt is the Spirit's word : their assemblies are tumultuous, and they " meditate " an empty thing. How much wiser is the " Blessed Man " of Psa. 1 : 2, who meditates on the law of the Lord ! The nations are out to get what they can for themselves ; whereas, if they sought what is given in God's Word, and acted accordingly, they would benefit themselves and others. What does the world itself want ? It wants a great ruler to consolidate things, and lead the nations. " The Times " some years ago said, " What is it that all Europe is looking for ? It is the King of men. . . . He must be a scholar, a statesman, a man of unflinching courage and irrepressible enterprise, full of resource and ready to look the world in the face of a rival." Such a man will be found in the Man of Sin, described in 2 Thess. 2 : 3-12.

Creation's Outlook Creation is waiting for " the manifestation of the sons of God " (Rom. 8 : 19). Believers are waiting for the Son of God, but creation is " waiting for the sons of God." God's fair creation was blasted and blighted by man's sin, and brought into bondage and limitation ; but when believers are glorified, creation will be delivered into the " liberty of the glory of the children of God " (Rom. 8 : 21, R.V.). One has well said, in speaking of creation's outlook : " Nature with its melancholy charm resembles a bride, who at the very moment when she was fully attired for marriage saw the bridegroom to whom she was to be united die on the very day fixed for the marriage. She still stands with her fresh crown and in her bridal dress, but her eyes are full of tears." But, besides the " tears," her eyes are full of hope, hence, she is waiting. The word " waiteth " is a compound one, and suggests one who is waiting to receive something out of the hands of another, who extends it to that one from afar. That " something " will be " liberty of the glory " when she will no longer

> " Be bathed in tears and blood,"

but

> " Be blessed with the sons of God."

The Jewish Outlook One has said, " Keep your eyes on Palestine. True in Disraeli's day, truer to-day. Jews,

Arabs, Turks, British, French, Italian, all realize that
Palestine is the coming centre. The Jews are gathering back
in thousands, millions of vines have been planted, property
is stabilised, the latter rain is falling, railways are spreading,
electric and other schemes developing, and the desert beginning once more to blossom as the rose. The land is
getting ready for the people, the city is getting ready for the
King. When ye see these things, ' Look up,' ' the coming
of the Lord draweth nigh.' ''

While all these things are in the present Jewish outlook,
before the Lord comes with His saints, the time of " Jacob's
trouble " must take place (Jer. 30 : 7), the like of which has
never happened before in the history of the world (Dan.
12 : 1 ; Matt. 24 : 21), when a covenant will be made with
the Antichrist (Dan. 9 : 26, 27), when two-thirds of the
inhabitants of the land will be " cut off " (Zech. 13 : 8) ;
but it is just at that time the Lord will appear in Person
and deliver His earthly people (Zech. 14), and the Jewish
nation will own Jesus of Nazareth, the pierced One of
Calvary, to be their Promised Messiah (Zech. 12 : 10).

The Personal Outlook When Christ came the first
time, there were those who were " looking for redemption,"
and among them was the godly Anna (Luke 2 : 36-38).
That same attitude should be ours in relation to Christ's
return. To this end we are exhorted to be " looking for that
Blessed Hope, and the glorious appearing of our great God
and Saviour Jesus Christ " (Titus 2 : 13). To be occupied
with present things only, is to become like the things with
which we are occupied. The word " look " in both of the
above passages signifies to receive to one's self, and when
used of things in the future, to wait for with an ardent
expectancy. In worldly callings men have recognized the
influence of looking ahead. The following incident illustrates :

" One day I ventured," said the secretary of the late
Lord Northcliffe, " to ask him, ' Tell me, did you ever imagine
in your very young days you would have such a successful
life ?' He replied, ' I attribute my success, as you call it,

to seeing ahead. I did not think my school-fellows were stupid, but I could always see further than they could.' "

Are we looking for the coming of our Lord personally ? This is a personal message. We cannot truly live in the present of our Christian life if we are not expecting Him.

Men's Outlook   A writer in " The Times " says of the future : " ' He hath set eternity in their hearts.' This phrase, as it stands, represents a truth of large significance. There is infinity outside us, and over against it we find eternity within us. We can never fully gauge or apprehend either. We are unable to reach far into their mysterious borders, but there is always something both within and without us beyond our understandings, our affections, and our moral powers. They are the source of the most real, the most powerful, the most awful and most inspiring experiences of life.   Professor Edward Caird declared that we must first discover the infinite in the impossibility of being satisfied with the finite, or limiting our thoughts to it. The recognition of the infinite is the silent presupposition of true manhood.   Man is never content to rest in an object which he can entirely apprehend.   He must go out into the unknown, into the infinite. And when he turns within himself, he finds that there also he is carried beyond the range of things temporal to experiences which imply the existence of spiritual realities deeper than those he is able to fathom. In the secret fountains of personality the supernatural is real and satisfying. We could have but little happiness in the world and could recognize but little of our meaning of human life if they did not lead us beyond ourselves."

The Condition for True Outlook   One other character who is mentioned, as well as Anna, who was looking for Christ's first coming, is Simeon ; and what is said of him and her may suggest the condition we should be in, in heart and life in order to be ready for His arrival.   Of Simeon it is said, " He was just and devout, and the Holy Spirit was upon him," and Anna is described as serving God with fastings and prayers, and that she also " spake " of Christ's advent (Luke 2 : 25-38). Simeon was " just," that is, he was a man who was in a right condition of life and was fulfilling all claims which were right and becoming. He is also described as being " devout," and to be devout means to be taking hold of things in a circumspect way in relation to the Lord. And further, the Holy Spirit is said to have been put upon him, as indicating the power which enabled him not only to wait for Christ, but to be what he was. Anna is described as serving God, and the word " serve " indicates to sacrifice ; hence, to truly worship the Lord. Coupled with her serving, she is said to have prayed and fasted. Fasting, of course, indicates abstinence from food, and prayer speaks of seeking aid in a consciousness of personal insufficiency. Further, it is said of Anna that she " spake " to others about the coming Christ.

Shall we not have the same characteristics if we are looking for Christ in His second Advent ? We shall be just in all our transactions with men, and righteous in our personal life ; and devout, that is, ardent in all the things which relate to the service of the Lord, recognizing the only power that can qualify us for the things of God is the Holy Spirit Himself ; serving the Lord in glad surrender till we feel its sacrifice ; abstinence from things which are proper and necessary in the ordinary course of things, but counting it a privilege to give up the ordinary for the Lord's extraordinary service ; prayer will ever express itself in a sense of personal need, for true prayer is ever the recognition of our inability which gives God the opportunity to display His efficiency and sufficiency ; and with these things operating in our hearts and lives, we cannot but speak of Him Who is coming again, and there will be response to our testimony, even as there was from Anna's, to all who are looking for the coming Christ.

THE IMPORTANCE OF THE PROPHETIC
OUTLOOK

The importance of any given thing may be seen by pondering its relationship. For instance, in the fictitious account of Robinson Crusoe, it was proof positive that the footprint upon the sand must have been made by an individual. The imprint declared the naked foot that made it. As the impression upon the seashore evidenced a relationship between it and the man Friday ; so, when we turn to the truths of the Bible, we find each one has a relationship to the advent of our Lord. There are at least nine great outstanding doctrines, namely :

> The Doctrine of the Bible.
> The Doctrine of God.
> The Doctrine of Christ.
> The Doctrine of the Holy Spirit.
> The Doctrine of Man.
> The Doctrine of Salvation.
> The Doctrine of Sin.
> The Doctrine of the Church.
> The Doctrine of the Last Things.

The Bible and Christ's Return One of the " take heeds " of the Spirit is, " Take heed to the sure Word of prophecy." We can better apprehend the importance of this injunction if we give the Revised reading, and leave out the word " made "—" And we have the word of prophecy, more sure " (2 Pet. 1 : 19). The Apostle has been speaking of the " power and coming of our Lord Jesus Christ." We are not all privileged to have visions, but we have something " more sure," that is, the " sure word of prophecy." The transfiguration was limited and passing. " The sure word " is lasting and for all. The vision was the flashing forth of the glory for a moment ; but the " sure word " is a " lamp," constant in its " shining," and it shines in its forth-gleaming " until the day dawn " of Christ's Millennial reign, and " until the day-star " of His coming for His own ; hence, we do well to " take heed to it in our hearts." Prophecy, according to modernism, is the application of history ; but we believe it is history made known before it comes to pass. It is " sure " because He, Who knows everything from the beginning, makes it known.

God, and Christ's Coming In the earliest of the apostolic writings, we find Paul closing his first epistle to

the saints in Thessalonica with these benedicting words:
" And the God of Peace Himself sanctify you wholly ; and
may your spirit and soul and body be preserved entire,
without blame, at the coming of our Lord Jesus Christ"
(I Thess. 5 : 23, R.V.). God and the coming of Christ are
the Genesis and Revelation of this verse. " The God of
Peace " is the God of Infinite Calm, and He alone can give
what He desires ; so we do well to pray with Augustine :
" Give, Lord, what Thou dost command, and then command
what Thou wilt." He can preserve, as the salt keeps the meat
from putrefaction, the spirit of our being in fellowship with
Himself, the soul of our affection, and the body of our senses,
so that they shall be " wanting in nothing," and be in " perfect soundness " (see Jas. I : 4 ; Acts 3 : 16, where the word
" whole " in A.V. and its cognate are rendered " entire " and
" perfect soundness "). As the altar, mentioned in Deut.
27 : 6, was to be built of unchipped or unbroken stones, so
the being of the believer is to be unbroken by the world of
sin, and unchipped by self-effort. This preservation is
emphasized by the word " preserved," which might be
rendered " kept," " reserved," and is so given in 2 Tim. 4 : 7
and I Pet. I : 4, and is used of Peter being " kept in prison "
(Acts 12 : 5, 6) ; and this keeping is to blamelessness (see
how the word is used in I Thess. 2 : 10 ; 3 : 13) ; and all this
is " unto the coming of our Lord," or, as it literally is, " in "
(ev), " the coming of our Lord." If He finds us when He
returns thus free from blame by God's preservation, it will
be seen what He has done for us, and we shall not be ashamed.

Christ, and His Return The last message of Christ
to John was, " Behold, I come quickly ; and My reward is
with Me, to give to every man according as his work shall
be " (Rev. 22 : 12). Christ calls special attention to His
return by the arresting injunction " Behold." He calls to
our direct notice that He is about to return. " I am coming "
is a better reading than " I come," for it proclaims the act
of His coming which will be consummated in the fact. Many
have wondered what Christ meant when He said, " Behold,
I come quickly." To us, in our hurry, " quickly " seems
slowly. May I suggest that there is an explanation to His

" I come quickly." When He starts He will come quickly, just as we might say to a friend, " When I come to you, I shall come by a quick train and not a slow one," meaning of course, the method of travelling, and not the time of starting.

Then He declares the purpose of His coming is to " reward every man according as His work shall be." This at once proclaims His personal interest in all we do, and His pledge to recompense all who do anything out of love to Him.

The Holy Spirit, and Christ's Coming   One of the promises of Christ was, the Holy Spirit would reveal to us " things to come " ; and one of the first things He uttered through the lips of the Apostle Peter, who, having first referred to the sufferings, resurrection and ascension of Christ, was, God would " send Jesus Christ " again, and lest we should be in any doubt about His meaning, he further states : " Whom the heavens must receive until the times of restitution of all things, which God hath spoken by the mouth of all His holy prophets " (Acts 3 : 21). The one outstanding feature of Peter's message is the identity of Christ's second coming with His first. The one cannot be denied without ignoring the other. Calvin says : " In plucking up the faith of Christ's coming, Satan aims directly at the throat of the Church. For to what end did Christ die and rise again, but that along with Himself He might redeem us from death, and gather us into eternal life ? " Christ's death, resurrection, and advent are the trinity of the Gospel. To leave out any one of them is to destroy the triangle of truth. Mark how the Spirit of God couples them in 1 Thess. 4 : 14 : " For since we believe Jesus died and rose again, even so them also who sleep in Jesus will God bring with Him." The Gospel is throttled when any one of the facts of Christ's Death, Resurrection, and Advent is omitted. If the above are carefully studied it will be found this triangle of truth is ever presented.

Man, and Christ's Coming   When God created man an indestructible spirit, His purpose was that man might " have dominion " over His works (Gen. 1 : 26). Absolute

dominion has been lost by man's sin, hence, " We see not all
things put under him, but we see Jesus, who was made a
little lower than the angels, for the suffering of death,
crowned with glory and honour." Some hold the " glory
and honour " (Heb. 2 : 9) have reference to Christ as being
coronated before His death ; but the whole tenor of Scripture indicates that the " glory and honour " are because of
His death, and this is certainly proved by the " For."
" Dia," rendered " for " when with the accusative signifies
the reason of an act, or the ground of something which
follows ; therefore, the reason of His being crowned with
" glory and honour " is because of His suffering unto death.
Then we should remember what the Spirit already had said
in connection with Christ's return, namely, " When He
bringeth again the First-begotten into the world " (Heb.
1 : 6, margin). When Christ first came, He was " the Only-
begotten " (John 3 : 16), but as the " First-begotten " He is
seen in resurrection as the One Who brings the many sons
to glory. The whole argument of Heb. 1 and 2 is, Christ as
the Man, has regained what man had lost by sin, and the
men who are identified with Him will share that dominion.

Salvation, and Christ's Coming There is a goal, as
well as a crisis and a process, in relation to salvation. There
is one sentence which expresses it, namely, " Unto salvation " (Heb. 9 : 28 ; 1 Pet. 1 : 5 ; Rom. 13 : 11 ; 1 Thess.
5 : 8, 9) ; hence we look for a body of glory (Phil. 3 : 20, 21).
This future salvation will be " revealed in the last time,"
that is, when our Lord arrives in Person. He alone can
accomplish the work of atonement, to free us from the
penalty of sin. He alone can fill the office of Priest, to save
us from the power and pollution of sin. He alone can live
out His life of holiness to reproduce His own character in us.
And He alone can complete our redemption, by freeing us
from the body of sin, and saving us to a body which shall
make us like to Him. He shall one day look upon us, and
see His likeness in us, then shall He be glorified in His saints,
and be admired in them. There will not only be a translation to be with Him, but a transformation, which will make
us like Him. " He shall fashion anew the body of our

humiliation," or, as someone has rendered it, " He will re-construct the body of our abasement." What that recon-struction will mean, we may gather from the glorified Christ, as seen on the Mount of Transfiguration, and the detailed description of Christ as given in Rev. 1.

Sin, and Christ's Coming In Heb. 9 : 26-28 we have two appearings mentioned. Christ's past purpose in coming into the world is distinctly and definitely stated : " He appeared to put away sin by the sacrifice of Himself." Sin was the hindrance that kept God from man, and man from God, and He, at the expense of His life, put it away ; removed it out of the way, so that man can now come to God. He shall appear the second time without sin ; that is, without a sin-offering. His atoning work on the Cross was complete, sufficient and eternal ; hence, there is no need to repeat it ; but He comes forth the second time to complete our salvation. As Aaron, after the great work of expiation on the day of atonement, came forth clothed again in his garments of glory and beauty to bless the people, so Christ shall come, not in humiliation, but in power and great glory, to receive His own to Himself, and vindicate Himself and His people.

The Church, and Christ's Coming When we speak of the Church, we mean what Robertson, of Brighton, indicated when he said : " According to the High Church party in the Established Church, it is the Church which makes Christians ; but we believe it is the Christians which make the Church." Men deal in labels and adjectives to describe the Church, but the Lord speaks of " My Church," and says, in so many words : " Life counts, not labels." In reading such a pas-sage as 1 Cor. 1, we find believers addressed as " the Church of God which is at Corinth, to them that are sanctified in Christ," and to these " saints " the Spirit urges, that they be " waiting for the coming of our Lord Jesus Christ " ; and in each of the Church epistles we find similar exhortations. It might be an interesting study to see in the Church epistles the relative importance, not only to the doctrines of the Word of God, but also to the ordinances and practices of the

Church. To note but one or two. The Lord's Supper is observed "till He come" (1 Cor. 11 : 26) ; discipline is exercised now, that the spirit may be saved in "the day of the Lord Jesus" (1 Cor. 5 : 5) ; saints are not to go to law, because they are going to judge angels, and the world (1 Cor. 6 : 1-8) ; saints are not to judge anything "until the Lord come" (1 Cor. 4 : 3-5) ; saints are to "wait for the Hope of Righteousness by faith" (Gal. 5 : 5) ; we are to be living in the light of the Blessed Hope (Titus 2 : 13) ; we are not to sleep, because the day of the Lord cometh (1 Thess. 5 : 1-9) ; we are to comfort one another in sorrow, with the hope of being caught up to meet Him (1 Thess. 4 : 13-18) ; and we are to be faithful in service and life, and love His appearing, that we may obtain the crown of righteousness (2 Tim. 4 : 1-8). Such injunctions are repeated again and again, and all in the light of the Lord's return.

The Last Things, and Christ's Return   The "last enemy" will be destroyed (1 Cor. 15 : 26), the "last trump" will be sounded (1 Cor. 15 : 52), the "last plagues" will be ended (Rev. 21 : 9), and the "last day" will arrive, when the Lord comes.

It is a mystery how anyone can honestly read the Bible without seeing the truth of the Second Advent. Sir Isaac Newton, in speaking of prejudice, said it was difficult to light a candle when the extinguisher was on. So when men place their self-made extinguishers upon the candle of truth, no light is possible ; but let an unbiassed mind and an unprejudiced reader ponder the pages of the Scriptures, and the Blessed Hope and the appearing of our Lord is evident beyond all dispute.

Further, let it be said, if any preacher or Christian worker fails to witness to this truth, he is keeping back part of the Divine Revelation. Christ's command to His disciples is : "Teach all things that I have commanded you." He promised He would come again, He has commanded us "all" to watch ; and He has pledged that the faithful servants shall be rewarded, and honoured, if He finds us faithful to Him.

LUMINOUS WORDS WHICH SPEAK OF THE OUTLOOK

There are certain great words in the New Testament which have a soul of embodying meaning, and from them there shines forth a revelation of conditions which relate to the life of the future. Some of these are " Translation," " Transformation," " Eternal Life," " Glory," " Conformation," " Immortality," and " Transfiguration."

" Eternal Life," or the life that is eternal, suggests a life that corresponds to God's nature. " Translation " conveys the thought of a removal to another sphere. " Transformation " embodies the fact of a changed condition. " Immortality " proclaims the incorruptibility of a glorified body. " Conformation " speaks of a likeness to a pattern. " Glory " is the excellence of anything in display. " Transfiguration " proclaims the outcome of the changed internal in a perfect luminosity of expression.

Eternal Life The positive blessing of the Gospel is Eternal Life. Christ declared that those who " believe on Him " possess this life, and that those who do not believe on Him shall not see life (John 3 : 16, 36). This life is more than existence. All men are indestructible spirits, because they are created in the image of God ; for, as Dale says, " The image of God in man refers to nature, and not to character." We must distinguish between survival after death, and a state of bliss forever. The unsaved survive after death, but they do not possess the life that is eternal. Here, again, we must distinguish between eternal existence and eternal life. Man, being a spirit, lives on as long as Jehovah lives, for " the spirit of man is the lamp of Jehovah " (Prov. 20 : 27), but the believer is eternally in union with the Father and the Son.

Dr. Westcott says on eternal life, " Eternal life is not an endless duration of being in time, but being of which time is not a measure. It is beyond the limitations of time : it belongs to the being of God." We need to emphasize the last sentence, " eternal life belongs to the being of God."

God in the essence of His Being " is love." The being of God
may be compared to a circle. Man is outside that circle, and
cannot get into it by himself. God, in the Person of His Son,
has broken the circle, and the entrance into it is by the
atoning work of Christ ; hence, Christ says, " I am the Way,
the Truth, and the Life, and no man cometh to the Father
but by means of Me."

Translation Of Enoch, it is said he was " Translated
that he should not see death, and was not found, because
God had translated him, for before his translation he had
this testimony, that he pleased God " (Heb. 11 : 5). The
meaning of " metatithemi " and " metathesis " embodies
two things, removal and change. These words are employed
to describe the carrying over of a body from one place to
another, as Jacob was " carried over " from Egypt to Sychem
(Acts 7 : 16) ; to denote those who are " removed " from
the position of the liberty of the Gospel to the legalism of
law, as Paul declared of the Galatians (Gal. 1 : 6) ; as
describing those who are " turning " the grace of God into
lasciviousness (Jude 4) ; as pointing to the " removing " of
one order of things to bring in another (Heb. 12 : 27) ; and
to the " change " effected by the bringing in of the Melchisedec priesthood, which displaced the Aaronic priesthood
(Heb. 7 : 12). Looking at these words, we find there are
two thoughts suggested. First, the removal of an object
from one place to another ; and second, an internal change
effected.

Enoch's translation, therefore, speaks of two things : the
removal of himself from the present life to a higher ; and
the necessary change to fit him for that new sphere in which
he found himself. This is implied in the qualifying statements, " He was not found," and " should not see death."
As to his body, it evidently was searched for, but he was not
found, and he had undergone a change, for he did not " see
death," that is, experience the dissolution caused by death.
Is not this a type of what will take place when Christ removes
His own to be with Himself ? A beloved brother, an M.D.,
is reported to have said, " When Christ comes for His own,
He will take their spirits to be with Himself ; but He will

leave their bodies behind in death, and their friends will find their dead bodies." Surely this cannot be in the light of the translation referred to ! But the translation is that for which we long, if, like Enoch, we walk with God, and we are well-pleasing to Him.

Transformation One of the things the Lord will do when He returns is, " He will fashion anew the body of our humiliation " (Phil. 3 : 21, R.V.). " Change " or " Fashion " means to change the form of anything ; hence, to transform. The word is " metaschematizo." " Meta " means " with " ; hence, an accompaniment, and the other part of the word is derived from " schema," which means a figure as seen in the external form, and is rendered " fashion " in referring to the " fashion " of the world in its present form, and to Christ as He appeared in " fashion " as a man (1 Cor. 7 : 31 ; Phil. 2 : 8) ; but the compound word, " meta-schematizo," means to " fashion with another," and is rendered " transformed " when Satan is identified with an angel of light and makes himself to appear as one (2 Cor. 11 : 13-15).

One has rendered the words, " fashion anew the body of our humiliation," as " He will reconstruct the body of our abasement." What that reconstruction will mean we have some idea from the transfiguration scene, and also from the description of Christ's glorified body in Rev. 1. We see something of what wonderful transformations God can accomplish in His works. Who would ever think that the beautiful dragon-fly, with its wings of gauze, with its sheen of brightness, with its coat of mail, with its variegated colour, with its lightning movement, with its wonderful body, and with its hum of pleasing sound, was once a grub which had its home in some muddy pool ! That is a picture of the change that will take place when the Lord transforms His saints.

Conformation " Change " or " fashion " does not convey all the Lord intends for the redeemed, so we have the added assurance we shall be " fashioned like His glorious body," or as the R.V., " Conformed to the body of His glory." The word " conformed " is " sum-morphos." The

prefix " sum " is from the preposition " sun," which means
" union with " ; and " morphos " is from " morphe," which
signifies " form," and is three times used of Christ, Who was
in the form of God, and yet took upon Him the " form of a
servant " (Phil. 2 : 6, 7), and who appeared to some of His
disciples, after His resurrection, " in another form " (Mark
16 : 12). In its compound form " sum-morphos " denotes
association with, and having form like to another. Therefore, when we are told Christ shall " change " or " fashion "
anew our body, it means to change into another form of
character, but this does not tell us what the character will
be ; hence the necessity for the positive statement, " That it
may be conformed to His body of glory." " Like Him "
expresses all that is meant, and all that is needed. He went
to heaven in the hey-day of His perfect manhood, and what
that body of glory is, we have described in a detailed unfolding
in Revelation, where Christ in His glory is unveiled as the
Son of Man (Phil. 3 : 20, 21, R.V.)

Immortality Man's thought of immortality is deathlessness ; hence, he speaks of " the immortality of the soul ; "
but the thought in the New Testament is the incorruptibility
of the body ; hence, what is meant by immortality is a state
of holiness and bliss in a glorified body, from which it will be
impossible to fall.

The late Dr. J. Anderson, of Brighton, says : " It is
important to distinguish between the survival of the soul
and spirit after the death of the body, and the alleged immortality of man by creation. That Adam, when first created
did not possess an absolute and inherent immortality is
clearly shown by the conditions imposed upon him, namely,
that he should not eat of the tree of knowledge of good and
evil. He might have had immortality, yet by disobeying
the Divine commands he lost the capacity to become
immortal, and was driven from Eden, lest he should put forth
his hand and take of the tree of life, and live forever. . . .
The believer's immortality does not arrive from a natural
immortality at his creation, but solely and entirely by reason
of his union and identification with the Lord Jesus Christ.

This union is an organic union, and the immortal life of the believer arises from the fact that 'because I live,' says Christ, 'ye shall live also.'"

The great resurrection chapter plainly indicates that it is not until Christ returns that the dead will be raised incorruptible, and the living ones will be changed. For it is "then," and not till then, that corruption shall put on incorruption. For that blissful hour we wait ; but it will arrive, for the sure word is, " This mortal must put on immortality," and it "shall come to pass," and then we shall know " Death is swallowed up in victory " (1 Cor. 15 : 50-55). Ponder the emphatic words, " must," " shall," and " is."

Transfiguration The scene on the Mount of Transfiguration is a type, as Peter declared, of the coming glory of Christ's kingdom.

" We made known unto you the power and coming of our Lord Jesus Christ, but were eye-witnesses of His majesty . . . when we were with Him in the Holy Mount " (2 Pet. 1 : 16-18). The different touches of that scene are suggestive. Matthew says, " He was transfigured . . . and His face did shine as the sun, and His raiment was white, as the light " (Matt. 17 : 2). Mark says, " His raiment became shining, exceeding white as snow, so that no fuller on earth can white them " (Mark 9 : 3). Luke records, " The fashion of His countenance was altered, and His raiment was white and glistening " (Luke 9 : 29). There also " appeared in glory with Him " Moses and Elijah. The word " transfigured " is rendered " transformed " in Rom. 12 : 2, and " changed " in 2 Cor. 3 : 18. Someone has defined life " as the continuous adjustment of internal relations to external conditions," which means the organs of the body within answer to the circumstances in which they move without. But those " internal relations " break down ; hence, death ensues. But in the glorified state the " internal conditions " are independent of " external relations," and the " internal relations " are so perfect and complete and work in such constant harmony, that they eternally harmonise. Take a simple illustration. The bulb of the tulip in its internal nature produces the beautiful and perfect flower. Supposing the bulb in its internal conditions was eternally vivacious in life-producing properties, there would be produced eternal flowering. So in the glorified condition, our natures will be so changed that the glory of that condition will be independent of our surroundings ; yet, as in the transfiguration, from that inner life will flash out a glorious luminosity.

Glory Seven times within the compass of a few verses Paul uses the word " glory " (1 Cor. 15 : 40-43) in calling attention to the different phases of glory as seen in the sun, moon, and stars, and takes these as indicating the difference between a natural body and the spiritual body. The soulish or animal body will cease to exist, and therefore death cannot be experienced ; but the spiritual body will be spiritual, although actual in substance. There will be a correspondence in likeness between the natural and spiritual, and therefore the identity of the individual. The bare grain in embryo has in it all the qualities of the beautiful corn which it produces ; but there is a great difference between the " bare grain " and the beautiful cluster of corn. Human language cannot describe eternal glories, but the description of the glorious City which John saw coming down from heaven, illustrates the fact, that glory is the excellence of anything in display.

In the golden age of Christ's perfect rule, after the Millennium, as unfolded in Rev. 21 to 22 : 6, there will be a perfect condition of things.

There is revealed in the following seven shalls :

PERFECT ENVIRONMENT All the imperfections of earth are because man does not give God His right place ; but in the golden age " The throne of God and the Lamb shall be therein " (22 : 3), says the Spirit, in speaking of the Lamb's wife as embodied in the New Jerusalem.

PERFECT SERVICE " His servants shall do Him service." The word for servant denotes one who is bound to serve, because he is a slave ; but, when used in a Christian sense, expresses the highest devotion of one who is bound by love because he has been purchased by the blood of Christ. This is brought out in the higher word for service, which signifies sacrifice, and one who worships God (see Heb. 12 : 28).

PERFECT VISION   " Shall see His face." To see His face is to enjoy His favour and fellowship. Not like Absalom, who was not allowed to see the King's face (2 Sam. 14 : 24), but like the Queen of Sheba, who was gladdened by seeing King Solomon and all his possessions, so that she was over-joyed and awed by the sight (1 Kings 10 : 5).

PERFECT NATURE   " His Name shall be in their fore-heads." The Name stands for nature and correspondence. As Moses and Elijah were transfigured with Christ, so we shall be like Him. He will look at us and see the corre-spondence to Himself. The mark of sin left its leprous stamp on the forehead of Uzziah (2 Chron. 26 : 19), but the out-shining of Christ's glory will cause us to shine with a luminosity like to His.

PERFECT DAY   " There shall be night no more." Night with all its evil associations of sin, robbery, preying beasts, and fear, will have fled away from the luminous presence of the Sun of Righteousness, and no more shall the watchman cry, " The night cometh !"

PERFECT ILLUMINATION   " The Lord God giveth them light," hence, no light of lamp of man's production will be needed, nor will nature's sun be required. The unchanging One in His infinite power is the One Who causes the endless light in all its radiating power to shine in endless beauty and benefit.

PERFECT RULE   " And they shall reign forever and ever." " Ever and ever," or unto the ages of the ages. How can we express such a sentence ? Certainly it conveys the thought without limitations of time or earth conditions. And their " reign " being stated as beyond limitations or opposi-tion, there is perfect dominance.

The Beyond need not trouble us. It is in the gracious Hands of Him Who died for us. He, Who is the Resurrec-tion and the Life, is also the Great I AM, so He can bring to pass all the gracious purpose of His love.

Beloved Samuel H. Wilkinson, on one occasion visited the late Robert Chapman. The former had only a minute to greet the latter, the latter in his own gracious way said, " The Best is yet to come." That is the message which the Holy Spirit gives to us, for the future is resplendent with coming glory. So amid all the shadows of earth and the sorrows of life, we find the rainbow of God's promise to cheer and stimulate us.

> The Best's to come, so do not fret,
>   Amid the stress of time,
> But list to what the Lord doth say,
>   " In glory thou shalt shine."
>
> The Best's to come, for Christ will come,
>   And end the strife of sin,
> He'll hush the woes, and quell the strife,
>   And all will bow to Him.
>
> The Best's to come beyond this vale
>   Of sorrow, tears and woe,
> For He will wipe all tears away,
>   And conquer every foe.
>
> The Best's to come, so look ahead,
>   Beyond this death-doomed shore,
> For Christ is Resurrection's Life,
>   So worship and adore.
>
> The Best's to come when war shall cease,
>   And men will fight no more,
> For Christ shall reign as Prince of Peace,
>   For time and evermore.
>
> The Best's to come, when earth shall rest,
>   From curse and shame of sin,
> And all created things shall know
>   That Christ the Lord doth win.
>
> So rest thy heart in Jesus, Lord,
>   And watchful for Him be,
> For He will make thee like to Him,
>   When thou His face shalt see.

1

INDEX OF AUTHORS

2

INDEX OF SCRIPTURE PASSAGES
ANNOTATED OR EXPLAINED

432

3

INDEX OF SUBJECTS, TOPICS, AND THEMES

A

Abiding in Christ, 233-235
Acceptance of the believer, 238-239, 308
"According to" (signifying design), 252-253
Actions as types, 243
Acts, Book of, 171-175
Acts, Book of, Holy Spirit in, 171-175, 179-180
Adam and Christ, 231-232
Adonai, (Lord), 111-114
Adoption, meaning of, 279, 407
Advents of Christ, 317-329
Age, golden, 428
Ages, periods of time, 350-352
"All," used in Ephesians, 249-251
Almighty God, 110-111
Altar of burnt offering, 30-31
Angels, 35
"Appearings" of Christ, the three, 265, 322-323
Assurance of the believer, 139
Atheism answered, 103-104
Atonement, 97, 378-379, 381-386
Atonement in relation to other doctrines, 30-36
Atonement in relation to second coming of Christ, 310-317
Attraction (gravitation) to Christ, 277
"Authority," use of word, 113

B

Bees, illustrating law and order, 1-2
Beginning, the, 399-402
"Behold," a keyword, 369-377
Belief and faith, 397-399
Believers, prophetic outlook of, 412
"Better," a keyword in Hebrews, 272
Bible, the; likened to a body, 4-7; likened to a building, 3-4; seven characteristics of, 288-289; Christ Himself the theme of, 260-261, 301-302; Christ's death revealed in, 31; doctrines of, 294-296; Godhead revealed in, 20-25; Grant's outline of the whole Bible, 223; requirements of the Bible interpreter, 299-305; and the second coming of Christ, 417; unity of its various books, 18-20; unity of its prophecy, 10-11; unity of its sections, 13-18; unity of its truths, 11-13; unity of the whole, 8-10; what the Bible is and what it does, 305-307

Blessing, promises of, 204-205
"Blood, the," 386-388
Body, the, compared to the vine, 276
Break or gap in prophecy, 360-361
Burnt offering, the, 47-52

C

Cause of judgment, 362-363
Central thoughts in the Bible, 225
Characteristic words and topics, 280-281
Charts or diagrams: The Holy Spirit, 182A; Judgments, 280A; the prophetic "days" of Scripture, 352A
Children of God and sons of God, distinction between, 279
Christ: His cross, 32-33; glorified in His saints, 140; God spoke through Him, 285-286; His outlook on prophecy, 411-412; His perfect reign or rule, 428-430; His superiority, 281; how Christians should behold Him, 375-376; the key to prophecy, 10-11; the King, 372-373; the Lamb of God, 371-372; the Lion of Judah, 374; the manifestation of Christ 377-381; our example, 274-275; the perfect Man, 370-371; portrayed in Revelation, 246-247; prophecy concerning, 410-411; revealed in the Passover and offerings, 36-39; revealed in the whole Bible, 260-261, 301-302; true Messiahship (Christship), 367-368; ultimate goal of prophecy, 366-368; the Word or *Logos,* 251.
Christlikeness, 159-160, 175
Church, the: and the cross, 34-35; doctrine of, in Thessalonians, 296; twelve facts concerning the church, 240-241; God's purpose for the church, 207-220; perspective or standpoint of, 254; relation to the second coming of Christ, 421-422.
Cleansing, twofold, 309
Climax in Scripture, 258-259
"Commandments," meaning of word, 15-16
Commentary, the best, 253
Commentary on the first chapter of Ephesians, 405-409
Commission, 23
Comparison and proportion of Scripture, 235-237, 238-239
Concentration of truth, 257-258

Index of Subjects, Topics and Themes / 437

G

"Generations," a keyword, 18-20
Genesis, book of, 18-20
Genesis to Kings, 36-37
Gentiles, Israel, and the Church, 183-220
Gentiles, times of the, 363-364
"Geographical" outlines, 279-280
"Geological" formation of words, 278-279
Gifts of the Holy Spirit, 268
God: basic names of, 103-141; doctrine of, in Ephesians, 405-409; doctrine of, in Thessalonians, 294; Fatherhood of, 129-141; His place in the prophetic outlook, 410-411; His plan for Israel, 194-207; His purpose for the church, 207-220; His relation to the cross, 31-32; His relation to the second coming of Christ, 417-418; His self-existence, 115-116; the Holy Spirit points men to God, 369-370; in relation to the manifestation of Christ, 378, 381; wisdom of, 26-30
Gospel, the, 183-184
Glorification, 22
Glory of Christ (enclosure), 251
"Glory," use of word, 428-430
Grace: contrasted with the law, 228; expounded in distinctive statement, 405-409; the gospel of, 26-31; impact of, on the life, 309; a keyword in Ephesians (comparison), 238
"Gravitation," attraction to Christ, 277
Greek prepositions, chart or diagram of, 182A
Greek prepositions concerning the Holy Spirit, 160-171

H

Healing, 120-121
Heaven, kingdom of, in Daniel, 358-359
Heavenlies (heavenly places) defined, 409
Hebrews, epistle to the, illustrating the law of eclipse, with its keyword, "better," 272
Hidden meaning in Scripture (enshrinement,) 361
Holy Spirit, the: chart or diagram of, 182A; and the death of Christ, 33; the doctrine of, 142-182; expounding the Word, 302-305; the gifts of, 268; His concern with the second coming of Christ, 419; His relation to the manifestation of Christ, 380-381; as the Infiller, 170-171; the law of, 247-248; Paul's teaching of, in Thessalonians, 295; personality of,

152-160; 180-182; pointing men to Christ with the word, "behold," 370-377
How to "behold" our Lord, 375-376
How to interpret the Scriptures, xiii-xvi, 241-281, 289-307, 358-368, 381-405
How to study the Word of God, 1-7

I

"'I AM" in the Gospel of John, 292-294
Identification with Christ, 264, 266-267
Illumination, 300; perfect in the future, 429
Illustrations, 1-2, 3-4, 4-7, 41, 43, 45, 46, 53, 64, 90, 92, 95-96, 148, 149, 150, 151, 153, 155, 156, 157-158, 158-159, 160, 188, 189, 191, 191-192, 193, 206, 210, 212, 239-240, 254, 286, 301, 347-348, 349, 366, 422
Immortality and the manifestation of Christ, 381
Immortality and the prophetic outlook, 426-427
Immutability of God and His Word, 205-207
Imprecatory psalms, difficulties solved, 255
Incarnation of Christ, 310-317
Independence of Jehovah, 115-116
Influence of a godly life, 148-151
Inheritance of Christ in the saints, 408-409
Inspiration of Scripture, verbal, 282-289, 299-300
Institutions (ceremonial), as types, 244
Intelligence in man, origin of, 103-104
Interpretation, detailed principles of:
  "According to," indicating design or standard, 252-253
  "All" as a comprehensive word, 249-251
  Amplification or ellipsis, 272-273
  Association and context, 230
  Attraction (gravitation), 277
  Background, Scriptural setting, 275-276
  Building up a truth with ellipsis, 272-273
  Central thought, 225-227
  Climax: the end in view, 258-259
  Commands, 270
  Comparison, 238-239
  Completion, 240-241
  Comprehensiveness, 249-251
  Concentration of truth, 257-258

Words of Coverdale, xiii-xvi
Words, "geological" formation of, 278-279
Words, topics, keywords, 280-281
Interpretation, laws or principles of, xiii-xvi, 224-281, 289-307, 358-368, 381-405
"In that day," 258-259
Inversion, parallel, 9-10
Ishmaelites and Midianites, 230-231
Israel, God's sevenfold plan for, 194-207; in future fulfillment of prophecy, 413-414; prophecy concerning, in relation to Abraham and David, 365-366
Italics in the English Bible, 277-278

J

Jehovah, 114-129
Jehovah's love, 206-207
Jesus, Messiahship or Christship of, 367-368
Jewish outlook in prophecy, 413-414
Joy, 23
Judgment defined, 16, 17, 96
Judgment, God's method of, 364-365
Judgment, sin the cause of, 362-363
Judgments, chart or diagram of, 280A
Justification, 235-237
Justification, twofold, 265-308

K

Keys to prophecy: Christ, 10-11, 366-368, 411-412, 418-419, 428-430; Israel, 194-207, 365-366, 413-414
Keys, words and topics as, 280-281
Kingdom of heaven in Daniel, 358-359
Kingdom and the Lord's Supper, 312-314

L

Lamb, the, in Revelation as conqueror, 323-324; the Lamb of God, 371-372
Last things, relative to the cross, 35-36; in Thessalonians, 296; in view of Christ's return, 422
Law, definition of, 2-3; keyword in psalms, 16; law and grace contrasted, 228; law of the Spirit, 247-248
Leviticus, the Book of, 383-385, 387
Life in the Holy Spirit, 142-145; in the Gospel of John, 231; in the First Epistle of John, 258, 279; twofold life, 309, 320-321; life in Christ, 379-380
"Like," a keyword in similes, 263
Logos, the Word, 251

"Lord" in relation to Christ, 402-405
Lord's inheritance, the, 408-409
Lord's Supper, the, 312-314
Love, the oneness of, 24; the Father's love, 140; the love of God, 183-220; expressed as pity, 263; as charity, 267-268; in relation to Christ's manifestation, 378

M

Man, in view of the cross, 32; his outlook in prophecy, 415; his relation to the second coming of Christ, 419-420
Manhood of Christ, the, 370-371
Manifestation of Christ, the, 321-323; great doctrines revealed in relation to, 377-381; his manifestation in regard to sin, 421
Maranatha, 271-272
Meal (meat) offering, 52-58
Messiahship (Christship) of Jesus, 367-368
Metaphor, 280
Millennium, Christ's rule after, 428-430
Millennium, the Lord's Supper in, 313-314
Mizpah 271
Moses as prophet, 284
Most High God, 126-127
Mysteries in the Bible, 245-246
Mysteries of the kingdom (enshrinement), 361

N

Names of God, 103-141
Names of the Holy Spirit, 175-182
Nations, judgment of the, 364-365
New, all things to be made, 376-377
Number "three," 2

O

Obedience: of Christ and of Christians, 136; of Christians to the Father, 139-140; consistently practiced, 304; emphasized in Deuteronomy, 248-249
Offerings, the, 13, 36-102
Offices (prophet, priest, king) as types, 243
Omnipotence, omnipresence, omniscience, 181
One King over Israel, 203-204
Oneness of the Father and Son, 21-25
Only begotten and firstbegotten, 255-256, 324-325, 420
Order, the law of, 254-255
Outlines: on abiding, 233-235; on the acts of God relative to Christ's death, 31-32; on the name, Adonai, 112-114; on vari-